History from Below

The Politics of
Historical Thinking

—

Edited by
Brigitta Bernet, Lutz Raphael, and Benjamin Zachariah

Advisory Board:
Amar Baadj, American University Cairo
Berber Bevernage, University of Ghent
Federico Finchelstein, New School for Social Research, New York
Kavita Philip, University of British Columbia
Dhruv Raina, Jawaharlal Nehru University
Indra Sengupta, German Historical Institute, London
Jakob Tanner, University of Zurich

Volume 6

History from Below

Between Democratisation and Populism

Edited by
Brigitta Bernet, Lutz Raphael, and Benjamin Zachariah

DE GRUYTER
OLDENBOURG

This publication has been supported by the German Research Foundation (DFG).

ISBN 978-3-11-150464-3
e-ISBN (PDF) 978-3-11-152218-0
e-ISBN (EPUB) 978-3-11-152247-0
ISSN 2625-0055

Library of Congress Control Number: 2025933998

Bibliographic information published by the Deutsche Nationalbibliothek
The Deutsche Nationalbibliothek lists this publication in the Deutsche Nationalbibliografie;
detailed bibliographic data are available on the internet at http://dnb.dnb.de.

© 2025 Walter de Gruyter GmbH, Berlin/Boston, Genthiner Straße 13, 10785 Berlin
Cover image: Lilly Chambers
Typesetting: Integra Software Services Pvt. Ltd.

www.degruyter.com
Questions about General Product Safety Regulation:
productsafety@degruyterbrill.com

The Politics of Historical Thinking

Historical thinking has a politics that shapes its ends. While at least two generations of scholars have been guided into their working lives with this axiom as central to their profession, it is somewhat of a paradox that historiography is so often nowadays seen as a matter of intellectual choices operating outside the imperatives of quotidian politics, even if the higher realms of ideological inclinations or historiographical traditions can be seen to have played a role. The politics of historical thinking, if acknowledged at all, is seen to belong to the realms of nonprofessional ways of the instrumentalisation of the past.

This series seeks to centre the politics inherent in historical thinking, professional and non-professional, promoted by states, political organisations, 'nationalities' or interest groups, and to explore the links between political (re-)education, historiography and mobilisation or (sectarian?) identity formation. We hope to bring into focus the politics inherent in historical thinking, professional, public or amateur, across the world today.

Editorial Board:
Brigitta Bernet, University of Zurich
Lutz Raphael, University of Trier
Benjamin Zachariah, Einstein Forum, Potsdam

Advisory Board:
Amar Baadj, American University Cairo
Berber Bevernage, University of Ghent
Federico Finchelstein, New School for Social Research, New York
Kavita Philip, University of British Columbia
Dhruv Raina, Jawaharlal Nehru University
Indra Sengupta, German Historical Institute, London
Jakob Tanner, University of Zurich

https://doi.org/10.1515/9783111522180-202

Contents

The Politics of Historical Thinking —— V

Part One: History from Below: Reflexions on a Global Phenomenon

Brigitta Bernet, Lutz Raphael, Benjamin Zachariah
1   **The Upside-Down World Turned Upside Down Again?** —— 3

Benjamin Zachariah
2   **History from Below and the Populist Temptation: Nationalism, Indigenism and Authenticity** —— 29

Part Two: National and Regional Varieties

Brigitta Bernet
3   **Microhistory and Micropolitics. The Political Background to a New Historiographical Approach** —— 59

Etta Grotrian
4   ***Barfußhistoriker*** **and** ***Geschichtswerkstätten*** **– History from Below in West Germany in the Late 1970s and the 1980s** —— 85

Dario Di Rosa
5   **Indigenous History from Below? Problems and Perspectives from the Pacific** —— 113

Olaf Kaltmeier
6   **Horizontality and Decolonisation of Knowledge: Doing Oral History in Latin America** —— 141

Part Three: Case Studies

Menachem Klein
7   **Jerusalem's History from Below – a History of Personal and Historiographical Transitions** —— 177

Irit Carmon Popper

8 Art "from Below": Activating Socially Engaged Art at a Site-in-Conflict – the Israeli-Palestinian Case —— 197

Yannick Lengkeek

9 Regimes at Play: Rethinking Games, Agency, and Power Relations under the Portuguese Estado Novo —— 227

Franziska Rueedi

10 Violence during the Transition "From Below" in South Africa —— 259

Biographical Notes —— 285

Selected Bibliography —— 289

Index —— 293

Part One: **History from Below: Reflexions on a Global Phenomenon**

Brigitta Bernet, Lutz Raphael, Benjamin Zachariah

1 The Upside-Down World Turned Upside Down Again?

Much of the historiography of the second half of the 20th century believed itself to be following the determined advances of processes of democratisation that began after the Second World War. Historians sought to embrace the lives, experiences, and subjectivities of people who were not priests, princes, lords, kings, dictators, capitalists, or statesmen, seeking out instead the worlds of slaves, vassals, women, peasants, and workers. The experiences of the latter groups, usually silenced in what was then the 'mainstream' which came to be somewhat disparagingly called 'history from above', were increasingly seen as the true, worthwhile histories to write; but what was 'below' depended very strongly on what was 'above', as a result of which the 'aboves' could often be preserved, reified, and potentially re-empowered by the focus on the 'belows' to which they were still the 'aboves'.

This volume attempts to follow a democratisation process that simultaneously, implicitly, and/or potentially, contained within it the seeds of a populism that drew its legitimation from the automatic and *a priori* importance of the people whose story it was telling. It maps many of the moves, in and across different parts of the world, of a loosely-coordinated trend that became a movement, and evolved into an academically self-evident practice, even as it insisted on its importance beyond the ivory tower.

1.1 The Making of a Movement

A shortened history of a radical movement that is now a form of academic legitimation might be useful in order to position this set of problems. History from below, *Geschichte von unten*, *Storia del basso*, *histoire d'en bas*, *historia a ras del suelo* – these and other terms represent a reorientation of historiography that began in the 1960s and 1970s. Sometimes also referred to earlier as "people's history" or "radical history", history from below is, as institutionalised in the definition of the Institute of Historical Research, a historiography that "seeks to take as its subjects ordinary people, and concentrates on their experiences and perspectives, contrasting itself with the stereotype of traditional political history and its focus on the actions of 'great men'. It also differed from traditional labour history in that its exponents were more interested in popular protest and culture than in

https://doi.org/10.1515/9783111522180-001

the organisations of the working class."[1] It is, therefore, and definitionally, by in-directions that we directions find: nothing is but what is not.

Although one could potentially trace the prerequisites for this form of think-ing back into the 19th century, one can claim that serious attempts to put the pro-ject into historiographical practice have only been formulated since the 1960s. In his programmatic essay "History from below", which appeared in a special issue of the *Times Literary Supplement* on "New Ways in History" in 1966, the British historian and former member of the Communist Party of Great Britain's (CPGB) "Historians' Group",[2] E.P. Thompson, made the case for a liberation of history. This new way would, he said, not only leave behind outdated political history, but also free itself from the shackles of a workers' history that was fixated on parties and institutions. Instead, it should turn to topics of "popular culture" and the "common people", and take the latter seriously as producers of history. Thomp-son emphasised the need to understand people in the past as far as possible in the light of their own experiences – and of their own interpretation of those experiences. Simultaneously, Thompson also called for a democratisation of his-tory that actively opposed tendencies toward specialisation. He concluded his essay with the warning words: "Perhaps it will prove most healthy for [history from below] if it remains somewhat disestablished, with an extra-mural audience still partly in mind. Otherwise it may become successful: grow fat and adopt Nor-man habits in its turn."[3] ("Norman habits", perhaps, was an allusion to the work of his fellow-member of the CPGB Historians' Group, on the "English Revolution" of 1640, in which he pointed out the importance of the themes and counterposi-tion of the "Norman yoke" and the "free-born yeoman" in the ideology of a revo-lution that had previously been called a Civil War.[4])

This "new way of history" quickly aroused great interest among historians who wanted to expand the boundaries of their subject, open up new areas of re-search and, above all, explore the historical experiences of those people whose ex-istence was so often ignored or only mentioned in passing in what was then inno-

---

1 "Archive History," accessed November 09, 2024, https://archives.history.ac.uk/makinghistory/themes/history_from_below.html.

2 On the CPGB Historians' Group, see Eric Hobsbawm, "The Historians' Group of the Communist Party (1978)," *Versobooks*, 9 June 2023, https://www.versobooks.com/blogs/news/the-historians-group-of-the-communist-party, accessed November 09, 2024. E.P. Thompson left the Communist Party in 1956.

3 E.P. Thompson, "History from below (1966)," in *The Essential E.P. Thompson*, ed. Dorothy Thompson (New York: New Press, 2001), 482–489.

4 Christopher Hill, *The English Revolution, 1640: An Essay* (London: Lawrence & Wishart, 1940); Christopher Hill, "The Norman Yoke," in *Puritanism and Revolution*, ed. Christopher Hill (London: Secker & Warburg, 1958), 50–122.

cently seen as "general history". The rise of perspectives from below can also be explained by the fact that demands for a history from below or a history from the bottom up were prominent in the New Left, whose catalysing can be dated to Khrushchev's de-Stalinisation speech and its fallout, shortly to be followed by the Soviet Hungarian invasion in 1956; or perhaps, for those within Communist or fellow-traveller circles who were slower on the uptake, to the 1968 invasion of Czechoslovakia that brutally ended the Prague Spring.[5]

These demands were raised with a similar thrust worldwide and not just in the academic field. For example, a collective of writers from Puerto Rico stated in a 1971 manifesto: "We face the problem, that the history presented as ours is only part of our history. What of the history of the 'historyless', the anonymous people who, in their collective acts, their work, their daily lives, and fellowships, have forged our society through many centuries?"[6] The oral history movement also belonged to the same community as History from Below, interested as it was in culture passed down orally and the perspectives contained in song lyrics and anecdotes that were at odds with established history. The investigations into factory life in France and Italy, the trade unionist "Dig where you stand" movement in Sweden, and a variety of cultural initiatives that made it their mission to make dissident voices heard – from Augusto Boal's "Theater of the Oppressed" in Brazil, to the films of the British filmmaker Ken Loach, to the global folk revival, and the practices of various and variously-defined self-awareness groups.[7] In all of these fields, participants were also interested in the collective experience of subordinate classes and marginalised groups because they were seen as pioneers of a politics of liberation that they wanted to build on in the present; and the point was to reduce the distance between the leaders and the led. The constellation of the "red decade" after 1968 opened up an international space of resonance that encompassed British history from below, Italian *microstoria*, West German *Alltagsgeschichte*, an epistemologically-oriented feminism, and (a belated entrant about a decade and a half later) Indian 'subaltern studies'. In the 1970s and 1980s, similar movements emerged in Western and Eastern Europe: in Britain, the Federal Republic of Germany, France, Switzerland, Sweden, Yugoslavia; and also in the

---

5 On exits from the CPGB and historians, see John Savile, "Edward Thompson, the Communist Party and 1956," *Socialist Register* (1994): 20–31, copy at: https://www.marxists.org/archive/saville/1994/xx/epthompson.htm, accessed November 08, 2024.
6 Angel Quintero Rivera, *Workers' Struggle in Puerto Rico. A Documentary Study* (New York: Monthly Review Press, 1976 (Spanish 1971)), 6–29, 6f.
7 Timothy Scott Brown, *Sixties Europe* (Cambridge: Cambridge University Press 2020), 67–101; John Brewer, "New Ways in History, or, Talking About My Generation," *Historein* 3 (2001): 27–46.

6 —— Brigitta Bernet, Lutz Raphael, Benjamin Zachariah

USA, South Africa, and India, though its extra-academic reach was in each case different.

Conceived in this way, history from below was closely linked to the emergence of the New Left and the social movements of the 1970s. It saw itself as a social-emancipatory project, seeking to transform not only academic debates, but also the social practice of historiography, and to reach an audience beyond the walls of the academy. An example of this are the "History Workshops", which emerged from the worker training courses that Raphael Samuel held from 1966 onwards at Ruskin College, the trade union workers' training institute at the University of Oxford. They, programmatically, were to encourage laypeople to research the history of their village, family or workplace. History should not be delegated to academic experts, but should be practiced and re-appropriated by those affected themselves.[8] "History is too important to be left just to the professional historians", we read in the founding manifesto of the *History Workshop Journal* in 1976, which Raphael Samuel edited together with Sally Alexander, Anna Davin and Gareth Stedman Jones.[9] The journal, now very much a part of the landscape of elite academic journals, initially served as a platform for the various local and national associations that had formed in England, Scotland and Wales based on the workshop model.[10] It quickly became an international hub. The History Workshop Movement was connected to related projects in South Africa, the USA, Sweden as well as in the Federal Republic of Germany, where history workshops spread in the 1980s and everyday history emerged.

This historiographical downward orientation was a global phenomenon, occurring not only in Western Europe and the USA, but also in the Eastern Bloc and what would now be called the Global South, the artiste formerly known as the Third World. Another pioneer of the new perspectives was certainly decolonisation, the liberation of Indochina, the Vietnam War and the Chinese Revolution.[11] In the political as well as in the historiographical field, liberation struggles, which at that time were led primarily by the rural classes, sparked a lively interest in the culture of the subaltern classes and motivated an intensive dialogue between historiography and anthropology. The aim was to rediscover buried knowledge and traditions that were independent of and resistant to the dominant culture. Although the impulses to rewrite history "from below" were realised in different

---

8 "History Workshop Journal," Making History, http://www.history.ac.uk/makinghistory/resour ces/articles/HWJ.html, accessed November 09, 2024.
9 Sally Alexander and Anna Davin, "Editorial," *History Workshop* 1 (1976): 6.
10 "History Workshop Journal."
11 See Benjamin Zachariah, *After the Last Post* (Berlin: De Gruyter, 2019), 32–33.

ways, they often moved within a (neo-)Marxist horizon of thought in which the criticism and renewal of historiography was seen as the key to social change: of the social practice of historiography, and ultimately of society.

1.2 Themes and a Canon

History from below, counter-canonical by self-definition, has by now its own canon: this includes E.P. Thompson's *The Making of the English Working Class* (1963), Christopher Hill's *The World Turned Upside Down* (1972), Carlo Ginzburg's *The Cheese and the Worms* (1976), or Natalie Zemon Davis' *The Return of Martin Guerre* (1982).[12] Often retrospectively-claimed predecessors to a history from below would include works such as C.L.R. James' *Black Jacobins: Toussaint L'Ouverture and the San Domingo Revolution* (1938) and Georges Lefebvre's *The Coming of the French Revolution* (1939), an indication, if one includes Christopher Hill's *The English Revolution 1640* (1940), of its emergence during the course of a leftist involvement in an anti-fascist war effort.[13] This would foreshadow the importance, later, of Antonio Gramsci's *Prison Notebooks*, which were of course published in excerpted English translation in 1971 and swiftly became a central point of reference.[14]

History from below also includes histories of women,[15] or the New World historical-literary trilogy *Memory of Fire* by Eduardo Galeano,[16] as well as works on the transatlantic slave trade by Marcus Rediker, one of today's most active representatives of history from below; and it is surviving protagonists

---

12 E.P. Thompson, *The Making of the English Working Class* (London: Penguin, 1963); Christopher Hill, *The World Turned Upside Down* (London: Penguin, 1975) [1972]; Carlo Ginzburg, *The Cheese and the Worms: The Cosmos of a Sixteenth-Century Miller* (London: Routledge & Kegan Paul, 1980) [1976]; Natalie Zemon Davis, *The Return of Martin Guerre* (Cambridge, MA: Harvard University Press, 1982).

13 C.L.R. James, *The Black Jacobins: Toussaint L'Ouverture and the San Domingo Revolution* (London: Penguin, 2001) [1938]; Georges Lefebvre, *The Coming of the French Revolution* (Princeton: Princeton University Press 2015) [1939]; Hill, *The English Revolution*.

14 The English-speaking world largely encountered Gramsci after the publication of Antonio Gramsci, *Selections from the Prison Notebooks*, ed. and trans. Quintin Hoare and Geoffrey Nowell Smith (New York: International Publishers, 1971).

15 For instance, Joan Scott, *Gender and the Politics of History* (New York: Columbia University Press, 1988); Silvia Federici, *Caliban and the Witch: Women, the Body and Private Accumulation* (Brooklyn: Autonomedia, 2004) or Marisa Fuente, *Dispossessed Lives: Enslaved Woman, Violence, and the Archive* (Philadelphia: University of Pennsylvania Press, 2018).

16 Eduardo Galeano, *Genesis: Memory of Fire* (New York: W.W. Norton, 1998).

from the early years such as he who are, today, writing a canon for history from below.[17] Although there are significant differences in approach across these different studies, they all start from the everyday life, experiences, self-interpretations and scope of action of people whose voices were missing from the previously mainstream historiography: workers, farmers, women, slaves, those discriminated against, 'subaltern' groups in general. Following E.P Thompson's call "to rescue" people whose life-worlds are difficult to include in an easy narrative of success "from the enormous condescension of posterity", historians from below are still concerned with multiplying the protagonists as well as the producers of history.[18] It would be wrong to believe that history from below ignores the balance of power or the powerful: as Geoff Eley has argued, contrasting history from below with the history of the "bosses, bankers and brokers who run the economy" is a false dichotomy: history from below cannot be written without looking up.[19] This is because "historians from below", as Marcus Rediker insists, "study power".[20] The importance of a non-reductionist idea of "power" will be clear from this, as is the fact that history from below is therefore a residual and contrasting category, and a relational one.

To demand a history "from below", then, apparently means to distance oneself from an elitist history "from above", and yet to remain dependent on it. The claims made by history from below rely on the idea of a "traditional" history: since ancient times history has traditionally been conducted as an account of the deeds of the great. Although a broader interest in social, cultural and economic history developed in the 19th century, the main subject of history remained the politics of the elites. Of course, even before Thompson's plea, there were voices who were dissatisfied with this situation. One of these was Lev Tolstoy: *War and Peace*, from 1867, contains an astute polemic against the understanding of history of his times, for which the battle represented the historical event *par excellence*. In contrast, Tolstoy emphasised that the banal, seemingly insignificant actions of all individuals (even microscopic everyday actions) are of crucial importance for

---

17 For instance, Markus Rediker and Peter Linebaugh, *The Many-Headed Hydra: Sailors, Laves, Commoners, and the Hidden History for the Revolutionary Atlantic* (Boston: Beacon Press 2000). The set of examples used here largely follows the reading list compiled by Marcus Rediker: How to write History from Below (graduate), https://www.marcusrediker.com/how-to-write-history-from-below-graduate/, accessed November 09, 2024.

18 E.P. Thompson, *The Making of the English Working Class*, 12.

19 Geoff Eley, "No Need to Choose: History from Above, History from below," *Viewpoint Magazine*, June 27, 2024.

20 C.G. Marin and M. Roy, "Narrative Resistance: A Conversation with Historian Marcus Rediker," *Workplace* 30 (2018): 54–69, 58.

1 The Upside-Down World Turned Upside Down Again? — **9**

the course of history, because it is not just big ideas or great personalities like Napoleon who determine the course of history. Tolstoy contrasts the fragmented everyday experiences of the characters in his story with passages from official reports or stories to demonstrate contradictions between empty generalisations and first-hand impressions.[21]

Nevertheless, there is no doubt that history from below was dominated by Marxist historians, even if they were Marxists of heterodox persuasion, or 'Marxian' historians, to distinguish (some of) them from party-line organised communists.[22] From Georges Lefebvre in France to Eric Hobsbawm, E.P. Thompson and Sheila Rowbotham in Great Britain, to Giovanni Levi and Carlo Ginzburg in Italy, to Eugene Genovese in the United States, and Charles van Onselen in South Africa,[23] the nature and method of history from below were defined by Marxist or Marxian social historians. They used the term "history from below" for the first time and distinguished its characteristics from conventional historiography. A central reference point for the left-wing tradition of history from below is still Walter Benjamin's insight that the traditional understanding of history expresses the interests of the victors and that a change in the prevailing social order necessarily involves a rewriting of history from a perspective from below – in Benjamin's case from the perspective of the "fighting, oppressed class". In his theses "On the Concept of History," written in 1940 while fleeing National Socialism, Benjamin sharply criticised historicism because its method of "empathy" inevitably led to "empathy with the victor", but his criticism was also directed at the vulgar Marxist progressive thinking of a social democracy that had placed hope for happiness and salvation in the future and had therefore become blind to past and present catastrophes. Instead, Benjamin called for "to brush history against the grain" and to show that "there is no document of civilisation which is not at the same time a document of barbarism".[24] Benjamin's demand remains at the heart of history from below, and at the same time it makes clear that it encompasses not only a historiographical but also a political project of emancipation.

---

21 Leo Tolstoy, *War and Peace* (Harmondsworth: Penguin, 2006) [1869].

22 This is a distinction we used in an earlier volume: Benjamin Zachariah, Lutz Raphael, and Brigitta Bernet, eds., *What's Left of Marxism* (Berlin: De Gruyter, 2020).

23 For instance, Eric Hobsbawm, *Bandits* (rev. edn., New York: Pantheon, 1981) [1969]; Sheila Rowbotham, *Hidden from History, 300 Years of Women's Oppression and the Fight Against it* (London: Pluto Press 1977); Giovanni Levi, *Inheriting Power: The Story of an Exorcist* (Chicago: University of Chicago Press, 1988); Eugene Genovese, *Roll, Jordan, Roll! The World the Slaves Made* (New York: Pantheon, 1974); Charles van Onselen, *The Seed is Mine. The Life of Kas Maine, A South African Sharecropper 1894–1985* (New York: Hill and Wang 1996).

24 Walter Benjamin, "Theses on the Philosophy of History (On the Concept of History)," in *Illuminations*, ed. Hannah Arendt, transl. Harry Zohn (New York: Schocken Books, 2007), 253–264: 256.

1.3 Reading Against the Grain

The question of what constitutes history from below is also a question of "how": of what methods historians use, what sort of sources they comb through, and which narratives they choose to use to tell history. Assuming that there are such things as verifiable facts and events (which is something many professional historians don't necessarily acknowledge), the questions of how these are documented and transmitted, how they are brought into a context, how they are described, weighted or inserted into a narrative are already part of empowered social processes. Following Walter Benjamin, History from Below attempts to "brush history against the grain" and to look for fragments and debris behind the scenes of official history and to piece together a different story from these traces. In fact, difficulties connected with sources that a history from below struggles with – whether it is primarily concerned with telling counter-history or with democratising history – are not trivial, since the sources preserved in archives were usually not written from the perspective they choose to highlight. The public archives of those who could most urgently need them as support and assurance for their own existence have often remained unwritten or fragmentary: those of the dominated, exploited, and undocumented. And yet: making unyielding sources yield the counter-narratives is essential to history from below. Despite poor or even non-existent sources, its pioneers, through extensive archival work, but also frankly admitting to using much imagination and insight when sources failed them or proved inadequate, found ways to get ordinary people from the past to say something to the present. E.P. Thompson did this by expanding the source corpus, which, in addition to the official documents from the state, also wove songs, toasts, proverbs and caricatures into the analysis and read the official sources "backwards", so to speak – which of course raises the question as to whether official sources themselves have a "forwards", a clear direction in which they tend, against which direction we can read them only by knowing their official direction. Carlo Ginzburg, in turn, addressed these difficulties with the suggestion of approaching the official sources – in his case inquisition protocols – according to a "hermeneutics of cracks"[25] and wrote: "The voices of the accused reach us strangled, altered, distorted; in many cases, they haven't reached us at all. Hence – for anyone unresigned to writing history for the nth time from the standpoint of the victors – the importance of the anomalies, the cracks that occasion-

---

25 Alexander Schnickmann, "Unter einem anderen Mond: Carlo Ginzburg und die Hermeneutik der Risse," *Weimarer Beiträge: Zeitschrift für Literaturwissenschaft, Ästhetik und Kulturwissenschaften* 1 (2020): 17–35, https://publikationen.ub.uni-frankfurt.de/opus4/frontdoor/deliver/index/docId/71481/file/WB_66-1_2020_Schnickmann.pdf, accessed November 09, 2024.

ally (albeit very rarely) appear in the documentation, undermining its coherence."[26] While Ginzburg tried to infer deeper, and otherwise invisible, realities through cracks or infinitely subtle traces, Natalie Zemon Davis explicitly added imagination to the arsenal of her methods. In the introduction to her 1982 book, *The Return of Martin Guerre*, she wrote: "What I offer you here is in part my invention, but held tightly in check by the voices of the past."[27] Zemon Davis' open declaration has provoked no small amount of criticism, which has often been greatly exaggerated and has reinforced two false ideas: that historiography can be purely objective;[28] or that history is "emplotment", with truth-*claims* that should be taken no more seriously than the truth-claims of literature.[29] Even if one may agree with certain points of Davis' comments, her observation remains correct that historiography has a narrative dimension that is by no means limited to the approaches taken by history from below. Criticism and defence would both probably have been less harsh if Davis' book had not been placed in the middle of the spiteful discussions about the linguistic turn, postmodernism, and the thesis that the discourse of history represents an arbitrary construction without reference to an extra-textual reality. It has taken some time for some of the smoke to clear from the many skirmishes and mock battles over truth and invention, over fact and fiction, over the impossibility of objectivity and the telling of deliberate lies, over postmodernism and the post-truth age; but the miasma continues to hang in the air.[30]

In the last two decades, however, these questions have become more pressing again. Especially in the study of the history of slavery – which is certainly the place where history from below is currently at its strongest – there are great difficulties in making the voices of the enslaved audible with the help of official archives and the sources to be found therein. There is also the problem that the dehumanising logic of the slave trade is often documented in a recording logic that degraded the enslaved people to the status of goods that had a certain age, weight, gender, ill-

---

26 Carlo Ginzburg, *Ecstasies: Deciphering the Witches' Sabbath* (New York: Pantheon Books 1991), 10.

27 Zemon Davis, *The Return of Martin Guerre*, viii-iv, 5.

28 See for instance Robert Finlay, "The Refashioning of Martin Guerre," *American Historical Review* 93/3 (1988): 553–571, https://www.jstor.org/stable/1868102, accessed November 09, 2024.

29 Hayden White, *The Content of the Form: Narrative Discourse and Historical Representation* (Baltimore: Johns Hopkins University Press, 1987).

30 For a recent return to these debates in the present-day context, which has resonances for our understanding of the dangers of populism, see Jason Stanley, *Erasing History: How Fascists Rewrite the Past to Control the Future* (New York: Simon & Schuster, 2024). The title is almost an exact paraphrase of George Orwell's remark in *1984* (London: Penguin, 1983) [1949], 199 – "who controls the past controls the future; who controls the present controls the past" – and Orwell was not referring exclusively to fascists at all.

ness, etc., but no subject status. In view of these difficulties, the American literary scholar Saidiya Hartman recently suggested taking the blank spaces in historical tradition as a starting point, and in order to counter the silences of the archives, fill the silence in a creative way with a "critical fabulation".[31] Instead of omitting from the historical narrative pasts about which sources provide inadequate or illegible information, or sources cannot be found to answer critical questions to which the easily-accessible sources will not yield answers (where at best it can be said: "We can't say anything about that"), "critical fabulation" is also intended to address these pasts and allow a place in the historical narrative. This is a point at which disciplinary boundaries might become relevant: many 'historical' interventions in the last half a century or so have come from literary scholars who are concerned with moral or affective 'truths' that allegedly trump documented or forensic truths, and affect is notoriously non-intersubjective. "Make it up" is a populist rule of thumb that many historians might wish to oppose. It might be said in parentheses that "the archives" is a static and mythical concept, and a serious set of historical questions requires an active and creative identification of sources from which to answer them: the idea of "the Archive" as a building representing Authority from Above is a fiction that belongs to the realms of "critical fabulation" itself.[32]

1.4 Class and/or Culture

If there is such a thing as a hymn to history from below, Bertolt Brecht has written it. His 1936 poem "Questions from a Worker Who Reads" succinctly captured the need for alternative perspectives to the dominant "history from above" when he asked: "Who built the seven-gate Thebes?"[33] His well-known answer: "The names of kings are written in the books." And subversively he continues: "Did the kings bring the boulders?" Brecht lets the reading worker's gaze wander across the continents and shake his head at what the history books record: "The young Alexander conquered India. He alone? Caesar defeated the Gauls. Didn't he at

---

31 Saidiya Hartman, "Venus in Two Acts," *small axe* 26 (2008): 1–14, https://warwick.ac.uk/fac/arts/history/research/centres/blackstudies/venus_in_two_acts.pdf, accessed November 09, 2024.
32 See Benjamin Zachariah, "Travellers in Archives, or the Possibilities of a Post-Post-Archival Historiography," in *After the Last Post*, ed. Benjamin Zachariah (Berlin: De Gruyter, 2019), 149–162.
33 "A Worker reads and asks," Times Literary Supplement, https://www.the-tls.co.uk/regular-features/poem-of-the-week/a-worker-reads-and-asks-bertolt-brecht-poem-of-the-week-andrew-mcculloch/, accessed November 09, 2024, provides a translation: there are several available, but we have a slightly different translation here, at our own risk and responsibility.

least have a cook with him?" The criticism of a historiography that has long been dominated by the victors is certainly a central starting point for the search for alternative historiographies in which the motley group – the bricklayer, the cook, the mother – and their contribution to the creation of "cultural assets", would be represented. This demand to multiply the subjects of history is just as central to history from below to this day as the power-critical question of the positions and resources which make hegemonic certain interpretations of history at the expense of others, which then succeeds in ignoring and keeping certain memories silent. A history from below, as can be seen in Benjamin and Brecht, focuses on the past with the express aim of breaking the historical continuum of the victors and exploring strategic spaces for liberating action. Historiography from below therefore questions the long chain of victories achieved by those in power and treats with empathy those who did not have the means to transmit their experiences in the same currency. And it does this not least in the interests of those who are now, in the present, dominated by the heirs of the ruling classes of the past. In this version of history from below, conflict and class struggle are important categories of analysis; and the apparent inheritors of those conflicts and class struggles are placed in a lineage that justifies or discredits their current position in history and society. If history from below emphasizes people's agency and their own role in shaping their lives and histories, some historians emphasize people's lived experiences rather than abstract notions of class to understand their behaviour. And, indeed, that was a central concern of the break with party-line histories that emphasised the vanguard role of the Communist Party in the mobilisation of workers or peasants; and that was why Antonio Gramsci became, retrospectively, a major theorist of history from below, with his formulation ,subaltern' avoiding the rigidities of a pre-ordained class category in which to place ordinary people's lived experiences. Gramsci, writing in defeat from a Fascist prison, sought to answer the question as to why the Italian peasantry had betrayed its own interests by siding with the Fascists – an outcome that could hardly have been extrapolated from the externalist class analysis of official Communist Party literature.[34]

We have already mentioned Tolstoy as a 19th-century precursor of history from below. His criticism of elitist historiography was also combined with a tendency to make heroes of the common people, the Russian farmers. Influenced by cultural-revolutionary as well as concepts of authentic folk traditions, which is to say, simultaneously by the Enlightenment and by Romanticism, and in particular

---

34 Antonio Gramsci, *Selections from the Prison Notebooks*, ed. and trans. Quintin Hoare and Geoffrey Nowell Smith (New York: International Publishers, 1971).

by intensified efforts from the 1870s to "go into the people", which characterised the revolutionary-populist movement of the "Narodniki" (from "Narod", the people), Tolstoy also attributed special moral qualities to the Russian people (such as fraternal solidarity, religiosity or even basic communist instincts).[35] Such idealising tendencies, with their diverse parallels to the German Romantic writings about the German people as well as to the populist movement in the USA in the late 19th century, remain present in the tradition of history from below up to the present day,[36] with the danger that its afterlives can be seen spilling over into what we might call *völkisch* history. The object of historical investigation can thus become a projection surface for the wishes of those who write the histories.

This danger is implicit in history from below: Raphael Samuel recognised this in 1981, when he acknowledged that the central categories of history from below, the "people" and "people's history", have had a long career and include a whole ensemble of different registers, some characterised by the idea of progress, others by cultural pessimism, some with left-wing and some with right-wing vectors, sometimes with unpleasant overlaps.[37]

Therefore, there are other versions or variations of this type of historiography from below. A right-wing or conservative interest in the history of the "common people" in terms of regions, ancestors, *Heimat* (an untranslatable German term for 'homeland' perhaps best explained in terms of another, mostly untranslated, German term, *völkisch*), and the preservation of local characteristics, also flared up in the 1970s and continues to exist. In this perspective, "below" is a kind of cultural commons always in danger of being appropriated by elites or other groups/ethnicities, and a kind of communitarian residuum to be detected and protected at the same time. Here, the relational element is much less prominent than in the Marxian tradition.

Often motivated by regionalist and separatist movements, local histories emerged "from below", which also referred to the people and popular culture, were based on "native knowledge" and provided escapist counter-histories to national, "official" and "Jacobin" histories of the state from above. A particular region's otherness was its response to the totalising discourse of the nation, the colonial power, and/or to "modernity" per se. With the rise of right-wing populism

---

35 See Isaiah Berlin, *The Hedgehog and the Fox: An Essay on Tolstoy's View of History*, ed. Henry Hard, Foreword by Michael Ignatieff (New Jersey: Princeton University Press, 2013).
36 See Franco Venturi, *Roots of Revolution. A History of the Populist and Socialist Movements in 19th Century Russia* (London: Phoenix Press, 2001), which remains a classic study on Russian Populism: See also Christopher Ely, *Russian Populism. A History* (London: Bloomsbury, 2021).
37 Raphael Samuel, "People's History," in *People's History and Socialist Theory*, ed. Raphael Samuel (London: Routledge & Kegan Paul, 1981), xv–xxxix: xvii.

after the reunification of Germany after 1989 and the collapse of "really existing socialism" in Eastern Europe, right-wing populist parties increasingly resorted to identity politics strategies, which were intended to strengthen a sense of unity oriented towards community rather than society, through a backward-looking view of history anchored in supposedly stable pre-modern popular values and traditions. In an age that claims to be one of denationalisation, in Europe, at least, they rely on collective identification as a guide for individual orientation, offering myths about the nation, its folk heroes and freedom struggles as narratives that create meaning and identity, as instructions for decoding the global here and now.[38] These histories are mirrored in 'decolonialist' thinking in the now-newly-self-identified 'Global South', in which a moral order attributed to 'colonialist' thinking is to be reversed – and questions of sources, rational argument, or grounded thinking is increasingly irrelevant.[39]

Such counter-histories do not aim at the further democratisation of the ideas of equality, freedom and fraternity, but on the contrary at the "decolonisation" of such ideology, at "cultural identity" and at a right to Otherness – not infrequently also due to ancestry. This, then, re-opened a process that brought such counter-histories in touch with what we can describe as 'populism', a term notoriously difficult to define. We do not want to engage here in a theoretical debate that is still going on and that is necessarily intertwined with a political debate about the future of emancipatory movements and democracy. There is a kind of minimal consensus describing "populism" as a particular form of politics combining the mobilisation of popular anti-establishment resentment with authoritarian or revolutionary visions of government blurring the lines between liberal parliamentary democracy and authoritarian dictatorship. "The concept of populism erases the distinction between left and right, thus blurring a useful compass to understand politics".[40] If a left populism is one that takes short-cuts to public sympathy by drawing on a shared emotive symbolism, and a right populism is a stage on the way to abolishing the democracy that brings its purveyors, via that public sympathy, to power,[41] we are often only able to establish this distinction in retro-

---

38 Andreas Audretsch, and Claudia Gatzka, eds., *Schleichend an die Macht: Wie die Neue Rechte Geschichte instrumentalisiert, um Deutungshoheit über unsere Zukunft zu erhalten* (Berlin: Dietz, 2020).

39 The works of Enrique Dussel, *Politics of Liberation: a Critical World History* (London: SCM Press, 2011); or Walter Mignolo, *The Politics of Decolonial Investigations (On Decoloniality)* (Durham: Duke University Press, 2021) are symptomatic of this trend.

40 Enzo Traverso, *The New Faces of Fascism: Populism and the Far Right* (London: Verso, 2019).

41 This is the distinction suggested by Federico Finchelstein, *From Fascism to Populism in History* (Berkeley: University of California Press, 2017).

spect. But it is this blurring effect, intentional or not (and historians don't have always adequate sources to read intention), that is the question at the heart of our concerns here. Does the blurring of history from below into populist-friendly categories destroy the leftish tendencies that drove it to its pre-eminent position in historiography? Does the focus on "authenticity", of experience, positionality, inheritance, or anything else, dehistoricise the histories that History from below retells?

The rise of populism reminds us of what one of the founders of history from below, Raphael Samuel, was conscious of, which Dario Di Rosa reminds us of in his contribution to this volume: "People's history, whatever its particular subject matter, is shaped in the crucible of politics, and penetrated by the influence of ideology on all sides. In one version it is allied with Marxism, in another with democratic liberalism, in yet another with cultural nationalism, and (. . .) the Left can make no proprietorial claim to it".[42]

1.5 Disciplinary Contexts

From a historiographical perspective, history from below can, on the one hand, be tied back to the social history from which it undoubtedly emerged, and on the other hand, it is also closely connected to the cultural or anthropological turn in the discipline of history. The emancipatory claim connects history from below with social history: a liberation from a historiography of great men and political events. The focus shifts to structures and processes, and, in particular, to the social or material situation of 'subaltern' classes, especially workers, peasants, and their collective struggles. Furthermore, interest was focused on labour relations and power structures under capitalism, as well as generally on the transition from agrarian, pre-industrial society to modern industrial society, and the social and human consequences of this modernisation process in all its aspects, with the analytical criteria often being provided by the social sciences, and often by the works by Karl Marx or Max Weber.

The second formative tradition is certainly anthropology. A characteristic of history from below is its preoccupation with everyday culture in the broader sense – that is, with everything that is not considered "high culture" or the "culture of the elites" (again a residual category), and the increased focus on consciousness, on everyday life, and the experiences of the "people". However, this "people" was imagined less as a social or ethnic collective body, but rather as a

---

42 Samuel, "People's History," xx.

pre-political subaltern plebeian in the sense of Populus: the people, *le peuple, il popolo*. Careful micro-studies, starting with the experiences, practices and meaning-making of "ordinary people", it was thought, should contribute to a systematic decentring of existing and well-rehearsed analysis and interpretation, and make it possible to understand more of the ambiguities and contradictions of the perception and behaviour of "ordinary people". The impact of anthropology on history from below has also been reciprocated in the other direction. E.P. Thompson's development of the idea of a "moral economy of the crowd", though not exclusively his, has, for instance, been very influential, well beyond what explicit citations might show.[43] As one commentator aptly put it, Thompson "might well have been a revered ancestor for today's anthropologists, but instead he is like a specter whose traces are ubiquitous but who remains almost invisible. Thompson was a social constructionist before social constructionism, a fervent antistructuralist before the poststructuralist turn, an early proponent of the importance of 'agency' and 'experience' in social analysis, and a tenacious polemicist and militant intellectual before anthropology embraced activism".[44]

The turn to the culture of the lower orders of society and to popular culture, which is so characteristic of history from below, was not, at least initially, synonymous with a turning away from history of a Marxian orientation or origin, based on class struggle and social conflicts, though perhaps it opened the doors to that trend. For E.P. Thompson, "plebeian culture" was not just a component of the ideological "superstructure", as it was in official Partyspeak, but a concept that was intended to capture the everyday lives of the lower classes and help to lift the veil of official ideologies. In his introduction to a series of key essays for history from below, Thompson wrote about his understanding of popular culture: "In these studies I hope that plebeian culture becomes a more concrete and usable concept, no longer situated in the thin air of 'meanings, attitudes and values', but located within a particular equilibrium of social relations, a working environment of exploitation and resistance to exploitation, of relations of power which are masked by the rituals of paternalism and deference. In this way (I hope) 'popular culture' is situated within its proper material abode".[45]

---

43 E.P. Thompson, "The Moral Economy of the English Crowd in the Eighteenth Century," *Past and Present* 50 (1971): 76–136.

44 Marc Edelman, "E.P. Thompson and Moral Economies," in *A Companion to Moral Anthropology*, ed. Didier Fassin (Chichester: Wiley-Blackwell, 2012), 49–66: 49.

45 E.P. Thompson, "Introduction: Custom and Culture," in *Customs in Common*, ed. E.P. Thompson (London: Penguin 1991), 1–15: 7.

For Thompson, culture is not the cream on the cake, but the yeast in the dough. It is intimately interwoven with the material world, not separated from it. It acts as a catalyst for social learning processes and changes, and is at the same time a stage in which the dependencies between social classes are manifested and negotiated. As has already become clear, the development of history from below can rightly be linked to specifically contemporary historical phenomena. The context in which it emerged can be seen in post-war Great Britain with its strongly institutionalised workers' movement, against which Thompson sought to reconstruct popular cultures of resistance that were neither absorbed into the established interest-representing institutions of the workers' movement nor into the belief in the progress of historical materialism.

1.6 Scholastic Fallacies

Despite some of its anti-academic self-positionings, history from below was from the beginning a cultural and political movement with a strong link to professional historians. These historians were often at the beginning of their academic career or situated at the margins of their academic field. In some countries, older historians mostly with strong and long-established links to parties of the left figured as some kind of protectors for projects and people engaged in history from below. Often, political publishers were the first to publish or edit the books that were produced.

This situation changed in the industrial countries of the western hemisphere during the 1980s, and somewhat later in South Asia, or in Latin America. In the former, the decline of working-class protests and strikes, but also a decline in trade union membership and activities was followed by a calming down of the so-called 'new social movements' and their protests.[46] But this change in protest culture did not bring to end the history from below movement. On the contrary, its voice and position in academia, but also inside the smaller worlds of the arts and literature, were strengthened: young activists turned into professional scholars and started their careers in universities; international links between the different nationally active circles were established that did not follow the lines of political internationalism, but rather constituted academic networks.

History from below was one of the topics that profited from the so-called linguistic and cultural turn that passed through the national fields of historical pro-

---

46 Lutz Raphael, *Beyond Coal and Steel. A social history of Western Europe after the Boom* (London: Verso 2023), 91–132.

duction in the western hemisphere, and shifted the interests and ambitions of (mostly younger) scholars towards themes that they believed had been marginalised in historiography up to that point: the culture of subaltern groups, the oral history of everyman, the stories of victims, or forgotten heroes of popular resistance against colonial, capitalist, or fascist repression.

The cultural turn was a professional turn for history from below in many countries. The implications and consequences were manifold: text production grew and became more standardised. An international market for academic books and careers emerged, and helped scholars of the Third World, and subsequently the global south, to find entrance into the until-then closed shops of academic centres in the US, UK, or France. International contacts and international fashions were pushed – with Italians and South Asians emerging as the hidden champions of this smaller subsection of the cultural history movement in international academia. "Scholastic fallacies"[47] were one of the unexpected, perhaps unintended, consequences resulting from this academic success: as early as 1989, the primacy of the text was re-established among historians from below: the search for hidden meaning in symbols and the interest in (their own) hermeneutic virtuosity in reading gestures or deeds as texts made progress as fast as the careers of former activists. "Agency" became a buzzword without clear references, and without any (or with very low) resonances in contemporary cultural and political movements.

These trends also found their early critics, and there ensued the first splits between political activists, hardcore defenders of economic and political emancipatory goals for their clientele, and the softer academic forms of a history from below that turned to directions such as 'subaltern studies' as a kind of late child of intellectual romanticism.[48] Scholars adhering to history from below tended to adapt to academic modes of thinking that Pierre Bourdieu characterised as "scholastic fallacy" – a term that sums up the consequences of projecting academic modes of thinking onto common people and their lives: It helped to integrate the heterodox outsiders and newcomers into the academic world; and we should not underestimate the "agency", or better still, the structural attraction forces of the liberal or centre-left academic mainstream dominating the national fields of historical production during these decades. Where this force was non-existent or much weaker, the fate of the movement was much less comfortable, as the example of the post-Soviet Memorial group shows very clearly.[49]

---

[47] Pierre Bourdieu, *Pascalian Meditations* (Stanford: Stanford University Press, 2000).

[48] Sumit Sarkar, "The Decline of the Subaltern in *Subaltern Studies*," in *Writing Social History*, ed. Sumit Sarkar (Delhi: Oxford University Press, 1997), 82–108.

[49] Evgenija Lezina, "Memorial und seine Geschichte," *Osteuropa* 11–12 (2014): 165–176.

Another effect of scholastic routinisation happened where history from below was institutionalised as a part of an official curriculum to serve the wishes and needs of groups whose right to education was realised via special and segregated programmes in academia. Identity claims were always present, and were an integral part of the history from below movement, but their meaning changed when they were transformed into official programmes, and became selection criteria for sources and narratives to be dealt with and legitimised, as authentic traces of one's own history. The institutionalisation of such interests followed the lines by which national prerogatives have been implemented in academic history during the 19th century: the evasion or ignoring of too-critical voices from inside one's own "community", defence against external critique (from "abroad"), and the romantic cult of the authentic voice of the people.

Such a critical reconstruction of the trends of the past decades does not suggest a history of decline because of depoliticisation, but it may serve as a critical reminder of the necessary effects produced by the combination of depoliticisation and connected academic success during the 1980s and 1990s. It opened up a period of transformation during which the old formulae turned from being critical into becoming ideological weapons to defend inner-academic positions; and in a second step, to defend established group interests, or sometimes in the other direction. There is no professional logic or functional necessity in this, but just a strong social logic of appropriation of what historical scholarship has established as critical facts and counter-narratives. Scholastic fallacies have made history from below a somewhat more normal or even fully "normal" form of scholarship. This opened the way to another trend that one could observe in western academia: its texts and positions were integrated into the pluralistic canon of approaches as examples of best-practice-scholarship when it came to studying the effects of hierarchy, inequality, violence or power, even when these effects were studied in the so-called 'global south', upon which academics positioned in western academia sought to project their assumptions.

None of this prevents new histories from below from starting elsewhere and restarting the cycle of discoveries, the creation of new links between history-research, cultural and social protest. Where such a cycle will lead is open to history. It starts from conditions different from the history from below that we took as our starting point in this volume, and we do not want to speculate about the directions or outcomes of this next round.

1.7 The Chapters

The essays presented in this volume are historical and historiographical, presenting the emergence of a set of research fields that collectively go by the name "history from below" and/or have emerged from it. Our focus also requires us, in the spirit of the origins of the field(s), to treat history from below not as an outcome of discussions internal to academia or to the discipline of history, but as a part and expression of historical cultures in which political questions play(ed) a role. Walter Benjamin suggested that "the events that surround the historian and in which he takes part" also underpin historians' writing "as a text written with invisible ink". Our volume aims to illuminate different contexts and worlds of experience that motivated a "downward" shift in historiographical perspective in the 1960s and 70s; to track some of the changes in the project(s) since the 1980s; and to reflect on how it has been reformulated or could be reformulated for the present.

Chapter 2, written by co-editor Benjamin Zachariah, "History from Below and the Populist Temptation: Nationalism, Indigenism and Authenticity", takes up one central aspect of the reflections we developed in this Introduction, on the political, cultural and intellectual implications of history from below under the changing political conditions worldwide during the last five decades. He argues that a number of the trends we now see developed in populist versions of history-writing were implicit in approaches to history from below, and were also dangers that did not go unnoticed among historians who were practitioners of those historiographical approaches. Using examples mainly from English and British historiography as it developed through the Communist Party of Great Britain's Historians' Group, and from the brief period of the South Asian Subaltern Studies collective in which that collective described itself as attempting a history from below, he suggests that the postulating of superior and authentic subjectivities from 'below' that serve to consolidate a preconceived collective identity, with historians as partisans for or members of that collective, or perhaps unable to escape the logic of their commitments, gives us a politics that is neither left nor right, and can be easily assimilated to right-wing or even *völkisch* projects.

The second part of the book, "National and Regional Varieties", brings together four chapters reflecting on the particularities of the regional or national contexts of the intellectual movement for history from below, emphasising the strong impact of the cultural and political motivations that shaped it as a movement. Brigitta Bernet's chapter, "Microhistory and Micropolitics: The Political Background to a New Historiographical Approach", reconstructs the changing political cultures of the Left in Italy in which the different groups of historians were embedded and which had a strong impact on the particularities of the Italian *micro-*

storia. It was the special blend of Italian Marxism and anthropology that inspired authors like Ginzburg, Levi or Passerini. That they found readers and followers all over the world should not let us lose sight of the fact that their perspectives are inseparably linked to dynamics and problems of the intellectual left in Italy, as they sought to liberate themselves from orthodox communist party versions of Marxism even in their very subtle form of Gramscian communism. The Italian move is more or less contemporaneous to the British wave of history from below and is strongly linked to the era of the Cold War and the economic and social transformations of Western Europe from the 1950s to the '70s. Here, languages of class, experiences of work, and structures of inequality were prominent topics dealt with in new ways and by new methods.

Somewhat later, the German variant of history from below started up in the 1970s, and its high season was in the 1980s, when the long shadow of the Nazi period and its traces at the local level and in the everyday life of common people could be made visible and studied by local initiatives. Etta Grotrian reconstructs, in the fourth chapter, *"Barfußhistoriker* and *Geschichtswerksstätten* – History from Below in West Germany in the Late 1970s and the 1980s", the political and academic struggles that shaped the profile of this movement. Unlike their famous Italian forerunners, they did not centrally confront Marxism as a paradigm, but had instead to contend with modernisation theory as the macro-historical master narrative. They were attacked from very early on by mainstream academic historiography, which described the products of the movement as a kind of poorly theorised and ill-reflected documentation of local histories. Besides being a controversy internal to academic historiography, the German debate was about the political uses of a mainly locally and regionally active movement among social democrats and members of new social movements such as ecologists or feminists.

Dario di Rosa describes quite a different setting in Chapter 5, "Indigenous History from Below? Problems and Perspectives from the Pacific". The political context is that of anti-colonialism and of post-colonial nation-building in a region where British and American anthropology had a strong impact on historians trying to move away from imperial history in the British or American style. Marxism did not play a prominent role in Pacific history from below, as it turned towards reconstructing local and/or traditional cultures as important sources for the postulating of the resistance and resilience of local agents in a time of decolonisation, and later of nation-building. Class, work, and inequality did not play a prominent role in a movement that tended to get involved in regional power networks and official views of the nations' pasts in the Pacific. Di Rosa emphasises the risk of a counter-narrative from below against colonial empire-history being transformed into a kind of official historiography of newly-created nation states, whose economic and social tensions are hidden under an umbrella of cultural identity.

We encounter another setting, though perhaps with some political similarities to the Pacific situation, when reading Olaf Kaltmeier's chapter on "Horizontality and Decolonisation in Latin America: Doing Oral History in Latin America". Kaltmeier insists on the fact that orality is the main form in which indigenous people have transmitted and still transmit their own history, and by means of which a history from below can be reconstructed in most parts of Latin America. Thus, a whole range of the classic problems that doing history from below entails worldwide are highly visible and are vividly discussed in Latin America: how to bridge the gaps in power, resources and culture between researchers and speakers of indigenous people; how to create conditions in which reciprocity and dialogue between academics and ordinary people are made possible in the face of strong forces of cultural inertia and of economic inequality. Kaltmeier discusses in detail the ambiguities resulting from a setting shaped by a longue durée of colonialism and racism and the political motivations of a mainly post-colonial "left" that gained momentum during the 1990s and 2000s. Again, the politics of cultural and national identity play an important role in the controversies on how to do oral history and through that route write an emancipatory history from below in Latin America.

The third part of this book comprises four chapters that deal with current uses of perspectives of history from below. Chapters 7 and 8 confront us with examples from conflict-ridden Israel and Palestine and their controversial overlapping histories. Menachem Klein's chapter, "Jerualem's History from Below – a History of Personal and Historiographical Transitions" is a reflection on the author's endeavour to write a counter-history of a Jerusalem as a city where Jews, Christians and Muslim families and communities lived together, a heritage that is under threat in times of political separation and distrust. It is exactly in the context of that contemporary struggle and confrontation that Irit Carmon Popper's chapter "Art 'from Below': Activating Socially Engaged Art at a Site-in-Conflict – the Israeli-Palestinian Case" is situated. It reconstructs the public intervention of the "Common Views" art collective, bringing together Israeli city dwellers and Palestinian Bedouins in the Negev desert in southern Israel. The reactivation of older, "traditional", techniques of water supply and the cultural re-evaluation of the corresponding sites follow the lines of history from below movements to reconstruct the lost heritage of marginalised people and to empower them to reappropriate their own, if sometimes forgotten, history. Carmon Popper critically discusses the chances and limits of such kinds of interventionism aiming at environmental and social reconciliation in times of political confrontation and war.

Yannick Lengkeek's chapter, "Regimes at Play: Rethinking Games, Agency, and Power Relations under the Portuguese Estado Novo", takes up a classic topic of history from below: that of the resistance and resilience of common people under conditions of political repression combined with cultural hierarchies and economic inequality. During the four decades of Salazar's dictatorship, called the "Estado Novo" (1930s to 1974), gaming and playing was heavily controlled by the state. The chapter discusses the social uses and cultural meanings players of billiards and popular gambling developed in confrontation with this kind of moralising and controlling state interventionism in their leisure-time and sports practices. More than a history of resistance, this perspective from below and of everyday practices reveals the micro-histories of the social decline of a seemingly strong police state.

The last chapter of this book, Franziska Rueedi's "Violence during the Transition 'from Below' in South Africa", uses the perspective of micro-history and the use of oral testimonies to reconstruct the often-hidden history of violence between different ethnic groups in the Townships of the Greater Johannesburg region. Rueedi uses a history from below approach to reconstruct the views and the agency of ordinary people confronted with organised violence by the opposed political forces of the Inkatha Freedom Party and the African National Congress in one small area in the township of Sebokeng. The micro-historical approach she uses helps to identify the mechanisms of inter-group violence and of civic self-defence and private survival in a long period of transition, before public order and security on the streets and in the neighbourhoods could be established – a micro-history deeply intermingled with the macro-history of regime change and democratic transition in South Africa. It serves as a kind of complementary counter-history to a political macro-history that is strongly marked by the official versions of the peaceful and democratic transfer of power narrative that informs today's multi-ethnical democracy in South Africa. In the process, it asks an important question: in situations of conflict, who exactly is "below"?

These four case-studies cover very different aspects and problems of writing history from below today, and they show different uses of the intellectual capital (in theory, methods and political awareness) accumulated during the last six decades. We may speak about a historical "tradition" that grew out of the first steps in the direction of history from below in the 1960s, and that spread to or were simultaneously adopted in many parts of the world. During its travels in space and time, this "tradition" was used under very different political and cultural circumstances, providing space for very different political interpretations by forces of the left, and also of the right. We offer this book to our readership not merely as critique, but also to underline the opportunities this tradition still offers – despite all the risks of academic normalisation and populist manipulation – as tools of investigation and as approaches to history that open the way to the emancipation of subaltern and plebeian, of oppressed or simply overlooked common people looking to be heard or overheard, and as routes in the direction of fair access to resources, by becoming people "with" instead of "without" history.

References

Alexander, Sally, and Anna Davin. "Editorial." *History Workshop* 1 (1976): 6.

Archive History. "History from below." https://archives.history.ac.uk/makinghistory/themes/history_from_below.html, accessed November 09, 2024.

Audretsch, Andreas, and Claudia Gatzka, eds. *Schleichend an die Macht: Wie die Neue Rechte Geschichte instrumentalisiert, um Deutungshoheit über unsere Zukunft zu erhalten.* Berlin: Dietz, 2020.

Benjamin, Walter. "Theses on the Philosophy of History (On the Concept of History)." In *Illuminations*, edited by Hannah Arendt, translated by Harry Zohn, 253–264. New York: Schocken Books, 2007.

Berlin, Isaiah. *The Hedgehog and the Fox: An Essay on Tolstoy's View of History.* New Jersey: Princeton University Press, 2013.

Bourdieu, Pierre. *Pascalian Meditations.* Stanford: Stanford University Press, 2000.

Brewer, John. "New Ways in History, or, Talking About My Generation." *Historein* 3 (2001): 27–46.

Dussel, Enrique. *Politics of Liberation: a Critical World History.* London: SCM Press, 2011.

Edelman, Marc. "E.P. Thompson and Moral Economies." In *A Companion to Moral Anthropology*, edited by Didier Fassin, 49–66. Chichester: Wiley-Blackwell, 2012.

Eley, Geoff. "No Need to Choose: History from Above, History from below." *Viewpoint Magazine*, June 27, 2024.

Ely, Christopher. *Russian Populism. A History.* London: Bloomsbury, 2021.

Federici, Silvia. *Caliban and the Witch: Women, the Body and Private Accumulation.* Brooklyn: Autonomedia, 2004.

Finchelstein, Federico. *From Fascism to Populism in History.* Berkeley: University of California Press, 2017.

Finlay, Robert. "The Refashioning of Martin Guerre." *American Historical Review* 93/3 (1988): 553–571, https://www.jstor.org/stable/1868102, accessed November 09, 2024.

Fuente, Marisa. *Dispossessed Lives: Enslaved Women, Violence, and the Archive.* Philadelphia: University of Pennsylvania Press, 2018.

Galeano, Eduardo. *Genesis: Memory of Fire.* New York: W.W. Norton, 1998.

Genovese, Eugene. *Roll, Jordan, Roll! The World the Slaves Made.* New York: Pantheon, 1974.

Ginzburg, Carlo. *The Cheese and the Worms: The Cosmos of a Sixteenth-Century Miller.* London: Routledge & Kegan Paul, 1980 [1976].

Ginzburg, Carlo. *Ecstasies: Deciphering the Witches' Sabbath.* New York: Pantheon Books, 1991.

Gramsci, Antonio. *Selections from the Prison Notebooks. Edited and translated by Quintin Hoare, and Geoffrey Nowell Smith.* New York: International Publishers, 1971.

Hartman, Saidiya. "Venus in Two Acts." *small axe* 26 (2008): 1–14, https://warwick.ac.uk/fac/arts/history/research/centres/blackstudies/venus_in_two_acts.pdf, accessed November 09, 2024.

Hill, Christopher. *The English Revolution, 1640: An Essay.* London: Lawrence & Wishart, 1940.

Hill, Christopher. "The Norman Yoke." In *Puritanism and Revolution*, edited by Christopher Hill, 50–122. London: Secker & Warburg, 1958.

Hill, Christopher. *The World Turned Upside Down*. London: Penguin, 1975 [1972].

Hobsbawm, Eric. *Bandits*. New York: Pantheon, 1981 [1969].

James, C.L.R. *The Black Jacobins: Toussaint L'Ouverture and the San Domingo Revolution*. London: Penguin, 2001 [1938].

Lefebvre, Georges. *The Coming of the French Revolution*. Princeton: Princeton University Press, 2015 [1939].

Levi, Giovanni. *Inheriting Power: The Story of an Exorcist*. Chicago: University of Chicago Press, 1988.

Lezina, Evgenija. "Memorial und seine Geschichte." *Osteuropa* 11–12 (2014): 165–176.

Making History. "History Workshop Journal." http://www.history.ac.uk/makinghistory/resources/articles/HWJ.html, accessed November 09, 2024.

Marin, C.G., and M. Roy. "Narrative Resistance: A Conversation with Historian Marcus Rediker." *Workplace* 30 (2018): 54–69.

Mignolo, Walter. *The Politics of Decolonial Investigations (On Decoloniality)*. Durham: Duke University Press, 2021.

Orwell, George. *1984*. London: Penguin, 1983 [1949].

Quintero Rivera, Angel. *Workers' Struggle in Puerto Rico. A Documentary Study*. New York: Monthly Review Press, 1976 (Spanish 1971).

Raphael, Lutz. *Beyond Coal and Steel. A social history of Western Europe after the Boom*. London: Verso, 2023.

Rediker, Markus. How to write History from Below (graduate), https://www.marcusrediker.com/how-to-write-history-from-below-graduate/, accessed 09.11.2024.

Rediker, Markus, and Peter Linebaugh. *The Many-Headed Hydra: Sailors, Laves, Commoners, and the Hidden History for the Revolutionary Atlantic*. Boston: Beacon Press 2000.

Rowbotham, Sheila. *Hidden from History, 300 Years of Women's Oppression and the Fight Against it*. London: Pluto Press, 1977.

Samuel, Raphael. "People's History." In *People's History and Socialist Theory*, edited by Raphael Samuel, xv-xxxix. London: Routledge & Kegan Paul, 1981.

Sarkar, Sumit. *Writing Social History*. Delhi: Oxford University Press, 1997.

Savile, John. "Edward Thompson, the Communist Party and 1956." *Socialist Register* (1994): 20–31, copy at https://www.marxists.org/archive/saville/1994/xx/epthompson.htm, accessed November 08, 2024.

Schnickmann, Alexander. "Unter einem anderen Mond: Carlo Ginzburg und die Hermeneutik der Risse." *Weimarer Beiträge: Zeitschrift für Literaturwissenschaft, Ästhetik und Kulturwissenschaften* 1 (2020): 17–35, https://publikationen.ub.uni-frankfurt.de/opus4/frontdoor/deliver/index/docId/71481/file/WB_66-1_2020_Schnickmann.pdf, accessed November 09, 2024.

Scott Brown Timothy. *Sixties Europe*. Cambridge: Cambridge University Press, 2020.

Scott, Joan. *Gender and the Politics of History*. New York: Columbia University Press, 1988.

Stanley, Jason. *Erasing History: How Fascists Rewrite the Past to Control the Future*. New York: Simon & Schuster, 2024.

Thompson, E.P. *The Making of the English Working Class*. London: Penguin, 1963.

Thompson, E.P. "History from below (1966)." In *The Essential E.P. Thompson*, edited by Dorothy Thompson, 482–489. New York: New Press, 2001.

Thompson, E.P. "The Moral Economy of the English Crowd in the Eighteenth Century." *Past and Present* 50 (1971): 76–136.

Thompson, E.P. *Customs in Common*. London: Penguin, 1991.

Times Literary Supplement. "A Worker reads and asks." https://www.the-tls.co.uk/regular-features/poem-of-the-week/a-worker-reads-and-asks-bertolt-brecht-poem-of-the-week-andrew-mcculloch/, accessed November 09, 2024.

Tolstoy, Leo. *War and Peace*. Harmondsworth: Penguin, 2006 [1869].

Traverso, Enzo. *The New Faces of Fascism: Populism and the Far Right*. London: Verso, 2019.

van Onselen, Charles. *The Seed is Mine. The Life of Kas Maine, A South African Sharecropper 1894–1985*. New York: Hill and Wang, 1996.

Venturi, Franco. *Roots of Revolution. A History of the Populist and Socialist Movements in 19th Century Russia*. London: Phoenix Press, 2001.

Versobooks. "The Historians' Group of the Communist Party." https://www.versobooks.com/blogs/news/the-historians-group-of-the-communist-party, accessed November 09, 2024.

White, Hayden. *The Content of the Form: Narrative Discourse and Historical Representation*. Baltimore: Johns Hopkins University Press, 1987.

Zachariah, Benjamin. *After the Last Post*. Berlin: De Gruyter, 2019.

Zachariah, Benjamin, Lutz Raphael, and Brigitta Bernet, eds. *What's Left of Marxism*. Berlin: De Gruyter, 2020.

Zemon Davis, Natalie. *The Return of Martin Guerre*. Cambridge, MA: Harvard University Press, 1982.

Benjamin Zachariah

2 History from Below and the Populist Temptation: Nationalism, Indigenism and Authenticity

2.1 Introduction

The precise moment when history from below came into being is difficult to trace. This may be because a historiographical tendency is often long present before it acquires a name, a set of institutions, a journal, adherents, professorships, and gatekeepers. With history from below, a further difficulty is manifest: as a tendency that claimed grass-roots, participatory, and politically activist roots, its legitimation claims tended to be based on its *not* being an academic phenomenon. Its entry into academia, sometimes heralded as a phenomenon indicative of the transformation and democratisation of academia itself, was a contradictory process. Many of its protagonists insisted that they cared not for the recognition of academic history-writing; many of the same people became academic celebrities by drawing on their extra- or pre-academic personas or avatars, and on the legitimation provided by their subjects. That history from below now aligns the voices of its writers with the voices of those written about, conflating or coordinating the voices to appear to be congruent, suggests that something has changed since its origins as a counter-hegemonic and counter-academic movement.

But it probably must be said that the idea of a history "from below", thereby implying an "above" that is predetermined along with the "below", and with "above" and "below" reciprocally defining each other, has an implicit populism built into it: "elite" versus "subaltern", the version that has done the rounds via Antonio Gramsci's formulation of the latter term, maps quite well onto the former binary.[1] That without a careful contextual reading, many cases can predetermine above and below, elite and subaltern, and read evidence according to a convenient template, is a danger that has materialised very often. Mapped onto recent trends in the social sciences, history, and public discourse more generally, of attributing 'power' and siding with 'victim' communities, the populist temptation has never been greater.

---

1 Antonio Gramsci, *Selections from the Prison Notebooks*, ed. and trans. Quintin Hoare and Geoffrey Nowell Smith (New York: International Publishers, 1971).

https://doi.org/10.1515/9783111522180-002

And yet, as an old-fashioned Marxian might be tempted to say, the "ripening of the contradictions" takes time: what might be implicit in the logic of a situation does not immediately manifest itself. We can see this unfolding of an implicit logic in the tendencies that we can now see, overlapping, and sometimes chronologically contiguous, but with backward-looping tendencies and some survivals, that provide reminders of what was once meant by history from below. While we need not believe that we can map or analyse an entire body of writing that has travelled under the history from below label, there are recognisable tendencies that we can indeed name, and they might awkwardly co-exist in the same text.

2.2 The Populist Temptation: An Attempt at a Description

These tendencies can be listed as follows: one: the acknowledging of a different subjectivity that problematises the "normal" view as a view from "above". Two: creating a different subjectivity that is normatively superior, because it establishes the perspective of the downtrodden and the oppressed, thereby giving that perspective voice. Three: the promotion and perpetuation of a postulated superior subjectivity "from below" that fixes the category of victim as a (person from) a group with a claim on the past, and on the future, as a corollary of her victimhood. Four: establishing the *historian of* histories from below as authentic and as equivalent to her subject of study – to use the terminology borrowed from Antonio Gramsci that accompanies much of history from below, the subalternist masquerading as the subaltern, perhaps convinced she is the subaltern. Five (possibly mainly as a corollary to four): the exclusion of persons writing histories from "below" from the writing of histories that are not "their" subaltern positions – not, in other words, histories of collective victimhood subjectivities that are the histories of the historian's own collective. We may speak of autobiographical collectivities with the individual effaced. This is of course a fundamental paradox: in attempting to give voice to the voiceless, the individual is effaced and subsumed into a collective, which s/he can "embody" or "represent".

Here, then, is the conflation and then the inflation of claims on behalf of history from below, what it does, and what it can do: from subjectivities acknowledged to authentic voices identified; from amplification of authentic voices to the creation of indigenism as the main basis for that authentic voice; to the identification of historians themselves with indigenist authenticity. Historians who cannot unproblematically identify themselves as indigenous and thereby authentic must content themselves with identifying *with* the indigenous and authentic, 'allies' in an imagined historiographical-political battle in which their inauthenticity is alleviated by their genuflection to properly indigenous and authentic authority.[2] In this process, self-reflexivity becomes autobiography, history becomes projection, subjects become the projection site for the historian's fantasies, fears, affect, neuroses.[3] "Lived experience" becomes an invocation that takes the place of truth or fact, whose existence at all in the universe of history from below is differentially shaky. The processes of mediation that deliver what claims to be not just a historiographical tendency, but a social and political movement on its own, to the academy, and then via the academy back to a public domain in which, after its academic sojourn, history from below is not a grassroots movement but a set of slogans, have become less than transparent in the process.

We can trace this tendency of slogans replacing sources, self-positioning replacing open-ended enquiries about subjectivities, literary reading overpowering historical contextualisation, to a moment in history (the post-1989 winding down of the Eastern Bloc, and the decline of the aspired-to collective we once called "class" or "classes"), sites of knowledge-production (the Australian National University in Canberra, the University of Chicago, and Columbia University in New York), or political and historiographical manoeuvres (the Subaltern Studies collective and its entanglements, which bring with it the weight of the historical conjuncture as well as the institutions we have just mentioned).[4] That would be the route away from its Marxian beginnings for history from below, and its later successors would not even claim the term as a distant legitimator. But, as we always remind ourselves as historians, correlation is not causation, and intentionality is usually unreadable: when it is readable at all, it is as proclaimed intention, framed within a given language of legitimation, and even the individual's own "authentic" intentions are often opaque to the individual herself.

And, strangely enough, and despite Marxian thinking's own discomfort with an idea of the "authentic voice",[5] it is true that given the Stalinist propensity to exalt the proletariat's authentic contributions to history and culture, there ap-

---

2 See Olaf Kaltmaier, in this volume, for a study of this problem and the inauthentic historian's place in it.

3 "The peasant acts here as a shorthand for all the seemingly nonmodern, rural, nonsecular relationships and life practices . . ." – see below (p. 46, fn. 50) for the source of this statement.

4 A symptomatic publication would include Edward W. Said, "Foreword", in *Selected Subaltern Studies*, eds. Ranajit Guha, and Gayatri Chakravarty Spivak (New York: Oxford University Press, 1988), v–x. Both Said and Spivak were at Columbia. See also the contribution of Dario de Rosa, in this volume, on Canberra as a site.

5 "Not the *invention* of a new proletarian culture, but the *development* of the best models, traditions and results of the *existing* culture, *from the point of view* of the Marxist world outlook and the conditions of life and struggle of the proletariat in the period of its dictatorship." VI Lenin,

pears to have been enough room for authenticity-based arguments *within* Marxian practices of history from below. This is a strain that, denounced in principle but only partially successfully repressed, returns in the form of other authentic collectivities, whose normative desirability or sacrosanct quality is not subject to historical scrutiny. If we were to attempt to reconstruct the path that led to these tendencies – from within Marxian traditions and among the Marxist left, as a major strand, but not the only strand, of history from below, we would be faced with an awkward question: did history from below contain a tendency to populism within itself from its inception?

The populist temptation, then, a short-cut that accepts certain categories as a priori legitimate, desirable, and normatively superior, cannot be easily assimilated to "left" or "right", politically speaking. Does the focus on "authenticity", of experience, positionality, inheritance, or anything else, dehistoricise the histories that history from below retells? Institutionalisation creates its own echo-chambers, shutting out the voices that could help the processes of self-doubt; and by now there are enough comforting semi-public spaces, journals, publishers, salons, that will keep the nostalgic left intellectual secure in her self-delusions. What might allow for a certain disruption is that (without the benefit of flattening concepts that conflate left and right) some of us might feel a little uneasy at the easy uses that both left and right can make of authenticity-based arguments, such that we can no longer tell the difference between the one and the other.

History from below as the democratisation and popularisation of history was intended to question what history really was, or is; this question often gets siphoned off into something that now passes as memory studies, where the axiom that is (strategically?) forgotten is that collective memory is *taught*, not remembered.[6] The need to give memory the status of history, we might want to note, owes something to the history from below scheme of things, in which listening to otherwise unheard voices might include recording memories, first or second hand, and then rendering them in print *as history* – and the parallel problem of the status of truth or fact in oral histories raises its head at the same time.

In the sections that follow, I attempt to trace the histories of history from below, told from the point of view of their protagonists' own historiographical commentaries, self-generated genealogies, and of the histories they wrote. Here, a strict separation of these genres is often impossible: memoirs, historiographical commentaries, political self-justifications, and self-criticism often can be found in

---

'Rough Draft of a Resolution on Proletarian Culture' (1920), https://www.marxists.org/archive/lenin/works/1920/oct/09b.htm, accessed November 17, 2024.

6 Maurice Halbwachs, *On Collective Memory* (Chicago: Chicago University Press, 1992) [1925].

the same texts. Two geographical and at the same time historiographical locations are used here as stalking horses of tendencies that can be seen across various varieties of history from below, but are here used as exemplary: the English (which contains within itself an awareness of its own failures to be British), and the "South Asian", the latter often a euphemism for "Indian".

2.3 The Relevant Collective: Marxist Roots, Marxian Routes and the English

The early history of history from below in Britain is bound to the Communist Party of Great Britain's (CPGB) Historians' Group (CPHG), which was a branch of the CPGB's National Cultural Committee. This used to be one of the best-known things about history from below in the Anglophone world. "In a sense, we saw ourselves as continuing the major national tradition of history, and many non-Marxists as prepared to join in this task with us."[7] The moment of 1956, when many or most of the CPHG left the CPGB after the Soviet Union's invasion of Hungary, in the aftermath of Khrushchev's de-Stalinisation speech, was a foundational moment: much of the CPHG, and E.P. Thompson, soon to be the unofficial head priest of history from below, migrated to what was now the 'New Left';[8] though John Savile, at least, believed that E.P. Thompson had not been particularly active in the CPHG; Dorothy Thompson had been.[9] The tracing of the heritage of 'people's history', one of the predecessor terms that history from below in its residual Marxian existence never abandoned,[10] was often attributed to A.L. Morton, whose *People's History of England* was published by the Left Book Club in 1938.[11]

---

7 Eric Hobsbawm, "The Historians' Group of the Communist Party," in *Rebels and their Causes: Essays in Honour of A.L. Morton*, ed. Maurice Cornforth (London: Lawrence & Wishart, 1978), reproduced at https://www.versobooks.com/blogs/news/the-historians-group-of-the-communist-party, accessed November 08, 2024.
8 Hobsbawm, "The Historians' Group of the Communist Party".
9 John Savile, "Edward Thompson, the Communist Party, and 1956," *Socialist Register* 1994, copy at https://www.marxists.org/archive/saville/1994/xx/epthompson.htm, accessed November 08, 2024.
10 Raphael Samuel, ed., *People's History and Socialist Theory* (London: Routledge, 1981).
11 Hobsbawm, "The Historians' Group of the Communist Party"; A.L. Morton, *A People's History of England* (London: Victor Gollancz, 1938). Raphael Samuel, "Editorial prefaces," in *People's History and Socialist Theory*, xviii, cites Morton as an influence on "people's history". A. Ramos Oliveira's *People's History of Germany* (London: Victor Gollancz, 1942), published four years later, does not seem to have made the same impact.

After most of the CPHG were expelled from the Party, or had resigned, they carried with them an attempt to maintain their Marxian commitments: "it is more important that we should remain loyal to our intellectual integrity as Marxists than to the Party under all circumstances. Our duty to the British working class as honest intellectuals is more important", E.P. Thompson wrote to John Savile in 1956.[12] What this amounted to was to continue to write histories of English working-class or "plebeian" social formations, without fitting them into a prefabricated template of a developed universal class without specific characteristics. "Plebeian" had the further advantage of not bearing the burden of a teleology of an emerging revolutionary class.

Starting from the 'national tradition', Hobsbawm himself might have later said, is potentially parochial and narrow;[13] but the CPHG was not merely national: it had local chapters, and a cyclostyled publication called "Our History", which might serve, if one is looking for precedents and ancestors, to indicate that a smaller parochialism might have been a stage on the way to a wider space, just as the 'national' was a stage on the way to the international. This default position of doing national history was perhaps what the exiting CPHG members took with them out of the party. "History, like love, is something about which all of us think we know something once we are old enough." Eric Hobsbawm wrote this line in self-ironic mode, in the course of his reminiscences about the CPHG and its early years, his account culminating in the acrimonious debates and splits around 1956–57: Hobsbawm, famously, was the one who did not leave. He continues:

> Moreover, history is a valued component of the labour movement, since its ideological tradition and continuity largely rest on the collective memory of old struggles. History is the core of Marxism, though some recent schools of Marxists appear to think otherwise. For us and for the Party, history – the development of capitalism to its present stage, especially in our own country, which Marx himself had studied – had put our struggles on its agenda and guaranteed our final victory. Some of us even felt that it had recruited us as individuals. Where would we, as intellectuals, have been, what would have become of us, but for the experiences of war, revolution and depression, fascism and antifascism, which surrounded us in our youth? Our work as historians was therefore embedded in our work as Marxists, which we believed to imply membership of the Communist Party. It was inseparable from our political commitment and activity. Eventually this very sense of unity between our work as historians and communists led to the crisis of 1956-7, for it was among the historians that the dissatisfaction with the Party's reactions to the Khrushchev speech at the Twen-

---

12 E.P. Thompson to John Savile, 4 April, 1956, quoted in Savile, "Edward Thompson, the Communist Party, and 1956".

13 Eric Hobsbawm, *Nations and Nationalism since 1780: Programme, Myth, Reality* (Cambridge: Cambridge University Press, 1990).

tieth Congress of the CPSU first came into the open. In the event many of the most active and prominent members of the Group left or were expelled from the Party . . .[14]

For most national Communist Parties, their need to operate within really-existing states, shaping and guiding struggles within those boundaries, was a structural constraint as well as a 'stage': the Italian case was a peculiar one in which, under Stalin's instructions, the revolution would not be attempted in Italy, a cultural movement that would be initiated and sustained by the Party would happen in its stead, paving the way for something important in the future.[15] And this, if it wasn't completely evident in the British case, was a greater problem in parts of the world where the struggle for 'national self-determination' was, according to Leninist doctrine, a necessary prior stage to the struggle for socialism.[16] The only trouble was, of course, that in this situation one could very easily get stuck in the politics of an earlier 'stage' and never emerge from it: either as a traditional Communist Party or as heterodox Marxians struggling with and against the legacies of a Stalinised communist movement and then its awkward aftermath in the Cold War. Here, pro-Moscow "Third World" regimes as diverse as Nehru's India, Nasser's Egypt, and Idi Amin's Uganda, found support from the Soviet Bloc; parts of the New Left looked to Maoist China and the Cultural Revolution for inspiration.

Perhaps it is the fate of E.P. Thompson, in his central focus on the *English* working class ("class is a cultural as much as an economic formation . . . I have been cautious as to generalising beyond English experience"[17]), to be incorporated into a reification of culture that suggests the *national* specificity of a working *class* that, in being specifically English, loses the abstraction of its revolutionary universalism. And it is the *national* as a formation, its Englishness, rather than class in its abstract universalism, that stands in the foreground.[18]

A fiftieth anniversary volume celebrating the impact and afterlives of E.P. Thompson's *The Making of the English Working Class* (1963) opens with the line

---

14 Hobsbawm, "The Historians' Group of the Communist Party".

15 For the historiographical implications of this, see Brigitta Bernet's chapter in this volume; also Brigitta Bernet, "The Postwar Marxist Milieu of Microhistory," in *What's Left of Marxism?*, eds. Benjamin Zachariah, Lutz Raphael and Brigitta Bernet (Berlin: de Gruyter, 2020), 37–64.

16 VI Lenin, *The Right of Nations to Self-Determination* (1914), https://www.marxists.org/archive/lenin/works/1914/self-det/ accessed November 08, 2024, and on the Lenin-Roy debates at the Second Comintern Congress in 1920, see https://www.marxists.org/history/international/comintern/2nd-congress/ch04.htm also accessed November 08, 2024.

17 E.P. Thompson, *The Making of the English Working Class* (Harmondsworth: Pelican, 1980) [1963], 12.

18 See Eric Hobsbawm, "Do Workers Have a Country?," in *On Nationalism*, ed. Eric Hobsbawm (London: Abacus, 2022), 87–106.

"Does a revolution need big books anymore?".[19] These chronological bookends, as it were, preserve a populist expectation: will the "real" below stand up and be recognised? Where, the anniversary-book asks, are the women, the people of colour, the colonised, in Thompson's account? These questions, in and of themselves, are predictably populist, in a book that opens with an invocation of Black Lives Matter.[20] It might serve as a reminder that the central 'big book' in question that appears to be the hovering text of the anniversary and its volume, for anyone who was politically conscious from 1965 to 1975, isn't, of course, *The Making*: it's a *little* book, a mass-produced set of quotations, an empty signifier to be waved and not read: Chairman Mao's *Little Red Book*.[21] That, of course, is a moment from the end of the beginning of history from below, in which intellectuals 'went to the countryside' to discover the authentic life of the authentic peasant, and to tell his story. But let us return to the first bookend, or the beginning of the beginning, or at least the beginning of *a* beginning, for a moment.

2.4 Cultural Revolutionaries: Subaltern Studies in South Asia

We shall return later to Thompson via his Indian comrades; but for now, before that return, let us turn briefly to a late flowering of the history from below movement, in the early phases of a movement that, using Gramscian terminology, called itself "Subaltern Studies".[22] Here, "elite" and "subaltern" mapped onto "above" and "below"; but any conception of class was soon overpowered by a version of Third Worldist (we would now say Global Southist) nationalism. The manifesto that Subaltern Studies began with denounced the "elitism" of both "colonialist" and "bourgeois-nationalist" historiographies, and demanded attention to the "politics of the people", hitherto missing from the picture. What *SS* sought to find,

---

19 Antoinette Burton and Stephanie Furtado, "Preface: The Revolution and the Book," in *Histories of a Radical Book: E.P. Thompson and The Making of the English Working Class*, eds. Antoinette Burton and Stephanie Furtado (Brooklyn: Berghahn, 2021), viii.

20 Burton and Furtado, "Preface," ix.

21 See Alexander C Cook, ed., *Mao's Little Red Book: A Global History* (Cambridge: Cambridge University Press, 2014).

22 Although it was not my intention to write on Subaltern Studies again, the populism theme cannot be addressed without some reference to Subaltern Studies. For my previous treatment of the subject, see for instance Benjamin Zachariah, "Identifying the Beast Within: Postcolonial Theory and History", in *After the Last Post: The Lives of Indian Historiography*, (Berlin: de Gruyter, 2019), 21–47, esp. 30–36.

however, was the contribution of the people *to nationalist struggle.*[23] This was a strange, predetermined question; and it may well have been a particular obsession of those parts of the world that tended to centre the national so quickly. The usefulness of the non-specific 'subaltern', whose consciousness and loyalties were not altogether known from the name used as analytic, in place of "worker" or "peasant", was immediately negated by the appropriation of the subaltern to serve the nation.

But the question of finding adequate sources to tell the stories of the 'politics of the people' raised its head very quickly. That most sources utilised by historians of India were from 'the colonial archive', or rather, the most obvious repository of official papers that could be found nearby, and that very few people were going to trouble themselves to find interesting new sources based on their new questions, emerged very early on in the "movement". Ranajit Guha's programmatic essay in *Subaltern Studies II* uses the idea of the 'prose of counter-insurgency' as a device to disinter the assumptions hidden in the writings of most historians of South Asia. Such historians' forays into 'the colonial archive' can, he wrote, only reproduce that prose, as a result of which the eponymous 'subaltern' only appears to the historian as the 'insurgent' of the colonial imagination, and is otherwise invisible. The historian, writing effectively from 'secondary' or (Guha's coinage) 'tertiary' sources, can therefore only reproduce the assumptions of the colonial state apparatus. His advice to historians was, therefore, a form of creative use of the pre-existing binary by reversal: to read the colonial archives' negative terminology to present 'the insurgent' as 'the peasant' in a positive light.[24]

Although this has retrospectively been described, paraphrasing Walter Benjamin, as reading 'against the grain',[25] Ranajit Guha doesn't appear to set much store by this phrase himself: in the passage where he juxtaposes 'colonialist discourse' with his other-side-of-the-binary counter-readings, he draws instead on Chairman Mao's text from 1927, *Report on an Investigation of the Peasant Movement in Hunan*: the piece whose title he borrows is called "'It's Terrible!" Or "It's Fine!"'.[26] Mao's *Report*, as even every pretend-Marxist knows, and every Bengali

---

23 Ranajit Guha, "On Some Aspects of the Historiography of Colonial India," in *Subaltern Studies I*, ed. Ranajit Guha (Delhi: Oxford University Press, 1982), 1–9.

24 Ranajit Guha, "The Prose of Counter-Insurgency," in *Subaltern Studies II*, ed. Ranajit Guha (Delhi: Oxford University Press, 1983), 1–42.

25 Walter Benjamin, "Über den Begriff der Geschichte" (1940), translated as "On the Concept of History" (2005), Thesis VII, https://www.marxists.org/reference/archive/benjamin/1940/history. htm accessed November 08, 2024. Translation by Dennis Redmond.

26 Mao Tse-Tung [Zedong], *Selected Works of Mao Tse-Tung* volume 1 (Paris: Foreign Languages Press, 2021) [Beijing: Foreign Languages Press, 1965], 14–15.

Marxist once had to pretend to have read, is the text that tells us the revolutionary's duty in the face of peasant self-mobilisation: should they "march at their head and lead them?" Should they "trail behind them, gesticulating and criticizing?" Or should they "stand in their way and oppose them?"[27] The future Great Helmsman believed that the first answer was the right one: on the "'it's terrible or it's fine' binary", as Guha called it, this is what Mao had actually said on the peasant committees' control in Hunan:

> Even quite progressive people said, "Though terrible, it is inevitable in a revolution." In short, nobody could altogether deny the word "terrible". But, as already mentioned, the fact is that the great peasant masses have risen to fulfil their historic mission and that the forces of rural democracy have risen to overthrow the forces of rural feudalism. . . . This is a marvelous feat never before achieved, not just in forty, but in thousands of years. It's fine. It is not "terrible" at all. It is anything but "terrible". . . . If your revolutionary viewpoint is firmly established and if you have been to the villages and looked around, you will undoubtedly feel thrilled as never before. Countless thousands of the enslaved – the peasants – are striking down the enemies who fattened on their flesh. What the peasants are doing is absolutely right, what they are doing is fine! "It's fine!" is the theory of the peasants and of all other revolutionaries. . . . Every revolutionary comrade must support it, or he will be taking the stand of counter-revolution.[28]

Ranajit Guha invokes this passage as he himself uses a logic of substitution, in which his "colonialist knowledge" texts are re-read to render "implied, though unstated terms" (Tab. 1):[29]

Tab. 1: Ranajit Guha's methodological table.

TERRIBLE	FINE
Insurgents	peasants
fanatic	Islamic puritan
daring and wanton atrocities on the Inhabitants	resistance to oppression
defying the authority of the State	revolt against zamindari
disturbing the public tranquil(l)ity	struggle for a better order
intention to attack, etc	intention to punish oppressors
one of their Gods to reign as a King	Santal self-rule

It should be clear that, as Chairman Mao had pointed out, it was only the true revolutionary who could correctly render "It's terrible!" as "it's fine!" in an accu-

---

27 *Selected Works of Mao Tse-Tung*, vol. 1, 12.
28 *Selected Works of Mao Tse-Tung*, vol. 1, 14–15.
29 Guha, "The Prose of Counter-Insurgency," 15.

2 History from Below and the Populist Temptation — **39**

rate translation. This is already a *moral* rather than an analytic claim: it is the historian with the correct vision who will be able to read his sources correctly.

We might wish to question whether the writing of history – in retrospect, when the actors are dead and their issues buried – is not too easily and somewhat facetiously paralleled to a revolutionary situation, or a revolutionary act, a parallel that swiftly becomes anointed as the act itself: "I do not think it is an exaggeration to say therefore that rewriting Indian history today is an extension of the struggle between subaltern and elite, and between the Indian masses and the British *raj.*"[30] And history-writing swiftly takes the form of Cultural Revolutionary populism, where the former Stalinists are now (and about a decade too late) convinced Red Guards throwing stones at little bottles: that which was revered must now be reviled; that which was worthwhile will now be worthless.

In retrospective accounts of history from below as a movement, it is unusual to find traces of the now-discredited genealogy of Maoism, which was available to contemporaries and near-contemporaries as a fascination for the "Chinese Cultural Revolution". The emulable example allegedly to be taken on board was that class could be unlearned by a series of declassing actions on the part of a suspect portion of the population, whose bourgeois or feudal proclivities had to be unlearned by doing. Whether this form of Maoism, whose histories were also well-received in the "west" (and which for this purpose ought to include India, not just because it lies to the west of China, but also because few first-hand accounts of the Cultural Revolution made their way directly to India, but returned eastward via a geographical point further "west"),[31] can still be

---

30 "Foreword," in *Selected Subaltern Studies,* eds. Gayatri Chakrabarty Spivak, and Ranajit Guha (Delhi: Oxford University Press, 1988), vii. The Foreword has no named author; we could probably attribute authorship to GCS, assuming that Ranajit Guha might not have been quite so immodest as to describe his own work in those terms. But it could be that the first-person singular used there is a deliberate misdirection, a necessary myth, or a strategic essentialism.

31 Among the few exceptions were Hemanga Biswas, *Abar Cheen Dekhe Elam* (Calcutta: Sribhumi, 1975) in Bengali. Parts of Joan Robinson's *The Cultural Revolution in China* (1969) were first published in the journal *Now* from Calcutta on December 22, 1967: Joan Robinson, "Preface," *The Cultural Revolution in China* (Harmondsworth: Pelican, 1970) [1969]. *Now* was edited from 1966 to 1968 by the Bengali poet, journalist, and translator (from Russian), Samar Sen (information confirmed from Subhas Ranjan Chakraborty, text message on November 11, 2024, from copies of the journal in his possession). This is perhaps not the place to introduce an oral history/ memory theme, but my mother recalls a conversation between an ardent enthusiast of the Chinese Cultural Revolution in Calcutta and a lawyer: the tailpiece of the conversation was her put-down of the enthusiastic proto-Maoist with "not having been there, I wouldn't know". The enthusiast in question, who later in his life became an ardent supporter of the Hindu fascist Bharatiya Janata Party, had also, of course, never been to China. Perhaps this fragment of memory will one day count as his-

40 —— Benjamin Zachariah

acknowledged publicly as a source of legitimacy for history from below, is doubtful.[32]

Here, a Cultural Revolution populism simply inverts the hierarchies of a moral or political order in a somewhat mechanistic way, and assumes that the world to win is contained in your words: there is nothing outside the (pre-)text. Just as values were already good or bad in Cultural Revolutionary Red Guard vigilantism, the new vigilante squads, confident in the rightness of their cause, and unable or unwilling to listen to outside voices, are convinced that they are the chosen ones who will find themselves "on the right side of history". This seems more like a religious cult than a historically- or philosophically-informed politics; and perhaps the roots of and routes to our present discontents lie in the Stalinised party-politics of an allegedly self-correcting democratic centralism, which requires periodic self-denunciation on the part of party members who find themselves out of joint with the party line, as historiography and official memory corrects itself to restore the correct view of history; or in a Cultural Revolution-like attempt to control the narrative by shutting out, shutting down, or taking out, one's opponents. After that, one is right by virtue of being on the right side of the moral consensus. How do we know we are? We don't; but we have learnt our shibbolethics well enough to know that we've said the right thing, and no one will break ranks in order to disagree, so all is safe: we have signalled true belonging to the collective.

And yet, in its early years, Subaltern Studies did produce some innovative histories from below: for instance, Ranajit Guha"s *Chandra's Death*, or Sumit Sarkar's *The Kalki-Avatar of Bikrampur*, among the essays.[33] Some years down the line, Partha Chatterjee's *A Princely Impostor* or Shahid Amin's *Event, Metaphor, Memory* could serve to show that "the subaltern" was not yet a purely abstract entity, and that sources that really existed, even in "the colonial archive", which would yield to the writer and reader of history something of a subaltern

---

tory, if a transcript of the conversation, at which I was present, aged about three, could be put in writing.

32 "Class" remained central to all "Western" adaptations of Maoism – but it meant peasants and/or workers. So "classism" was at the forefront, and the goal of the struggle would be an avant-gardist replacement of the petit bourgeois intellectual with the true worker/peasant. But this could not be a solution in an anti-colonial "national cause" and of a claiming of leadership for oneself: hence the emphasis on declassing.

33 Ranajit Guha, "Chandra's Death," in *Subaltern Studies V*, ed. Ranajit Guha (Delhi: Oxford University Press, 1987), 135–165; Sumit Sarkar, "The *Kalki-Avatar* of Bikrampur," in *Subaltern Studies VI*, ed. Ranajit Guha (Delhi: Oxford University Press, 1989), 1–53.

life.[34] And if some of the narrative strategies or story-lines used were slightly too close to Carlo Ginzburg, *The Cheese and the Worms,* or Natalie Zemon Davis, *The Return of Martin Guerre,* the fact that these were already classics of the history from below genre, and of microhistory, could be said to provide a defence against the derivative nature of some of the Subaltern Studies' discourse.[35] The visibility of their 'subalterns' in these cases, owed much to the affairs of courts of law of various description, in which subaltern testimony appears in the public record because of the need to establish legal culpability. This obviates the need for the injunction to render "it's terrible" as "it's fine", or to be "reading against the grain", which of course can also accommodate a variety of different approaches. For the most part, a straightforward reading of 'colonialist' sources was used when it would yield good results: Shahid Amin's essay *Gandhi as Mahatma* took colonial officials' reportage about the myths and quasi-religious practices that grew up around the personality of Mohandas Gandhi during the Non-Cooperation Movement of 1920–1922 pretty much at face value.[36]

Be that as it may: the prophetic voice was what counted in producing injunctions as to how to do history from below. Partha Chatterjee's subaltern was an impostor attempting to claim the inheritance of a large *zamindari,* an estate that yielded much by way of land-rents (his eponymous "Princely Impostor"). This would require the below to start at a relatively high level, but fortunately the author had already coined the term "the subalternity of an elite", in which, because of the colonial state above him (usually him), the "Indian", whether of a lower or higher status within most contexts, was always possible to depict as a subaltern.[37] That a colleague from literary studies (Partha Chatterjee himself was trained as a political scientist), Gayatri Chakravarty Spivak, had already suggested that subalternity is a pure position of voicelessness ('the subaltern cannot speak' unless spoken for by someone who stands in for the subaltern; and in speaking, the subaltern ceases to be the subaltern), and had thereby created a kind of literary Absolute Zero subaltern (we might remember from our school-level physics clas-

---

34 Partha Chatterjee, *A Princely Impostor? The Strange and Universal History of the Kumar of Bhawal* (Princeton: Princeton University Press, 2002); Shahid Amin, *Event, Metaphor, Memory: Chauri Chaura 1922–1992* (Delhi: Oxford University Press, 1995).

35 Natalie Zemon Davis, *The Return of Martin Guerre* (Cambridge, MA: Harvard University Press, 1982); Carlo Ginzburg, *The Cheese and the Worms: The Cosmos of a Sixteenth-Century Miller* (London: Routledge & Kegan Paul, 1980) [1976].

36 Shahid Amin, "Gandhi as Mahatma: Gorakhpur District, Eastern U.P., 1921–22," in *Subaltern Studies III,* ed. Ranajit Guha (Delhi: Oxford University Press, 1984), 1–61.

37 Partha Chatterjee, *The Nation and its Fragments: Colonial and Postcolonial Histories* (Princeton: Princeton University Press, 1993).

ses that Absolute Zero cannot be attained in any real-world situation), made things contradictory, as far as the larger pronouncements were concerned. Now, the subaltern*ist* must stand forth as the subaltern, (re)present her, and bring her, kicking and screaming, into History.[38] How the subalternist acquired this right, except by virtue of common *national* belonging (with the 'subaltern' already appropriated to an *Indian* national cause), to speak for 'her subalterns', was a difficult question to raise, in an era already beginning to see the effects of affect-claims in academia. But this was no longer about how to read difficult archives, if it ever had been: it was about the self-positioning of the academic.

Let us return to our list of tendencies that beset history from below as it grew: the first two were arguably fellow-travellers in a project that sought to foreground the actual histories of those usually excluded from history – the acknowledgement of a different subjectivity; and the implied attribution to that subjectivity of normative superiority. The second is implicit in the methodologies, or some of them, of history from below: for instance, oral history, or oral testimonies that, when written down, turn (uncertain) memory into (written) history, with the concurrent danger that the subjectivities thus recorded are those that will win a place in history, silencing the many divergent views that are not thus recorded. Volumes have been written on this subject, in which over-sympathetic oral historians amplify positions that suit their often-romanticised views of their interlocutors' lives.[39] This is a situation where sources have to be found that "give voice" to the "silenced": but when perspectives are *a priori* derived from abstract positions *on the authority of* a (self-proclaimed) speaker *for* the subaltern, we are in the realms of tendencies three and four.

The third tendency, let us remind ourselves, is the promotion and perpetuation of a postulated superior subjectivity from below that fixes the category of victim as a (person from) a group with a claim on the past, and on the future, as a corollary of her victimhood. In a well-publicised exchange of historiographical polemic, one subalternist questioned the idea that his adopting of a subjectivity of a particular group led to his blindness to other victims of history, stating that it was perfectly possible to draw analogies between different victimhoods, and thereby to offer solidarity to them, extrapolating from the positions that he

---

38 Gayatri Chakraborty Spivak, "Can the Subaltern Speak?," in *Marxism and the Interpretation of Culture*, eds. Cary Nelson, and Lawrence Grossberg (Basingstoke: Macmillan, 1988), 271–313.
39 For my attempt to understand these debates, see Benjamin Zachariah. "The Tongue is Mightier than the Printing Press? Reflections on the Production of Oral Histories and on Languages of Legitimation," *Dve Domovini* 50 (2019): 71–88.

knew.[40] The implication of his argument was that victimhoods, extrapolated from their positionality ("below"), and in the case of the analogous victims, extrapolated without the benefit of any primary sources, could be lined up in coalition. This gives us no principle of adjudication in a situation where victims or victimhoods are in conflict.[41]

The fourth, and implied fifth tendency, are best represented in the polemics of the literary critic Gayatri Spivak: establishing the *historian of* histories from below as authentic and as equivalent to her subject of study – who gets to speak for whom?[42] Here, to use the terminology borrowed from Antonio Gramsci that accompanies much of history from below, the subalternist can be seen to be masquerading as the subaltern, perhaps convinced she is the subaltern. And the fifth: the exclusion of persons writing histories from below from the writing of histories that are not of their subaltern positions, is also implied here. 'White man saving brown woman from brown man' is Spivak's succinct summary of the agonised debates and moral, political, and legal battles surrounding the abolition of Sati, the rite of burning a widow alive on the funeral pyre of her husband: the ban was put in place by the East India Company in 1829. There is a curious politics of choice here: it appears that the brown man and brown woman are both "below", and the "white man" is "above", therefore illegitimate in his exercise of (state) authority. The brown woman, of course, according to Gayatri Spivak's scheme, is the pure subaltern, unable to speak at all. That not all brown men agreed on the necessity of burning widows, and indeed campaigned against the rite, thereby taking on the burden of being reviled as inauthentic traitors to their religion and race; that the legal doctrine of the widow's 'free will' was difficult to establish in practical terms before a court of law, especially in the absence of the key witness herself, leading up to the ban; or any other complexities of this particular example, were relegated to the background.[43] History, in this view, was both nationalised and racialised: it had inauthentic foreign interventionists and authentic defenders of tradition; in retrospect, it had legitimate writers and illegitimate interlopers; and there was no way to connect subjectivities. The national claim trumped the claim of the (dead?) widow (she could not speak, and the sub-

---

40 Gyan Prakash, "Can the Subaltern Ride? A Reply to O'Hanlon and Washbrook," *Comparative Studies in Society and History* 34 (1992): 168–184.

41 See also Rueedi in this volume.

42 Spivak, "Can the Subaltern Speak?"; for an earlier version of this argument, see Lata Mani, "Contentious Traditions: The Debate on Sati in Colonial India," *Cultural Critique* 7 (1987): 119–156.

43 For a primary-source-based re-evaluation from a former member of the Subaltern Studies collective, see Tanika Sarkar, "Something like rights? Faith, law and widow immolation debates in colonial Bengal," *The Indian Economic & Social History Review* 49, 3 (2012): 295–320.

alternist would not speak for her?). This is a curious outcome for a movement that avoided the terminology of class, because it was already too predeterminedly structured in terms of a telos (a making, one might add, already has this predetermination), in favour of an open-ended, undefined "subaltern".

Consistency, fortunately, was not the aim of this school of thought; and the impossibility of mixing Partha Chatterjee's relational elite-as-subaltern with Spivak's Absolute-Zero-(cannot-be-attained) subaltern with Gyan Prakash's analogous-solidarity subaltern, or other variants, could safely be ignored. After all, if Gramsci used "subaltern" as a term that did not pre-ordain the person thus described to be a member of a class, the term could mean whatever it could be bent to. "Gramsci was a shibboleth", one writer once wrote;[44] and subaltern became a shibboleth too. The tendency among intellectuals to imagine themselves as "representatives" of the subalterns was of course an illusion that was sustainable mainly when becoming cosmopolitan academics outside of the territories whose subalterns they would speak for: thus, the subaltern*ist* became one of the imaginary heads of a hydra of united victims of imperialism, westernisation, colonialism, and oppression; and identifying *with* the victims often became interchangeable with identifying *as* the victims themselves. Given their claims to being avant-gardists of a post-modern, and then post-colonial world situation, "from below" become an intra-academic code for the still-dominated but soon to be at the commanding heights of academia. The shifting subaltern had risen; and new elites had to be imagined who dominated the increasingly dominant subalternist.

2.5 The Splitting of the Subaltern(ist), and an Attempted Return to E.P. Thompson

We are left here, then, with a curious tendency. Abandoning the pre-destined category of class in a structural sense for "plebeian" or "subaltern" had the advantages of non-specificity in that it could use an analytic that was more actor-centric, less teleological. The shift from class to culture opened a way to leave the nation frame behind and step towards other points of reference. But at the same time, given that the nation-*state* poses its candidature implicitly and also often explicitly as the custodian of authentic culture, the dangers of a culturalism that

---

44 Walter Baier, "Gramsci was a Shibboleth," *International Gramsci Journal*, 3, No. 1 (2018): 55–67.

2 History from Below and the Populist Temptation — **45**

gravitates towards nation-statism is always present. When not anchored in the telos of class, do nation and culture become the relevant units of analysis? These difficulties were becoming evident in the movement called Subaltern Studies, more and more affectively nationalised, when Sumit Sarkar announced in the 1990s that an implicit split in Subaltern Studies had become explicit, in an article called 'The Decline of the Subaltern in *Subaltern Studies*'.[45] This was a major breach of the democratic-centralist principles of SS, with differences that had apparently been clear for some time making it into the open, and this led to recriminations and polemics; but we are not concerned with the quasi-Stalinist structures of the collective here. We are concerned with the lenses with which Sumit Sarkar returned history from below to its beginnings, and tried to provide a normative and prescriptive reading of history from below through the works and life of E.P. Thompson. Written on the occasion of E.P. Thompson's death and then enlarged for publication, Sarkar's long tribute,[46] in the anthology in which it appeared, can be paired with a chapter on Thompson's father, also Edward, who had been a missionary in India, a friend of Jawaharlal Nehru, and a biographer of Rabindranath Tagore.[47] The younger Thompson had also appeared in person at one of the Indian History Congress' sessions, in Trivandrum (as it was then still called) in 1976, making him an honorary commentator on historiography in India, at least in an indirect reading.[48] E.P. Thompson, indeed, late in his life, himself wrote a piece on the Indian connection of his father's, *Alien Homage*: reading his father's tribute to a Bengali poet whose language he did not understand.[49]

This moment of the partitioning of the subaltern marked a different rendering of the subalternist's birth-right: on the one hand, with their Marxian underpinnings still pinned on, one group believed that the culturalism, and implicit elitism, of studying "subalterns" who were relatively better off in social and economic terms turned the grandiose proclamations of the "movement" of giving a voice to the voiceless into a bit of a bad joke. On the other hand, those who abandoned even the implicit understandings of how class was made, in favour of a now-post-Cold-War world's preference for cultural categories that had no specific class enemy, and therefore no implied call to active politics, were perfectly happy with this

---

45 Sumit Sarkar, "The Decline of the Subaltern in *Subaltern Studie*," in *Writing Social History*, ed. Sumit Sarkar (Delhi: Oxford University Press, 1997), 82–108.

46 Sumit Sarkar, "The Relevance of E.P. Thompson," *Writing Social History*, 50–81.

47 Sumit Sarkar, "Edward Thompson and India: The Other Side of the Meda," in *Writing Social History*, 109–158.

48 Sarkar, "The Relevance of E.P. Thompson," 54.

49 E.P. Thompson, *'Alien Homage': Edward Thompson and Rabindranath Tagore* (Delhi: Oxford University Press, 1993).

move. This latter story, where "the subaltern" is s/he who cannot speak without being spoken for, and therefore, in speaking without a(n authentic) ventriloquist's services, ceases to be a subaltern, picked up on an 'agency'-based view of historical actors. It also turned a situation that was a historical and historiographical conjuncture (the post-Cold War discrediting of "communism" and "socialism" and the consequent reticence to speak of "class" or "classes") into an act performed in circumstances of one's choosing, more or less with historical figures behaving as if they were all discerning consumers in late capitalist societies: they determined, and actively chose, their "identities".

Thus, chronologically speaking, at the mark of the end of the Cold War and the decline of an organised left with a rootedness in struggles for liberation, once-politically-charged categories like "the peasant", still being read in the 1970s as the possible vanguard class for the world revolution, were now symbolic of something completely different.

> The "peasant" acts here as a shorthand for all the seemingly nonmodern, rural, nonsecular relationships and life practices that constantly leave their imprint on the lives of even the elites in India and on their institutions of government. The peasant stands for all that is not bourgeois (in a European sense) in Indian capitalism and modernity.[50]

We are not now going to go down the rabbit-hole of the strange conflations presented to us here by the writer of the above passage: but we can see here that the idea of the "subaltern" (treated as synonymous with this shorthand peasant) as an actual person has vanished from the agenda. And why should it not have done so, given that for the post-Great Schism Subaltern Studies, history from below is not on the agenda, abandoned along with the idea of history itself, as a Eurocentric claim with its corresponding cultural-supremacist assumptions? This was not the first instance in Subaltern Studies that history from below rendered an unspecified, archetypical "peasant" without specific characteristics, well before Subaltern Studies abandoned history from below: Ranajit Guha had already delivered such a peasant to the readers in a peculiar book in which "peasants" knew that moneylender, government, and landlord were actually the same group of people; whose "elementary aspects" of insurgency could be a typology, and whose struggles could be captured "in its general form" in six simple modalities.[51]

Let us turn instead to the prescriptive implications of Sumit Sarkar's return to E.P. Thompson, siding, if you like, with the secessionists rather than the Party-

---

50 Dipesh Chakravarty, *Provincializing Europe* (Princeton: Princeton University Press, 2000), 11.
51 Ranajit Guha, *Elementary Aspects of Peasant Insurgency in Colonial India* (Delhi: Oxford University Press, 1983); the "general form" statement is from p. 11.

2 History from Below and the Populist Temptation ⸺ **47**

Line Subaltern Studies. A series of warnings against the postulate of "authenticity" emanated from Sarkar's pen: "postulating traditional catholicities . . . 'authentic community consciousness' . . . against 'communalisms' ultimately attributable to colonial discourses" provided a rather simplistic picture of authentic indigenous resistance versus foreign colonial constructions.[52] This trend was accompanied, according to Sarkar, by a refusal to learn from History Workshop experiments in Britain, or even to follow the work of the "barefoot historians" in Germany (and to take seriously the work of Alf Lüdke in particular), in order to find an innovative way to give voice to the silenced, rather than to hide in *a priori* theories.[53] In this respect, E.P. Thompson, according to Sarkar, was an exemplary user of innovative sources. He also managed to work without a fixed notion or economically-determined formula for class, as befits an anti-Stalinist and a Gramscian. Sarkar was nevertheless critical of Thompson's "elevating 'experience' into a kind of master-key that as a 'junction concept' could somehow unproblematically link together social being with social consciousness, structure with process and agency".[54]

And yet, in what was now the immediate post-Cold War age, "much of Thompsonian social history, in this changed milieu, seemed tainted by the sins of Eurocentrism and gender-blindness, philosophically naïve and hopelessly dated by the linguistic turn, and guilty of complicity with liberal humanism and rationalism – for which the Enlightenment has become, today, the convenient, if homogenizing, polemical shorthand."[55] Sarkar makes several references to the attempts to substitute historical sources for readings of discourses via Edward W. Said and Michel Foucault. He concedes that Thompson was not particularly alert to the gender and race aspects of his narratives of "plebeians", Thompson's own preferred word when he was attempting to avoid a predetermined picture of a well-formed class or the amorphous undescribed abstraction of the subaltern. And he suggests that others close to Thompson had done this better: Peter Linebaugh or Catherine Hall, for instance.[56]

---

52 Sumit Sarkar, "The Many Worlds of Indian History," *Writing Social History*, 1–49: 44: he is summarising Gyanendra Pandey, *The Construction of Communalism in Colonial North India* (Delhi: Oxford University Press, 1992).

53 Sarkar, "The Many Worlds of Indian History," *Writing Social History*, 47.

54 Sarkar, "The Relevance of E.P. Thompson," *Writing Social History*, 64–65. Sarkar cites E.P. Thompson, "The Politics of Theory," in *People's History and Socialist Theory*, ed. Raphael Samuel (London: Routledge, 1981), 396–408.

55 Sarkar, "The Relevance of E.P. Thompson," *Writing Social History*, 65

56 Sarkar, "The Relevance of E.P. Thompson," *Writing Social History*, 65

This set of reflections relates to Sarkar's discomfort with the indigenous-authenticity emphasis of the Subaltern Studies group as it abandoned class as a category of analysis altogether, replacing it with religious-inflected community-consciousness assumptions, and (this is more of an implicit critique in his reading) the decline of sources in Subaltern Studies, which accompanies the slippage "from subaltern through peasant to community".[57] He noted that attempts at what he would consider 'microhistory' seldom led to attempts to place these micro-histories in wider contexts, with the result that they remained "fragments"; the closeness of later Subaltern Studies to "neo-traditionalist anti-modernism" as represented by writers like Ashis Nandy; and the distance that Subaltern Studies now had from anything one might recognise as social history, or history from below at all.[58] But how much of this tendency to valorise the authentic and indigenous, and to anoint specific ventriloquists who could give voice to the voiceless subaltern, had already existed before?

2.6 Sources, Authenticity, and the Return of the Repressed (Patriotism/Nationalism)

The two historiographical locations that we have discussed so far in this piece, although aware of and feeding off each other, appear to have had one major difference. In a British, or English, history from below, the tendency of the historian to become a partisan for the histories s/he tells is less pronounced, and/or is seen as a potential danger. In South Asia, it is seen as a virtue. And with these two comparators simultaneously operating against one another, it would be possible to claim that the substitution of "community" for "class" was not necessarily an act of self-censorship or opportunist self-refashioning on the part of historians after the Cold War ended and the "West" had declared the victory of capitalism. The dangers, in the English examples we could draw upon, stretch back to earlier times, and exist in the prehistories of history from below that are claimed from the days of the CPHG itself: Christopher Hill, notably, drawing on R.H. Tawney's reading of Max Weber for England, *Religion and the Rise of Capitalism*[59] to demonstrate (perhaps against the spirit of Weberianism) how Puritanism was a proto-class consciousness, and "the Norman yoke", used as an explanatory concept for

---

57 Sarkar, "The Decline of the Subaltern in Subaltern Studies," *Writing Social History*, 87.
58 Sarkar, "The Decline of the Subaltern in Subaltern Studie," *Writing Social History*, 98, 99.
59 R.H. Tawney, *Religion and the Rise of Capitalism* (London: John Murray, 1948) [1926].

the loss of liberties of the true-born English yeoman, could be a factor in "the English Revolution".[60] If what was effectively a parochial fixing of an enemy within – apparently unproblematic for early modern contexts – raised its head in the twentieth century, it would have very different implications: the automatic positive connotations of this ability to achieve plebeian solidarity at the expense of an axiomatic outsider, marked indelibly by origin.

Misgivings about the categories that the new histories from below were using were also voiced, notably, by those who were considered its pioneers and its most loyal defenders. And here we confront a problem of the practitioner of a critical craft that he knows is failing to maintain the critical standards that the craft requires, and yet can do nothing about it. Raphael Samuel is a good instance of this.[61] In *Perils of the Transcript*, an early oral history piece from 1972, warned against the tendency among historians using oral testimony to clean up their sources, taking out the hesitations, completing sentence fragments, and removing "the cadences of speech". "It would be helpful," he suggested, "if historians could be dissuaded from transcribing speeches according to the conventions and constrictions of written prose". This is all the more important because "[t]he collector of the spoken word – of oral memory and tradition – is in a privileged position. He is the creator, in some sort, of his own archives, and he ought to interpret his duties accordingly".[62] The responsibility of the historian, therefore, was to ensure that s/he did not identify too strongly or merge with the sources s/he used. It wasn't clear whether there was a way of escape other than that dictated by one's own self-reflection or scholarly conscience, both of which might at times be at odds with an activist self, which, after all, is what made history from below a movement, different from academic histories.

Two other concerns of Raphael Samuel's, the teaching of history and its connections with nationalism and the "national curriculum",[63] and with the relationship between history and memory,[64] are worth noting in this connection. A teach-

---

60 Christopher Hill, "The Norman Yoke," in *Puritanism and Revolution*, Christopher Hill (London: Secker & Warburg, 1958), 50–122; Christopher Hill, *The English Revolution, 1640: An Essay* (London: Lawrence & Wishart, 1940).

61 See Susan Scott-Brown, *The Histories of Raphael Samuel: A Portrait of a People's Historian* (Canberra: Australian National University Press, 2017).

62 Raphael Samuel, "Perils of the Transcript," *Oral History*, Vol. 1, No. 2 (1972), 19–22: 21–22. See also Kaltmeier, in this volume, as an indication of what the logic of this position now tends towards.

63 Raphael Samuel, "A Case for National History," published posthumously in *International Journal of Historical Teaching, Learning and Research*, Volume 3 Number 1 (January 2003), 81–88.

64 Raphael Samuel, ed., *Patriotism: The Making and Unmaking of British National Identity* (London: Routledge, 1989); Raphael Samuel, *Theatres of Memory: Past and Present in Contemporary*

ing of national histories in wider contexts, he felt, would be a desirable outcome of the debates of the late 1980s and early 1990s on what a national history curriculum at school and then at university should look like: he was perceptive in recognising that anti-racist histories could also be flattening, with schools "stigmatising non-black children as 'whites', and therefore by definition the bearers of prejudice"; although "[a]nti-racism', like 'anti-sexism', has the merit of undermining consensus views of the past, and putting into question history's unified totalities – not only the 'nation' and the 'nation-state' of the traditional textbooks but also, as Paul Gilroy argues . . ., the alternative terms favoured in the lexicon of 'history from below' – 'class', 'community', 'the people'."[65] And yet, it is a *national* framing of the past, familiar, safe, that is to be preferred as a pedagogical and political imperative:

> Many teachers and scholars, especially perhaps those engaged, like History Workshop, in 'history from the bottom up', have attempted to sidestep the issue of 'nation', advancing the claims of local and regional studies, or culture and community – 'lived experience' – against the record of high politics and statecraft. . . . Yet history, whether we like it or not, is a national question and it has always occupied a national space. Even in teaching of local history it remains, or ought to remain, an inescapable point of reference. Nor can the history of minorities escape it, since it is in relations of opposition to majorities that minorities are defined.[66]

He was consistent in this respect when he said this of "grand narratives": "The contours of the national past are continuously changing shape" – and obviously in a world where he was thinking of school and university curricula in history he did not look beyond the national, perhaps only seeking to place it in a larger set of contexts.[67]

On the relationship between history and memory, he was also not overoptimistic that the two could be that easily reconciled, though they had points of similarity and overlap: "memory, so far from being merely a passive receptacle or storage system, an image bank of the past, is rather an active, shaping force; that it is dynamic – what it contrives symptomatically to forget is as important as what it remembers – and that it is dialectically related to historical thought, rather than being some kind of negative other to it. What Aristotle called anamnesis, the conscious act of recollection, was an intellectual labour very much akin to

---

Culture (London: Verso, 1994); Raphael Samuel, *Island Stories: Unravelling Britain* (London: Verso, 1998).

65 Samuel, "A Case for National History," 84. He cites Paul Gilroy, *There Ain't No Black in the Union Jack* (London: Hutchinson, 1987)

66 Samuel, "A Case for National History," 85.

67 Raphael Samuel, "Grand Narratives," *History Workshop*, No. 29 (Spring, 1990): 120–133: 120.

that of the historian: a matter of quotation, imitation, borrowing and assimilation. After its own fashion it was a way of constructing knowledge." And "[i]t is also my argument that memory is historically conditioned, changing colour and shape according to the emergencies of the moment . . ."[68]

In introducing his volumes on British patriotism, published in 1989 when the moment had passed, Samuel said that the volumes were a response to the outburst of British patriotism that followed the Falklands War of 1982: "born out of anger at the Falklands War", with a "deconstructive" aim; but to a large extent it was the historians themselves who had failed "to come to terms with, or address, the patriotic sentiments in ourselves".[69] A response to the populist use of British patriotism in the service of a banal war, as it was seen at the time, then, was a three-volume critical anthology of different forms of British patriotism (a late replacement for *English* patriotism as a subject for the volumes) that sought to provide alternatives to its tabloid headlines version. And Samuel found that what they were doing, in effect, was to call history from below itself into question:

> History Workshop and the causes with which it is associated – "people's history" or "history from below" in particular – was part of what we were attacking, or at the least putting into question. Folk-radical in its sympathies, local and regional in its subject matter, people's history is deeply attached to that spirit of place which, according to Conservative philosophy . . . is the touchstone of "true" national feeling. It treats "the common people" as a collective subject, transposing the national epic from the field of high politics to that of everyday life.[70]

It would not be unreasonable to trace this tendency to compromise with nationalism, or indeed to lose perspective on the distinction between a left nationalism and a nationally-organised left, back to the imperatives of Popular Front politics from the mid-1930s, which itself might be seen as the origins of the CPHG. As one commentator rather aptly put it, "Two threads were central to the recovery of this national-popular tradition: the assumption that the 'authentic' national culture was democratic (and thus that the true national culture was national because it was popular); and that the dominant culture fleeced 'the people' of their heritage and heroes."[71] Posterity, then, might well receive history from below as a search for people's heroes for the nation, and a bunch of historians writing *Volksgeschichte* for the *Volk*.

---

68 Raphael Samuel, *Theatres of Memory: Past and Present in Contemporary Culture* (London: Verso, 2012) [1994], 64.

69 Samuel, ed., *Patriotism*, vol. 1, Preface, xi.

70 Samuel, ed., *Patriotism*, vol. 1, Preface, xi.

71 Kynan Gentry, "'The Pathos of Conservation': Raphael Samuel and the politics of heritage," *International Journal of Heritage Studies*, 21:6 (2015): 561–576: 563.

2.7 Conclusions

The drawing together of historians and histories in history from below is a curious situation also matched by their drawing apart. If the point of history from below is to enable the hitherto unheard to bring their voices to the forefront, then the emphasis on collectivities that appears to have ensued from the need to amplify the voices of victims, those hidden from history, has had the contrary effect of silencing voices that do not conform to a pre-identified collective.

What are the amplified collectives? The nation, for sure, is one of them. The lack of a defined and pre-theorised figure as prototype for the 'subaltern' or 'plebeian' could render unto the writer or reader of history from below a person or persons who defied typologies (the individual as historical fragment) or a part to be fit into the collective whole. That whole tended to be, or to gravitate back towards, the national, by default, for ex-Marxists, Marxians, and anti-Marxians: when it was less than national, it could contribute to a larger national entity, but it was, at least, no longer larger than the national. And so it came to pass that the universal, internationalist, implication of a class in and for itself was not available as a potential historical player. A CPHG trend to see the progressive nation in its people, a subaltern studies belief that it was the authentic co-national and fellow-oppressed (formerly) colonised intellectual that could speak for the subaltern, and a right-wing assumption that the authentic people exist and must be seen as authentic by virtue of shared cultural-religious beliefs, could merge or be confused with one another.

For historians to abandon the idea of the superior subjectivities of the plebeians below, they would have to abandon the idea of the automatically progressive nature of movements from below, which is itself a populist assumption; they would have to abandon, too, the idea that something like a class that could lead a revolution was in the making through these processes. And those doing the history-writing would, themselves, in the interests of not imposing inauthentic subjectivities on the histories they write, have to weigh the importance of their personal backgrounds, their "identities", and the extent to which they wanted to mobilise those details as part of their historians' personae. Raphael Samuel's Jewishness, while not hidden, makes no intrusive appearance as an essential part of his legitimacy to write the histories he chooses to (and given the diversity of those, it would be a great imaginative leap on anyone's part to connect them to his "identity"). The average postcolonial global southist position would of course be very different: the writers' qualification to write history, to be ventriloquists delivering the authentic voice from below to the higher-ups, rests on the claim that they are themselves authentic. We are now very far from history from below, or even from history; and sources, at least, are irrelevant. And yet it is a residue of history from below that we can see here: the implicit nationalism of popular folklore, the Cultural Revolution self-erasures of intellectuals in their journeys to the countryside that ensure their return as now-authentic proto-peasants.

References

Amin, Shahid. "Gandhi as Mahatma: Gorakhpur District, Eastern U.P., 1921–22." In *Subaltern Studies III*, edited by Ranajit Guha, 1–61. Delhi: Oxford University Press, 1984.

Amin, Shahid. *Event, Metaphor, Memory: Chauri Chaura 1922-1992*. Delhi: Oxford University Press, 1995.

Baier, Walter. "Gramsci was a Shibboleth." *International Gramsci Journal*, 3:1 (2018): 55–67.

Benjamin, Walter. *Über den Begriff der Geschichte* (1940). Translated as "On the Concept of History" (2005), Thesis VII, https://www.marxists.org/reference/archive/benjamin/1940/history.htm, accessed November 08, 2024. Translation by Dennis Redmond.

Bernet, Brigitta. "The Postwar Marxist Milieu of Microhistory." In *What's Left of Marxism?*, edited by Benjamin Zachariah, Lutz Raphael, and Brigitta Bernet, 37–64. Berlin: de Gruyter, 2020.

Biswas, Hemanga. *Abar Cheen Dekhe Elam*. Calcutta: Sribhumi, 1975.

Burton, Antoinette, and Stephanie Furtado. "Preface: The Revolution and the Book." In *Histories of a Radical Book: E.P. Thompson and The Making of the English Working Class*, edited by Antoinette Burton, and Stephanie Furtado, vii–xii. Brooklyn: Berghahn, 2021.

Chakravarty, Dipesh. *Provincializing Europe*. Princeton: Princeton University Press, 2000.

Chatterjee, Partha. *A Princely Impostor? The Strange and Universal History of the Kumar of Bhawal*. Princeton: Princeton University Press, 2002.

Cook, Alexander C., ed. *Mao's Little Red Book: A Global History*. Cambridge: Cambridge University Press, 2014.

Davis, Natalie Zemon. *The Return of Martin Guerre*. Cambridge, MA: Harvard University Press, 1982.

Gentry, Kynan. "'The Pathos of Conservation': Raphael Samuel and the politics of heritage." *International Journal of Heritage Studies*, 21:6 (2015): 561–576.

Gilroy, Paul. *There Ain't No Black in the Union Jack*. London: Hutchinson, 1987.

Ginzburg, Carlo. *The Cheese and the Worms: The Cosmos of a Sixteenth-Century Miller*. London: Routledge & Kegan Paul, 1980 [1976].

Gramsci, Antonio. *Selections from the Prison Notebooks. Edited and translated by Quintin Hoare, and Geoffrey Nowell Smith*. New York: International Publishers, 1971.

Guha, Ranajit. "Chandra's Death." In *Subaltern Studies V*, edited by Ranajit Guha, 135–165. Delhi: Oxford University Press, 1987.

Guha, Ranajit. "On Some Aspects of the Historiography of Colonial India." In *Subaltern Studies I*, edited by Ranajit Guha, 1–9. Delhi: Oxford University Press, 1982.

Guha, Ranajit. "The Prose of Counter-Insurgency." In *Subaltern Studies II*, edited by Ranajit Guha, 1–42. Delhi: Oxford University Press, 1983.

Guha, Ranajit. *Elementary Aspects of Peasant Insurgency in Colonial India*. Delhi: Oxford University Press, 1983.

Halbwachs, Maurice. *On Collective Memory*. New edition, Chicago: Chicago University Press, 1992 [1925].

Hill, Christopher. "The Norman Yoke." In *Puritanism and Revolution*, edited by Christopher Hill, 50–122. London: Secker & Warburg, 1958.

Hill, Christopher. *The English Revolution, 1640: An Essay*. London: Lawrence & Wishart, 1940.

Hobsbawm, Eric. "Do Workers Have a Country?." In *On Nationalism*, 87–106. London: Abacus, 2022.

Hobsbawm, Eric. "The Historians' Group of the Communist Party." In *Rebels and their Causes: Essays in Honour of A.L. Morton*, edited by Maurice Cornforth. London: Lawrence & Wishart, 1978, reproduced at https://www.versobooks.com/blogs/news/the-historians-group-of-the-communist-party, accessed November 08, 2024.

Hobsbawm, Eric. *Nations and Nationalism since 1780: Programme, Myth, Reality*. Cambridge: Cambridge University Press, 1990.

Lenin VI. *Rough Draft of a Resolution on Proletarian Culture (1920)*. https://www.marxists.org/archive/lenin/works/1920/oct/09b.htm, accessed November 08, 2024.

Lenin VI. *The Right of Nations to Self-Determination (1914)*. https://www.marxists.org/archive/lenin/works/1914/self-det/, accessed November 08, 2024.

Mani, Lata. "Contentious Traditions: The Debate on Sati in Colonial India." *Cultural Critique* No. 7 (1987): 119–156.

Morton, A.L. *A People's History of England*. London: Victor Gollancz, 1938.

Oliveira, A. Ramos. *A People's History of Germany*. London: Victor Gollancz, 1942.

Pandey, Gyanendra. *The Construction of Communalism in Colonial North India*. Delhi: Oxford University Press, 1992.

Partha Chatterjee. *The Nation and its Fragments: Colonial and Postcolonial Histories*. Princeton: Princeton University Press, 1993.

Prakash, Gyan. "Can the Subaltern Ride? A Reply to O'Hanlon and Washbrook." *Comparative Studies in Society and History* 34 (1992): 168–184.

Robinson, Joan. *The Cultural Revolution in China*. Harmondsworth: Pelican, 1970 [1969].

Roy, MN. "Supplementary Theses on the National and Colonial Questions." In *Minutes of the Second Congress of the Communist International*, Fourth Session, July 25, 1920. https://www.marxists.org/history/international/comintern/2nd-congress/ch04.htm, accessed November 08, 2024.

Said, Edward W. Foreword to *Selected Subaltern Studies*, edited by Ranajit Guha, and Gayatri Chakravarty Spivak, v–x. New York: Oxford University Press, 1988.

Samuel, Raphael, ed. *Patriotism: The Making and Unmaking of British National Identity*. London: Routledge, 1989.

Samuel, Raphael, ed. *People's History and Socialist Theory*. London: Routledge, 1981.

Samuel, Raphael. "A Case for National History." *International Journal of Historical Teaching, Learning and Research*, 3:1 (January 2003): 81–88.

Samuel, Raphael. "Grand Narratives." *History Workshop*, No. 29 (1990): 120–133.

Samuel, Raphael. "Perils of the Transcript." *Oral History*, 1:2 (1972): 19–22.

Samuel, Raphael. *Island Stories: Unravelling Britain*. London: Verso, 1998.

Samuel, Raphael. *Theatres of Memory: Past and Present in Contemporary Culture*. London: Verso, 1994.

Sarkar, Sumit. "Edward Thompson and India: The Other Side of the Medal." In *Writing Social History*, edited by Sumit Sarkar. Delhi: Oxford University Press, 1997.

Sarkar, Sumit. "The Decline of the Subaltern in Subaltern Studies." In *Writing Social History*, edited by Sumit Sarkar, 82–108. Delhi: Oxford University Press, 1997.

Sarkar, Sumit. "The Kalki-Avatar of Bikrampur." In *Subaltern Studies VI*, edited by Ranajit Guha, 1–53. Delhi: Oxford University Press, 1989.

Sarkar, Sumit. "The Many Worlds of Indian History." In *Writing Social History*, edited by Sumit Sarkar, 1–49. Delhi: Oxford University Press, 1997.

Sarkar, Sumit. "The Relevance of E.P. Thompson." In *Writing Social History*, edited by Sumit Sarkar, 50–81. Delhi: Oxford University Press, 1997.

Sarkar, Tanika. "Something like rights? Faith, law and widow immolation debates in colonial Bengal." *The Indian Economic & Social History Review* 49, 3 (2012): 295–320.

Savile, John. "Edward Thompson, the Communist Party, and 1956." *Socialist Register* 1994, copy at https://www.marxists.org/archive/saville/1994/xx/epthompson.htm, accessed November 08, 2024.

Scott-Brown, Susan. *The Histories of Raphael Samuel: A Portrait of a People's Historian*. Canberra: Australian National University Press, 2017.

Spivak, Gayatri Chakrabarty, and Ranajit Guha, eds. *Selected Subaltern Studies*. Delhi: Oxford University Press, 1988.

Spivak, Gayatri Chakraborty. "Can the Subaltern Speak?" In *Marxism and the Interpretation of Culture*, edited by Cary Nelson, and Lawrence Grossberg, 271–313. Basingstoke: Macmillan, 1988.

Tawney, R.H. *Religion and the Rise of Capitalism*. London: John Murray, 1948 [1926].

Thompson, E.P. *'Alien Homage': Edward Thompson and Rabindranath Tagore*. Delhi: Oxford University Press, 1993.

Thompson, E.P. "The Politics of Theory." In *People's History and Socialist Theory*, edited by Raphael Samuel, 396–408. London: Routledge, 1981.

Thompson, E.P. *The Making of the English Working Class*. Harmondsworth: Pelican, 1980 [1963].

Zachariah, Benjamin. "Identifying the Beast Within: Postcolonial Theory and History." In *After the Last Post: The Lives of Indian Historiography*, edited by Benjamin Zachariah, 21–47. Berlin: de Gruyter, 2019.

Zachariah, Benjamin. "The Tongue is Mightier than the Printing Press? Reflections on the Production of Oral Histories and on Languages of Legitimation." *Dve Domovini* 50 (2019): 71–88.

Zedong, Mao. *Selected Works of Mao Tse-Tung* volume 1. Paris: Foreign Languages Press, 2021 [Beijing: Foreign Languages Press, 1965].

Part Two: **National and Regional Varieties**

Brigitta Bernet

3 Microhistory and Micropolitics. The Political Background to a New Historiographical Approach

3.1 Reading Ginzburg in Chiapas

In autumn 1995, just over a year after the uprising of the *Ejército Zapatista de Liberación Nacional (EZLN)* in the Mexican state of Chiapas, the Argentinian-Mexican historian and activist Adolfo Gilly published a slim book entitled *Discusión sobre la historia*.[1] It documents a debate on questions of historical theory between Gilly and the most prominent figure in the EZLN, Subcomandante Marcos. At the centre of the exchange is one of Carlo Ginzburg's best-known texts, first published in Italian in 1978 under the title *Spie. Radici di un paradigma scientifico,* (published in English in 1979 as *Clues. Roots of a Scientific Paradigm*).[2] Gilly sent Marcos a copy of the essay while the uprising was still in its most intense phase – firmly convinced that there were strong affinities between Neo-Zapatism and Ginzburg's *Microstoria*. The comment he sent Marcos with the text was that it appeared to provide the theory for the practice of the indigenous liberation movement.[3]

Marcos was unable to agree with this view. Unlike Gilly, he did not recognise Ginzburg's "evidential paradigm" as an attempt to rediscover the oppressed culture 'from below' as a resource for political resistance. On the contrary, he accused Ginzburg of being a "sad apologist for neoliberalism", completely lacking

---

1 Adolfo Gilly, Subcomandante Marcos, and Carlo Ginzburg, *Discusión sobre la historia* (Mexico: Taurus, 1995). For an interpretation of this correspondence see Jerôme Baschet, "(Re)discutir sobre la historia," *Chiapas* 10 (2000): 7–39, and David Mayer, "Gute Gründe und doppelte Böden. Zur Geschichte 'linker' Geschichtsschreibung," *Sozial.Geschichte Online* 14 (2014): 62–96, https://duepublico2.uni-due.de/receive/duepublico_mods_00036456, accessed February 20, 2024.
2 A first, slightly shorter version appeared in 1978 in *Rivista di storia contemporanea* VII (1978), 1–14. Gilly and Marcos discussed an extended version which appeared in Spanish translation in 1983: Carlo Ginzburg, "Señales. Raíces de un paradigma indiciario," in *Crisis de la razón. Nuevos modelos en la relación entre saber y actividades humanas*, ed. Aldo Gargani (Mexico: Siglo Veintiuno Editores, 1983), 55–99. For the first English translation see: Carlo Ginzburg, "Clues: Roots of a Scientific Paradigm," *Theory and Society* 7/3 (May, 1979), 273–288.
3 "Con todo cariño, va esta teorización sobre el pensamiento del viejo Antonio [y de Heriberto] [y el tuyo, a veces . . .]," in Gilly, Marcos and Ginzburg, *Discusión sobre la historia*, 38. See also, Baschet, "(Re)disutir sobre la historia," 161.

https://doi.org/10.1515/9783111522180-003

the appropriate "attitude to class". In an eight-page statement, Marcos mocked the Italian historian's "mundane drivel" *(todología)*. He wanted nothing to do with the idea of a close relationship between Neo-Zapatism and microhistory.[4]

Gilly, in turn, could not accept this. In his detailed reply he portrayed microhistory as part of a revival of Marxism which had become urgent after the Cuban revolution, both in Latin America and Europe.[5] Gilly was particularly familiar with developments in Italy. As a member of the Trotskyist *Buró Latinoamericano*, he had been active in the milieus of the radical left in Rome and Turin in the 1960s and '70s at the same time as the evolution of microhistory there. The experiences and perspectives of these milieus reflected a revolutionary left that had been striving to expand Marxist ideas of class struggle since the 1960s. It criticised the optimistic notion of progress based on the state and the party as portrayed in official labour history and cultivated by the Italian Communist Party (PCI).[6] Carlo Ginzburg, whose publications focussed on repressed popular cultures of resistance, from witch trials to his evidential paradigm, was a classic example of this new approach. He provides a shift in perspective away from orthodox party-based Marxism's claim to authority towards the spontaneous resistance of the subaltern classes. Gilly was convinced that the EZLN was following this tradition of thought – consciously or unconsciously. It was therefore logical for him to equate the uprising of the indigenous farmers in Chiapas with the struggle of the Friulian miller Menocchio in sixteenth-century Italy, which Ginzburg had portrayed in his 1976 book "Il formaggio e i vermi" (The Cheese and the Worms).[7] The proximity of microhistory to Neo-Zapatism was thus sufficiently proven for him.

For historians trained in Western Europe there are many surprising aspects to this exchange of letters. The most significant is the simultaneity of the non-simultaneous, that is the fact that Gilly so unquestioningly declared a text that is part of the canon of cultural history and the history of science in Western Europe to be the meta-text of an indigenous liberation movement. It is quite clear that Gilly read Ginzburg's essay through a prism of experiences that were markedly

---

4 Gilly, Marcos and Ginzburg, *Discusión sobre la historia*, 15–20. See also: Baschet, "(Re)discutir sobre la historia," 8. On the intellectual biography of Rafael Guillén resp. Subcomandante Marcos and his relationship to Gramsci cf. Nick Henck, "The Subcommander and the Sardinian: Marcos and Gramsci," *Mexican Studies / Estudios Mexicanos* 29/2 (2013): 428–458.

5 Gilly, Marcos and Ginzburg, *Discusión sobre la historia*, 25–71. For Gilly's life, see Adolfo Gilly, "What exists cannot be true (Interview)," *New Left Review* 64 (2010): 29–46.

6 Gilly, "What exists cannot be true," 56.

7 Carlo Ginzburg, *Il formaggio e i vermi. Il cosmo di un mugnaio del '500* (Torino: Einaudi, 1976); Carlo Ginzburg, *The Cheese and the Worms: The Cosmos of a Sixteenth-Century Miller*, trans. John Tedeschi and Anne Tedeschi (Baltimore: John Hopkins University Press, 1992).

different from those of Marcos. Marcos also read the text politically but positioned it in a different, namely a neoliberal, context.[8] The situation in Western Europe was completely different. In 1995, it would hardly have occurred to anyone there to interpret Ginzburg's text politically or in any way associate it with militant guerrillas and indigenous revolt. In Germany at least, where his essay was reissued in that same year, it was read within the academic community as an inspiring yet abstract contribution to historical epistemology in the context of the "cultural turn".[9] By then the political references that Gilly invoked in Chiapas had disappeared from historiographical culture in Western Europe. What makes this correspondence so interesting, however, is precisely Gilly's broad contextualisation of Ginzburg's work in an "imagined community" that transcends the boundaries of narrow academic disciplines and in which historical and political culture frequently overlap.[10]

This article takes up the trail laid by Gilly and analyses the emergence of microhistory as an intellectual processing of political-social experiences in a different temporal and spatial context: Italy in the 1960s and '70s.[11] To this end, I do not reconstruct microhistory as a primarily inner-academic debate, but as part of a social movement reflecting and catalysing experiences in the field of political culture. Historiographical paradigms are neither the result of individual conviction nor the consequence of an increase in knowledge within academia. Rather, academic historical research is also situated in a "historical culture" and thus closely

---

8 Cf. Richard Stahler-Sholk, "Resisting Neoliberal Homogenization: The Zapatista Autonomy Movement," *Latin American Perspectives* 34/2 (2007): 48–63.

9 As Volker Depkart has shown, this unpolitical interpretation applies to the 'cultural turn' overall. In German historiography the cultural turn was treated as "a largely academic affair which seems to lack a political dimension that goes beyond the scholarly field". Volker Depkat, "The 'Cultural Turn' in German and American Historiography," *Amerikastudien / American Studies* 54/3 (2009): 425–450, 437.

10 Stephanie Jed uses this term in her review of the correspondence, see Stephanie Jed, "Proof and Transnational Rhetorics: Opening up the Conservation (Review)," *History and Theory* 40/3 (2001): 372–384, 377–79.

11 Important references to the contextualisation of microhistory in the social and political context of Italy are provided by Thomas Kroll, "Die Anfänge der microstoria: Methodenwechsel, Erfahrungswandel und transnationale Rezeption in der europäischen Historiographie der 1970er und 1980er Jahre," in *Perspektiven durch Retrospektiven: Wirtschaftsgeschichtliche Beiträge*, ed. Jeanette Granda and Jürgen Schreiber (Köln: Böhlau, 2013), 267–287; Maurizio Gribaudi, "La lunga marcia della microstoria," in *Microstoria: A venticinque anni da 'L'eredità immateriale'*, ed. Paola Lanaro (Milano: Franco Angeli, 2011), 9–23; Brigitta Bernet, "The Postwar Marxist Milieu of Microhistory. Heterodoxy, Activism and the Formation of a Critical Historiographical Perspective," in *What's Left of Marxism. Historiography and the Possibilities of Thinking with Marxian Themes and Concepts*, ed. Benjamin Zachariah et al. (Berlin: De Gruyter Oldenbourg, 2020), 37–64.

tied to social constellations, worlds of experience, and forms of practice.[12] In other words, their paradigms and practices are deeply embedded in political and social developments and discourses. This article is based on a broad concept of knowledge that does not separate the academic from the political dimensions of historical culture but rather allows their interaction, overlaps and conflicts to be exposed. It reconstructs the beginnings of microhistory with reference to the claims, practices, and perspectives of a radical Italian left seeking to establish its political orientation, including in the field of historiography.

In a first step, I introduce microhistory and its currently accepted historiographical positioning. Secondly, I look back to post-war Italy and outline the historiographical context that was fundamental to the emergence of microhistory. Thirdly, I analyse the political impulses for this new intellectual development. As I will show, its pioneers adopted the practices and perspectives (such as anthropological field work, oral history, and participatory research, both inside and outside the factory) of a radical left-wing movement that critically distanced itself from party communism. Italian microhistory was – as will be shown – the medium and expression of the political culture of the New Left. This article aims to historicise microhistory and thus to uncover its political traces in its current manifestations.

3.2 Does Cultural History Depoliticise History?

Microhistory is regarded nowadays as an innovative method of the "new cultural history", whose rise is certainly one of the most remarkable and most controversial historiographical developments in recent decades. It was an approach that flourished in the mid-1980s and in historiography it was soon dubbed the "cultural turn" or "anthropological turn". As it evolved, its focus of interest became ordinary men and women, their experiences and agency, as well as the interac-

---

12 Here I follow perspectives of Intellectual History and the Cultural History of Intellectual Practices. Cf. Peter Burke, "The Cultural History of Intellectual Practices. An Overview," in *Political Concepts and Time: New Approaches to Conceptual History*, ed. Javier Fernándes Sebastián (Santander: Cantabria University Press, 2011), 103–130, 108–9; Georg G. Iggers, Q. Edward Wang and Supriya Mukherjee, eds., *A Global History of Modern Historiography* (New York: Routledge, 2008); Bernard Guénée, *Histoire et culture historique dans l'Occident médiéval* (Paris: Aubier, 1980).

tion of elite and popular culture.[13] Since the 1980s, Italian microhistory has been perceived as a particularly influential branch of this approach. It distances itself from traditional historiography with its focus on large-scale politics and dominant economic classes. It also distances itself from the generalisations of a macrohistory, whether of Marxist or modernisation-theoretical/socio-historical provenance. As a variant of history from below it seeks to discover the great in the small by examining it under the microscope, as it were. In its search for generalisations, its starting point is not outside or beyond individuals but always with them and their experiences. It also turns away from elites and ideas as well as from structures and processes to focus on seemingly irrelevant, insignificant and backward phenomena such as everyday life, the family, and popular culture.[14] The academic credentials for this shift in perspective were established through the reception of approaches from the social sciences and the incorporation of research findings and methods from Cultural Anthropology.

Theoretical texts and major works of microhistory by Carlo Ginzburg, Giovanni Levi, Edoardo Grendi, Luisa Passerini and Gianna Pomata considerably enriched history from below by adding the factor of popular culture. This is particularly true of Ginzburg's 1976 book *The Cheese and the Worms*, which has since been translated into twenty-five languages. Ginzburg takes the case of a Friulian miller executed as a heretic in the sixteenth century and uses Inquisition records to reconstruct his world view, which was intractably steeped in rural folk culture. The miller, Domenica Scandella, known as Menocchio, was able to read and write, and had his own ideas about God and the universe which were radically different from those of Catholic orthodoxy. Not only did he reject the notion of God as the Creator in his world view, he also condemned the church's pomp, championed egalitarian ideas, and announced in public that he "wished for a new world and way of life".[15] These and other such statements led to him being branded a heretic and burnt at the stake in 1599. In spite of this bitter outcome it is still a pleasure to follow how Ginzburg uncovers his protagonist's universe layer by layer. Using scant historical resources he meticulously reconstructs the

---

13 Depkat, "Cultural Turn," 427; Geoff Eley, *History Made Conscious: Politics of Knowledge, Politics of the Past* (London/New York: Verso Books, 2023); Marco Santoro, "Culture As (And After) Production," *Cultural Sociology* 2/1 (2008): 7–31.

14 For microhistory, see Giovanni Levi, "On Microhistory," in *New Perspectives on Historical Writing*, ed. Peter Burke (Cambridge: Polity Press, 2001), 97–119, 97; Carlo Ginzburg, "Microhistory: Two or Three Things I Know about it," *Critical Inquiry* 20, no. 1 (Autumn, 1993): 10–35; Sigurdur Gylfi Magnússon and István M. Szijártó, eds., *What is Microhistory? Theory and Practice* (London, New York: Routledge, 2013).

15 Ginzburg, *The Cheese and the Worms*, 77.

subaltern world to which Menocchio belonged and the intellectual trends influencing him. His study is programmatic for microhistory, as it shows how specific details within sources can be decoded to disclose voices and experiences excluded from official histories. In this approach, and in the use of concepts such as "subaltern classes" and "popular culture", Ginzburg followed the ideas of Antonio Gramsci, who in his prison notebooks (published by Einaudi from 1948) called for the fragmentary testimonies of the subaltern classes to be reconstructed as part and expression of a potentially revolutionary counterculture.

The social reasons for the cultural turn in historiography rather than its purely academic basis have still hardly been investigated. It is usually explained as an inner-academic push intending to correct and compensate for the dehumanised macro analyses and structural functionalism of New Economic History, social history, and the Annales school, and during which the weight shifted to culture – i.e. to the ideas, beliefs, and world views of the lower classes.[16] For historiography, microhistory is the flagship of the cultural turn and, as such, has always provoked particular controversy. In contrast to British history from below, with which it has much in common, Italian microhistory is still often unthinkingly equated with a primarily descriptive approach that is limited to the private and non-political. As a result it risks being branded as a step towards the depoliticisation of historiography.[17] In his autobiography, Eric Hobsbawm, for instance, quotes Ginzburg's book *The Cheese and the Worms* as a symptom of a regrettable cultural turn which had caused "a shift away from historical models or 'the large *why* questions', a shift from 'the analytical to the descriptive mode', from economic and social structure to culture, from recovering fact to recovering feeling, from telescope to microscope . . ." and had thus lost its feeling for the essential.[18] Wolfgang Reinhard has argued similarly that microhistory (which he as-

---

16 Stated explicitly by Stefan Jordan, who sees the rise of microhistory as a purely academic corrective to the Annales and maintains that, in contrast to West German history of everyday life *(Alltagsgeschichte)*, microhistory was not influenced by political ideas, see, Stefan Jordan, *Theorien und Methoden in der Geschichtswissenschaft* (Paderborn: Ferdinand Schöningh, 2018), 159. For a similar inner-academic contextualisation, see also, Doris Bachmann-Medick, "Cultural Turns (Version: 2.0)," in *Docupedia-Zeitgeschichte*, 17.6.2019, doi: http://dx.doi.org/10.14765/zzf.dok-1389.

17 Christophe Charle, "Micro-histoire sociale et macro-histoire sociale: Quelques réflexions sur les effets des changements de méthode depuis quinze ans en histoire sociale," *Histoire sociale – histoire globale? Actes du colloque de l'IHMC*, ed. Christophe Charle (Paris: Editions de la MSH, 1993), 45–57; Winfried Schulze, "Mikrohistorie versus Makrohistorie? Anmerkungen zu einem aktuellen Thema," *Historische Methode*, ed. Christian Meier, and Jörn Rüsen (München: dtv, 1988), 319–341.

18 Eric Hobsbawm, *Interesting Times: A Twentieth-century Life* (London: Allen Lane, 2002), 294.

signs to historical anthropology) can be seen as a kind of "apolitical science, legitimising an individualistic society", in which the subject concentrates only on its own limited happiness and has ultimately adapted to the anonymous processes of power.[19]

3.3 Orthodox Party-based Marxism and Popular Culture

This kind of interpretation of microhistory is largely incompatible with the self-perception of this school of thought. Before considering this disparity, it makes sense to look at the areas in left-wing, post-war Italy where historical culture and political culture overlapped and in which microhistory developed. Until the 1960s, the prevailing left-wing understanding of history was strongly influenced by the Italian Communist Party (PCI). On the one hand it followed Marxist principles, interpreting historical events as the history of class struggle, but on the other it remained influenced by the idealistic historicism of Benedetto Croce, which focused on the political sphere.[20] After 1945, as part of a rigorous "unity of action" pact, the left-wing parties swiftly promoted the adaptation and rewriting of Italy's history as part of the country's cultural renewal.[21] Following their expulsion from the government in May 1947 and their crushing election defeat against the Christian Democratic Party (DCI) in 1948, the PCI resorted to Antonio Gramsci's concept of "cultural hegemony" and were thus convinced that cultural activities could lead to a radical reform of Italian society. The General Secretary of the PCI, Palmiro Togliatti, called for the transformation of the PCI from being a cadre party to a national people's party, as well as the creation of a new integrative narrative of Italian history with the party at its centre.[22] To further this aim, the PCI launched a variety of initiatives after 1948 to build a "national-popular" counterculture that would arouse a socialist consciousness among the broad masses, par-

---

19 Wolfgang Reinhard, *Lebensformen Europas: Eine historische Kulturanthropologie* (Munich: Beck C. H., 2004), 31.

20 Daniela Coli, "Idealismo e marxismo nella storiografia italiana degli anni '50 e '60," in *La storiografie contemporanea: Indirizzi e problemi*, ed. Pietro Rossi (Milan: Il Saggatore, 1987), 39–58.

21 Paolo Favilli, *Marxismo e storia: Saggio sull'innovazione storiografica in Italia (1945–1970)* (Milan: Franco Angeli, 2006). For an overview of post-war Italian history see, Paul Ginsborg, *A History of Contemporary Italy: Society and Politics 1943–1988* (London: Penguin Books, 1990).

22 Alexander Höbel, "Storia d'Italia e PCI nell'elaborazione di Palmiro Togliatti," in *Il Risorgimento: Un'epopea? Per una ricostruzione storico-critica*, ed. Cristina Carpinelli, and Vittorio Gioiello (Milan: Zambon editore, 2012), 185–205.

ticularly among farmers, the largest group in the population at the time. These initiatives ranged from organising summer *Feste dell' Unità* where people sat on long benches in the open air, eating, drinking and singing, through supporting neo-realist perspectives in film and literature, to encouraging the sciences and historiography to focus on the everyday struggles of "ordinary people".[23]

Orthodox party-based Marxism, however, did not acknowledge the autonomy of the people, but saw them as bearers of "false consciousness". In the south in particular, where under fascism large sections of the rural proletariat had defected to Mussolini – against their own objective class interests, so to speak – the PCI intensified its educational efforts through external avant-gardes.[24] It assumed, with Kautsky and Lenin, that class consciousness among the proletariat could not arise spontaneously but had to be introduced to them "from outside" and organised by the party.[25] From this perspective, progressive historical change had to originate from the party. By contrast, social movements and forms of resistance not organised by the party were seen as pre-political, pre-modern phenomena, sitting, as it were, in an imaginary "waiting-room of history".[26]

In the 1950s, a proliferation of journals, publishing houses, and archives dedicated themselves to the task of reassessing and rewriting the history of Italy from below – that is from the point of view of the workers' movement. Its focus was, however, on the history of the organised workers' movement, its parties and institutions. It was, in other words, still a history from above, leading to the formation of the PCI and increasingly limiting itself to the national framework of Italy. This was a party historiography that emphasised the leading role of the communists in the anti-fascist resistance movement and claimed for the PCI the historical position of the legitimate heir and consummator of the *Risorgimento* (literally: the Resurgence – the nineteenth-century movement for Italian unification). The general secretary of the PCI, Palmiro Togliatti, in particular, never tired of describing the Resistenza as a second Risorgimento – a genuine national popular

---

23 David Forgacs, "The Italian Communist Party and Culture," *Culture and Conflict in Postwar Italy. Essays on Mass and Popular Culture*, ed. Robert Lumley, and Zygmunt G. Baranski (Houndmills: The Macmillan Press, 1990), 97–114.

24 Höbner, "Storia d'Italia," 200.

25 Vladimir. I. Lenin, "What is to be done?" *Essential Works of Lenin*, ed. Henry M. Christman (New York: Dover Publications, 1987), 53–175. See also: Stephen Eric Bronner, "Was tun? und Stalinismus," *UTOPIE kreativ* 151 (2003): 425–434.

26 Dipesh Chakrabarty, *Provincializing Europe: Postcolonial Thought and Historical Difference* (Princeton: Princeton University Press, 2000), 7. Chakrabarty made this comment about John Stuart Mill's writings, but it is equally applicable to orthodox Marxist historiography. On the usage by Chakrabarty, see: Amit Chadhuri, "In the Waiting-Room of History," *London Review of Books* 26 (2004): 3–8.

movement that under communist leadership could finally realise the project of Italian unification, which had been started in the nineteenth century but betrayed by the bourgeoisie. However, it actively excluded other areas from its history.[27] Among these were not only the continuities of fascism in post-war Italy, but also entire areas of the history of the socialist movement (council communism, anarchism, the women's rights movement and the farmers' movement), which it was unable to fit into the self-image of a workers' movement led by the PCI.[28]

3.4 The 'Anthrological Turn' and Italy's Liberal-socialist Tradition

Even at the height of the "unity of action" pact, this understanding of history provoked opposition on the left, usually connected to fundamental criticism of the PCI's direction. This became apparent over the *Questione Meridionale*, the 'Southern Question', which had remained contentious since the unification of Italy in 1861. This was the question of how the unbearable poverty and exploitation of the rural population in the agrarian *Mezzogiorno*, southern Italy, could be explained and overcome.[29] The issue became all the more critical since between 1943 and 1953, fierce struggles over the redistribution and self-administration of landowners' fields shook the south.[30] For the PCI, the peasant movement, which aimed to overthrow the ruling land ownership system, soon became a problem. Togliatti, having returned to Italy from exile in Moscow in March 1944, had received clear instructions from Stalin to renounce a socialist revolution in Italy and instead promote a policy of "national unity". Stalin had already made a pact with the Western Allies for the division of Europe after the war, according to which Italy was to be part of the Anglo-American zone of influence.[31] Togliatti

---

27 Cf. Filippo Focardi, *La guerra della memoria: La Resistenza nel dibattito politico italiano dal 1945 a oggi* (Rome: GLF editori Laterza, 2005).

28 Bruno Groppo, "Die Kommunistische Partei Italiens und ihre Historiographien," *Jahrbuch für Historische Kommunismusforschung* (2013): 191–210.

29 Christian Jansen, "Uneiniges Italien. Die 'Südfrage' als Strukturproblem vom Risorgimento bis heute," in *150 Jahre einiges Italien*, ed. Massimo Minelli, and Rainer Schlösser (Munich: Meidenbauer, 2012), 179–202.

30 Peter Kammerer, "Bauernkämpfe und Landreform 1943–1953 in Süditalien," in *Produktion und Lebensverhältnisse auf dem Land*, ed. Onno Poppinga (Wiesbaden: Springer, 1979), 236–252.

31 Silvio Pons, "Stalin, Togliatti, and the Origin of the Cold War in Europe," *Journal of Cold War Studies* 3/2 (2001), 3–27.

met with quite a bit of opposition – not only within his own ranks, but also from the southern Italian peasants and their supporters. They were frequently anti-capitalist in their orientation and so were repeatedly challenged by the limits of the strategy of unity outlined by the left-wing parties, which was to consent in essence to the capitalist reconstruction of the country. The PCI cadre rejected these "spontaneous" revolts on principle and regarded their demands for *autogoverno* (self-government) as a threat to the PCI's cooperation with the DCI, who were courting them with their "policy of the outstretched hand". For others, however, it was clear that Italian socialism had to be achieved by strengthening these struggles and grassroots initiatives from below. This approach was further supported by the anti-colonial liberation struggles in the emergent 'Third World', which opened a new perspective on the Italian South – as a third world country within Italy – and brought a fresh urgency to the question of the autonomy of popular culture.[32]

Against this backdrop, dissenting left-wing intellectuals and cultural figures such as Carlo Levi (an uncle of Giovanni Levi) and Manlio Rossi-Doria (Carlo Ginzburg's father-in-law), Rocco Scotellaro and Pier Paolo Pasolini, developed a dissident view of peasant folk culture and its history. Unlike the PCI, they did not see it as a mainly reactionary element, but as a progressive force whose agency and autonomy should be taken into account, from a historiographical as well as a political angle. In many cases, this view was rooted in an anti-fascist, liberal-socialist tradition.[33] A classic example of the type of person thus imagined as representing such a tradition is found in Carlo Ginzburg's father Leone, a Slavic specialist, writer and journalist, who was born in Odessa in 1908 and murdered in 1944 by the Gestapo in a prison in Rome as a member of the *Resistenza*. In the 1930s he was an active member of the anti-fascist resistance movement *Giustizia e Libertà*; and in 1942, he co-founded the underground liberal-socialist Action Party (*Partito d'Azione*), in which his wife (Carlo Ginzburg's mother), the writer Natalia Ginzburg, was also an activist. According to Carlo Ginzburg, his father was strongly influenced by Russian populism and, like the revolutionary *Narodniki*, had a deep moral and intellectual affinity with the peasant classes and their

---

32 Pier Paolo Pasolini, "La Resistenza negra," in *Letteratura negra*, ed. Mario De Andrade (Roma: Editori Riuniti, 1961), XXII; Gabriella Gribaudi, "Images of the South: The Mezzogiorno as Seen by Insiders and Outsiders," in *The New History of the Italian South*, ed. Robert Lumley, and Jonathan Morris (Exeter: University of Exeter Press, 1997), 83–114.

33 Mariamargherita Scotti, *Da sinistra: Intellettuali, Partito socialista italiano e organizzazione della cultura (1953–1960)* (Rome: Ediesse, 2011), 23–80.

values.[34] In 1933, Leone Ginzburg and Giulio Einaudi founded the legendary Turin publishing house Einaudi, which in post-war Italy – now with Natalia Ginzburg as editor – became the centre of a utopian Mediterranean socialism. In 1945 it published the autobiographical novel *Cristo si è fermato a Eboli*[35] by the writer Carlo Levi, who was also active in the Action Party with the Ginzburgs. After 1948 Einaudi also printed Antonio Gramsci's *Prison Notebooks*, and the studies of the religious historian and anthropologist Ernesto De Martino, who in many ways provided a breeding ground for the historical culture of the New Left. His writings had an immense influence on the pioneers of microhistory, and on Carlo Ginzburg in particular.

Ernesto De Martino had encountered the peasant struggles during the *Resistenza* and completely revised his view of the south after the war.[36] Initially a member of the Partito d'Azione, after its dissolution in 1949 he joined the PCI, read the recently edited writings of Gramsci and turned to the seemingly primitive cultural forms of the *Mezzogiorno*: magic, death cults, the tarantella, and superstition. His major concern was to view them not as pre-political and primitive, but as historically and dialectically comprehensible responses to living conditions that in the south of Italy – in contrast to the more favoured north – were particularly miserable and hopeless.[37] Like Gramsci, De Martino was also convinced that the ruling class secured its hegemony by means of historiography and that, as a result, the struggle for liberation must take place here too. He called for a radical new historiography that renounced the distinction between indigenous and civilised peoples, so convenient for colonialism, including and especially in the historiographical topography of relevance. De Martino thus called for the equivalent of an anthropological or cultural turn in historiography, whose first step would have to be to overcome its strict separation from anthropology. In the 1950s, under the slogan "progressive

---

34 Carlo Ginzburg, "Witches and Shamans," *New Left Review* 200 (July/Aug 1993), 75–85, 77. On Leone Ginzburg and Einaudi Press see Maike Abath, *Der Geist von Turin. Pavese, Ginzburg, Einaudi und die Wiedergeburt Italiens nach 1943*, (Berlin: Wagenbach, 2010). For Russian populism, see, Franco Venturi, *Roots of Revolution. A History of the Populist and Socialist Movements in 19th Century Russia* (London: Phoenix Press, 2001).

35 Carlo Levi, *Christ Stopped at Eboli*, trans. Frances Frenaye (New York: Farrar, Straus and Company, 1947).

36 For Ernesto De Martino, see, Dorothy Louise Zinn, "An Introduction to Ernesto de Martino's Relevance for the Study of Folklore," *The Journal of American Folklore* 128 (2015): 3–13; George R. Saunders, "'Critical Ethnocentrism' and the Ethnology of Ernesto De Martino," *American Anthropologist* 95.4 (1993): 875–893.

37 Ernesto De Martino, "Intorno a una storia del mondo popolare subalterno," *Società* 5, no. 3 (1949): 411–35, included in *Il dibattito sul folkore in Italia*, ed. Pietro Clemente, Maria Luisa Meoni, and Massimo Squillacciotti (Milan: Edizioni di cultura popolare, 1976), 63–81.

folklore", he charged historiography with the task of discovering and documenting the hidden and repressed popular cultures of resistance and utopias and making them relevant in the present as a catalyst of progressive cultural change.[38]

With claims such as these, formulated in books like *Il mondo magico* (1948) and *Sud e magia* (1959), De Martino differed markedly from the interpretations of the PCI, where popular beliefs (like the magical cults of southern Italian peasants) could only be seen as a disorderly pile of exotic curiosities or as a symptom of false consciousness.[39] By contrast, De Martino criticised this "reactionary" understanding of folklore and called for a "progressive" approach that was willing to discover aspects of agency and resistance in the traditional forms of popular culture.[40] His theories of progressive folklore triggered a fierce innerparty debate which was partly responsible for his leaving the PCI in 1956.[41] While in the 1950s he was associated with a dissident minority, in the early 1960s he was received by the avant-garde of a revisionist New Left. This group hoped to revise the theory of the party and its connection to the masses, using the autonomy of workers and peasants as its basis.[42] The idea of discovering forms of genuine resistance in the alleged backwardness of a subaltern culture also inspired Carlo Ginzburg. He read *Il mondo magico* as an eighteen-year-old and repeatedly cited it as a central reference point for his research.[43] This influence is evident in his early studies on witch trials, which Ginzburg sought to interpret as a form of class struggle.[44] His contribution to the prestigious *Storia dell'Italia* (1972) was also based on the idea, inspired by De Martino, Gramsci and Mikhail Bakhtin, that there was a much older folk culture underlying the "official" religion of the Catholic Church. This comprised a "potentially revolutionary principle", so his claim, nourished by hopes of redemption and notions

---

38 Ernesto De Martino, "Il folklore progressivo: Note lucane," *Unità* (June 28, 1951): 3; also in Clemente, *Il dibattito sul folklore*, 123–124.

39 Ernesto De Martino, *Il mondo magico: Prolegomeni a una storia del magismo* (Torino: Einaudi, 1948); English: Ernesto De Martino, *The World of Magic*, trans. Paul Saye White (New York: Pyramid Communications, 1972), 1948; Ernesto De Martino, *Sud e magia* (Milan: Feltrinelli, 1959).

40 Ernesto De Martino, "Il folklore progressive: Note lucane," *Unità* (June 28, 1951): 3; also in *Il dibattito sul folklore in Italia*, ed. Pietro Clemente, Maria Luisa Meoni, and Massimo Squillacciotti (Milan: Edizioni di cultura popolare, 1976), 123–124.

41 Valerio Salvatore Severino, "Ernesto de Martino nel Pci degli anni Cinquanta tra religione e politica culturale," *Studi Storici* 44/2 (2003): 527–553.

42 Clemente, *Il dibattito sul folklore*, 26.

43 Carlo Ginzburg, preface to *The Night Battles: Witchcraft and Agrarian Cults in the Sixteenth and Seventeenth Centuries*, ed. Carlo Ginzburg, trans. John and Anne C. Tedeschi (Baltimore: Johns Hopkins University Press, 2013), ix–xii, ix.

44 Ginzburg, *Night Battles*, x.

3 Microhistory and Micropolitics — 71

of justice, which the clergy had always feared, always appropriated and eviscerated, but could never completely eradicate.[45] It was this deep zone of a subversive popular culture that Ginzburg was seeking to reconstruct in his 1976 study, based on the case of the miller Menocchio.[46]

3.5 Grassroots Culture and the History Workshops of the New Left in the 1960s

This interest in a better understanding of popular culture was connected in a diverse and at times indirect way with a heterodox Marxist Left that in the long 1960s developed new research practices, institutional structures, and interpretations of the past. This grassroots culture was grounded in a network of history workshops self-described as *Circoli* or *Leghe di cultura,* extending over northern Italy. This included the circle known as *Incontri di cultura* founded in 1960 in Piacenza around Piergiorgio Bellocchio and which after 1962 published the journal *Quaderni Piacentini;* also the *Lega di Cultura di Piadena* started by Giuseppe Morandi and Gianfranco Azzali in 1967, and the *Istituto Ernesto de Martino per la conoscenza critica e la presenza alternative del mondo popolaro e proletario* established in 1966 in Milan by the historian Gianni Bosio and the anthropologist Alberto Cirese.[47] Ernesto de Martino featured here as the driving force behind historical initiatives dedicated to developing and cultivating a subaltern counterculture. Gianni Bosio, mentioned above, was a particularly active representative of this movement. Since the early 1950s, when he was still editor of the magazine *Mondo Operaio,* he had been a critic of the omissions and constrictions of orthodox party-based Marxist historiography focussing on elites and the nation.[48] In the 1960s, Bosio became a pioneer of oral history and a cultural organiser who sought new ways of communi-

---

45 Carlo Ginzburg, "Folklore, magia, religione," in *Storia d'Italia: I caratteri originali,* vol. 1, ed. Ruggiero Romano, and Corrado Vivanti (Turin: Einaudi, 1972), 603–676, 611.

46 Ginzburg, *The Cheese and the Worms,* xi.

47 Matteo Rebecchi, "La lega di cultura di Piadena: Cronaca di un'esperienza," *Storie in movimento* 7 (2015): 108–111; Giacomo Pontremoli, *I 'Piacentini': Storia di una rivista (1962–1989)* (Rome: Edizioni dell'Asino, 2017); Cesare Bermani, *Una storia cantata: Trentacinque anni di attività del Nuovo Canzioniere Italiano/ Istituto Ernesto de Martino (1962–1997)* (Milan: Jaca Book, 1997).

48 Stefano Merli, *L'altra storia: Bosio, Montaldi e le origini della nuova sinistra* (Milan: Feltrinelli, 1976). See also, Gianni Bosio, *L'intellettuale rovesciato: Interventi e ricerche sulla emergenza d'interesse verso le forme di espressione e di organizzazione 'spontanee' nel mondo popolare e proletario, 1963–1971* (Milano: Edizioni Bella Ciao, 1975).

cating history and popular culture.[49] He organised theatrical performances and concerts, produced records, and was one of the initiators of the Italian folk revival. Bosio assumed that the experiences of the oppressed which had been excluded from the official (written) historical culture of the elites had left traces in popular oral culture – particularly in songs, fairy tales and proverbs – from which counter-histories and, not least, alternative paths for the future could be indirectly reconstructed. Microhistory shared this interest in popular culture with the oral history movement, as it did the understanding of historical research as a political intervention, cultivated by Bosio (and other history activists such as Danilo Montaldi, Sergio Bologna and Cesare Bermani).[50]

It was not only perspectives and practices that moved between these grass-roots milieus and microhistory, but also people. One of these was Alessandro Portelli, who founded the *Circolo Gianni Bosio* in Rome in 1972 and whose oral history portrait of his home town of Terni was published by Einaudi in the *Microstorie* series in 1985. In the 1960s, Portelli, like many others of his generation, did voluntary social work in the *Borghetti* (the working-class suburbs) of Rome, conducted interviews with resident migrant workers from southern Italy, and collected their protest songs as part of a counterculture of resistance.[51] Another example is Luisa Passerini, who was involved in a similar milieu, joining a *Circolo Culturale* in Asti made up of workers and students in 1960. As she narrates in her autobiographical retrospective of the 1968 generation in northern Italy, her group sought out former resistance fighters to hear their stories about the *Resistenza* and to join them in singing protest songs and old Piedmontese folk songs. Although many of the former partisans were communists, they had distanced themselves from the party and criticised the "*Resistenza* myth" cultivated by the PCI, with its blindness to the continued existence of fascism in the present. Many kept weapons in secret, since in their eyes the war was not yet over. According to Passerini, it was in this context that she became interested in oral culture – in the experiences and views found in anecdotes and songs that clashed with established history and were not represented in it. This interest was combined with her increasing politicisation.[52] As a history student in Turin in the

---

49 Alessandro Portelli, "Oral History in Italy," in *Oral History: An Interdisciplinary Anthology*, ed. David K. Dunaway, and Willa K. Baum (Walnut Creek: AltaMira Press, 1996), 391–416.

50 Cesare Bermani, "Dieci anni di lavoro con le fonti orale," *Primo Maggio* 5 (1975): 35–50.

51 Miroslav Vanek, "Alessandro Protelli," in *Around the Globe: Rethinking Oral History with its Protagonists*, ed. Miroslav Vanek (Prague: Charles University, 2013), 122–134.

52 Luisa Passerini, *Autobiography of a Generation: Italy 1968* (Middletown, Connecticut: Wesleyan University Press, 1988), 20–25; Luisa Passerini, "A Passion for Memory," *History Workshop Journal* 72 (2011): 241–250, 243.

early 1960s, Passerini was a member of a Situationist group whose focus was on the "revolutionisation of everyday life". In 1967, she travelled to Africa (Kenya, Zambia, Tanzania and later Egypt) for two years to join the liberation movements there and to document the "memory of resistance". At the University of Dar es Salaam, in collaboration with the Mozambican liberation movement *Frelimo*, she compiled a book composed of newspaper articles, leaflets, songs, and her own oral history portrayals of militant struggles.[53] When she returned to Turin in 1969, she seamlessly implemented this form of historiography in various groups of the New Left to support their political aims.[54] Before becoming an assistant professor at the university and a member of the "Turin Group" around Giovanni Levi in 1974, her various activities included distributing leaflets outside factories in northern Italy as a founder-member of the Workerist (*Operaismo) Gruppo Gramsci*, joining a women's group, and contributing to an edition of Clara Zetkin's writings on the history of the women's rights and proletarian women's movements.[55]

3.6 From the Factory to Everyday Life: the Turin Group

Contrary to the standard interpretations of many handbooks and introductions to microhistory, the chief concern of its pioneers in the early years was not internal academic debate. Their analytical perspectives were in fact grounded in militant intellectual practices in the political arena. The case of Giovanni Levi is a prime example. His path to microhistory led initially from the peasant struggles of the south to the factories of the north, where labour migration had generated a completely new "class composition", a key term used by Raniero Panzieri, the founder of the Workerist *Quaderni Rossi* (Red notebooks) group, in whose circles Giovanni Levi moved.[56] Before becoming a student of history in Turin in 1960,

---

53 Luisa Passerini, *Colonialismo portoghese e lotta di liberazione nel Mozambico* (Torino: Einaudi, 1970).

54 Passerini, *Autobiography of a Generation*, 108; Passerini, "Passion for Memory," 244.

55 Luisa Passerini, *Clara Zetkin, La questione femminile e la lotta al riformismo* (Milano: Mazzotta, 1972), 9–24.

56 These changing perspectives between Northern and Southern Italy, typical for a generation of the New Left, are explained by Goffredo Fofi in his diary: Goffredo Fofi, *Strana Gente: Un diario tra Sud e Nord nell'Italia del 1960* (Rome: Donzelli Editore, 1993). See also: Angelo Ventrone, '*Vogliamo tutto': Perché due generazioni hanno creduto nella rivoluzione 1960–1988* (Roma/Bari: Laterza, 2012).

Levi spent an interim semester as a volunteer in the suburbs of Palermo, where he conducted interviews with day labourers for the social reformer Danilo Dolci.[57] Levi took these survey and oral history techniques to Turin, where a wave of violent labour struggles – led by radical southern Italian migrants – had broken out in the Fiat factories. Levi was a member of the left wing of the Italian Socialist Party (PSI) but was also active in the Workerist centre of the Italian New Left, the Turin-based *Quaderni Rossi* group.[58] The aim of this group was to provide a new and effective impetus to the struggle of the workers' movement outside the established left, and to this end they carried out several investigations in factories, including Fiat plants, in which Levi was involved.[59] Levi left the PSI after it formed a centre-left coalition with the DCI in 1963, but remained a member of a Turin student-worker group that existed until 1973. In an interview he said that this group was anti-Leninist, basically anarchist and close in outlook to *Lotta Continua*, but less hierarchically organised. They studied the situation of the workers in the factories so that they could stimulate the trade union struggles.[60] In the course of several interviews, Levi placed direct responsibility for his interest in microhistory on this long-standing political involvement. When he was campaigning in Val Susa at the beginning of the 1970s and distributing leaflets on piecework wages, he said he was deeply disturbed by the reaction of one of the workers to whom the leaflet was addressed. This worker was adamant that its content was of no interest to him and explained that the factory was by no means as central to the workers as Levi and his comrades assumed, and that the really interesting part of their lives was outside the factory. Levi was keen to emphasise the fact that this brief episode had made him realise that his view of reality was essentially Leninist, and that after that it became clear to him that the only way to understand the working class was to study their everyday lives. He had under-

---

57 The connection between field studies, life course research and worker studies is demonstrated in, Marcelo Hoffmann, *Militant Acts: The Role of Investigations in Radical Political Struggles* (Albany: State University of New York Press, 2019), 68–79.

58 On the *Quaderni Rossi* group see, Nello Ajello, *Il lungo addio. Intellettuali e PCI dal 1958 al 1991* (Roma/Bari: Laterza, 1997), 37–47. On Italian Workerism (Operaismo), see, Steve Wright, *Storming Heaven. Class Composition and Struggle in Italian Autonomist Marxism*, 2. Edition (London: Pluto Press, 2017).

59 Giovanni Levi, "Entrevista a Giovanni Levi," *Estudios sociales: Revista Universitaria de Santa Fe Semestral* 9 (1995): 111–124, 114; Giovanni Levi, "Entrevista con Giovanni Levi," *Salud mental y cultura: Revista de la Asociación Española de Neuropsiquiatria* 71 (1999): 483–492, 487. See also: Giovanni Artero, *Il punto di Archimede: Biografia politica di Raniero Panzieri da Rodolfo Morandi ai 'Quaderni rossi'* (Cernusco sul Naviglio: Giovane Talpe, 2007); Romolo Gobbi, *Com'eri bella classe operaia* (Milan: Longanesi, 1989), 80–88.

60 Levi, "Entrevista a Giovanni Levi," 115.

stood that reality had to be analysed on a small scale in order to reach generalisations and not the other way round.[61]

As a result, in 1975 Levi launched a major research project on the Turin working-class district of Borgo San Paolo during the interwar period. In contrast to the early Workerist analyses, this examined not the factories but everyday life, and it anticipated many of the central demands of microhistory – the reduction of scale, the focus on interpersonal relationships, and the awareness of ordinary people's scope for action in everyday life.[62] In a joint essay in 1977, Levi, Luisa Passerini, and Lucetta Scaraffia made it clear that it was not their intention to write a Marxist social history of parties, organisations, or working methods, but rather to reconstruct the thinking of a class before it had been shaped by party-based Marxist schemata.[63] As the research group explained, under fascist rule and the rationalisation of work, the culture of resistance had shifted from the factories to leisure time. It was here – and not in the factory (let alone in the party) – that the antagonistic potential of the working class was to be located. In their everyday attitudes and beliefs, in their festivals and spectacles, the Turin group recognised moments of rebellion and the potential for upheaval, which, drawing on Ernesto de Martino, they considered analogous to the magical cults of southern Italian peasants.[64] In historiographical terms, this was a plea to take popular culture seriously as an independent field that was not only subject to historical change, but also caused it; in political terms, it was a call to seek – and mobilise – collective resistance, not primarily in production, but above all in the field of culture. According to Maurizio Gribaudi, who was involved in the study, the Turin group tried to use their research to analyse the theoretical and practical dead ends of a left whose strategies were anchored in an extremely conservative and economistic view of history.[65] The debate was therefore not primarily about inner-academic problems, but about political questions concerning the development of strategies for action in the face of seemingly overpowering economic realities – in the past as well as in the present.

---

61 This interpretation follows Kroll, "Die Anfänge," 282.

62 Giovanni Levi, "Il piccolo, il grande, il piccolo: Intervista con Giovanni Levi," *Meridiana* 10 (1990): 211–234, 223.

63 Giovanni Levi, Luisa Passerini, and Lucetta Scaraffia, "Vita quotidiana in un quartiere operaio di Torino fra le due querre: L'apporto della storia orale," *Quaderni storici* 12.35 (1977): 433–449, 434.

64 Levi, Passerini, Scaraffia, "Vita quotidiana," 447.

65 Gribaudi, "La lunga marcia," 11.

3.7 Contexts of the Reception of Microhistory

It has become clear that the analysis of actors' interpretations of themselves and the world, which is a chief characteristic of microhistory, should in no way be understood as a rejection of the political relevance of historiography. Microhistory's approaches were situated in a community of shared theory and practice which was socially diverse and comprised various disciplines within a "heated" political culture involving student and worker groups, university seminars, trade unions, history workshops, and magazine projects. Contrary to the claims made in numerous handbooks and introductory courses, it was never the main aim of microhistorians for their studies to trigger an internal academic debate. Rather, their aim was to provoke a political debate. As Thomas Kroll rightly remarked, their purpose was not introspection for its own sake nor the celebration of happy private lives. On the contrary, microhistory hoped to provide present-day "ordinary people" with an understanding of the everyday world and therefore a knowledge of the fact that opportunities for concrete political intervention were open to them.[66] With this in mind, microhistory cannot be equated with a depoliticisation of history. Its political leanings have, however, prevented it from ever being able to establish an institutional base within Italian historiography. According to Maurizio Gribaudi, microhistory was faced with rejection on two fronts. It was arrogantly disregarded by traditional historians, but it also came under fierce public attack from historians from the traditional left. This was, he suggests, because they recognised its dangerous challenge to the Marxist models which were the inspiration they were not prepared to forgo. Microhistorians were isolated politically and in Italian academia. This forced them to take their approaches abroad, where they often went straight to the heart of academic debate. Many, such as Maurizio Gribaudi, Simona Cerutti, Carlo Ginzburg and Gianna Pomata, who had been among those thinking and acting together politically in the 1970s, left Italy in the 1980s to move to France, Britain, and North America and pursue their academic careers there.[67]

In the course of this successful move abroad, microhistory gained more acceptance as an academic approach. It became disengaged from its original geographical and social contexts and thus gradually disassociated from the political milieus, issues, and debates with which it had originally been linked. One of the reasons why the microhistory paradigm was so successful internationally in the 1990s was that it was not based on any consolidated school of thought that would

---

66 Kroll, "Die Anfänge der microstoria," 282.
67 Gribaudi, "La lunga marcia," 11, 14.

have defended a "correct" approach. As a result it could be adapted to different historiographical milieus and applied in a variety of ways

Nevertheless, there was at times fierce resistance to microhistory in other countries. In West Germany, for example, it was harshly criticised by the leading Bielefeld school of historical social science.[68] This was soon followed, however, by a first stage of its academic reception, particularly in the area of early modern history, with such research as the massive studies by Jürgen Schlumbohm and Hans Medick.[69] The *École des Hautes Études en Sciences Sociales (EHESS)* in Paris, on the other hand, had always had close links to Italy and was receptive to the microhistorical approach. Its reception began in the context of the Annales school at the end of the 1980s, a time when the macroscopic tenets of *Nouvelle Histoire* were proving increasingly too rigid, too general, and too heedless of experience. French historians such as Bernard Lepetit and Jacques Revel used approaches from microhistory to revive social history by redirecting it from structures to practices.[70]

The overall outcome of this process of inclusion in academia is not undisputed. While on the one hand it ensured that the tools of microhistory would be to a certain extent sustained, it also contributed to the complete transformation of microhistory from a politically-based intellectual project into an experimental methodological approach.[71] David Blackbourn has pointed out that applying the label "microhistory" did not necessarily mean that a study was boldly experimental. Even historians using conservative methods have occasionally labelled their work microhistory. According to Blackbourn, for example, when he was a student in Cambridge in the 1970s, although there was a general intellectual antipathy towards theory, it was deemed interesting to refer to microhistory as a contrasting position to the structural history stemming from Weber, Marx, and others. "Narrow-minded empiricists" saw their "scepticism towards theory" confirmed, and used microhistory as a label that permitted them to continue as before, with an

---

68 Cf. Winfried Schulze, ed., *Sozialgeschichte, Alltagsgeschichte, Mikro-Historie: Eine Diskussion* (Göttingen: Vandenhoeck & Ruprecht, 1994); Jürgen Schlumbohm, ed., *Mikrogeschichte – Makrogeschichte: Komplementär oder inkommensurabel?* (Göttingen: Wallstein, 1998).

69 See Otto Ulbricht, "Divergierende Pfade der Mikrogeschichte. Aspekte der Rezeptionsgeschichte," *Jahrbuch für Geschichte des ländlichen Raumes* 9 (2012): 22–36.

70 Jacques Revel, ed., *Jeux d'échelles: La micro-analyse à l'expérience* (Paris: Gallimard, 1996); Jacques Revel, "L'histoire au ras du sol," introduction to Giovanni Levi, *Le Pouvoir au village: Histoire d'un exorciste dans le Piémont du xviie siècle*, trad. Maurice Aymard (Paris: Gallimard, 1989), i–xxxiii.

71 Cf. Sandro Lardi, "Traduire la microstoria," *Traduire. Revue française de la traduction* 236 (2017): 71–74 and Paul-André Rosental, "Microstoria," in *Notionnaires, Vol. II, Idées*, (Paris: Encyclopaedia Universalis, 2005), 530–532.

anti-structural approach to the histories of events and ideas.[72] Francesca Trivellato shows that in the USA, on the other hand, in a historical environment where biographical historical research had always played a significant role, microhistory flourished. This, Trivellato suggests, explains how microhistorians such as Natalie Zemon Davis and to some extent David Warren Sabean could act "antithetically to microhistory", in that they studied historical context in order to interpret a single individual's fate and not the other way round.[73] In California, microhistory had even united with an anti-positivist scepticism that doubted the reality behind the text as a matter of principle.[74] Whether one agrees with these interpretations in detail or not, it is clear that microhistory joined the repository of accepted historiographical approaches in Europe and North America during the 1990s and became established as one of many possible research methods.

In other parts of the world, however, the reception of microhistory followed a different pattern. In some places such as Central and South America and India, its political leanings were less resolutely ignored. In India, where it was conveyed mainly through Carlo Ginzburg, microhistory had a moment of recognition in the early phases of Subaltern Studies.[75] Ginzburg realised how close he was to his Indian colleagues when he attended a history symposium in Calcutta at the end of the 1980s. A simple reason for their strong affinity soon became clear, namely that the Indian scholars were also Marxists and had read Antonio Gramsci in English.[76] In Latin America Marxism and Gramsci also paved the way for the acceptance of microhistorical perspectives.[77] Carlos Antonio Aguirre Rojas has shown that the reception of microhistory began on a considerable scale in the 1990s but branched off in various directions with different reference points. While in Argentina and Uruguay the works of the Turin group around Giovanni Levi at-

---

72 David Blackbourn, "Mikrogeschichte," in *Landschaften der deutschen Geschichte: Aufsätze zum 19. und 20. Jahrhundert*, ed. David Blackbourn (Göttingen: Vandenhoeck & Ruprecht, 2016), 353–367, 361.
73 Francesca Trivellato, "Microstoria/ Microhistoire/ Microhistory," *French Politics, Culture & Society* 33 (2015): 122–134, 128.
74 Trivellato, "Microstoria/ Microhistoire/ Microhistory," 129.
75 Sumit Sarkar, "The Decline of the Subaltern in Subaltern Studies," in *Writing Social History*, ed. Sumit Sarkar (Delhi: Oxford University Press, 1997), 92–108, 94.
76 Carlo Ginzburg, "In history as in cinema, every close-up implies an off-screen scene," Interview with Carlo Ginzburg, conducted by Nicolas Weill for 'Le Monde', 3 October 2022, https://www.versobooks.com/en-gb/blogs/news/5536-carlo-ginzburg-in-history-as-in-cinema-every-close-up-implies-an-off-screen-scene, accessed November 09, 2024.
77 Juan Maiguashca, "Latin American Marxist History: Rise, Fall and Resurrection," *Storia della Storiografia* 62 (2012): 105–120.

tracted a good deal of attention, in Mexico and Brazil it was mainly the work of Carlo Ginzburg that was translated and debated.[78]

It is worth examining the direction taken by Mexico in conclusion, since this is where Adolfo Gilly is situated. Gilly, who is still considered one of the most important representatives of "history from below" in Mexico and was then teaching at the *Universidad Nacional Autónoma de México (UNAM)*, was of course the activist within the politics of historiography who sent the text by Carlo Ginzburg to the subcommander Marcos in the summer of 1995. For Gilly, as we have seen, this text was a symbol of the revival of the old Marxist models and perspectives that he saw materialising in the Chiapas uprising. Since the end of the 1970s, Gilly had been increasingly focussed on a perspective "from below", which emphasised both the validity of the distinct world in which the exploited lower classes lived, and their lack of representation, in official historiography as in orthodox Marxist history writing. His 1980 text *Historia como crítica o como discurso del poder* was a call for the reconstruction of a history of the oppressed based both on material finds and oral sources such as songs. It reads as a surprisingly sweeping criticism of the alleged rationality of an episteme that was compliant to power and had from the outset to exclude the "alternative histories" of the powerless.[79]

Marcos, however, as we have seen, rejected Ginzburg's text as yet another case of the prevailing neoliberal ideology and read it as an outspoken attack on historical materialism, which he professed to champion. It is remarkable that in this way he disclosed his advocacy for a strikingly rigid form of Marxism, which was hardly in keeping with the international image soon to be presented by the media of him as a fighter influenced by poststructuralism, and with a poetic inclination. What is also remarkable is that two left-wing intellectual militants were discussing an article by probably the best-known now-academic microhistorian and restoring it to the level of political argument. Gilly and Marcos unwittingly embroiled Ginzburg in an intense debate about the relation between theory and practice, about the particular and the general, about the politics of historiographical epistemology and about the role of intellectuals in social movements. Ginzburg's text sparked a controversial debate about the present and the options for political action open to individuals in a situation which was very different from the context in which microhistory had developed.

---

[78] Carlos Antonio Aguirre Rojas, *Microhistoria italiana: Modo de empleo* (Rosario: Prohistoria Ediciones, 2017), 25.

[79] Adolfo Gilly, "La historia como crítica o como discurso del poder," in *Historia, ¿para qué?*, ed. Carlos Pereyra et al. (Mexico City: Siglo Veintiuno Editors, 1980), 195–225. See as well: Mayer, Gute Gründe und doppelte Böden, 92.

At issue was also the political function of microhistory and the ways in which it could be co-opted. This is another factor made clear by the dispute between Ginzburg (via Gilly) and Marcos, namely that certain central recurring themes in microhistory, such as the hope for social regeneration by including marginalised counter-histories from below, have been increasingly adopted since the 1990s by the populist political right and given an autocratic twist. In the same way, the right-wing of the mainstream neo-liberal project has attempted to take the idea of popular culture out of its Marxist context and alienate it to such an extent that it appears to fit into the individualist, identitarian self-realisation utopias of neoliberal provenance. Ultimately the dispute serves as a reminder that the construction of historical meaning does not take place in the secluded ivory towers of academia, but in a public political space which it also helps to shape. Within this political space it is a process that not only has to stand the test as a scientific method but also has to systematically scrutinise the political dimensions of its own actions. As a critical constituent of the self-understanding of the democratic process, its task is also to refute the one-dimensional interpretation of society and history conveyed by authoritarian movements. Instead, it must constantly reinterpret the complexity and plurality of past and present worlds by means of critical interrogation of sources. Apart from deepening knowledge of the past, this also allows a distancing from the imperatives and self-evident teleologies of the present and permits other futures to be conceived. Nothing else seems to correspond more closely to microhistory's aspirations, then as now.

References

Abath, Maike. *Der Geist von Turin: Pavese, Ginzburg, Einaudi und die Wiedergeburt Italiens nach 1943*. Berlin: Wagenbach, 2010.

Aguirre Rojas, Carlos Antonio. *Microhistoria italiana: Modo de empleo*. Rosario: Prohistoria Ediciones, 2017.

Ajello, Nello. *Il lungo addio: Intellettuali e PCI dal 1958 al 1991*. Roma/Bari: Laterza, 1997.

Artero, Giovanni. *Il punto di Archimede: Biografia politica di Raniero Panzieri da Rodolfo Morandi ai 'Quaderni rossi'*. Cernusco sul Naviglio: Giovane Talpe, 2007.

Bachmann-Medick, Doris. "Cultural Turns (Version: 2.0)." *Docupedia-Zeitgeschichte*, 17.6.2019. https://dx.doi.org/10.14765/zzf.dok-1389.

Baschet, Jerôme. "(Re)discutir sobre la historia." *Chiapas* 10 (2000): 7–39.

Bermani, Cesare. "Dieci anni di lavoro con le fonti orale." *Primo Maggio* 5 (1975): 35–50.

Bermani, Cesare. *Una storia cantata: Trentacinque anni di attività del Nuovo Canzioniere Italiano/ Istituto Ernesto de Martino (1962–1997)*. Milan: Jaca Book, 1997.

Bernet, Brigitta. "The Postwar Marxist Milieu of Microhistory: Heterodoxy, Activism and the Formation of a Critical Historiographical Perspective." In *What's Left of Marxism: Historiography*

3 Microhistory and Micropolitics — **81**

and the Possibilities of Thinking with Marxian Themes and Concepts, edited by Benjamin Zachariah, Lutz Raphael and Brigitta Bernet, 37–64. Berlin: De Gruyter Oldenbourg, 2020.

Blackbourn, David. "Mikrogeschichte." In *Landschaften der deutschen Geschichte: Aufsätze zum 19. und 20. Jahrhundert*, edited by David Blackbourn, 353–367. Göttingen: Vandenhoeck & Ruprecht, 2016.

Bosio, Gianni. *L'intellettuale rovesciato: Interventi e ricerche sulla emergenza d'interesse verso le forme di espressione e di organizzazione 'spontanee' nel mondo popolare e proletario, 1963-1971*. Milan: Edizioni Bella Ciao, 1975.

Bronner, Stephen Eric. "Was tun? und Stalinismus." *UTOPIE kreativ* 151 (2003): 425–434.

Burke, Peter. "The Cultural History of Intellectual Practices: An Overview." In *Political Concepts and Time: New Approaches to Conceptual History*, edited by Javier Fernándes Sebastián, 103–130. Santander: Cantabria University Press, 2011.

Chaudhuri, Amit. "In the Waiting-Room of History." *London Review of Books* 26 (2004): 3–8.

Chakrabarty, Dipesh. *Provincializing Europe: Postcolonial Thought and Historical Difference*. Princeton: Princeton University Press, 2000.

Charle, Christophe. "Micro-histoire sociale et macro-histoire sociale: Quelques réflexions sur les effets des changements de méthode depuis quinze ans en histoire sociale." *Histoire sociale - histoire globale? Actes du colloque de l'IHMC*, edited by Christophe Charle, 45–57. Paris: Editions de la MSH, 1993.

Coli, Daniela. "Idealismo e marxismo nella storiografia italiana degli anni '50 e '60." In *La storiografie contemporanea: Indirizzi e problemi*, edited by Pietro Rossi, 39–58. Milan: Il Saggatore, 1987.

De Martino, Ernesto. *Il mondo magico: Prolegomeni a una storia del magismo*. Torino: Einaudi, 1948.

De Martino, Ernesto. "Intorno a una storia del mondo popolare subaltern." In *Il dibattito sul folkore in Italia*, edited by Pietro Clemente, Maria Luisa Meoni, and Massimo Squillacciotti, 63–81. Milan: Edizioni di cultura popolare, 1976.

De Martino, Ernesto. "Il folklore progressivo: Note lucane." In *Il dibattito sul folkore in Italia*, edited by Pietro Clemente, Maria Luisa Meoni, and Massimo Squillacciotti, 123–124. Milan: Edizioni di cultura popolare, 1976.

De Martino, Ernesto. *Sud e magia*. Milan: Feltrinelli, 1959.

De Martino, Ernesto. *The World of Magic*. Translated by Paul Saye White. New York: Pyramid Communications, 1972.

Depkat, Volker. "The 'Cultural Turn' in German and American Historiography." *Amerikastudien / American Studies* 54/3 (2009): 425–450.

Eley, Geoff. *History Made Conscious: Politics of Knowledge, Politics of the Past*. New York: Verso Books, 2023.

Favilli, Paolo. *Marxismo e storia: Saggio sull'innovazione storiografica in Italia (1945-1970)*. Milan: Franco Angeli, 2006.

Focardi, Filippo. *La guerra della memoria: La Resistenza nel dibattito politico italiano dal 1945 a oggi*. Rome: GLF editori Laterza, 2005.

Fofi, Goffredo. *Strana Gente: Un diario tra Sud e Nord nell'Italia del 1960*. Rome: Donzelli Editore, 1993.

Forgacs, David. "The Italian Communist Party and Culture." In *Culture and Conflict in Postwar Italy: Essays on Mass and Popular Culture*, edited by Robert Lumley, and Zygmunt G. Baranski, 97–114. Houndmills: The Macmillan Press, 1990.

Gilly, Adolfo. "La historia como crítica o como discurso del poder." In *Historia, ¿para qué?*, edited by Carlos Pereyra, Luis Villora, Luis Ganzález, Joé Joaquin Blanco, Enrique Florescano, Arnaldo Córdova, Héctor Aguilar Camin, Carlos Monsiváis, Adolfo Gilly, and Guillermo Bonfil Batalla, 195–225. Mexico City: Siglo Veintiuno Editors, 1980.

Gilly, Adolfo, Subcomandante Marcos, and Carlo Ginzburg. *Discusión sobre la historia*. Mexico: Taurus, 1995.

Gilly, Adolfo. "What exists cannot be true (Interview)." *New Left Review* 64 (2010): 29–46.

Ginsborg, Paul. *A History of Contemporary Italy: Society and Politics 1943–1988*. London: Penguin Books, 1990.

Ginzburg, Carlo. "Folklore, magia, religione." In Vol. 1 of *Storia d'Italia: I caratteri originali*, edited by Ruggiero Romano, and Corrado Vivanti, 603–676. Turin: Einaudi, 1972.

Ginzburg, Carlo. *Il formaggio e i vermi: Il cosmo di un mugnaio del '500*. Turin: Einaudi, 1976.

Ginzburg, Carlo. "Señales: Raíces de un paradigma indiciario." In *Crisis de la razón: Nuevos modelos en la relación entre saber y actividades humanas*, edited by Aldo Gargani, 55–99. Mexico: Siglo Veintiuno Editores, 1983.

Ginzburg, Carlo. "Clues: Roots of a Scientific Paradigm." *Theory and Society* 7/3 (May, 1979): 273–288.

Ginzburg, Carlo. *The Cheese and the Worms: The Cosmos of a Sixteenth-Century Miller*. Translated by John Tedeschi, and Anne C. Tedeschi. Baltimore: John Hopkins University Press, 1992.

Ginzburg, Carlo. "Witches and Shamans." *New Left Review* 200 (July/Aug 1993): 75–85.

Ginzburg, Carlo. "Microhistory: Two or Three Things I Know about it." *Critical Inquiry* 20 (Autumn, 1993): 10–35.

Ginzburg, Carlo. *The Night Battles: Witchcraft and Agrarian Cults in the Sixteenth and Seventeenth Centuries*. Translated by John Tedeschi, and Anne C. Tedeschi. Baltimore: John Hopkins University Press, 2013.

Gobbi, Romolo. *Com'eri bella classe operaia*. Milan: Longanesi, 1989.

Gribaudi, Gabriella. "Images of the South: The Mezzogiorno as Seen by Insiders and Outsiders." In *The New History of the Italian South*, edited by Robert Lumley, and Jonathan Morris, 83–114. Exeter: University of Exeter Press, 1997.

Gribaudi, Maurizio. "La lunga marcia della microstoria." In *Microstoria: A venticinque anni da 'L'eredità immateriale',* edited by Paola Lanaro, 9–23. Milano: Franco Angeli, 2011.

Groppo, Bruno. "Die Kommunistische Partei Italiens und ihre Historiographien." *Jahrbuch für Historische Kommunismusforschung* (2013): 191–210.

Guénée Bernard. *Histoire et culture historique dans l'Occident medieval*. Paris: Aubier, 1980.

Henck, Nick. "The Subcommander and the Sardinian: Marcos and Gramsci." *Mexican Studies / Estudios Mexicanos* 29/2 (2013): 428–458.

Hobsbawm, Eric. *Interesting Times: A Twentieth-century Life*. London: Allen Lane, 2002.

Höbel, Alexander. "Storia d'Italia e PCI nell'elaborazione di Palmiro Togliatti." In *Il Risorgimento: Un'epopea? Per una ricostruzione storico-critica*, edited by Cristina Carpinelli, and Vittorio Gioiello), 185–205. Milan: Zambon editore, 2012.

Hoffmann, Marcelo. *Militant Acts: The Role of Investigations in Radical Political Struggles*. Albany: State University of New York Press, 2019.

Iggers, Georg G., Q. Edward Wang, and Supriya Mukherjee, eds. *A Global History of Modern Historiography*. New York: Routledge, 2008.

Jansen, Christian. "Uneiniges Italien: Die 'Südfrage' als Strukturproblem vom Risorgimento bis heute." In *150 Jahre einiges Italien*, edited by Massimo Minelli, and Rainer Schlösser, 179–202. Munich: Meidenbauer, 2012.

Jed, Stephanie. "Proof and Transnational Rhetorics: Opening up the Conservation (Review)." *History and Theory* 40/3 (2001): 372–384.

Jordan, Stefan. *Theorien und Methoden in der Geschichtswissenschaft*. Paderborn: Ferdinand Schöningh, 2018.

Kammerer, Peter. "Bauernkämpfe und Landreform 1943–1953 in Süditalien." In *Produktion und Lebensverhältnisse auf dem Land*, edited by Onno Poppinga, 236–252. Wiesbaden: Springer, 1979.

Kroll, Thomas. "Die Anfänge der microstoria: Methodenwechsel, Erfahrungswandel und transnationale Rezeption in der europäischen Historiographie der 1970er und 1980er Jahre." In *Perspektiven durch Retrospektiven: Wirtschaftsgeschichtliche Beiträge*, edited by Jeanette Granda, and Jürgen Schreiber, 267–287. Köln: Böhlau, 2013.

Lardi, Sandro. "Traduire la microstoria." *Traduire: Revue française de la traduction* 236 (2017).

Lenin, Vladimir. I. "What is to be done?" In *Essential Works of Lenin*, edited by Henry M. Christman, 53–175. New York: Dover Publications, 1987.

Levi, Carlo. *Christ Stopped at Eboli*. Translated by Frances Frenaye. New York: Farrar, Straus and Company, 1947.

Levi, Giovanni, Luisa Passerini, and Lucetta Scaraffia. "Vita quotidiana in un quartiere operaio di Torino fra le due querre: L'apporto della storia orale." *Quaderni storici* 35 (1977): 433–449.

Levi, Giovanni. "Il piccolo, il grande, il piccolo: Intervista con Giovanni Levi." *Meridiana* 10 (1990): 211–234.

Levi, Giovanni. "Entrevista a Giovanni Levi." *Estudios sociales: Revista Universitaria de Santa Fe Semestral* 9 (1995): 111–124.

Levi, Giovanni. "Entrevista con Giovanni Levi." *Salud mental y cultura: Revista de la Asociación Española de Neuropsiquiatria* 71 (1999): 483–492.

Levi, Giovanni. "On Microhistory." In *New Perspectives on Historical Writing*, edited by Peter Burke, 97–119. Cambridge: Polity Press, 2001.

Magnússon, Sigurdur Gylfi, and István M. Szijártó, eds. *What is Microhistory? Theory and Practice*. London, New York: Routledge, 2013.

Maiguashca, Juan. "Latin American Marxist History: Rise, Fall and Resurrection." *Storia della Storiografia* 62 (2012): 105–120.

Mayer, David. "Gute Gründe und doppelte Böden: Zur Geschichte 'linker' Geschichtsschreibung." *Sozial.Geschichte Online* 14 (2014): 62–96, https://duepublico2.uni-due.de/receive/duepublico_mods_00036456, accessed February 20, 2024.

Merli, Stefano. *L'altra storia: Bosio, Montaldi e le origini della nuova sinistra*. Milan: Feltrinelli, 1976.

Passerini, Luisa. *Colonialismo portoghese e lotta di liberazione nel Mozambico*. Turin: Einaudi, 1970.

Passerini, Luisa. *Clara Zetkin, la questione femminile e la lotta al riformismo*. Milan: Mazzotta, 1972.

Passerini, Luisa. *Autobiography of a Generation: Italy 1968*. Middletown, Connecticut: Wesleyan University Press, 1988.

Passerini, Luisa. "A Passion for Memory." *History Workshop Journal* 72 (2011): 241–250.

Pasolini, Pier Paolo. "La Resistenza negra." In *Letteratura negra*, edited by Mario De Andrade, and Léonard Sainville, Vol 1, XV-XXIV. Rome: Editori Riuniti, 1961.

Pons, Silvio. "Stalin, Togliatti, and the Origin of the Cold War in Europe." *Journal of Cold War Studies* 3/2 (2001): 3–27.

Pontremoli, Giacomo. *I 'Piacentini': Storia di una rivista (1962–1989)*. Rome: Edizioni dell'Asino, 2017.

Portelli, Alessandro. "Oral History in Italy." In *Oral History: An Interdisciplinary Anthology*, edited by David K. Dunaway, and Willa K. Baum, 391–416. Walnut Creek: AltaMira Press, 1996.

Rebecchi, Matteo. "La lega di cultura di Piadena: Cronaca di un'esperienza." *Storie in movimento* 7 (2015): 108–111.

Reinhard, Wolfgang. *Lebensformen Europas: Eine historische Kulturanthropologie*. Munich: Beck C. H., 2004.

Revel, Jacques "L'histoire au ras du sol." Introduction to *Le Pouvoir au village: Histoire d'un exorciste dans le Piémont du xviie siècle*, edited by Giovanni Levi, translated by Maurice Aymard, i–xxxiii. Paris: Gallimard, 1989.

Revel, Jacques, ed. *Jeux d'échelles: La micro-analyse à l'expérience*. Paris: Gallimard, 1996.

Rosental, Paul-André. "Microstoria." In *Notionnaires*, Vol. II, 530–532. Paris: Encyclopaedia Universalis, 2005.

Santoro, Marco. "Culture As (And After) Production." *Cultural Sociology* 2/1 (2008): 7–31.

Sarkar, Sumit. "The Decline of the Subaltern in Subaltern Studies." In *Writing Social History*, edited by Sumit Sarkar, 92–108. Delhi: Oxford University Press, 1997.

Saunders, George R. "'Critical Ethnocentrism' and the Ethnology of Ernesto De Martino." *American Anthropologist* 95.4 (1993): 875–893.

Schlumbohm, Jürgen, ed. *Mikrogeschichte – Makrogeschichte: Komplementär oder inkommensurabel?* Göttingen: Wallstein, 1998.

Schulze, Winfried. "Mikrohistorie versus Makrohistorie? Anmerkungen zu einem aktuellen Thema." In *Historische Methode*, edited by Christian Meier, and Jörn Rüsen, 319–341. München: dtv, 1988.

Schulze, Winfried, ed. *Sozialgeschichte, Alltagsgeschichte, Mikro-Historie: Eine Diskussion*. Göttingen: Vandenhoeck & Ruprecht, 1994.

Scotti, Mariamargherita. *Da sinistra: Intellettuali, Partito socialista italiano e organizzazione della cultura (1953-1960)*. Rome: Ediesse, 2011.

Severino, Valerio Salvatore. "Ernesto de Martino nel Pci degli anni Cinquanta tra religione e politica culturale." *Studi Storici* 44/2 (2003): 527–553.

Stahler-Sholk, Richard. "Resisting Neoliberal Homogenization: The Zapatista Autonomy Movement." *Latin American Perspectives* 34/2 (2007): 48–63.

Trivellato, Francesca. "Microstoria/ Microhistoire/ Microhistory." *French Politics, Culture & Society* 33 (2015): 122–134.

Ulbricht, Otto. "Divergierende Pfade der Mikrogeschichte. Aspekte der Rezeptionsgeschichte." *Jahrbuch für Geschichte des ländlichen Raumes* 9 (2012): 22–36.

Vanek, Miroslav. "Alessandro Portelli." In *Around the Globe: Rethinking Oral History with its Protagonists*, edited by Miroslav Vanek, 122–134. Prague: Charles University, 2013.

Ventrone, Angelo. *'Vogliamo tutto': Perché due generazioni hanno creduto nella rivoluzione 1960-1988*. Rome/Bari: Laterza, 2012.

Venturi, Franco. *Roots of Revolution: A History of the Populist and Socialist Movements in 19th Century Russia*. London: Phoenix Press, 2001.

Wright, Steve. *Storming Heaven: Class Composition and Struggle in Italian Autonomist Marxism*, 2. Edition. London: Pluto Press, 2017.

Zinn, Dorothy Louise. "An Introduction to Ernesto de Martino's Relevance for the Study of Folklore." *The Journal of American Folklore* 128 (2015): 3–13.

Etta Grotrian

4 *Barfußhistoriker* and *Geschichtswerkstätten* – History from Below in West Germany in the Late 1970s and the 1980s

In the Federal Republic of Germany, the idea and practice of a "history from below" are primarily linked to *Geschichtswerkstätten* and similar initiatives that shared a common interest in history. *Geschichtswerkstätten* can be translated as history workshops – and this term should be understood as plural, unlike the History Workshop at Ruskin College, which can be seen as one of the role models for the groups in West Germany.[1] These regional associations and groups were founded from the late 1970s; and especially in the 1980s, they could be found all over the Federal Republic of Germany.[2] They have been labeled a new history movement and have referred to themselves as such, but it was a movement that was the sum of quite different activities and groups, including both academic-dominated groups and citizen initiatives that consisted of interested lay researchers, and often a mix of academically-oriented students and academic mid-level professionals, and other interested people. Their goal was to research history as it was on the ground, with a regional emphasis, which amounted to the history of everyday life; and to involve all those interested in history, in other words, aiming for a historiography beyond and also in opposition to the academic historical sciences.

In addition to the many small initiatives, there was a nationwide association, "Geschichtswerkstatt e.V.", in existence since 1983, which functioned as a network for these initiatives and for individual historians as well. This association was founded based on the initiative of academic historians who originally wanted to give space to and establish new approaches in academic historical research, and

---

1 Barbara Taylor, "History of History Workshop," *(published online on 22 November 2012)*, https://www.historyworkshop.org.uk/the-history-of-history-workshop/, accessed December 31, 2022; Logie Barrow, "On getting involved in History Workshop," *Geschichtswerkstatt* 7 (1985): 60–63; Richard J. Evans, "Die 'History-Workshop' -Bewegung in England," in *Geschichte entdecken. Erfahrungen und Projekte der neuen Geschichtsbewegung*, ed. Hannes Heer et al. (Reinbek: Rowohlt, 1985), 37–45; Raphael Samuel, "Wahrheit ist parteiisch. Zur Entstehung des 'History Workshop'," *Journal für Geschichte* 3 (1981): 36–38.

2 A list of initiatives and groups founded since the late 1970s in Western Germany has been published online by the author, https://www.barfuss-oder-lackschuh.de, accessed July 2, 2022.

https://doi.org/10.1515/9783111522180-004

for this purpose wanted to found an academic periodical. Through personal contacts, a network was thus created to link individual academically-practicing historians and non-academic history groups. The local groups were to be integrated into and networked with it.[3] The name "Geschichtswerkstatt", history workshop, for this association was controversial, because the association was not actually exactly that: a locally active initiative. It was more of an association in which individuals from the local groups tried to achieve a supraregional impact. It had been founded to provide a network for a variety of local initiatives, and also for individual historians, in which they could exchange ideas and find support for their work and their approaches.

But even though the association named "Geschichtswerkstatt e. V." was more of a network than a local workshop initiative, the statement of principles (*Selbstverständnispapier)* that the association published in the academic journal "Geschichtsdidaktik" in 1984 summarised the essential points to which the local initiatives also felt attached.[4] *Geschichtswerkstätten* set out to look at the "Geschichte der Ausgeschlossenen, Unterdrückten und Beherrschten" [history of the excluded, the oppressed and the dominated] beyond the established historical sciences. In doing so, they claimed to distinguish themselves from the academic establishment and to include all those interested in history.

Other crucial points in this statement were that the inclusion of everyone in historical work should serve to ensure that those "die in der bisherigen Geschichtsschreibung an den Rand gedrängt wurden, ein neues kollektives Gedächtnis entwickeln und sich ihre Geschichte wieder aneignen" [those marginalised by hitherto-existing historiography develop a new collective memory and re-appropriate their own history]. The everyday history approach, as it is named in the paper, served to bridge the gap between big politics and the experience of the individual, often using regional examples. The initiatives wanted: "Alltagswirklichkeiten in ihren Veränderungen nachspüren und dem Bild entgegenarbeiten, daß Politik nur jenseits des individuellen Lebens stattfindet, der Alltag und die Menschen aber immer gleich blieben" [to trace everyday realities in their historical changes and counteract the image that politics only takes place beyond individual life, while everyday life and people always remained the same]. And that,

---

3 Detlef Siegfried, "Subversiver Alltag. Geschichtswerkstätten zwischen Politik und Wissenschaft," in *25 Jahre Galerie Morgenland. Geschichtswerkstatt Eimsbüttel (Festschrift)*, ed. Geschichtswerkstatt Eimsbüttel, (Hamburg: Morgenland, 2003), 101; Rainer Wirtz, "Geschichtswerkstatt – die andere Geschichte?," *Journal für Geschichte* 5 (1983): 64.
4 "Selbstverständnispapier der Geschichtswerkstatt, beschlossen auf der Gründungsversammlung am 28.5.1983 in Bochum," *Geschichtsdidaktik* 9 (1984): 193.

4 *Barfußhistoriker* and *Geschichtswerkstätten* – History from Below in West Germany

finally, was to help overcome the previous separation between local and "macro" history as they described it.[5]

In this conception, engagement with history had a significant part to play in coming to terms with a present that felt increasingly complicated, with the awareness of the crises of the times, and in finding both visions from and orientation in the past. The historical perspectives of the various *Geschichtswerkstätten* and initiatives were not always as precisely formulated as in the conception of the "Geschichtswerkstatt e. V." Often, theirs was a very heterogeneous and spontaneous *Spurensuche*, 'search for traces', which involved diverse and unconventional forms of conducting interviews as "oral history", or a search for and interpretation of historical sources motivated by activism. On the other hand, there also existed a very literate and theory-driven set of publication activities directed at academic debates. Exhibitions and alternative city tours, projects supported by local cultural policy, and the development of innovative and unusual ways to convey history topics, add to the picture. The activities of these *Geschichtswerkstätten* were diverse, and so were the motives and personal and social objectives of those involved in them.

The association "Geschichtswerkstatt e. V." took on the task of organising a joint publication from the local initiatives.[6] And through the association, annual *Geschichtsfeste* 'history festivals' were also organised, in which the initiatives could exchange information about their topics: These were, for example, the local post-war history, the National Socialist history of a city or town and its continuing residues, the history of industrialisation and the changes caused by contemporary restructuring of industrial society. Other topics were linked more closely to contemporary protest movements: the transformation of cities through modern urban politics and the processes of displacement of historically developed structures and neighborhoods, ecology and environmental history. But they also exchanged ideas about their methods: on interviewing local communities, exhibition practices, unconventional forms of local historical research and outreach, history games, city tours, and alternative commemorative activities.

The first *Geschichtsfest* took place in Berlin in 1984 and was organised by the *Berliner Geschichtswerkstatt*, 'Berlin History Workshop' for initiatives throughout the Republic.[7] The idea was developed from the experience gained in Berlin, when many local history and cultural initiatives were involved in a decentralised

---

5 "Selbstverständnispapier," 193.

6 Peter Schöttler, "Die Geschichtswerkstatt e.V. Zu einem Versuch, basisdemokratische Geschichtsinitiativen und -forschungen zu 'vernetzen'," *Geschichte und Gesellschaft* 10 (1984): 423.

7 About Berliner Geschichtswerkstatt: Jenny Wüstenberg, "Vom alternativen Laden zum Dienstleistungsbetrieb: the Berliner Geschichtswerkstatt. A Case Study in Activist Memory Politics,"

commemoration concept to remember the National Socialist "seizure of power" in 1933 on its fiftieth anniversary, and in this way received funding for exhibitions, publications and actions in 1983. In many regions and cities, 1983 was an initial spark for the founding of new groups.[8] The way in which the commemoration of National Socialist history was being dealt with in many local and regional initiatives also shows that the willingness of West German society to come to terms with its own history had changed since the end of the 1970s, in contrast to the immediate postwar period.[9] Another model for the concept of the *Geschichtsfest* was the *Berliner Volksuni* 'Berlin people's university', which was founded in 1980 and had some similarities in approach to that of the *Geschichtswerkstätten*. It pursued the goal of discussing academic ideas and analyses with interested participants from the non-academic public. Representatives from the university, trade unions, workplaces, and the so-called new social movements were to meet for events, discussions, and diverse cultural offerings, and to practice a rapprochement of the academic with the non-academic world; the idea of the *Kritische Universität* 'critical university' of the West German student movement was cited as precedent. Already at its second meeting in 1981, the Volksuni had given itself the motto "Aus der Geschichte lernen – Leben lernen" [learning from history – learning to live]. It was intended to convey that learning from history can make it possible, in a time of social disorientation, to place one's own goals in a long-term and historical-social continuity.[10]

Gräv där du står 'Dig where you stand', was the title and motto of a 1978 Swedish handbook written by the publicist and author Sven Lindqvist, which was frequently received in the *Geschichtswerkstätten*.[11] This book provided an essen-

---

German Studies Review 32 (2009): 590–618; Anthony McElligott, "The German History Workshop Festival in Berlin, May-June 1984," *German History* 2 (1985): 21–22.

8 A list of the initiatives can be found in the documentation ". . . *Geschichte zurechtrücken, Unbekanntes aufdecken . . .*". *Dokumentation der lokalhistorischen Projekte in der BRD und in Berlin (West) anläßlich des 50. Jahrestages der Machtübergabe an die Nationalsozialisten,* ed. Berliner Geschichtswerkstatt, (Berlin, 1984).

9 Etienne François, "L'Allemagne Fédérale se penche sur son passé," *Vingtième Siècle,* 7 (1985): 160–161.

10 Volksuni. "Bilder und Texte von der ersten Volksuni Pfingsten 1980," ed. Erwin Seyfried, (Berlin, 1980), 5–6; Lars Grüterig, and Alexander Kastner, "Volk + Uni = Volksuni?," in *Experiment: Politische Kultur. Berichte aus einem neuen gesellschaftlichen Alltag,* ed. Gerd Koch (Frankfurt/ Main: Extrabuch 1985), 137–146.

11 Sven Lindqvist, *Gräv där du står. Hur man utforskar ett jobb* (Stockholm: Albert Bonniers Förlag, 1978), a German version of the book has been published in the late 1980s, translated by the German SPD politician Manfred Dammeyer: Sven Lindqvist, *Grabe wo du stehst. Handbuch zur Erforschung der eigenen Geschichte,* trans. Manfred Dammeyer (Bonn: Dietz, 1989), Lindqvist's approach has been published in several essays in German already in the early 1980s.

4 *Barfußhistoriker* and *Geschichtswerkstätten* – History from Below in West Germany — **89**

tial approach for the work of the history groups: Lindqvist argued that if the corporate history of a company, for example, is told from the perspective of those who pay for the historiography, meaning the entrepreneurs, then it follows that the readers' perceptions of history are shaped by their perspective. In this way, developments that bring about an improvement for the entrepreneurs are understood as progress. But the perspective of those who may suffer from production conditions and whose workplace affects their health and life prospects is not researched and written up. Lindqvist challenged workers to write down the history of their workplace themselves: To visit archives, to interview people, to study historical newspapers, to shed light on their own experience. In this way, according to Lindqvist's approach, a new perspective on historical developments can emerge from the richness of the historical narrative of those "affected." *Betroffene* 'those affected' and *Betroffenheit* 'being affected', were the contemporary terms used to describe those affected by marginalisation in history and in historiography. And it was very common in the alternative movements of the 1970s and 1980s to use these terms in describing the process of bringing one's authentic experience into political work and culture.[12]

From this perspective, history from below – and this is very important to emphasise – means two things: It means, on the one hand, looking at those who are supposedly "at the bottom" in society, the "excluded, oppressed," but also those forgotten by historiography, and this definition names the object of research. It also means that the subject of research changes, namely that this view is taken in deliberate contradistinction to academic research at the universities, by anyone who is interested in it.

Two very different examples of local initiatives illustrate how diverse the new history movement in West Germany was, how varied the occasions for its activity were, and also how different the motives and backgrounds of those involved and the spokesmen and their objectives were.

---

12 Sven Reichardt, "Authentizität und Gemeinschaftsbindung. Politik und Lebensstil im linksalter- nativen Milieu vom Ende der 1960er bis zum Anfang der achtziger Jahre," *Forschungsjournal Neue Soziale Bewegungen* 21 (2008): 122, 124; Sven Reichardt, and Detlef Siegfried, "Das Alternative Milieu. Konturen einer Lebensform," in *Das Alternative Milieu. Antibürgerlicher Lebensstil und linke Politik in der Bundesrepublik Deutschland und Europa 1968–1983*, ed. Sven Reichardt et al. (Göttingen, 2010), 17–18; *Sven Reichardt*, "Authentizität als Selbstbeschreibungskategorie im linksalternativen Milieu," in *Die „andere" Provinz. Kulturelle Auf- und Ausbrücke im Bodenseeraum seit den 1960er Jahren*, ed. Heike Kempe (Konstanz: UVK, 2014), 14.

4.1 The "Museum der Arbeit" Initiative in Hamburg

One example from Hamburg is meant to express how a practical concept has been developed from the spirit of the *Geschichtswerkstätten*, for a new way of telling history and collecting heritage in a museum. It also illustrates how the claim of pushing the boundaries of responsibility and competency for historical interpretation and narrative changed, as activism became more institutionally established and successfully. The aim of this group was to create a "Museum der Arbeit" [museum of labour], which was not to collect and display the machines and tools and show the technical development of work processes, but to focus on work as the experiences of the people who filled a workplace.[13] The context of this initiative was structural economic changes that threatened the professional existence of working people in Hamburg, such as changes in the production conditions and demand in shipbuilding, for example, or changes in the publishing industry, where the introduction of phototypesetting and computerisation led to changes in professional practice, qualifications and payment.[14] The structural changes in the work environment were taken as an inspiration to found a museum that would transform the experiences of these changes into a museum concept. The founding idea of the museum was triggered by the closure of Zeise, a ship's propeller factory, in 1979, and the idea was to transform the disused factory building into a museum that would document those changes in the workplace and musealise jobs that were no longer needed.[15] A group of people around architect Dieter Glienke sought support from local political representatives, and then founded the initiative as a registered association in 1980.

The association was to carry on the conceptual work, and initiated the formation of working groups for this purpose, which consisted of former professionals, people interested in history, and, from 1984, employed staff, who were at first

---

13 Gernot Krankenhagen, "Hamburg plant ein Museum der Arbeit – seit 1980 oder: Warum ist es so schwer, ein Museum der Arbeit zu realisieren?," in *Geschichte der Arbeit im Museum. Dokumentation einer Tagung im Rahmen der Ruhrfestspiele Recklinghausen 11. bis 13. Mai 1987*, ed. Bernd Faulenbach et al. (Recklinghausen, 1987), 40–41.
14 Arndt Neumann, *Unternehmen Hamburg. Eine Geschichte der neoliberalen Stadt* (Göttingen: Vandenhoeck & Ruprecht, 2018): 137–146 and 159–161.
15 The first logo of the group showed the face of a Zeise worker, later a crane hook of the *Howaldtswerft* shipyard, which was occupied during the labour dispute in 1983, was the symbol of the initiative. Harald Meier-Weigand, "Der Kranhaken, der Zeise-Arbeiter und das Rot. Das erste Logo des Vereins Museum der Arbeit," *mitarbeit* 15 (2015): 37–39. The Zeise factory finally did not become the location of the museum.

4 *Barfußhistoriker* and *Geschichtswerkstätten* – History from Below in West Germany — **91**

placed at the "Museum für Hamburgische Geschichte" [Museum for Hamburg History]. At the same time, the association made efforts to gain political support and funding for the museum, which was officially founded in 1990 and opened its doors as a Hamburg museum with permanent and temporary exhibitions in 1997. The political initiative was mainly supported by the Hamburg trade unions, which obtained regular representation on the board of the association, and also demanded their conceptual participation through it. Referring to the *DGB-Projekt "Geschichte von unten"* 'DGB's project history from below', which will be explained below, guidelines for the support of museum work were developed, which made clear how important the shaping of historical perceptions was considered to be for the trade union's position.[16]

In Sweden, Lindqvist's book, already discussed above, sparked a flurry of local activity in union-organised local groups, and with the support of the Swedish trade union movement, sparked off the so-called *Grävrörelsen* 'digging-movement' or *Gräv-där-du-står-rörelsen* 'Dig-where-you-stand movement'. Although Lindqvist also had great influence on the concepts and visions of the German *Geschichtswerkstätten*, trade union influence was marginal, although there were efforts by the *Deutsche Gewerkschaftsbund (DGB)* 'German Trade Union Confederation' to network and coordinate initiatives in the *DGB-Projekt "Geschichte von unten"*, funded by the *DGB*'s *Hans-Böckler-Stiftung* 'Hans Böckler foundation' from 1985 to 1987. The perception that the *DGB* project or those responsible for the content of the project had of the initiatives was rather static; they were not actually that static. The *DGB* considered them to be an educational initiative, in which amateurs in scientific research, who do research on their workplace were to be guided by professional historians.[17] The *DGB* project wanted to initiate working groups, but had difficulties with the coordination and support of already existing *Geschichtswerkstätten*, many of which had organised themselves nationwide in the network "Geschichtswerkstatt e.V." The unions also found it difficult to cope with the fact that *ABM* positions, *Arbeitsbeschaffungsmaßnahme* 'Work procurement measure', were necessary in most of the *Geschichtswerkstätten* to ensure the continuity and success of the work. Trade union organisations were

---

16 Deutscher Gewerkschaftsbund. Bundesvorstand, ed., *Vorstellungen des DGB zur Kulturpolitik und Kulturarbeit* (Düsseldorf, 1981).

17 Manfred Scharrer, "Zum Selbstverständnis einer gewerkschaftlichen Geschichte von unten," in *Macht Geschichte - von unten. Handbuch für gewerkschaftliche Geschichte vor Ort*, ed. Manfred Scharrer (Köln: Bund, 1988), 32 und 33; Wilfried Busemann, "Ausgelaufen! Bericht vom Abschlußseminar des DGB-Projektes 'Geschichte von unten', Hattingen, 4–6. Mai 1987," *Geschichtswerkstatt* 13 (1987): 67–68.

not open to applying for these positions because they did not support the *ABM* programme in their official argument that it created precarious employment.[18]

Here, too, it is worth looking to Sweden: In Norrköping, Sweden, a *Arbetets Museum* 'Museum of Labour' had been founded and sustained by the Swedish Trade Union Organisation and the Workers' Education Association, which had a close relationship with the decentralised organisation of *Gräv där du står*. It served as an organisational center for participation and collaboration among museum professionals and experts in workplace practices, and at the same time was able to make visible the experience of workers.[19]

Also the *Sozialdemokratische Partei Deutschlands (SPD)* 'Social Democratic Party of Germany' made efforts to activate grassroots historical work in the local groups of the party and developed a handbook for this purpose.[20] The *SPD* and also the party-affiliated *Friedrich Ebert Stiftung*, 'Friedrich Ebert Foundation', organised conferences on history from below, providing a useful platform for exchanging themes and methods.[21] The impression could arise that the history movement was driven by the SPD.[22] But, as one of the participants from the *Berliner Geschichtswerkstatt* put it, the impression predominated that the *SPD* was jumping on a train that was already running.[23]

For the "Museum der Arbeit" initiative, however, the local trade union influence was significant, but also led to conflicts, which illustrates the diversity of the different interests and approaches. In the political process of establishing the mu-

---

18 Manfred Scharrer, "Bericht über das DGB-Projekt Geschichte von unten nach zweijähriger Laufzeit (vorgelegt auf der Abschlußtagung des Projektes vom 4.-6. Mai 1987)," cited after *Weller* 20 (1987): 32 and 33.

19 Erik Hofrén et al., "Museum from below – history from below," in *Europa im Zeitalter des Industrialismus. Zur ‚Geschichte von unten' im europäischen Vergleich. Beiträge zur gleichnamigen wissenschaftlichen Tagung im Dezember 1990 (3. bis 7.12.1990),* ed. Museum der Arbeit (Elisabeth von Dücker) (Hamburg, 1993), 267.

20 Bildungsvereinigung Arbeit und Leben Niedersachsen, eds., *Geschichte und Kulturarbeit. Arbeiter erforschen ihre Geschichte* (Hannover, 1983); Historische Kommission beim SPD-Parteivorstand, ed., *Historische Spurensuche in der politischen Praxis. Leitfaden* (Bonn, 1987); Horst Schmidt, "'Heißhunger auf Geschichte'. Ortsvereine entdecken ihre Vergangenheit (Original: Die Neue Gesellschaft 30.1983, 900–906)," in *Identität durch Geschichte. Leitziel Emanzipation,* ed. Malte Ristau (Marburg, 1985), 11.

21 Dingliang Fan, "SPD und Geschichtswissenschaft in der Bundesrepublik Deutschland 1959–1989. Die Kommunikation zwischen einer politischen Partei und professionellen Historikern" (PhD diss., University of Trier, 2012), 201.

22 Axel Vornbäumen, "Die Ortsvereine und der Blick in den Rückspiegel," *Frankfurter Rundschau,* April 23, 1986, cited after: *Weller* 18 (1986): 42–43.

23 Bernhard Müller, "Die Sozialdemokraten entdecken die Geschichte von unten (Stimmungsbericht eines Frustrierten von einem Kongreß in Bonn)," *BGW-Rundbrief* 1 (1985): 12.

4 *Barfußhistoriker* and *Geschichtswerkstätten* – History from Below in West Germany — **93**

seum, the voice of the people who supported the project conceptually as volunteers based on their work experience had less weight than that of the political actors. This illustrates what is also significant for a larger perspective on *Geschichtswerkstätten* and their institutionalisation. Because with successful museum founding and institutionalisation, the perspective between amateurs of museum work, called *Praxisexperten* 'experts of practice', and the appointed experts, called *Museumsexperten* 'museum experts', became imbalanced. The practitioners in the working groups, who had developed the initial exhibitions and public events to publicise the museum initiative and solicit support, played a role in the actual museum concept as volunteers to operate the machines, but the museum's storytelling was entrusted to museum professionals. This development also led to conflicts, because in the early stages it had been their professional contacts and experience that contributed expertise in acquiring and documenting collection items and helped secure machines from closed-down businesses. The first director of the museum, Gernot Krankenhagen, summarises this conflict and the different perspectives from his point of view:

> I would not like to exclude the remark that such cooperation can, of course, also be conflictual. One example: older colleagues have come to us and helped us to rebuild the letterpress area. For them, the museum is finished when the book printing plant looks the way they remember it from 30 or 40 years ago. In my opinion, this is not yet a museum, it is, so to speak, the starting point for a certain part of a museum, and there is then quite quickly a dispute when one then says: But there must be disruptions in there, because otherwise the nostalgia floods the visitors so much, because they forget for all the happiness about the machine that it is actually about something else. For me, this is also an example of the following: in Hamburg, in the trade unions, there is and has always been the consideration that this museum does not need academics, a museum of labour could be built by the colleagues themselves. I think we should neither make exhibitions as academics in isolation, nor let workers build up their museum on their own, who know a lot about the subject, but nothing about making exhibitions to begin with. We should use everyone's qualifications and bring them together to form a good whole.[24]

---

24 Original Quote: "Nicht ausklammern möchte ich die Bemerkung, daß derartige Zusammenarbeit natürlich auch konfliktbeladen sein kann. Ein Beispiel: ältere Kollegen sind zu uns gekommen und haben uns geholfen, den Bereich Buchdruckerei wieder aufzubauen. Für sie ist das Museum fertig, wenn die Buchdruckerei so aussieht, wie sie sie von vor 30 oder 40 Jahren in Erinnerung haben. Für meine Begriffe ist dies noch kein Museum, ist sozusagen Ansatz für einen bestimmten Teil eines Museums, und da gibt es dann ganz schnell Krach, wenn man dann sagt: Da müssen aber Brechungen rein, weil sonst die Nostalgie die Besucher so überschwemmt, da sie vor lauter Glück über die Maschine ganz vergessen, daß es eigentlich um etwas anderes geht. Für mich ist dies auch ein Beispiel für folgendes: es gibt und gab in Hamburg, in den Gewerkschaften, immer wieder die Überlegung, daß dieses Museum keine Wissenschaftler braucht, ein Museum der Arbeit könnten die Kolleginnen und Kollegen selbst aufbauen. Ich denke, wir sollten

4.2 Arbeitskreis Regionalgeschichte Konstanz

The Hamburg example shows a very specific constellation that had emerged in one place and on one topic. The diversity of the initiatives, however, offered very different characteristics both of the topics and of the people involved. The second example from Konstanz illuminates an important point for the new history movement in West Germany, namely the very clearly expressed orientation towards academic historical research in many initiatives. Sometimes, as in the example of the *Arbeitskreis Regionalgeschichte Konstanz,* 'Working Group for the Regional History of Konstanz,' it was also the founding impulse that was linked to a critique of the academic organisation; in other cases, which also applies to the specific case in Konstanz, it was also different points of view within the history group that led to conflicts. For some, it was the criticism of academic research, namely the organisation of academic work and the methods, which they made the starting point of the approach of the *Geschichtswerkstätten*. Others had no interest in the academic controversies and topics, and were only looking for regional work in a citizens' initiative that corresponded to their interest in history and their conviction that looking at history can change actions in the present.

The *Arbeitskreis Regionalgeschichte Konstanz* was founded in early 1979 as an outgrowth of a project at the still young Konstanz Reform University and was intended to perpetuate a university project that had existed from 1972 to 1985 and to carry it into the public and the region. The university project was originally run by Martin Broszat, director of the *Institut für Zeitgeschichte,* 'Institute of Contemporary History,' who passed it on to his colleague Gert Zang, but remained connected to the project. The project shared its approach of having students engage more fully in research-based practice while still undergraduates with the idea of the History Workshop at the Ruskin College. An important sub-project of the university project was dedicated to Oral History, in which students conducted interviews in the region from 1980, in close cooperation with institutions in the region such as local archives. This represented an opening of the university to the region. The methodology changed the perspective of the participants to a "Geschichte von innen" [history from within], which should complement the concept of a history from below or from above. It was significant that the participants valued oral history as "learning from each other" of the participants, overcoming generational differences and differences in people's experience, important pre-

---

weder als Wissenschaftler isoliert Ausstellungen machen, noch Arbeiterinnen und Arbeiter ihr Museum allein aufbauen lassen, die ja von der Sache viel verstehen, aber vom Ausstellungmachen zunächst einmal nichts. Wir sollten die Qualifikationen aller nutzen und sie zu einem guten Ganzen zusammenführen." Krankenhagen "Hamburg plant ein Museum," 38–39.

4 *Barfußhistoriker* and *Geschichtswerkstätten* – History from Below in West Germany — 95

requisites for being able to actively use history for social change.[25] It was thus considered by some representatives of the new history movement to be the perfect incarnation of history from below.[26]

The difficulties of presenting their first publication to a broader audience motivated those responsible for the project to establish a regional working group that would also include teachers and others interested in history.[27] Among academics, British historian Geoff Eley praised the work, and the historian Otto Dann complimented the book's frank reflection of the work processes.[28] But there had also been criticism.[29] The biggest criticism, however, from the participants themselves, was that it did not find a broad audience: it was too academically oriented and some contributions were overloaded with too much theoretical background, according to those involved.[30] Gert Zang already describes this first publication from 1978, which was based primarily on written sources and focused on early industrialisation in the region using individual examples, as an essential experience for students to move from the theory-driven perspective that had still strongly influenced the previous generation of the student movement to a direct engagement with the sources and with small-scale regional historical examples. He also hoped that this would help to bridge the conflicts that could arise from a historical perspective derived from grand theoretical concepts and abstract models of interpretation of societal processes.[31] Another important motive for the

---

25 Werner Trapp, "Sich am eigenen Schopf aus der Geschichtslosigkeit ziehen. Mündliche Geschichte als Versuch kommunaler historischer Kulturarbeit," *Literatur und Erfahrung* 10 (1982): 85.

26 Gerhard Paul et. al, "Geschichte und Heimat," in *Die andere Geschichte. Geschichte von unten, Spurensicherung, ökologische Geschichte, Geschichtswerkstätten*, ed. Gerhard Paul et al. (Köln: Bund, 1986), 25.

27 Gert Zang, "Gedanken tausendmal gedacht, Gefühle tausendmal gefühlt . . .? Versuche sich der Lebens- und Gedankenwelt kleiner Gemeinden zu nähern: Mündliche Geschichte in der Bodenseeregion," *Literatur und Erfahrung* 10 (1982): 65.

28 Geoff Eley, "Provinzialisierung einer Region. Regionale Unterentwicklung und liberale Politik in der Stadt und im Kreis Konstanz im 19. Jahrhundert. Untersuchungen zur Entstehung der bürgerlichen Gesellschaft in der Provinz ed. by Gert Zang," *The Journal of Modern History* 54 (1982): 798–802; Otto Dann, "Die Region als Gegenstand der Geschichtswissenschaft," *Archiv für Sozialgeschichte* 23 (1983): 657–658.

29 Ralf Dahrendorf, "Region als 'Provinz' und als Hoffnung," *Frankfurter Allgemeine Zeitung*, July 31, 1979.

30 Arbeitsgruppe des Projekts ‚Regionale Sozialgeschichte', "Regionalgeschichte: Neue Chancen für Gesellschaftsanalyse," *Das Argument* 131 (1982): 59.

31 Gert Zang, "Vorbemerkung," in *Provinzialisierung einer Region. Zur Entstehung der bürgerlichen Gesellschaft in der Provinz*, ed Gert Zang (Frankfurt/Main: Syndikat, 1978), 14; Gert Zang, "Subjektive Reflexionen über ein Projekt und seine organisatorische, methodische und inhaltliche Entwicklung. Überlegungen zu einer kritischen Regionalgeschichtsschreibung für das 19.

founding of the *Arbeitskreis Regionalgeschichte Konstanz*, and at the same time a conclusion from the book project, was to provide publication methods and activities for freelance historians, beyond the university setting.

The founding of the *Arbeitskreis* was also related to the rediscovery of the "Provinz" [province] by protest movements in the 1970s and 1980s.[32] The intention was to attract people who were committed to issues of the region without academic-institutional affiliations. History was considered to have a potential for regional history that detached it from a backward-looking attachment to the *Heimat*, a term for 'home' or 'homeland' which had romantic and conservative overtones. The working group also attempted to create a critical regional history, in which they also wanted to involve teachers, and which sought to distinguish itself from the efforts of Baden-Württemberg cultural policy to understand *Heimat* as a place with which to identify without the intrusion of disruptive elements into the identification.[33]

In the practice of the *Arbeitskreis*, which in the 1980s regularly published several volumes of a series of publications and, until 2012, produced a periodical for its members, the ambitious goals of questioning the practice of the historical sciences and achieving a participatory historiography in which their recipients take part, have met with little success. There were many local activities on various topics that were very well attended. It was mostly individuals who brought these topics into the working group, e.g. bicycle tours to the site of the former concentration camp in Überlingen, on which a history teacher, who was a member of the *Arbeitskreis*, did research.[34] Überlingen is an example of one of the many regional history topics that have been made visible by groups in the new history movement. Another is the publication on Jewish history in Gailingen emerging from the *Arbeitskreis*.[35] In discussions about its own self-perception, however,

---

und 20. Jahrhundert," in *Provinzialisierung einer Region. Zur Entstehung der bürgerlichen Gesellschaft in der Provinz*, ed. Gert Zang (Frankfurt/Main: Syndikat, 1978), 475; Martin Broszat, "Geleitwort," in *Provinzialisierung einer Region. Zur Entstehung der bürgerlichen Gesellschaft in der Provinz*, ed. Gert Zang (Frankfurt/Main: Syndikat, 1978), 11.

32 Bertolt Gießmann, "Die Wiederentdeckung der Provinz. Die 'Provinzbewegung' der 1970er Jahre und ihre Perzeption von Stadt und Land," in *'Bewegte Dörfer'. Neue soziale Bewegungen in der Provinz 1970–1990*, ed. Julia Paulus (Paderborn: Ferdinand Schöningh, 2018), 44–45.

33 Arbeitsgruppe des Projekts 'Regionale Sozialgeschichte', "Regionalgeschichte," 61–63.

34 "Materialien zu einer Fahrradtour," *arbeitskreis regional geschichte* 4 (1981): 2–24.

35 Eckhardt Friedrich et al., eds., *Die Gailinger Juden. Materialien zur Geschichte der jüdischen Gemeinde Gailingen aus ihrer Blütezeit und den Jahren der gewaltsamen Auflösung* (Konstanz: Konstanz Arbeitskreis f. Regionalgeschichte 1981); Regina Schmid, *Verlorene Heimat. Gailingen - ein Dorf und seine jüdische Gemeinde in der Weimarer Zeit* (Konstanz: Konstanz Arbeitskreis f. Regionalgeschichte 1988).

4 Barfußhistoriker and Geschichtswerkstätten – History from Below in West Germany

there was also criticism of the fact that the group's topics were shaped by the interests of individuals, and that there was hardly any common programe beyond the original one of the participants in the university project. The *Arbeitskreis*, which no longer exists, can still be considered successful on the basis of its richness of activities and publications. In addition, the goal to publish, or to organise conferences or excursions, as a field of activity for historians beyond the usual history-producing institutions was successfully realised by the *Arbeitskreis*. Judging by the aspirations of some of its founders, the different interests gathered together in the group also stood in the way of the implementation of a shared emancipatory historical output. While some complained of a theory deficit, this complaint was in tension with the "Weitervermittlung und der Anstiftung zu regionalhistorischer Laienarbeit im emanzipatorischen Sinne." [further mediation and instigation of the study of regional history by amateurs in an emancipatory sense].[36] This tension existed in many history workshops and could rarely be resolved productively.

In the West German movement, demarcation from the academic discipline was multi-layered: many of those involved had a connection to a university. Their need for separation had to do with their own experiences and their own desire for change. Another reason for this was the growing unemployment of academics in the Federal Republic of Germany, which also increased the need to find new ways to make history one's main occupation and perhaps a profession that existed beyond a university career.[37] Already at its point of origin there were different interests represented, namely those of academic historians and those of non-academic people engaged in history. In the course of the association's history, this conflict was not smoothed out; rather, it intensified, both within the nationwide association "Geschichtswerkstatt e.V." and sometimes within the individual groups. While some, for example, clearly and decisively aimed at local cultural work with a historical focus, others had a change and an opening up of the academic discipline in mind from the beginning. Disputes over the association's periodical shows this conflict: some wanted a diverse, colorful newsletter with reports from individual groups, the volumes of which could look different each time. Others, however, tried to standardise, edit, and professionalise reviews and contributions to debates.[38]

---

36 "Protokoll der Mitgliederversammlung des Arbeitskreises am Samstag, dem 27.6.1981, im Haus der Evangelischen Studentengemeinde, ab 14.30 Uhr," *arbeitskreis regional geschichte* 5 (1982): 4.

37 Roger Fletcher, "History from below comes to Germany. The new history movement in the Federal Republic of Germany," *Journal of Modern History* 60 (1988): 559; Lutz Raphael, "Der Beruf des Historikers seit 1945," in *Geschichtswissenschaften. Eine Einführung*, ed. Christoph Cornelißen, (Frankfurt/Main: Fischer, 2000), 40–41.

38 "Arbeitskreis zum Projekt einer Zeitschrift auf dem Dortmunder Geschichtsfest," *Geschichtswerkstatt* 11 (1987): 134–135; Ursula Nienhaus et. al, "Einige Überlegungen zu den Tendenzen in

4.3 The Academic Debate on *Alltagsgeschichte* (Everyday History) and *Barfußhistoriker* (Barefoot Historians)

From the side of the academic discipline of history, these developments did not go unnoticed. On the one hand, there was a lively exchange of academics with some institutions, research projects, and researchers, and a great interest also in the results of the work of the *Geschichtswerkstätten* and similar groups. But there was also harsh and polemical criticism. One particularly strong line of criticism came from Hans-Ulrich Wehler, who, together with Jürgen Kocka, was a representative of *Geschichte als Historische Sozialwissenschaft*, 'history as a historical social science', and thus of a theory-oriented research perspective focussing on socio-cultural developments. Wehler belittled the history workshops as *Barfußhistoriker*, 'barefoot historians', and warned that the distinction between a naïve and alternative-culture actionism and a theory-driven social science needed to be maintained.[39]

In the West-German historical sciences, too, international developments within the historical discipline had caused controversies and new methodological approaches in studies and debates. This intra-academic controversy was not initiated by the *Geschichtswerkstätten*; it had, as mentioned, international contexts and, to a certain extent, brought about the catching-up of West German historical sciences to international developments that had been delayed by a constrictingly nationalist perspective.[40] There were links between *Geschichtswerkstätten* and academic con-

---

der Geschichtswerkstatt e. V.," *Geschichtswerkstatt* 12 (1987): 87–89; "Mitteilungen des Ausschusses," *Geschichtswerkstatt* 12 (1987): 96–99; "Aus der Berliner Rezensionsredaktion," *Geschichtswerkstatt* 14 (1988): 72; Christa Jancik et al., "Zur Gründung eines Rezensionsteils," *Geschichtswerkstatt* 12 (1987): 91. To summarise the conflict: Michael Wildt, "WerkstattGeschichte – ein Zeitschriftenprojekt," in *Geschichtswerkstätten gestern – heute – morgen. Bewegung! Stillstand. Aufbruch?*, ed. Forschungsstelle für Zeitgeschichte in Hamburg und Galerie Morgenland/ Geschichtswerkstatt Eimsbüttel (Hamburg: Dölling & Galitz, 2004), 31–43, and Michael Wildt, "Die große Geschichtswerkstattschlacht im Jahr 1992 oder: Wie WerkstattGeschichte entstand," *WerkstattGeschichte* 50 (2008): 73–81.

39 Hans-Ulrich Wehler, "Geschichte – von unten gesehen. Wie bei der Suche nach dem Authentischen Engagement mit Methodik verwechselt wird," *Die Zeit*, May 3, 1985.

40 François, "L'Allemagne Fédérale," 154–155; Paul Nolte, "Die Historiker in der Bundesrepublik. Rückblick auf eine 'lange Generation'," *Merkur* 53 (1999): 420; *Christoph Cornelißen*, "Deutsche Geschichtswissenschaft nach 1945. Zwischen nationalen Traditionen und transnationalen Öffnungen," in *Die Rückkehr der deutschen Geschichtswissenschaft in die 'Ökumene der Historiker'. Ein wissenschaftsgeschichtlicher Ansatz*, ed. Ulrich Pfeil (München: Oldenbourg Verlag, 2008), 18,

troversy, and some debates were taken up at a wider level. Approaches that played a role in intra-academic controversy were the "Revival of Narrative", Oral history as a theoretically grounded research method for the production of historical sources, but also the transfer of methods from Italian *microstoria*, 'micro-history', and the still very diverse *Alltagsgeschichte*, 'history of everyday life,' which struggled to establish legitimate theoretical foundation in a number of very productive controversies.[41] History from below has often been associated with some of these approaches, e.g., with an extension of social history.[42] Hans Medick and Alf Lüdtke of the *Max-Planck-Institut für Geschichte*, 'Max Planck Institute for History' in Göttingen, also among the initiators of the founding of the "Geschichtswerkstatt e.V.", had made an outstanding contribution to *microstoria* and to the use of ethnological methods in the historical sciences. They also used the publications of the *Geschichtswerkstätten* to promote these developments in Germany and were interested in using the network and its publications to bring about discussions on these themes.[43] *Historische Sozialwissenschaft* represented by Wehler was a target of critique within the publications of the *Geschichtswerkstätten*: it was seen as being distanced from the public interest in history, and as a perspective that excluded people's everyday lives, beyond big politics, from the historical narrative.[44] The terms *Alltagsgeschichte*, *Mentalitätsgeschichte*, 'history of thought', and *Frauengeschichte*, 'women's history', became prominent words in the German publications of the 1980s, a trend that subsided in the 1990s. And the regular conference of the Association of Historians in Germany, the *Historikertag*, in 1984, expressed this

---

21–22, 29; *Roger Fletcher*, "Recent Developments in West German Historiography. The Bielefeld School and Its Critics," *German Studies Review* 3 (1984): 472–474.

41 Lawrence Stone, "The Revival of Narrative. Reflextions on a New Old History," *Past and Present* (85) 1979: 4–5, 12–13; Lutz Niethammer, "Fragen – Antworten – Fragen. Methodische Erfahrungen und Erwägungen der Oral History," in ‚*Wir kriegen jetzt andere Zeiten.' Auf der Suche nach der Erfahrung des Volkes in nachfaschistischen Ländern*, ed. Alexander von Plato et al. (Berlin, Bonn: Dietz, 1985), 392–445.

42 Roger Fletcher, "History from below," 558.

43 For example, they reprinted an article by Ginzburg and Poni about *microstoria* in the volume of the periodical of the "Geschichtswerkstatt e.V.," that they edited: Carlo Ginzburg et al., "Was ist Mikrogeschichte?," *Geschichtswerkstatt* 6 (1985): 48–52. Their role was also reflected in Hans Medick, "'Geschichte für wen?' Zu einem anstößigen Text von Alf Lüdtke und Hans Medick aus dem Jahr 1977," in *Alltag, Erfahrung, Eigensinn. Historisch-anthropologische Erkundungen*, ed. Belinda Davis et al. (Frankfurt/Main: Campus, 2008), 29–43.

44 Gert Zang, *Die unaufhaltsame Annäherung an das Einzelne. Reflexion über den theoretischen und praktischen Nutzen der Regional- und Alltagsgeschichte* (Konstanz: Arbeitskreis für Regionalgeschichte, 1985).

trend by taking these terms as its thematic focus.[45] A controversial debate about history from below ended the conference.[46]

Hans-Ulrich Wehler, one of the doyens of the historical profession in Germany, was one who turned on history from below in a polemical assault that is still remembered, He took *Alltagsgeschichte* as an example. Wehler acknowledged the enrichment of historiography provided by *Alltagsgeschichte*, and he also acknowledged problems with a social history analyzing processes and structures. Especially targeting the *Geschichtswerkstätten* in his critique, however, he spoke slightingly of "Selbstfindungs- und Selbstererweckungserlebnissen" [self-discovery and self-awakening experiences], and of "gefühlsstarken Barfußhistorikern" [emotive bare-foot historians], who in his opinion were seeking a new form of idyll in history under "alternativkulturellen, linkspluralistischen" [alternative cultural, left-wing pluralist] banners. Wehler called *Alltagsgeschichte* a fashionable trend, an approach that promised a new form of *Heimat*, identity, orientation, and the creation of meaning out of a skepticism concerning progress and a "Kritik an den Schattenseiten der ökonomischen Modernisierung" [critique of the dark sides of economic modernisation].[47]

But such an outburst of polemics as Wehler's was rather the exception. And such an outburst was also a welcome occasion for those in the initiatives who wanted to have a critical go at academic historicity and its scientistic pretensions. For this, too, was an opportunity to become the subject of scholarly debate. The label *Barfußhistoriker* was also appropriated as a self-designation. A – also controversial – response to this article by Wehler, written by the *Geschichtswerkstatt Dortmund* 'History Workshop of Dortmund', shows this very clearly:

> Mr. Wehler has understood nothing, absolutely nothing. The abused barefoot historians do not intend to enrich the usual historiography as it is taught and practiced at the universities, with the history of the little people. It is much worse: they are fundamentally critical of traditional academia. They are no longer interested in an apparatus of knowledge that, in the ivory tower of university arrogance, conducts history that bypasses those who act in and suffer from history. History concerns us all, not only some 'educated'(!) historians. The specialisation of the sciences so far has led to the majority of people not only becoming more and more uninterested, but also cut off from their history. This has devastating consequences for the self-awareness of our society. Those who do not know their past cannot plan their future in a meaningful way.

---

45 Olaf Blaschke et al., "Der Verband zwischen den Krisenjahren und der Rückkehr der Geschichte," in *Die versammelte Zunft. Historikerverband und Historikertage in Deutschland 1893–2000*, ed. Olaf Blaschke et al. (Göttingen: Wallstein, 2018), 565–590.

46 "Bericht über die 35. Versammlung deutscher Historiker in Berlin. 3. bis 7. Oktober 1984," (Stuttgart: Klett 1985), 249.

47 Wehler, "Geschichte – von unten gesehen".

4 *Barfußhistoriker* and *Geschichtswerkstätten* – History from Below in West Germany   **101**

> The history workshops are not interested in a theorizing "rationally disciplined" historiography, which, detached from political relevance, gets lost and confused in retrospect, supposedly objectively and neutrally, meticulously detailed. Our everyday history, on the other hand, is based on the history that is alive in people's minds, that helps decide the history of the future.[48]

This statement shows something else: The great public interest in history, which became manifest in the Federal Republic of Germany since the 1970s in exhibitions, book publications, television, was in contrast to an academic, 'scientific' historiography, which was considered one that could not reach a broad audience, because it was not very illustrative, was theory-heavy, difficult to access, abstract. The historical interest referred to in this quote was an interest in people, in stories, in regional and local references – in a history that had to do with oneself.

For many contemporary analysts – including Hans-Ulrich Wehler – and also for the *Geschichtswerkstätten* and history groups themselves, the experience of different crises in the 1970s and 1980s was an important reason why *Alltagsgeschichte* and a small-scale perspective on history were so appealing. History provides orientation. And in this case, the interest in history was not formulated as backward-looking nostalgia and the desire to preserve a status quo; rather, it was also the search for historical role models, for a supposedly proximate – even premodern – lifeworld to which one wanted to refer for orientation towards the challenges of the future and with which one wanted to justify the need for change

---

48 "Eine Stellungnahme der Geschichtswerkstatt Dortmund zu dem Beitrag von Hans-Ulrich Wehler in DIE ZEIT vom 3.5.1985, von dem viele überzeugt sind, daß er es nicht wert ist," *Geschichtswerkstatt* 7 (1985): 42, Original quote: "Herr Wehler hat nichts begriffen, aber auch gar nichts. Die geschmähten Barfußhistoriker haben zum großen Teil jedenfalls keineswegs vor, die übliche Geschichtsschreibung, wie sie an den Universitäten gelehrt und betrieben wird, zu bereichern um die Geschichte der kleinen Leute. Es ist viel schlimmer: sie üben fundamentale Kritik an der traditionellen Wissenschaft. Sie haben kein Interesse mehr an einem Wissenshaftsapparat [sic!], der im Elfenbeinturm universitärer Arroganz Geschichte an denen, die in der Geschichte handeln und sie erleiden, vorbei betreibt. Geschichte geht uns alle an, nicht nur einige „ausgebildet" (!) Historiker. Die bisherige Spezialisierung der Wissenschaften hat dazu geführt, daß die Masse der Menschen nicht nur immer uninteressierter, sondern auch von ihrer Geschichte abgeschnitten wurden. Das hat aber für das Bewußtsein unserer Gesellschaft verheerende Folgen. Wer seine Vergangenheit nicht kennt, kann auch seine Zukunft nicht sinnvoll planen.

Die Geschichtswerkstätten sind nicht an einer theoretisierenden „rational-disziplinierten" Geschichtsschreibung interessirt [sic!], die losgelöst von der politischen Aktualität, im Nachhinein, vermeintlich objektiv und neutral, akribisch detailliert sich verirrt und verliert. Unsere Alltagsgeschichte stützt sich dagegen auf die Geschichte, die in den Köpfen der Menschen lebendig ist, die über die Geschichte der Zukunft mitentscheidet."

and substantiate the motivation to activism. This interest in the *Geschichte des kleinen Mannes*, 'history of the small people', as it was rather mockingly referred to, was also seen by critics as a starting point for their accusation of romanticisation and idealisation.[49] *Alltagsgeschichte* as a whole was accused of being hostile to theory, of being depoliticised, and of being escapist. And in this debate, *Geschichtswerkstätten* also had the function of a catalyst, because their practices could be accused of being unscientific and activist, and this was then also transferred to *Alltagsgeschichte* in the intra-scholarly controversy. After all, in the *Geschichtswerkstätten* themselves there were both trends present: well-founded academic discussions as well as a more emotional *Betroffenen* culture. And there were also both approaches within one and the same initiative!

In order to distinguish between the intra-scholarly controversy and the polemics towards the history workshops, of which the latter obviously also served a purpose in the intra-scholarly debate, the approach of Thomas Lindenberger is helpful. Lindenberger was himself a long-time member of the *Berliner Geschichtswerkstatt* and is now director of the *Hannah-Arendt-Institut für Totalitarismusforschung*, 'Hannah Arendt Institute for Research on Totalitarianism', in Dresden. He has examined the controversy concerning the methodological approaches to *Alltagsgeschichte* as one of the relevant controversies in historiography in the Federal Republic of Germany. In doing so, he demonstrates that the controversy he analyses actually involved two disputes: one within the discipline that dealt with the new methodological approaches of *Alltagsgeschichte*, and another in which the professional scholarly discipline dealt with the non-university activities of the *Geschichtswerkstätten*. What is to be emphasised about Lindenberger's perspective is that he stresses the importance of developments in the international history of historiography that provide the context for methodical innovations within German academic history. In this respect, his analysis includes an important clarification, namely that the methodological innovations in the discipline did not result from the demands of the *Geschichtswerkstätten* and their protagonists.[50] This differentiation by Lindenberger is so helpful precisely because these two disputes, both contemporarily and in retrospective judgements of the historiographical disputes of the 1980s, are often linked.

---

49 Ernst Köhler, "Der kleine Mann und seine Liebhaber," *Freibeuter* 24 (1985): 98; Michael Zimmermann, "Haben Geschichtswerkstätten Zukunft?," in *Geschichtswerkstätten gestern – heute – morgen. Bewegung! Stillstand. Aufbruch?*, ed. Forschungsstelle für Zeitgeschichte in Hamburg und der Galerie Morgenland/Geschichtswerkstatt Eimsbüttel (Hamburg, 2004), 84.
50 Thomas Lindenberger, "'Alltagsgeschichte' oder: Als um die zünftigen Grenzen der Geschichtswissenschaft noch gestritten wurde," in *Zeitgeschichte als Streitgeschichte. Große Kontroversen seit 1945*, ed. Martin Sabrow et al. (München: Beck, 2003), 75 and 80.

4.4 *Geschichtswerkstätten* as a "soziale Bewegung im Miniformat" (Social Movement in Miniature)

Another important aspect of these debates was the fact that many initiatives were close to the new social movements of the 1970s and 1980s: In addition to the search for historical models for protests, the protest movements also gave rise to the desire to preserve their own protest culture. Numerous left-wing archives emerged, as well as an examination of the processes and acts of archiving themselves.[51] How does one become the object of historical records and how can one avoid being forgotten by history? By becoming a professional handler/actor, an archivist, a historian in one's own right. This idea is closely related, for example, to the thinking that motivated the Swedish *Gräv där du står* model: Adding a new perspective to the historical picture by having workers in the Swedish industry research the history of their workplace. The critical analysis of the present and of the need for change, e.g. of policies to secure peace or of policies to better protect the environment and nature from the consequences of industrial growth, was the starting point of some history initiatives, motivated by the experience of the transformation of society around them, and which motivated them to research the historical process and the coming into being of the present circumstances.

The programmatic claim of many history initiatives was to achieve forms of activism and change in the present through learning to understand history. Identification with historical groups and experiences was an important motive for finding orientation in the present, at a time when loss of orientation and the search for identity were important societal issues. In this respect, examples can be found in the study of the *Geschichtswerkstätten* that the participants tried to strengthen themselves for the conflicts of the present based on historical examples and precedents, to learn from them, to make use of resistance role models, for example, and to tie in with traditions. This becomes particularly clear in the following quote from an edited volume with project presentations on "Die andere Geschichte" [the alternative history]:

> Where one has dug in, one takes root and is difficult to knock down. Historical knowledge about the changes of the natural environment, for example, is able to sharpen the mind and create sensitivity towards the ecological threats of the present and the future. [. . .] To dig

---

51 Frauke Hansen, "Bericht vom Archiv-Seminar in Salecina," *BGW-Rundbrief* 5 (1986): 22–23. "Archiware [sic!] aller Länder . . .," *BGW-Rundbrief* 2 (1981), 8; "aktiv – Archiv – alternativ. Ankündigung des Salecina-Seminars vom 18. bis 24. Mai 1986," *Weller* 17 (1986): 31.

into everyday life, but also into the natural and spatial environments of the 'little people', to grasp the remnants of a different way of dealing with nature, to reconstruct the development of an almost entirely functionalistic relationship to nature in the course of industrialisation 'on the spot', to make visible conflicting interests of different societal groups in the use of nature, that would give a new substance to the ecological discussion. Whoever becomes familiar with the region, develops an awareness of our relationship to nature on the basis of actual visible signs of environmental threats, and gains insights into historical-ecological alternatives, will have a greater interest in his or her immediate environment, and will be inclined to intervene.[52]

In the *Berliner Geschichtswerkstatt*, for example, certain urban quarters were studied with these aims, the people who lived there were interviewed – and the results were presented in exhibitions, e.g. also as part of the decentralised cultural-political, publicly-funded programme of events for the 750th anniversary of the city, which was celebrated in 1987.[53] In a further example, protests were initiated by the *Berliner Geschichtswerkstatt* to prevent a German Historical Museum, which the German government established as a national history museum in the 1980s, because it was felt that it was a local historical perspective and a decentralised remembering that brought people closer to their history in a more immediate way than via a centralised museum perspective.[54] And this immediacy should,

---

52 Gerhard Paul et. al, "Geschichte und Heimat," 23, 26, Original quote: „Dort, wo man sich eingegraben hat, treibt man Wurzeln und ist nur mehr schwer umzuschlagen. Das historische Wissen um die Veränderungen der konkret natürlich-räumlichen Umwelt beispielsweise, vermag den Verstand und die Sensibilität zu schärfen gegenüber den ökologischen Bedrohungen der Gegenwart und der Zukunft. [. . .] Sich dort, wo man lebt, nicht nur in den Alltag, sondern auch in die natürlich-räumliche Umwelt der ‚kleinen Leute' einzugraben, Spuren eines anderen Umgangs mit Natur zu sichern, die allmähliche Entstehung eines ausschließlich funktionalistischen Verhältnisses zur Natur im Zuge der Industrialisierung 'vor Ort' zu rekonstruieren, Interessengegensätze sozialer Gruppen bei der Nutzung von Natur sichtbar zu machen, das würde der ökologischen Diskussion eine neue Substanz geben. Wer sich auch in diesem Bereich heimatkundig macht, ein Bewußtsein unseres Verhältnisses zur Natur anhand konkret sichtbarer Spuren der Umweltbedrohungen entwickelt, Phantasie für historisch-ökologische Alternativen gewinnt, der hat ein größeres Interesse an seiner unmittelbaren Umwelt und wird geneigt sein, sich einzumischen."
53 Berliner Geschichtswerkstatt, ed., *"Das war 'ne ganz geschlossene Gesellschaft hier". Der Lindenhof: Eine Genossenschaftssiedlung in der Großstadt* (Berlin: Nishen, 1987). About the funding concept of the 750th anniversary: Krijn Thijs, *Drei Geschichten, eine Stadt. Die Berliner Stadtjubiläen von 1937 und 1987* (Köln, Weimar, Wien: Böhlau, 2008), 171–172.
54 Andreas Ludwig, "Gesucht, gesammelt, gepflegt, geforscht, geputzt und schließlich . . .? Utopien für ein anderes Museum," *Geschichtswerkstatt* 11 (1987): 125, 127; And the nationwide association published "Wider die geplanten historischen Wiederaufbereitungsanlagen der Bundesregierung. Entschließung des Vorstands der Geschichtswerkstatt e. V.," *Geschichtswerkstatt* 9 (1986): 6.

the opponents of the museum felt, also call for immediate action and for changing the state of society.

And history initiatives were also founded quite directly as a concomitant to protest movements, just as their respective experiences and approaches were very close. When in Wyhl in the Kaiserstuhl region, the local population occupied the building site to prevent the construction of a nuclear power plant, protesters who had traveled from university towns together with the local communities spent a lot of time together and organised the *Volkshochschule Wyhler Wald*, where lectures by experts in alternative energy sources were heard, and historical examples of resistance and their consequences for protest were worked out together: Protest songs and historical sources from the time of the *Bauernkriege*, 'German Peasants' War' from 1524–25 as a consequence of the Reformation, were referred to in order to deal with one's own situation in the present.[55] The protest alliances that were forged in the very immediate neighborhood during the protests were also alliances that sought to learn from each other. The experience of questioning the knowledge of experts who were not addressing the public, and shedding light on one's own experiences in order to find solutions to current problems, was a shared experience of many of those involved in the so-called new social movements. As emphasised earlier with regard to the *Berliner Volksuni*, this approach was also one that motivated many involved in the new history movement in their programmatic approaches.

Detlef Siegfried has described the history movement as a "soziale Bewegung im Miniformat" [social movement in miniature]: the changed perspective of history toward a stronger focus on the individual can be explained not only from within the discipline of history, but from the point of view of societal processes of change.[56] This emphasis on subjectivity, which is also expressed in the view of the *Betroffenen*, is characteristic of this change in the historical perspective that focuses more on a close, manageable, and thus local, area, which makes it possible to trace larger developments on a small scale, while at the same time referring to concrete experiences and also practical actions.

---

55 Heiko Haumann, ed., *Vom Hotzenwald bis Whyl. Demokratische Traditionen in Baden* (Köln, 1977); Walter Mossmann, "'Die Bevölkerung ist hellwach!' Erfahrungen aus dem Kampf der badisch-elsässischen Bevölkerung gegen ein Atomkraftwerk in Whyl und ein Bleichemiewerk in Marckolsheim," *Kursbuch* 39 (1975): 130–136, 143.

56 Detlef Siegfried, "Die Rückkehr des Subjekts. Gesellschaftlicher Wandel und neue Geschichtsbewegung um 1980," in *Geschichte und Geschichtsvermittlung. Festschrift für Karl Heinrich Pohl*, ed. Olaf Hartung et al. (Bielefeld, 2008), 126.

4.5 Cultural Impact in the Neighborhood vs Critical Academic Perspectives

Both examples, Hamburg and Konstanz, have shown that it is significant that the *Geschichtswerkstätten* related their historical work to current topics, and to contemporary events and matters of importance that they identified in their near environment or in their neighbourhood. These often referred to larger processes and global problems, but were examined and contextualised locally. Historical practice was often part of a local activism with a specific purpose. History from below was understood as an approach that could potentially change perceptions of history and historical narratives, and thus also influence changes in society. And academic historiography, of course, was not unaffected by these social developments and movements; political and generational experiences shaped the perspectives taken in academic work. This is even more the case since some of those active in the new history movement took up academic careers, in some cases after their engagement in the history group, for which their on-the-ground practical historical research sometimes provided topics, approaches, practical experience, and specialisations. Others, however, established themselves in historical-political educational work in the urban neighborhood as providers of city tours or local history information, and thus as part of the local culture, such as the more than twenty *Geschichtswerkstätten* or local archives that are still active in Hamburg today – half of them founded in the 1980s, two even earlier.

The discussions and disputes of the "Geschichtswerkstatt e.V." at the end of the 1980s illustrate that there were very different interests that were articulated in the history workshops. And these point the way for the development of the new history movement after the end of the 1980s. When, as already mentioned, in the late 1980s and early 1990s, there were fights in the nationwide association about how the periodical could be organised more professionally in the future, these different interests were clearly voiced. Some wanted to standardise the review section of the periodical via a central editorial board and thus wanted to move away from the concept that, as in the past, the group responsible for editing changed from issue to issue, each being taken over by a different local *Geschichtswerkstatt*. Others feared a professionalisation that in fact aimed at establishing a new scholarly periodical that could compete in the academic world.[57] The periodical could become the im-

---

57 "Arbeitskreis zum Projekt einer Zeitschrift," 134–135; Jancik, "Zur Gründung eines Rezensionsteils," 91; "Aus der Berliner Rezensionsredaktion," 72.; Michael Zimmermann, "Protokoll Jahreshauptversammlung der Geschichtswerkstatt e.V. Samstag 26.05.1990, 9.30 bis 13.30 Uhr, Haus der Jugend Stintfang, Hamburg," *Geschichtswerkstatt* 21 (1990): 71–73.

4 *Barfußhistoriker* and *Geschichtswerkstätten* – History from Below in West Germany — **107**

portant periodical for *Alltagsgeschichte*, some of them hoped, which could then fill an important gap in the canon of scientific periodicals.[58]

After many *Geschichtswerkstätten* had written statements in which these conflicts were clearly expressed, a remarkable discussion took place, which was summarised by Michael Zimmermann under the title "Rückkehr der Gartenzwerge" [Return of the Garden Gnomes]. Dieter Thiele from the *Geschichtswerkstatt Barmbek* explained in this discussion that there were those who wanted to have an effect on urban neighborhoods and were not interested in discussions in academic history, did not understand anything about them, and did not consider themselves to be the avant-garde here. The others engaged in history from below as a branch of academic history at an international level. Thomas Lindenberger from the *Berliner Geschichtswerkstatt*, on the other hand, highlighted the influence that *Geschichtswerkstätten* would have had on the peripheries of academic history and what influence they could have had in their nationwide association "Geschichtswerkstatt e.V.". The urban research and the academic projects, such as *LUSIR – Lebensgeschichte und Sozialkultur im Ruhrgebiet*, 'Life History and Social Culture in the Ruhr Area', a groundbreaking Oral History project by Lutz Niethammer and others, have had a mutually beneficial effect on each other. As a conclusion, the discussants stated that everyone was withdrawing to their own terrain, and the discussions between the two groups were dying down.[59]

In terms of its foreshadowing further developments, this discussion is a landmark, and its descriptions are to the point. *Geschichtswerkstätten* continue to work in the communities, as already mentioned for Hamburg, they operate district archives, offer city tours, and secure historical knowledge with a local focus. Some of the participants, who were active in *Geschichtswerkstätten* as students or research assistants, are employed in museums or scientific research institutions, and also in some cases in professorships, or have by now retired. They have contributed their experiences and perspectives, and are invited as testimonies to their success by the still existing initiatives when they celebrate their anniversaries.[60] As already described, many historiographical innovations have found pub-

---

58 "Vorlage zum 2. Teil der Mitgliederversammlung und zur Heftkonferenz der Geschichtswerkstatt e.V. am 7. Juli 1990 in Essen von Eva Brücker und Michael Wildt im Juli 1990" Stadtarchiv Konstanz, Depositum Dr. Zang (Bestand Arbeitskreis Regionalgeschichte Bodensee e.V. und bundesweite Geschichtswerkstatt).

59 Michael Zimmermann, "'Die Rückkehr der Gartenzwerge?' Sieben Jahre Institutionalisierung: Kritik und Perspektiven der Geschichtswerkstätten. Ein Forumsgespräch auf dem Jahrestreffen der Geschichtswerkstätten," *Geschichtswerkstatt* 21 (1990): 80–82.

60 So as part of the event "30 Jahre Geschichtsarbeit 'von unten' – Reicht das jetzt?" of the *Berliner Geschichtswerkstatt*, https://www.berliner-geschichtswerkstatt.de/news-reader/items/mo-27022012-um-1900-uhr.html, accessed December 31, 2022.

lication forums and networking opportunities in the new history movement, but the academic debates that have taken place have been conducted by the participants as part of international developments in the historical sciences, in which the method of oral history, for example, has also established itself on the basis of international exchange; and the taking into account of the views of the "subjects in history" is part of the diversity of cultural anthropological methods. Many participants, who have also been involved in the new history movement, have contributed to this.

The perception that is often now derived from the historiography of the *Geschichtswerkstätten* as a new history movement, from their publications and the perspective of those who have written a significant amount about the work of the initiatives, is that historians with an academic background were the driving forces behind these initiatives. This is true in many cases, but not in all of them: the many groups were very different – the dynamics, the driving forces, and also the topics and objectives varied significantly.

References

Arbeitsgruppe des Projekts 'Regionale Sozialgeschichte'. "Regionalgeschichte: Neue Chancen für Gesellschaftsanalyse." *Das Argument* 131 (1982): 55–67.

"Arbeitskreis zum Projekt einer Zeitschrift auf dem Dortmunder Geschichtsfest." *Geschichtswerkstatt* 11 (1987): 134–135.

"aktiv – Archiv – alternativ. Ankündigung des Salecina-Seminars vom 18. bis 24. Mai 1986." *Weller* 17 (1986): 31.

"Archiware [sic!] aller Länder . . ." *BGW-Rundbrief* 2 (1981): 8.

"Aus der Berliner Rezensionsredaktion." *Geschichtswerkstatt* 14 (1988): 72.

Barrow, Logie. "On getting involved in History Workshop." *Geschichtswerkstatt* 7 (1985): 60–63.

"Bericht über die 35. Versammlung deutscher Historiker in Berlin. 3. bis 7. Oktober 1984." Stuttgart: Klett 1985.

Berliner Geschichtswerkstatt, ed. ". . . *Geschichte zurechtrücken, Unbekanntes aufdecken . . .". Dokumentation der lokalhistorischen Projekte in der BRD und in Berlin (West) anläßlich des 50. Jahrestages der Machtübergabe an die Nationalsozialisten*, (Berlin, 1984).

Berliner Geschichtswerkstatt, ed. *"Das war 'ne ganz geschlossene Gesellschaft hier". Der Lindenhof: Eine Genossenschaftssiedlung in der Großstadt*. Berlin: Nishen, 1987.

Berliner Geschichtswerkstatt, "30 Jahre Geschichtsarbeit 'von unten' – Reicht das jetzt?" https://www. berliner-geschichtswerkstatt.de/news-reader/items/mo-27022012-um-1900-uhr.html, accessed December 31, 2022.

Bildungsvereinigung Arbeit und Leben Niedersachsen, ed. *Geschichte und Kulturarbeit. Arbeiter erforschen ihre Geschichte*. Hannover, 1983.

Blaschke, Olaf, and Jens Thiel. "Der Verband zwischen den Krisenjahren und der Rückkehr der Geschichte." In *Die versammelte Zunft. Historikerverband und Historikertage in Deutschland*

4 *Barfußhistoriker* and *Geschichtswerkstätten* – History from Below in West Germany ■■ **109**

1893-2000, edited by Olaf Blaschke, Matthias Berg, Martin Sabrow, Jens Thiel, and Krijn Thijs, 565–590. Göttingen: Wallstein, 2018.

Broszat, Martin. "Geleitwort." In *Provinzialisierung einer Region. Zur Entstehung der bürgerlichen Gesellschaft in der Provinz*, edited by Gert Zang, 9–12. Frankfurt/Main: Syndikat, 1978.

Busemann, Wilfried. "Ausgelaufen! Bericht vom Abschlußseminar des DGB-Projektes ‚Geschichte von unten', Hattingen, 4–6. Mai 1987." *Geschichtswerkstatt* 13 (1987): 66–68.

Cornelißen, Christoph. "Deutsche Geschichtswissenschaft nach 1945. Zwischen nationalen Traditionen und transnationalen Öffnungen." In *Die Rückkehr der deutschen Geschichtswissenschaft in die 'Ökumene der Historiker'. Ein wissenschaftsgeschichtlicher Ansatz*, edited by Ulrich Pfeil, 17–34. München: Oldenbourg, 2008.

Dann, Otto. "Die Region als Gegenstand der Geschichtswissenschaft." *Archiv für Sozialgeschichte* 23 (1983): 652–661.

Dahrendorf, Ralf. "Region als 'Provinz' und als Hoffnung." *Frankfurter Allgemeine Zeitung*, July 31, 1979.

Deutscher Gewerkschaftsbund Bundesvorstand, ed.. Vorstellungen des DGB zur Kulturpolitik und Kulturarbeit. Düsseldorf, 1981.

"Eine Stellungnahme der Geschichtswerkstatt Dortmund zu dem Beitrag von Hans-Ulrich Wehler in DIE ZEIT vom 3.5.1985, von dem viele überzeugt sind, daß er es nicht wert ist." *Geschichtswerkstatt* 7 (1985): 41–44.

Eley, Geoff. "Provinzialisierung einer Region. Regionale Unterentwicklung und liberale Politik in der Stadt und im Kreis Konstanz im 19. Jahrhundert. Untersuchungen zur Entstehung der bürgerlichen Gesellschaft in der Provinz ed. by Gert Zang." *The Journal of Modern History* 54 (1982): 798–802.

Evans, Richard J., "Die 'History-Workshop' – Bewegung in England." In *Geschichte entdecken. Erfahrungen und Projekte der neuen Geschichtsbewegung*, edited by Hannes Heer, and Volker Ullrich, 37–45. Reinbek: Rowohlt, 1985.

Fan, Dingliang. "SPD und Geschichtswissenschaft in der Bundesrepublik Deutschland 1959-1989. Die Kommunikation zwischen einer politischen Partei und professionellen Historikern." PhD diss., University Trier, 2012.

Fletcher, Roger. "History from below comes to Germany. The new history movement in the Federal Republic of Germany." *Journal of Modern History* 60 (1988): 557–568.

Fletcher, Roger. "Recent Developments in West German Historiography. The Bielefeld School and Its Critics." *German Studies Review* 3 (1984): 451–480.

François, Etienne. "L'Allemagne Fédérale se penche sur son passé." *Vingtième Siècle* 7 (1985): 151–163.

Gießmann, Bertolt. "Die Wiederentdeckung der Provinz. Die‚Provinzbewegung' der 1970er Jahre und ihre Perzeption von Stadt und Land." In *"Bewegte Dörfer". Neue soziale Bewegungen in der Provinz 1970-1990*, edited by Julia Paulus, 43–56. Paderborn: Ferdinand Schöningh, 2018.

Ginzburg, Carlo, and Carlo Poni. "Was ist Mikrogeschichte?" *Geschichtswerkstatt* 6 (1985): 48–52.

Grüterig, Lars, and Alexander Kastner. "Volk + Uni = Volksuni?" In *Experiment: Politische Kultur. Berichte aus einem neuen gesellschaftlichen Alltag*, edited by Gerd Koch. Frankfurt/Main: Extrabuch, 1985.

Hansen, Frauke. "Bericht vom Archiv-Seminar in Salecina." *BGW-Rundbrief* 5 (1986): 21–25.

Haumann, Heiko, ed.. *Vom Hotzenwald bis Whyl. Demokratische Traditionen in Baden*. Köln: Pahl-Rugenstein, 1977.

Hofrén, Erik, and Maths Isacson. "Museum from below – history from below." In *Europa im Zeitalter des Industrialismus. Zur "Geschichte von unten" im europäischen Vergleich. Beiträge zur gleichnamigen wissenschaftlichen Tagung im Dezember 1990 (3. bis 7.12.1990)*, edited by Museum der Arbeit (Elisabeth von Dücker), 266–271. Hamburg: Dölling und Galitz, 1993.

Historische Kommission beim SPD-Parteivorstand, ed. *Historische Spurensuche in der politischen Praxis. Leitfaden*. Bonn, 1987.

Jancik, Christa, Thomas Lindenberger, Andreas Ludwig, and Peter Schöttler. "Zur Gründung eines Rezensionsteils." *Geschichtswerkstatt* 12 (1987): 91.

Köhler, Ernst. "Der kleine Mann und seine Liebhaber." *Freibeuter* 24 (1985): 88–99.

Krankenhagen, Gernot. "Hamburg plant ein Museum der Arbeit – seit 1980 oder: Warum ist es so schwer, ein Museum der Arbeit zu realisieren?" In *Geschichte der Arbeit im Museum. Dokumentation einer Tagung im Rahmen der Ruhrfestspiele Recklinghausen 11. bis 13. Mai 1987*, edited by Bernd Faulenbach, and Franz-Josef Jelich, 34–54. Recklinghausen: FIAB, 1987.

Lindenberger, Thomas. "'Alltagsgeschichte' oder: Als um die zünftigen Grenzen der Geschichtswissenschaft noch gestritten wurde." In *Zeitgeschichte als Streitgeschichte. Große Kontroversen seit 1945*, edited by Martin Sabrow, Ralph Jessen, and Klaus Große Kracht, 74–91. München: Beck, 2003.

Lindenberger, Thomas, and Michael Wildt. "Radikale Pluralität. Geschichtswerkstätten als praktische Wissenschaftskritik." *Archiv für Sozialgeschichte* 29 (1989): 393–411.

Lindqvist, Sven. *Grabe wo du stehst. Handbuch zur Erforschung der eigenen Geschichte*. Edited by Manfred Dammeyer. Bonn: Dietz, 1989.

Lindqvist, Sven. *Gräv där du står. Hur man utforskar ett jobb*. Stockholm: Albert Bonniers Förlag, 1978.

Ludwig, Andreas. "Gesucht, gesammelt, gepflegt, geforscht, geputzt und schließlich . . .? Utopien für ein anderes Museum." *Geschichtswerkstatt* 11 (1987): 124–128.

McElligott, Anthony. "The German History Workshop Festival in Berlin, May-June 1984." *German History* 2 (1985): 21–29.

Medick, Hans. "'Geschichte für wen?' Zu einem anstößigen Text von Alf Lüdtke und Hans Medick aus dem Jahr 1977." In *Alltag, Erfahrung, Eigensinn. Historisch-anthropologische Erkundungen*, edited by Belinda Davis, Thomas Lindenberger, and Michael Wildt, 29–42. Frankfurt/Main: Campus, 2008.

Meier-Weigand, Harald. "Der Kranhaken, der Zeise-Arbeiter und das Rot. Das erste Logo des Vereins Museum der Arbeit." *mitarbeit* 15 (2015): 37–39.

"Materialien zu einer Fahrradtour." *arbeitskreis regional geschichte* 4 (1981): 2–24.

"Mitteilungen des Ausschusses." *Geschichtswerkstatt* 12 (1987): 96–99.

Mossmann, Walter. "'Die Bevölkerung ist hellwach!' Erfahrungen aus dem Kampf der badisch-elsässischen Bevölkerung gegen ein Atomkraftwerk in Whyl und ein Bleichemiewerk in Marckolsheim." *Kursbuch* 39 (1975): 129–153.

Müller, Bernhard. "Die Sozialdemokraten entdecken die Geschichte von unten (Stimmungsbericht eines Frustrierten von einem Kongreß in Bonn)." *BGW-Rundbrief* 1 (1985): 11–12.

Neumann, Arndt. *Unternehmen Hamburg. Eine Geschichte der neoliberalen Stadt*. Göttingen: Vandenhoeck & Ruprecht, 2018.

Nienhaus, Ursula, Gabriele Wohlauf, Frank Thomas Gatter, and Stefan Weigand. "Einige Überlegungen zu den Tendenzen in der Geschichtswerkstatt e. V." *Geschichtswerkstatt* 12 (1987): 87–89.

Niethammer, Lutz. "Fragen – Antworten – Fragen. Methodische Erfahrungen und Erwägungen der Oral History." In *"Wir kriegen jetzt andere Zeiten." Auf der Suche nach der Erfahrung des Volkes in nachfaschistischen Ländern*, edited by Alexander von Plato, and Lutz Niethammer, 392–447. Berlin, Bonn: Dietz, 1985.

Nolte, Paul. "Die Historiker in der Bundesrepublik. Rückblick auf eine 'lange Generation'." *Merkur* 53 (1999): 413–431.

Paul, Gerhard, and Bernhard Schoßig. "Geschichte und Heimat." In *Die andere Geschichte. Geschichte von unten, Spurensicherung, ökologische Geschichte, Geschichtswerkstätten*, edited by Gerhard Paul, and Bernhard Schoßig, 15–32. Köln: Bund, 1986.

4 Barfußhistoriker and Geschichtswerkstätten – History from Below in West Germany — 111

"Protokoll der Mitgliederversammlung des Arbeitskreises am Samstag, dem 27.6.1981, im Haus der Evangelischen Studentengemeinde, ab 14.30 Uhr." *arbeitskreis regional geschichte* 5 (1982), S. 2–10, hier S. 4.)

Raphael, Lutz. "Der Beruf des Historikers seit 1945." In *Geschichtswissenschaften. Eine Einführung*, edited by Christoph Cornelißen, 39–52. Frankfurt/Main: Fischer, 2000.

Reichardt, Sven. "Authentizität und Gemeinschaftsbindung. Politik und Lebensstil im linksalternativen Milieu vom Ende der 1960er bis zum Anfang der achtziger Jahre." *Forschungsjournal Neue Soziale Bewegungen* 21 (2008): 118–130.

Reichardt, Sven, and Detlef Siegfried. "Das Alternative Milieu. Konturen einer Lebensform." In *Das Alternative Milieu. Antibürgerlicher Lebensstil und linke Politik in der Bundesrepublik Deutschland und Europa 1968–1983*, edited by Sven Reichardt, and Detlef Siegfried, 510–511. Göttingen: Wallstein, 2010.

Reichardt, Sven. "Authentizität als Selbstbeschreibungskategorie im linksalternativen Milieu." In *Die "andere" Provinz. Kulturelle Auf- und Ausbrücke im Bodenseeraum seit den 1960er Jahren*, edited by Heike Kempe, 11–20. Konstanz: UVK, 2014.

Samuel, Raphael. "Wahrheit ist parteiisch. Zur Entstehung des 'History Workshop'." *Journal für Geschichte* 3 (1981): 36–38.

Scharrer, Manfred. "Bericht über das DGB-Projekt Geschichte von unten nach zweijähriger Laufzeit (vorgelegt auf der Abschlußtagung des Projektes vom 4.-6. Mai 1987)." Cited after *Weller* 20 (1987): 30–35.

Scharrer, Manfred. "Zum Selbstverständnis einer gewerkschaftlichen Geschichte von unten." In *Macht Geschichte – von unten. Handbuch für gewerkschaftliche Geschichte vor Ort*, edited by Manfred Scharrer, 25–35. Köln: Bund, 1988.

Schmidt, Horst. "'Heißhunger auf Geschichte'. Ortsvereine entdecken ihre Vergangenheit (Original in: Die Neue Gesellschaft 30.1983, S. 900–906)." In *Identität durch Geschichte. Leitziel Emanzipation*, edited by Malte Ristau. (Marburg, 1985).

Schmid, Regina. *Verlorene Heimat. Gailingen – ein Dorf und seine jüdische Gemeinde in der Weimarer Zeit*. Konstanz: Eigenverl. d. Arbeitskreises für Regionalgeschichte, 1988.

Schöttler, Peter. "Die Geschichtswerkstatt e.V. Zu einem Versuch, basisdemokratische Geschichtsinitiativen und -forschungen zu 'vernetzen'." *Geschichte und Gesellschaft* 10 (1984): 421–424.

"Selbstverständnispapier der Geschichtswerkstatt, beschlossen auf der Gründungsversammlung am 28.5.1983 in Bochum." *Geschichtsdidaktik* 9 (1984): 193.

Seyfried, Erwin, ed. *Volksuni. Bilder und Texte von der ersten Volksuni Pfingsten 1980*. Berlin, 1980.

Siegfried, Detlef. "Die Rückkehr des Subjekts. Gesellschaftlicher Wandel und neue Geschichtsbewegung um 1980." In *Geschichte und Geschichtsvermittlung. Festschrift für Karl Heinrich Pohl*, edited by Olaf Hartung, and Katja Köhr, 125–146. Bielefeld: Verlag für Regionalgeschichte, 2008.

Siegfried, Detlef. "Subversiver Alltag. Geschichtswerkstätten zwischen Politik und Wissenschaft." In *25 Jahre Galerie Morgenland. Geschichtswerkstatt Eimsbüttel (Festschrift)*, edited by Geschichtswerkstatt Eimsbüttel, 99–106. Hamburg: Morgenland, 2003.

Stone, Lawrence. "The Revival of Narrative. Reflextions on a New Old History." *Past and Present* (85) 1979: 3–24.

Taylor, Barbara. History of History Workshop (published online on 22 November 2012), https://www.historyworkshop.org.uk/the-history-of-history-workshop/, accessed December 31, 2022.

Thijs, Krijn. *Drei Geschichten, eine Stadt. Die Berliner Stadtjubiläen von 1937 und 1987*. Köln, Weimar, Wien: Böhlau, 2008.

112 —— Etta Grotrian

Trapp, Werner. "Sich am eigenen Schopf aus der Geschichtslosigkeit ziehen. Mündliche Geschichte als Versuch kommunaler historischer Kulturarbeit." *Literatur und Erfahrung* 10 (1982): 77–86.

"Vorlage zum 2. Teil der Mitgliederversammlung und zur Heftkonferenz der Geschichtswerkstatt e.V. am 7. Juli 1990 in Essen von Eva Brücker und Michael Wildt im Juli 1990." *Stadtarchiv Konstanz, Depositum Dr. Zang (Bestand Arbeitskreis Regionalgeschichte Bodensee e.V. und bundesweite Geschichtswerkstatt).*

Vornbäumen, Axel. "Die Ortsvereine und der Blick in den Rückspiegel." *Frankfurter Rundschau,* April 23, 1986, cited after: *Weller* 18 (1986): 42–43.

Wehler, Hans-Ulrich. "Geschichte – von unten gesehen. Wie bei der Suche nach dem Authentischen Engagement mit Methodik verwechselt wird." *Die Zeit,* May 3, (1985).

"Wider die geplanten historischen Wiederaufbereitungsanlagen der Bundesregierung. Entschließung des Vorstands der Geschichtswerkstatt e. V." *Geschichtswerkstatt* 9 (1986): 6.

Wildt, Michael. "Die große Geschichtswerkstattschlacht im Jahr 1992 oder: Wie WerkstattGeschichte entstand." *WerkstattGeschichte* 50 (2008): 73–81.

Wildt, Michael. "WerkstattGeschichte – ein Zeitschriftenprojekt." In *Geschichtswerkstätten gestern – heute – morgen. Bewegung! Stillstand. Aufbruch?,* edited by Forschungsstelle für Zeitgeschichte in Hamburg und Galerie Morgenland/Geschichtswerkstatt Eimsbüttel. Hamburg: Dölling & Galitz, 2004.

Wirtz, Rainer. "Geschichtswerkstatt – die andere Geschichte?" *Journal für Geschichte* 5 (1983): 64–65.

Wüstenberg, Jenny. "Vom alternativen Laden zum Dienstleistungsbetrieb: the Berliner Geschichtswerkstatt. A Case Study in Activist Memory Politics." *German Studies Review* 32 (2009): 590–618.

Zang, Gert. *Die unaufhaltsame Annäherung an das Einzelne. Reflexion über den theoretischen und praktischen Nutzen der Regional- und Alltagsgeschichte.* Konstanz: Arbeitskreis für Regionalgeschichte, 1985.

Zang, Gert. "Gedanken tausendmal gedacht, Gefühle tausendmal gefühlt . . .? Versuche sich der Lebens- und Gedankenwelt kleiner Gemeinden zu nähern: Mündliche Geschichte in der Bodenseeregion." *Literatur und Erfahrung* 10 (1982): 65–76.

Zang, Gert. "Subjektive Reflexionen über ein Projekt und seine organisatorische, methodische und inhaltliche Entwicklung. Überlegungen zu einer kritischen Regionalgeschichtsschreibung für das 19. und 20. Jahrhundert." In *Provinzialisierung einer Region. Zur Entstehung der bürgerlichen Gesellschaft in der Provinz,* edited by Gert Zang, 465–538. Frankfurt/Main: Syndikat, 1978.

Zang, Gert. "Vorbemerkung." In *Provinzialisierung einer Region. Zur Entstehung der bürgerlichen Gesellschaft in der Provinz,* edited by Gert Zang, 13–14. Frankfurt/Main: Syndikat, 1978.

Zimmermann, Michael. "Haben Geschichtswerkstätten Zukunft?" In *Geschichtswerkstätten gestern – heute – morgen. Bewegung! Stillstand. Aufbruch?,* edited by Forschungsstelle für Zeitgeschichte in Hamburg und der Galerie Morgenland/Geschichtswerkstatt Eimsbüttel. Hamburg: Dölling & Galitz, 2004.

Zimmermann, Michael. "Protokoll Jahreshauptversammlung der Geschichtswerkstatt e.V. Samstag 26.05.1990, 9.30 bis 13.30 Uhr, Haus der Jugend Stintfang, Hamburg." *Geschichtswerkstatt* 21 (1990): 71–73.

Zimmermann, Michael. "'Die Rückkehr der Gartenzwerge?' Sieben Jahre Institutionalisierung: Kritik und Perspektiven der Geschichtswerkstätten. Ein Forumsgespräch auf dem Jahrestreffen der Geschichtswerkstätten." *Geschichtswerkstatt* 21 (1990): 80–82.

Dario Di Rosa

5 Indigenous History from Below? Problems and Perspectives from the Pacific

Commenting upon the various forms of historical knowledge produced under the rubric "people's history", Raphael Samuel observed that, although this historiography "[i]mplicitly or explicitly (. . .) is oppositional, (. . .) the terms of that opposition are necessarily different in different epochs and for different modes of work".[1] Starting from this characteristically materialist position, I offer in this chapter a comparison between the field of Pacific history and the British Marxist tradition of history from below.[2] Because Pacific historiography is lesser-known than the other term of comparison, its development and transformation from the 1950s is given the lion's share of space in this chapter. Moreover, the reader must be warned that mine is *per force* a selective reading. The Pacific is a region with over a thousand languages, which has known a plethora of colonial powers (Spain, Portugal, Holland, France, Germany, Japan, Great Britain and its dominions, and the United States of America); and it has long been separated into sub-regions (Melanesia, Micronesia, and Polynesia), which, despite the problematic nature of such a classification, continue to shape the specialisation and concerns of scholars.[3]

From a European perspective, the Pacific islanders' past has largely been the preserve of the field of anthropology, broadly conceived.[4] History, as a discipline, is a relative late-comer to the region. Anthropology has been – and in many

---

1 Raphael Samuel, "People's History," in *People's History and Socialist Theory*, ed. Raphael Samuel (London: Routledge, 2016 [1981]), xvi.
2 As Bryan Palmer has argued, the very notion of *the* British Marxist tradition is an all too comfortable shorthand for a much more complex constellation of methods, interests, and political positions. For reasons of space, since British social history is more a point of comparison with Pacific historiography, I have to surrender to the use of the shorthand. Bryan D. Palmer, "Reasoning Rebellion: E.P. Thompson, British Marxist Historians, and the Making of Dissident Political Mobilization," *Labour/Le Travail* 50, no. Fall (2002): 187–216.
3 See Nicholas Thomas et al., "The Force of Ethnology: Origins and Significance of the Melanesia/Polynesia Division [and Comments and Replies]," *Current Anthropology* 30, no. 1 (1989): 27–41 and the special issue of *The Journal of Pacific History*, vol. 38, no. 2 (2003) on Dumont d'Urville's division of Oceania into these three macro-areas.
4 In this instance I use the term 'anthropology' to embrace the whole range of theoretical interests and methodologies that have characterised the discipline since its inception as part of 'the

https://doi.org/10.1515/9783111522180-005

respect still is – crucial for the study of the region's past, and such disciplinary hegemony has left an enduring legacy in the way scholars of the Pacific have conceptualised local communities. From Branislaw Malinowski's functionalism and its endeavour to "grasp *the* native's point of view", to later instances (either structuralist or hermeneutical) of symbolic approaches in search of coherent cultural universes, up until more recent preoccupations heralded by the 'ontological turn', the discipline of anthropology has – unwittingly or otherwise – fostered representations of local communities as relatively homogenous.[5] It is such a non-articulation of internal power- and indeed class-dynamics that, as argued below, has hampered Pacific history from elaborating a kind of history from below as it developed in the Marxist tradition. Moreover, anthropology's focus on "culture" has led to the reification of this term, and its becoming the common denominator under which to subsume internal differences, thus fostering a populism that has reverberations both in the political life of the islands, as well as in the politics of academia. In fact, as shown below, it is through appeals to "culture", reminiscent of Herder's cultural nationalism, that indigenous scholars (especially in the diaspora) have claimed an exclusive source of insight into the workings of local societies and minds. In the following pages I trace the history of the formation and transformation of the field called Pacific History.

5.1 The Formation of an Autonomous Field (1950s–1970s)

The origin story of Pacific history as an autonomous sub-field coincides with the appointment in 1950 of James W. Davidson to the Foundation Chair of Pacific History at the Australian National University (hereinafter ANU). Davidson arrived at the ANU with a doctorate from Cambridge University, lair of British imperial history, and after a spell in Samoa as adviser to the high chiefs of West Samoa.[6]

---

natural history of man' in the nineteenth century up to modern anthropology. It is not by chance that I came to Pacific history in my doctorate via an anthropological training.

5 Branislaw Malinowski, *Argonauts of the Western Pacific: An Account of Native Enterprise and Adventure in the Archipelagoes of Melanesian New Guinea* (London: Routledge and Kegan Paul, 1922), 25 (my italics). For an intelligent critique of mainstream anthropological research in the Melanesian region see James Carrier, ed., *History and Tradition in Melanesian Anthropology* (Berkeley/Los Angeles/Oxford: University of California Press, 1992).

6 A most useful intellectual biography of Davidson can be found in Doug Munro, *The Ivory Tower and Beyond: Participant Historians of the Pacific* (Newcastle upon Tyne: Cambridge Scholars Publishing, 2009), chap. 2.

5 Indigenous History from Below? Problems and Perspectives from the Pacific — **115**

From his position at a markedly research-based institution,[7] for two decades Davidson fostered generations of scholars who came to dominate the scholarly landscape for quite some time. Indeed, as Brij Lal and Doug Munro write, these historians, "armed with a doctorate and an island-oriented theology, branched out to preach their new gospel".[8] The content of this gospel was spelled out in Davidson's programmatic Inaugural Lecture: having started off in British Imperial history, Davidson thought it necessary to move away from the metropoles and their concerns, shifting the gaze toward the islands themselves.[9] This island-centred history, in Davidson's view, would enable scholars to read the decisions taken in the metropoles as responses to the lived realities of the Europeans on the ground, with their various interests, especially in their interactions with Pacific Islanders. By fixing its gaze on the islands, then, Pacific history shaped itself as a history from below in relation to imperial history. Moreover, the change of perspective led Pacific historians to focus on "the study of multi-cultural situations",[10] hence coming to terms with indigenous agency. This second aspect has probably been the most influential tenet of what later will be variously termed the "Canberra-school" or "Davidson school".

The work of many historians trained at the ANU between the 1950s and 1970s focused on eliciting the role of indigenous agency in shaping the projects of different "waves" of colonial agents: explorers, beachcombers and castaways, traders, missionaries, and colonial administrators.[11] Many PhD dissertations were turned into monographs, and *The Journal of Pacific History* – the flagship journal of the ANU Department of Pacific History since 1966 – provided a publication outlet to

---

7 Founded in 1946, the ANU was conceived as a research based institution with the clear scope of guiding the Australian governments in devising policies. With no undergraduate teaching load and substantial government funds the department of that institution had plenty of resources to support its vision of what Pacific History ought to be. A further consolidation of Canberra's reproductive power of the intellectual labour force came with the publication in 1966 of *The Journal of Pacific History*.

8 Brij V. Lal, and Doug Munro, "The Text in Its Context: An Introduction," in *Texts and Contexts: Reflections in Pacific Islands Historiography*, ed. Doug Munro, and Brij V. Lal (Honolulu: University of Hawaii Press, 2006), 2.

9 J. W. Davidson, *The Study of Pacific History: An Inaugural Lecture Delivered at Canberra on 25 November 1954* (Canberra: Australian National University, 1955); later published in revised form in the first issue of the ANU department's flagship journal as J. W. Davidson, "Problems of Pacific History," *The Journal of Pacific History* 1 (1966): 5–21.

10 See Davidson, "Problems of Pacific History," 10, 13.

11 The metaphor of different waves of Europeans entering the Pacific has been fruitfully deployed by Kerry R. Howe to organise his general history of the Pacific Islands; Kerry R. Howe, *Where the Waves Fall: A New South Sea Islands History from First Settlement to Colonial Rule*, (Honolulu: University of Hawaii Press, 1984).

build up reputable academic credentials for young scholars. The unquestionable value of these works rests on a thorough and eclectic combing of various kinds of archives in order to show the extent of indigenous manipulation of Europeans' own projects for local ends.[12] Moreover, the emphasis on indigenous agency in shaping relations with colonial actors, captured the political mood carried by the so-called winds of change: "As the peoples of the Pacific (. . .) move towards self-government or independence, the study of their own role in the processes of political change has become a subject of great interest and importance".[13] Yet, the indigenous agency which finds place in many works is that of those indigenous people (mostly men) who occupied key positions in the local structure of power. Such histories thus reproduce the gaze of colonial archives which themselves reflect the dependence of colonial administrators on indigenous elites. Because colonialism, especially British colonialism with its preference for indirect rule, froze in time indigenous power structures that would later constitute the basis for the emergence of postcolonial elites, Simione Durutalo could plausibly assert that "orthodox A.N.U. scholars (. . .) are *but historians of the status quo*".[14] With this assertion, the Fijian intellectual was taking issue with the predominant historiography of Fiji's colonial history that had privileged the easterly chiefs of the archipelago, the same chiefs whose power British colonialists helped to maintain, over other polities less inclined to accommodate Britain's forcible intrusions.[15] Moreover, the *status quo* Durutalo was referring to is a thinly veiled critique of Sir Ratu Kamisese Mara, first Prime Minister of Fiji after independence, who occupied that office for over two decades, and who represented the continuation of eastern chiefly traditional politics in modern government. A celebration of the latter's place in Fiji's colonial history mirrored the appreciation of the (then) current political elite.[16] Darutalo had

---

12 The interested reader can find a useful historiographical discussion of a selection of influential works from this period in Doug Munro and Brij V. Lal, eds., *Texts and Contexts: Reflections in Pacific Islands Historiography* (Honolulu: University of Hawaii Press, 2006).

13 Davidson, "Problems of Pacific History," 16.

14 Simione Durutalo, "The Liberation of the Pacific Island Intellectual," *Review* 4, no. 10 (1983): 11; see also Simione Durutalo, "Bucaneers and Chiefly Historians," *Journal of Pacific Studies* 11 (1985): 117–56 and the exchange between Nicholas Thomas ("Taking Sides: Fijian Dissent and Conservative History-writing," *Australian Historical Studies* 24, no. 95 (1990): 239–51) and Deryck Scarr ("Secret Disharmonies and 'Scholarly Discourse': The Case of Nicholas Thomas," *Australian Historical Studies* 24, no. 97 (1991): 447–51).

15 Only relatively recently has such geographical and political bias been countered by Robert Nicole in his *Disturbing History: Resistance in Early Colonial Fiji* (Honolulu: University of Hawai'i Press, 2011): by a scholar who mentions his intellectual debt to the history from below tradition.

16 It should be noted that Sir Ratu Kamisese Mara, in his speech in front of the UN General Assembly 25th session (October 21, 1970), stressed the non-violent and amicable terms of the devolu-

5 Indigenous History from Below? Problems and Perspectives from the Pacific — **117**

no doubt that "History should be the *people's* history. Official history is written by the ruling class in its own image. [. . .] It arrogates to the leaders of this ruling class all the credit for the advances of society and [. . .] pays scant attention to the participation of the inarticulate – the masses".[17]

There is little question about Davidson's school being engaged outside the walls of academia. For instance, the focus on indigenous responses to the colonial situation and the resilience of certain cultural institutions and practices was a challenge to the (Gramscian) commonsense that Pacific societies and cultures – if not the people who embodied them – were doomed to vanish as a consequence of the "fatal impact" of the colonial encounter.[18] This was one of the ways in which ANU-trained historians made a direct intervention (whether or not successful) into the public domain. Davidson was aware that historians cannot but be implicated in the society they work in, as can be surmised from his recollection of his early days as a student at Victoria University College (Wellington). After having been steered away from researching the origins of the Maori wars (on the ground that he did not know the Maori language well enough), Davidson opted for the history of Scandinavian settlers in New Zealand as research topic for his Honours thesis. He recalls that "my work benefited from the fact that I was able to walk over the farms that the settlers had laboriously cut out (. . .) and to talk to the few survivors of the original migrants".[19] Davidson carried to the ANU his emphasis on direct experience in informing scholarship, valuing first-hand knowledge of the islands in the scholars he recruited. A particularly significant case in point is Henry E. Maude, who served for several years (from 1929 to 1956) in the British

---

tion of sovereignty from Great Britain to Fiji, dubbing this 'the Pacific way', establishing an implicit contrast with how decolonisation had been achieved elsewhere through struggles for liberation (not uncommonly under socialist banners). On the conservative character of "the Pacific way" ideology, see Stephanie Lawson, "'The Pacific Way' as Postcolonial Discourse: Toward a Reassessment," *The Journal of Pacific History* 45, no. 3 (2010): 297–314.

17 Durutalo, "The Liberation of the Pacific Island Intellectual," 11.

18 See Kerry R. Howe, "The Fate of the 'Savage' in Pacific Historiography," *The New Zealand Journal of History* 11, no. 2 (1977): 137–54. The expression 'fatal impact' is taken from the title of Alan Moorehead's popular book *The Fatal Impact: An Account of the Invasion of the South Pacific, 1767–1840*, [1st ed.] (New York: Harper & Row, 1966). Questions of demography and epidemics had a central place in the debates around the "fatal impact" thesis. Yet, for most Pacific historians, the technicalities of demographic research remained an article of faith; see Ian C. Campbell, "More Celebrated than Read: The Work of Norma McArthur," in *Texts and Contexts: Reflections in Pacific Islands Historiography*, ed. Doug Munro, and Brij V. Lal (Honolulu: University of Hawaii Press, 2006), 98–110.

19 J. W. Davidson, "Understanding Pacific History: The Participant as Historian," in *The History of Melanesia: Second Waigani Seminar*, ed. Research School of Pacific Studies (Canberra/Port Moresby: Australian National University/The University of Papua New Guinea, 1969), 2.

Colonial Office before arriving at the ANU armed with a wealth of practical experience in the islands. For example, Maude drew on his direct knowledge as Acting District Officer to depict the events relating to quasi-millenarian activities on Onotoa (in today's Kiribati) in 1930 which had worried the colonial administration and endangered the life of Koata, an indigenous Native Magistrate.[20] For those who could not show previous knowledge of the islands, fieldwork was regarded as highly desirable, if not essential. Reliance on ethnographic works was the second-best option, and indeed the boundaries of the two disciplines were blurred.[21]

Interestingly, Davidson makes a passing, yet explicit, parallel between his notion of "participation" and the leftist tradition of history from below.

> I had been irritated by the emphasis ordinarily placed upon the British origins of New Zealand society. Both topics [the origins of the Maori wars and the Scandinavian settlers in New Zealand] had been attractive to me because they would give me a chance of studying non-British elements in the country's heritage. The attraction had been similar to that which has drawn *Left-wing British historians to the English Civil War* and their *Australian counterparts* [. . .] toward studies of *the Labor Party and the trade union movement.*[22]

The reference is of course to Christopher Hill's work, and to socialist historians more in general. But was it, as Davidson suggested, the same kind of engagement? Hill drew on the Marxist tradition and sought in the English Civil War antecedents to popular protest and socio-political change. Davidson's engagement, instead, appears to be grounded more on "ethnic" identities; in translating this idea into his vision of Pacific history, the below/above dialectic was played out between on the one hand the Maori and non-Anglo European migrants and on the other British settlers. One wonders, with the advantage of hindsight, if this did not prefigure the terms of indigenous engagement with Pacific history in the 1990s (as we shall see below).

---

20 H. E. Maude, "The Swords of Gabriel: A Study in Participant History," in *The Journal of Pacific History* 2 (1967): 113–36.

21 For instance, speaking about the state of the art of historical knowledge in Papua New Guinea, Donald Denoon wrote that "some anthropologists have taken the opportunity to write what amounts to very sophisticated history," Donald Denoon, *People's History*, Inaugural Lecture (Boroko, P.N.G.: University of Papua New Guinea, 1973), 14–15.

22 Davidson, "Understanding Pacific History," 2.

5.2 The Paradigm Reaches its Limits (1970s)

In an important article, David Chappell invited Pacific historians to ponder the limitations of the "active agent paradigm" – so central to the ANU programme – for decolonising Pacific history.[23] As others have noted, the equation of "victimhood" with "passivity" is highly problematic, especially since the negation of either of these aspects or both means to deny the material impact of colonialism on the lives of Pacific Islanders. An instructive case in point, in this regard, is the historiography of Melanesian labour trade to Queensland, one of the few topics that generated debates outside the confines of specialised publication outlets.[24]

From the 1860s to 1906 a large number of Melanesians went to Queensland as indentured labourers. Missionaries, at the time, criticised the import of Melanesians to colonial plantations, accusing recruiters of blackbirding – kidnapping and deception – reminiscent of the Atlantic slave trade. It was in reaction to such views, still current long after the end of the trade, that Pacific historians Deryck Scarr and Peter Corris revisited the issue, showing the low incidence of actual kidnappings (largely confined to the very early phase of the trade), and the Melanesians' willingness to sign those contracts in order to advance local agendas.[25] From an island-centred perspective, the labourers recruited had a significant degree of agency in dealing with recruiters. A later generation of scholars, not associated with the ANU, challenged the idea that if the recruitment was not based on coercion, then Melanesians were engaged in free labour. By focusing on the plantation itself, rather than the islands where Melanesians were recruited, Kay Saunders and Adrian Graves showed the constraints that the politico-economic structure of the plantation system imposed on the workers.[26] For in-

---

23 David A. Chappell, "Active Agents versus Passive Victims: Decolonized Historiography or Problematic Paradigm?," *The Contemporary Pacific* 7 (1995): 303–26.

24 This is by no means the only aspect of the labour history of the Pacific but it contributed to shape much of the labour scholarship in the region; see Doug Munro, "Labour Trade Studies: What and Where?," in *Messy Entanglements: The Papers of the 10th Pacific History Association Conference*, ed. Alaima Talu, and Max Quanchi (Pacific History Association Conference, Brisbane: Pacific History Association, 1995), 131–39; Jacqueline Leckie, "Crossing the Boundaries – Labour Migration in the Eastern Pacific," in *Messy Entanglements: The Papers of the 10th Pacific History Association Conference*, ed. Alaima Talu, and Max Quanchi (Pacific History Association Conference, Brisbane: Pacific History Association, 1995), 141–47.

25 Deryck Scarr, "Recruits and Recruiters: A Portrait of the Pacific Islands Labour Trade," *The Journal of Pacific History* 2 (1967): 5–24; Peter Corris, *Passage, Port and Plantation: A History of Solomon Islands Labour Migration, 1870–1914* (Carlton: Melbourne University Press, 1973).

26 Kay Saunders, *Workers in Bondage: The Origins and Bases of Unfree Labour in Queensland, 1824–1916* (St Lucia: University of Queensland Press, 1982); Adrian Graves, *Cane and Labour: The*

stance, Graves analysed the structural functions of the so-called "truck system" and how this system went through several permutations to circumvent state-promulgated laws.[27] The truck system exploited the Melanesian labourers' desire to bring European commodities back home when their contracts expired, so that they could invest these objects in the local exchange system, ensuring the payment for brideprice and thus transition into full manhood. Plantation- and shop-owners also profited from this form of payment which, *de facto,* meant fewer expenses for labour and profit for shopkeepers, ensuring the survival of the sugar cane industry through periods of global low prices and the consequent restructuring of the production process.[28] Apparently, this was to the advantage of both parties,[29] but in fact the truck system "was a means by which workers were tied to their employers through debt".[30] And yet, as Graves notes, "One of the system's most interesting features was (. . .) the way in which colonial capitalism co-opted mechanisms in the pre-capitalist economy to its service", pointing to the fact that "as long as truck was transformed into gifts in the region, Melanesia remained not the beneficiary, not even the partner of colonial economic development, but its servant".[31] Graves' monograph, which took issue with the paradigm developed by ANU scholars, received criticism from Pacific history quarters, especially for the thesis that Melanesian labourers enlisted because the islands were proletarianised; a fair criticism also picked up by a Marxist reviewer, Tom Brass, though for different reasons.[32]

An attempt at adjudicating this debate is outside the scope of this chapter; suffice to say that it had the positive effect of mitigating the praise for the entrenched island-centred position, in favour of a middle-ground. It was after this historiographic exchange that Corris' *Passage, Port and Plantation* – which Doug

---

Political Economy of the Queensland Sugar Industry, 1862–1906 (Edinburgh: Edinburgh University Press, 1993).

27 Adrian Graves, "Truck and Gifts: Melanesian Immigrants and the Trade Box System in Colonial Queensland," *Past & Present*, no. 101 (1983): 87–124. In the 'truck system', payment of the worker's wage was deferred to the end of the contract, while at the same time allowing workers to buy goods on credit at specific retailers.

28 Graves, "Truck and Gifts," 116–18.

29 "The perceived purpose of the [1880 Pacific Island Labourers] act was therefore to ensure that the immigrants were successfully repatriated with a stock of trade box commodities. Deferred pay actually contributed to this goal and the workers did not object to truck since they wanted their earnings in the form of goods anyway", Graves, "Truck and Gifts," 111.

30 Graves, "Truck and Gifts," 120.

31 Graves, "Truck and Gifts," 123–24.

32 Tom Brass, "Contextualizing Sugar Production in Nineteenth Century Queensland," *Slavery & Abolition* 15, no. 1 (1994): 107–9.

Munro qualifies as "the first real attempt at applying 'history from below' to the Pacific labor trade" – could be seen as exemplary of "both the strengths and the weaknesses of the new Pacific historiography: detailed research and sharpness of focus was accompanied by a narrowness of concerns and an over-particularizing empiricism. The spotlight was on the Islander at the expense of wider contexts".[33] Yet, what ought to be stressed is that one of the issues Pacific historians took with Graves was that he had been "allowing theory to drive the argument".[34] Indeed the rejection of theory – the same theory that enabled Graves to see how debt-bondage was created and affected Melanesians' lives – in favour of empiricism is often cast in a positive light: "the *Journal* [*of Pacific History*] is standing testimony to the detailed empirical research and a corresponding disdain of theory which has always characterised Canberra scholarship".[35]

5.3 Early Critiques

With the passing of Davidson in 1973, some voiced a feeling that research in Pacific history had stagnated. In 1979, Kerry Howe diagnosed Pacific history as suffering from "monograph myopia": an excessive focus on islands or a portion of them at the expense of works of synthesis (and thus an evaluation of what Davidson's island-centred history had accomplished).[36] In the same year, appeals to move forward from Davidson's programme emerged from a stimulating conversation among practitioners of Pacific history, which appeared in a volume on Australian historiography.[37] Some of the structural limitations of the Davidsonian paradigm must have become evident before Davidson's death, if Alan Ward, after having emphasised the eclectic training history undergraduates received at La

---

33 Doug Munro, "The Labor Trade in Melanesians to Queensland: An Historiographic Essay," *Journal of Social History* 28, no. 3 (1995): 611–12. Corris, *Passage, Port and Plantation*.

34 Doug Munro, "Review Article: Revisionism and Its Enemies: Debating the Queensland Labour Trade," *The Journal of Pacific History* 30, no. 2 (1995): 240–49. It should be noted here that Graves' book, a revision of his 1979 doctoral thesis, was published in 1993 due to events outside his control; a fact acknowledged by his reviewers Munro, "Review Article: Revisionism and Its Enemies," 242; Tom Brass, "Contextualizing Sugar Production in Nineteenth-century Queensland," *Slavery & Abolition* 15, no. 1 (1994): 109–10, fn. 2.

35 Munro, "The Labor Trade in Melanesians to Queensland," 610.

36 Kerry R. Howe, "Pacific Islands History in the 1980s: New Directions or Monograph Myopia?," *Pacific Studies* 3, no. 1 (1979): 81–90.

37 Gavan Daws, "On Being a Historian of the Pacific," in *Historical Disciplines and Culture in Australasia: An Assessment*, ed. John A. Moses (St Lucia: University of Queensland Press, 1979), 119–29.

Trobe University in Melbourne and its relevance for history students at the University of Papua New Guinea (where he moved from Melbourne), could convey to his readers the

> grumblings among Ph.D. graduates from the Department of Pacific History at ANU that the supervision *they* received, while excellent in many respects, did not fully equip them to escape sufficiently from the confines of documentary history, and history which, because of the nature of the documentary record is still something of a footnote to empire and focused heavily on the nineteenth century.[38]

One of the most scathing and articulated critiques of Davidson's programme and research agenda was penned by Jacqueline Leckie in 1983. She called for more social history in order to reinvigorate the field and appealed to Eric Hobsbawm's seminal 1971 article "From social history to the history of society".[39] Leckie's appeal, though, was drowned in the clamour caused by the publication of Greg Dening's and Marshall Sahlins' works of historical anthropology in 1980 and 1981 respectively.[40]

5.4 Symbolic Anthropology (1980s–1990s)

Dening's and Sahlins' works offered a way out of the impasse reached by "Davidson's school", while maintaining indigenous agency at centre stage. Moreover, both authors anchored Pacific History to global historiographical trends prompted by the "rapprochement" between the disciplines of history and anthropology. While Canberra's (now waning) hegemony over the field extended regionally,[41] Dening and other historians at La Trobe University – named "the Melbourne Group" – received international recognition from none other than Clifford Geertz, leading proponent of an interpretative anthropology, who praised

---

38 Alan Ward, "Pacific History and Inter-Disicplinary Studies; Some Recent Trends," *Research in Melanesia* 1, no. 2 (1975): 26 (italics in original).
39 Jacqueline Leckie, "Toward a Review of History in the South Pacific," *The Journal of Pacific Studies* 9 (1983): 9–69; E. J. Hobsbawm, "From Social History to the History of Society," *Daedalus* 100, no. 1 (1971): 20–45.
40 Greg Dening, *Islands and Beaches: Discourse on a Silent Land : Marquesas, 1774–1880* (Melbourne: Melbourne University Press, 1980); Marshall Sahlins, *Historical Metaphors and Mythical Realities: Structure in the Early History of the Sandwich Islands Kingdom* (Ann Arbor: University of Michigan Press, 1981); Marshall Sahlins, *Islands of History* (Chicago and London: University of Chicago Press, 1985).
41 It could be said that Pacific history had more impact on the anthropological scholarship of the Pacific than it had on the discipline of history.

their hermeneutic approach to historical texts.[42] This change in institutional hegemony was mirrored in historiographical practice: a shift from the empiricism characteristic of the first phase of Pacific history to ethnographic history, with its theoretically-grounded reading of colonial texts as a means to recover the meaning of historical actors' actions.[43] Dening's work has clear parallels with Geertz's own hermeneutical project.[44] Dening explicitly says that history is ultimately "a conversation about ourselves", and he offers a 'Reflection' as counterpoint to each chapter of his *Islands and Beaches*.[45] The theoretical brooding of ethnographic history was not to everyone's liking but – questions of style aside – the key issue was the "arbitrary and dissatisfying (. . .) decision that culture should be explored essentially, if not only, in terms of symbols".[46] The flavour of idealism is perhaps best captured in Dening's explanation of the two key metaphors structuring his monograph:

> 'Islands and beaches' is a metaphor for the different ways in which *human beings construct their worlds* and for *the boundaries they construct between them*. (. . .) the islands and beaches I speak of *are less physical than cultural*. They are the islands men and women make by *the reality they attribute to their categories*, their roles, their institutions, and the beaches they put around them with their definitions of "we" and "they".[47]

Yet, as one of the few Pacific historians who critically reviewed Dening's work has written, "when getting down to the nuts and bolts of culture contact in the Marquesas, i.e. what happened on the beach" these metaphors "seem more de-

---

42 Clifford Geertz, "History and Anthropology," *New Literary History* 21, no. 2 (1990): 321–35. Beside Dening, the 'Group' comprised Rhys Isaac (who worked on colonial Virginia) and Inga Clenninden (who at that time worked on the Inca and Aztec encounter with Spanish *conquistadores*).

43 Rhys Isaac, "Ethnographic Methods in History: An Action Approach," *Historical Methods* 13, no. 1 (1980): 43–61; June Philipp, "Traditional Historical Narrative and Action-Oriented (or Ethnographic) History," *Historical Studies* 20, no. 80 (1983): 339–52; for an appraisal see Bronwen Douglas, "Doing Ethnographic History: Reflection on Practices and Practising," in *Pacific Islands History: Journeys and Transformations*, ed. Brij V. Lal (Canberra: The Journal of Pacific History, 1992), 92–106. Such reading against the grain was akin to the methodological innovations elaborated by Ranajit Guha at the ANU in those same years: "The Prose of Counter-Insurgency," in *Selected Subaltern Studies*, ed. Ranajit Guha and Gayatri Chakravorty Spivak (New York/Oxford: Oxford University Press, 1988), 45–86.

44 Geertz's most popular work among historians is surely his *The Interpretation of Cultures* (New York: Basic Books, 1973). See footnote 62 below.

45 Dening, *Islands and Beaches*, 6.

46 David Potts, "Two Modes of Writing History: The Poverty of Ethnography and the Potential of Narrative," *Australian Historical Association Bellettin* 66–67 (1991): 10.

47 Dening, *Islands and Beaches*, 3 (my italics).

scriptive[,] even perhaps decorative[,] than explanatory."[48] *How* social change came about and the material conditions that engendered it remains unexplained, we find ourselves confronted with texts with no contexts, or, to borrow Aletta Biersack's formulation in her critique of Geertz's hermeneutics, we are left with "[t]he webs, not the spinning; the culture, not the history; the text, not the process of textualizing."[49]

Arguably Sahlins has been the most prominent scholar of this period to put the Pacific region at the centre-stage of global historiographical trends by promising a framework to reconcile structure and agency, or the *longue durée* and the *événementiel*. Among the many examples one could provide, probably the most famous is Sahlins' explanation of Captain James Cook's death in 1779, following a confrontation that ensued after the taking hostage of a local chief, through the lenses of Hawaiian cosmology. Sahlins argued that Hawaiians identified Cook as Lono, deity of peace and fertility, due to his arrival in the area at the beginning of a specific period of the yearly ritual cycle. At this time the British navigator and his crew received a warm welcome, and their presence on the island to take provisions went smoothly. With the eventual departure of Cook/Lono from the island, the ritual season of peace was over. Hence, when Cook was forced to go back in order to repair the mast of his ship, this constituted a breach in the local ritual calendar, threatening the cosmological order. In fact, according to Sahlins interpretation, Cook came back in a calendrical time associated with the deity Kū, the god of strangers from which the ruling chiefs descend. Hence the kidnapping of the Hawaiian chief – which ultimately led to Cook's death – was a cosmological confrontation between Lono and Kū which, according to the cosmological order, could not but result in the death of Lono. In Sahlins' structuralist framework, symbols are the stuff of cognitive systems, hence they account for both structure and human agency.[50] Sahlins' structuralist semiotic is ultimately a theory of social change through "working misunderstandings", positing change in terms of a re-

---

48 Kerry K. Howe, "Review *Islands and Beaches. Discourse on a Silent Land: Marquesas 1774–1880* by Greg Dening," *New Zealand Journal of History* 15, no. 2 (1981): 192. For a different take on this portion of the history of the Marquesas Islands see Nicholas Thomas, *Marquesan Societies. Inequality and Policital Transformation in Eastern Polynesia* (Oxford: Clarendon Press, 1990).

49 Aletta Biersack, "Local Knowledge, Local History: Geertz and Beyond," in *The New Cultural History*, ed. Lynn Hunt (Berkeley/Los Angeles/London: University of California Press, 1989), 80. By the word 'web', Biersack is referring to Geertz's famous formulation that "man is an animal suspended in webs of significance he himself has spun"; Geertz, *The Interpretation of Cultures*, 5.

50 See Sahlins, *Historical Metaphors and Mythical Realities*; idem, *Islands of History*.

structuring of the relations among categories constituting a cognitive/cosmological system.[51]

As seen above, Pacific history always courted anthropology for the access it (supposedly) provided to local cultures and societies. At a surface level, the 1980s rapprochement between the two disciplines in Pacific scholarship looked like the encounter of two long-time acquaintances. But anthropological paradigms are not all the same, and often are not compatible with each other, as Hildred Geertz in her polemic against Keith Thomas' use of disparate anthropological theories indicated.[52] In the early days of Pacific history, anthropology mainly catered to the need "to know the social structure of indigenous peoples, the ways in which it changes in contact with Europeans, and the ways in which the European activity *is affected by* indigenous culture and the changes which occur within it".[53] E. P. Thompson, on several occasions, warned against "the wooden taking-over of unprocessed terminology and categories from one favoured school of sociology, and imposing these upon existent historical knowledge", since "the anthropological impulse is chiefly felt (. . .) in locating new problems, in seeing old problems in new ways".[54] What symbolic anthropology enabled Pacific historians to do was to pursue the "old" issue of indigenous agency with different tools, but at the cost of not being able to account for or explore processes occurring over time-spans longer than "first contact", the point of cultural encounter. To borrow Ronald Walters' words in his critique of Geertz, by describing "reality as a drama in which the focus is upon symbolic exchanges, not social consequences" we run the risk "to reinforce the impulse to burrow in and not to try to connect the dots."[55] The issue here is not to substitute the material for the ideal, but to look at the

---

51 Sahlins describes 'working misunderstandings' as "a sort of symbolic serendipity, or at least a congruent attribution from two different cultural orders of a special meaningful value to the same event" Marshall D. Sahlins, " The Apotheosis of Captain Cook," in *Between Belief and Transgression: Structuralist Essays in Religion, History, and Myth*, ed. Michel Izard, and Pierre Smith (Chicago: University of Chicago Press, 1982), 82; originally published as Marshall D. Sahlins, 'L'apothéose Du Capitaine Cook', in *La Fonction Symbolique. Essais d'anthropologie*, ed. Michel Izard, and Pierre Smith (Paris: Gallimard, 1979), 307–39.

52 Hildred Geertz, "An Anthropology of Religion and Magic, I," *The Journal of Interdisciplinary History* 6, no. 1 (1975): 71–89; Keith Thomas, "An Anthropology of Religion and Magic, II," *The Journal of Interdisciplinary History* 6, no. 1 (1975): 91–109.

53 Francis James West, "The Study of Colonial History," *Journal of Southeast Asian History* 2, no. 3 (1961): 73 (my italics).

54 The quotes are respectively from E. P. Thompson, "History from Below," *Times Literary Supplement*, 7 April 1966, 280 and E. P. Thompson, "Folklore, Anthropology and Social History," *Indian Historical Review* 3, no. 2 (1978): 248.

55 Ronald G. Walters, "Signs of the Time: Clifford Geertz and the Historians," *Social Research* 47, no. 3 (1987): 553, 551.

interplay of the two. In works such as Dening's or Sahlins' we find (authors' caveats notwithstanding) the dramatised encounter of two largely homogenous cultural universes, the local and the foreign. In this vein, conflict took place only between these two cultural worlds, thus obscuring internal fractures and interests within each. As many scholars have noted, the rapprochement between history and anthropology entailed a selective engagement with symbolic anthropology at the expense of other approaches that took into account conflicts and power relations in the production of 'culture'.[56] One of the consequences of such erasure of internal articulations in favour of homogenous cultural universes was that, in Pacific History and more so for Pacific Studies (as we shall see below), 'culture' has become the main category of analysis to understand the unfolding of local histories.[57]

5.5 Identity with the Politics Left Out

If Pacific history grew out of the early phase of the region's decolonisation, soon yet another shift in perspective was called for; from island-centred to islander-centred history. With the formal independence of Pacific Island countries and the growth of the tertiary education system, Islander scholars voiced their discomfort with the emphasis on the colonial period in Pacific history and began to question their own marginal places within the field. As new nation-states were emerging from a long period of European domination of the educational sector, their intellectuals stressed that "History, thus, has a therapeutic role to play in promoting the rehabilitation of Pacific peoples because it restores their confidence and self-respect (. . .). This psychological value of history should not be under-rated", especially since "it will produce a comforting sense of identity, especially if *we are not sure of our place in a changing world*".[58] This view was also held by European

---

56 For a critical appraisal of the influence of Geerz, Sahlins and other anthropologists working in the symbolic tradition (notably Mary Douglas and Victor Turner) in shaping the dialogue between history and anthropology see Biersack, "Local Knowledge, Local History"; Nicholas B. Dirks, "Is Vice Versa? Historical Anthropologies and Anthropological Histories," in *The Historic Turn in the Human Sciences*, ed. Terence J. McDonald (Ann Arbor: The University of Michigan Press, 1996), 17–51; William Roseberry, "The Unbereable Lightness of Anthropology," *Radical History Review* 65, no. 5 (1996): 5–25.
57 For a discussion of this in reference to Pacific history see Dario Di Rosa, "*Microstoria*, Pacific History, and the Question of Scale: Two or Three Things That We Should Know About Them," *The Journal of Pacific History* 53, no. 1 (2018): esp. 37–39.
58 Sister Mary Stella, Asesela Ravuvu, and Raymond Pillai, "Pacific History and National Integrity," *Pacific Perspective* 1, no. 2 (1973): 2–3 (my italics).

scholars, especially by Ron Crocombe at the University of the South Pacific, who did much to promote Islanders' history-writing

> Perhaps the greatest value of all these studies is basically psychological, for they not only give confidence and experience to the writers, they also give confidence to the readers [. . .] to know themselves better, to know that their own kind can do what they had thought could only be done by foreigners, to face the world more effectively.[59]

The stress on healing and recovering from what Franz Fanon and others saw as the psychological injuries of colonialism is not surprising at the time of and immediately after political independence. But the meaning of similar statements voiced since the 1990s has to be framed within a novel political, social, and economic context.

The insider/outsider dichotomy turned into a fracture widening with the passing years. In institutional memory, the 1996 Pacific History Association conference held at Hilo (Hawaii) constitutes the peak of such fracture. This intellectual venue was "split down the middle between an old guard of traditionalists and a new wave of post-modernists and/or Islanders".[60] The new hiatus eventually became entrenched in the creation and growth of Pacific Studies, an outlet that diverted indigenous intellectual energies away from Pacific history. Pacific Studies' interdisciplinarity was better suited to deal with contemporary issues and the more recent past. Pacific history, with its focus on the early period of colonialism, struggled to satisfy those. The past, that "scarce resource" as Arjun Appadurai aptly qualified it,[61] remained at the centre of scholarly and political contestation; history, as discipline, could not claim any monopoly over it.[62]

The stakes of the managing and control of the representation of the past can be grasped by looking at the heated scholarly debates over the "invention of tradition" predominant in the 1980s and 1990s.[63] Especially in ethnically plural

---

59 Ron Crocombe, "Pacific History: Perceptions from Within," *Pacific History Association Newsletter*, no. 12 (1984): 5.

60 Lal and Munro, "The Text in Its Context: An Introduction," 4.

61 Arjun Appadurai, "The Past as a Scarce Resource," *Man* 16, no. 2 (1981): 201–19.

62 Writing about the Hilo conference, Berrie Macdonald made the following comment: "Although in many senses, this was a Pacific Studies rather than Pacific history conference, the primary unifier was *history*, a perspective of, and interest in, the past", "'Now an Island Is Too Big': Limits and Limitations of Pacific Islands History," *Pacific Studies* 20 (1996): 26 (italics in original).

63 Roger M. Keesing, and Robert Tonkinson, eds., "Reinventing Traditional Culture: The Politics of Kastom in Island Melanesia (Special Issue)," *Mankind* 13, no. 4 (1982). A wealth of articles appeared in response to this special issue, which predates Hobsbawm and Ranger's more famous book *The Invention of Tradition* (Cambridge: Cambridge University Press, 1983); listing them all would take too much space but see Margaret Jolly, "Specters of Inauthenticity," *The Contempo-*

states, reference to "traditional culture" as source of a shared identity became a key political symbol to foster a sense of national unity. Anthropologist Roger Keesing has shown in several publications the process of reification of "culture" during the colonial period, and has argued that such recent construction of tradition has been deployed by indigenous elites to promote cultural nationalism.[64] Keesing alerted his audience to the phenomenon that "discourses of cultural identity in the contemporary Pacific, although they depict the precolonial past and claim to produce countercolonial images, are in many ways derived from Western ideologies", further observing that "those in the Pacific who in their rhetorical moments espouse these idealised views of the past are mainly (in their political actions and life-styles) hell-bent on technology, progress, materialism, and 'development'".[65] Hawaiian scholar and activist Haunani-Kay Trask wrote a bitter response to what she considered "a gem of academic colonialism".[66] Trask inscribed Keesing in what she sees as a long tradition of anthropologists who "seek to take away from us the power to define who and what we are, and how we should behave politically and culturally".[67] Keesing replied to this attack saying that "The stark 'insider' versus 'outsider' dichotomy (. . .) strikes me as a great leap backward in what purports to be radical discourse", insisting on his point:

> "The battle lines in the contemporary Pacific have more to do with issues of class and interest (. . .) than with issues of culture or skin color; in fact, cultural nationalist rhetoric is increasingly deployed by Pacific elites to camouflage these issues of power and interest".[68]

This episode draws attention to internal fractures within the "indigenous Pacific"; while Keesing articulated his analysis from the vantage point of his long

---

rary Pacific 4, no. 1 (1992): 49–72; Jonathan Friedman, "Will The Real Hawaiian Please Stand: Anthropologists and Natives in the Global Struggle for Identity," *Bijdragen Tot de Taal-, Land- En Volkenkunde* 149, no. 4 (1993): 737–67.

64 Roger M. Keesing, "Creating the Past: Custom and Identity in the Contemporary Pacific," *The Contemporary Pacific* 1, no. 1/2 (1989): 19–42; "Colonial and Counter-Colonial Discourse in Melanesia," *Critique of Anthropology* 14, no. 1 (1994): 41–58; "Class, Culture, Custom," in *Melanesian Modernities*, ed. Jonathan Friedman, and James G. Carrier (Lund: Lund University Press, 1996), 162–82. Keesing has also penned pungent critiques of depictions of cultures as well-ordered symbolic systems; see "Conventional Metaphors and Anthropological Metaphysics: The Problematic of Cultural Translation," *Journal of Anthropological Research* 41, no. 2 (1985): 201–17; "Anthropology as Interpretive Quest [and Comments and Reply]," *Current Anthropology* 28, no. 2 (1987): 161–76.

65 Keesing, "Creating the Past," 22, 23.

66 Haunani-Kay Trask, "Natives and Anthropologists: The Colonial Struggle," *The Contemporary Pacific* 3, no. 1 (1991): 159.

67 Trask, "Natives and Anthropologists," 162.

68 Roger M. Keesing, "Reply to Trask," *The Contemporary Pacific* 3, no. 1 (1991): 168.

5 Indigenous History from Below? Problems and Perspectives from the Pacific — **129**

engagement with the Solomon Islands, an independent nation-state, Trask composed her critique from Hawaii where *kanaka maoli* (indigenous Hawaiians) live effectively under US domination. Claims of pan-Pacific identity obscure the different legal, political, and economic structures that characterise settler colonial societies and former colonies. Moreover, such claims downplay the existing tensions between Melanesia and Polynesia.[69] The differential impact of different politico-economic structures on the politics of decolonisation can perhaps be best appreciated by Brij Lal's recollection of the time when, while working at the University of Hawai'i, he conducted seminars on the 1987 coup in Fiji. Following the victory of a multi-ethnic Labour coalition, which ended a two-decade-long period of indigenous conservative government, Lieutenant Colonel Stiveni Rabuka ousted the elected Prime Minister and seized power with a military coup. By 1990 a new constitution was ratified, assigning a large majority of seats both in the Senate and in the House of Representative to iTaukei (indigenous Fijians).[70] Yet, Lal recalls, "My graduate students (. . .) were adamant that what happened in Fiji was just and necessary, a struggle for indigenous rights against the political and economic dominance of an immigrant majority".[71] This "immigrant majority" was composed of descendants of Indian indentured labourers who had moved there to work on sugar plantations, a measure made necessary by the colonial policy of protection of iTaukei "traditional" culture.[72] Clearly, for Lal's graduate students, belonging to the Pacific is a matter of *ius sanguinis* rather than *ius soli*.

Political exclusivism is not the only outcome of the erasure of difference by means of appeals to the past in the form of "traditional culture"; the notion of class –

---

69 Postcolonial discourses such as "the Pacific Way" or "the Melanesian Way" perform a similar role of suppression of class differences and especially conflict. For instance, Michael C. Howard has shown how Walter Lini, a prominent figure in Vanuatu's independence who became the country's first Prime Minister, has used the notion of a conflict-free Melanesian socialism (a permutation of the Melanesian and Pacific Ways) to suppress workers' demands, "Vanuatu: The Myth of Melanesian Socialism," *Labour, Capital and Society / Travail, Capital et Société* 16, no. 2 (1983): 176–203. A critical take on the Pacific Way and the Melanesian Way can be found in Lawson, "'The Pacific Way' as Postcolonial Discourse' and '"Melanesia: The History and Politics of an Idea'," *The Journal of Pacific History* 48, no. 1 (2013): 1–22.
70 Lal was a member of the Fiji Constitution Review Commission (1995–1996) which revised the 1990 Constitution. Along with Davidson, and Alan Ward, Lal is part of a small but significant tradition of "participant historians" who engaged in constitutional and policy matters: see Peter Hempenstall, "Tasman Epiphanies: The 'Participant History' of Alan Ward," *Journal of New Zealand Studies* 4–5 (2005–2006): 65–80; Munro, *The Ivory Tower and Beyond*.
71 Brij V. Lal, "From Across the Horizon: Reflections on a Sojourn in Hawai'I," *The Journal of Pacific Studies* 20 (1996): 235.
72 See Brij V. Lal, *Broken Waves: A History of the Fiji Islands in the Twentieth Century* (Honolulu: University of Hawaii Press, 1992).

130 —— Dario Di Rosa

and indeed its analysis – is another "victim". For instance, as Colin Filer has convincingly argued, from the late 1980s, in Papua New Guinea, demands for compensation for land use associated with natural resources' exploitation by foreign companies – claims made possible by a legislation that recognises "customary landownership" – have been often exploited by an emerging class of landowners who accumulate capital in the form of rent, and "whose consumption of the proceeds may or may not leave a surplus which may [. . .] pay the price of their admission to the accumulation strategies of an existing "national bourgeoisie" – most commonly through the purchase of urban real estate or the formation of 'joint ventures' with foreign entrepreneurs".[73] The ideological role of appeals to "culture" is readily evident in the ways in which the category of "landowner" is constructed. In Filer's words:

> The growth of public debate about resource compensation is intricately linked with the development of "landownership" as the principal vehicle of national populism. Once released from their colonial subjection, Papua New Guineans (or "Melanesians") have been learning to think of themselves as people who are distinguished from other nations or races by their singular physical and emotional relationship to "the land" which all of them possess. The "automatic citizen" who has no customary land rights is a contradiction whose existence cannot be admitted.[74]

Filer here is making reference to what has become known as "the Melanesian Way", a turn of phrase coined by Papua New Guinean jurist and politician Bernard Narokobi. On the eve of Papua New Guinean independence, Narokobi contributed to the emerging national debate from the columns of the newspaper *Post-Courier*, articulating a discourse that attempted to balance "tradition" and "modernity" as a way to navigate the country's future when Australian rule ended.[75] Narokobi's intellectual endeavour was nothing unusual among intellectuals from nation-states emerging from the process of decolonisation; indeed, one could easily justify his claims to a "Melanesian" exceptionalism as a simple overcorrection of the colonial negative rep-

---

73 Colin Filer, "Compensation, Rent and Power in Papua New Guinea," in *Compensation for Resource Development in Papua New Guinea*, ed. Susan Toft (Boroko: Law Reform Commission, Monograph 6, Canberra: Australian National University, and National Centre for Development Studies, Pacific Policy Paper 24), 171. See also Rebecca Monson, *Gender, Property and Politics in the Pacific: Who Speaks for Land?* (Cambridge: Cambridge University Press, 2023).
74 Filer, "Compensation, Rent and Power," 165.
75 Narokobi's articles, along with some of the resposes they elicitated, have been collected in Bernard Narokobi, *The Melanesian Way. Total Cosmic Vision of Life / Bernard Narokobi, and His Critics and Supporters* (Boroko: Institute of Papua New Guinea Studies, 1980). A recent issue of the *Journal of Pacific History* (vol. 55, no. 2, 2020) dedicated to "The Legacy of Bernard Narokobi and the Melanesian Way" has substantially celebrated the role played by "culture" in Narokobi's oeuvre; see *Journal of Pacific History* 55 (2020).

5 Indigenous History from Below? Problems and Perspectives from the Pacific — 131

resentations of Papua New Guineans. Yet, the long-term consequences of such an exceptionalism rooted in "culture" become evident when we consider that

> "[t]he identification of 'the people' as (customary) 'landowners' is also the flipside denial that there is such a thing as 'poverty' or 'peasantry' in Papua New Guinea. It is because 'we' are all petty landlords that we can neither be peasants nor be poor", and thus transforming "Papua New Guinea, [. . .] once a nation of gardeners, [. . . into] a nation of gatekeepers and rentcollectors – or at least a nation of female gardeners and male rentcollectors."[76]

The link between decolonisation and control over the past has less dramatic, but not less profound, effects on historical scholarship. The political implications are evoked rather than stated. For example, in his scathing review of the 1997 edition of *The Cambridge History of the Pacific Islanders*, Terence Wesley-Smith correctly notes that "the transfer of formal constitutional authority had done little to liberate the islands from imposed economic and political structures, structures which did not appear to serve the material and cultural interests of ordinary Islanders particularly well".[77] Such a statement, though, sits uncomfortably with how he perceives the decolonisation project in relation to history-making. According to Wesley-Smith "The colonial nature of Pacific history lies not so much in the ethnicity of its authors (. . .) as in the larger narratives that frame and inform their work".[78] Hence, the solutions he proposes for truly decolonising Pacific history are either a) "to abandon 'history' as it is usually conceived in western academic institutions in favour of reconstructing or preserving indigenous genres of representing Pacific pasts", b) to unsettle the historian's authorship as Klaus Neumann did for the Tolai people's past , or c), as Epeli Hau'Ofa indicated, to allow indigenous people to "regain control of representations of the peoples and cul-

---

76 Filer, "Compensation, Rent and Power," 165, 171. On the use of another key signifier of "culture" in Papua New Guinea as a prism to articulate hopes and anxieties about the balancing images of"tradition"with capitalist relations and aspirations, see Colin Filer, "What is This Thing Called 'Bridgeprice'?," *Manikind* 15, no. 2 (1985): 163–83.

77 Terence Wesley-Smith, "Historiography of the Pacific: The Case of The Cambridge History," *Race & Class* 41, no. 4 (2000): 105; Donald Denoon et al., eds., *The Cambridge History of the Pacific Islanders* (Cambridge: Cambridge University Press, 1997).

78 Wesley-Smith, "Historiography of the Pacific: The Case of The Cambridge History," 112. A statement which allows him to pronounce the following on the Indigenous scholars' contributions to the volume: "for the most part, it is difficult to identify in these contributions approaches, perspectives or interpretations that are distinctively 'indigenous' in that they could only have been produced by individuals intimately connected to island cultures, cosmologies and ways of life. Rather than subvert the narratives produced by expatriate authors (. . .) these inserted island voices serve instead to legitimise and reinforce the dominant discourse" Wesley-Smith, "Historiography of the Pacific," 106.

tures of Oceania".[79] How any of these shifts should affect the "imposed economic and political structures" is not spelled out, nor is it easy to envision.

Most recently, Marcia Leenen-Young lamented the absence of Pacific voices (read "authors") in historical scholarship in general, and history-teaching in Aotearoa-New Zealand more specifically.[80] The appeal to redress the imbalance is grounded in notions of cultural specificity and indigenous epistemologies and ontologies:

> No matter the intentions, perspectives, exposure to Indigenous communities, or allyship of Pālāgi [white], they are still not writing *from the perspective of a Pacific person. Our worldviews* are infused and influenced by many things, especially in the diaspora, but *our cultural values* and positionalities guide us in unique ways.[81]

Despite the declining of "Pacific voices" in the plural, the notion of an indigenous Pacific remains firmly singular. It would be easy to dismiss issues of "ownership" over history by declaring oneself against private property. Yet, precisely because these scholarly issues have ramifications that branch out in Pacific societies, forming an entrenched ideology of Pacific exceptionalism, I find it necessary to engage with them. History, not as a discipline but as a practice, is a powerful form of cultural capital that can be invested and transformed into social, political, and economic capital. In this regard, the Pacific is not an exception.[82] For instance, looking back at their attempt to publish a bilingual history of Samoa, Malama Meleisea and Penelope Schoeffel had direct experience of coming face to face with "how contentious history and written descriptions of past events can be

---

79 Wesley-Smith, "Historiography of the Pacific," 113–14; Klaus Neumann, *Not the Way It Really Was: Constructing the Tolai Past* (Honolulu: University of Hawaii Press, 1992); Epeli Hau'ofa, "Epilogue: Pasts to Remember," in *Remembrance of Pacific Pasts: An Invitation to Remake History*, ed. Robert Borofsky (Honolulu: University of Hawaii Press, 2000), 453–71.

80 Mainly she criticises *The Journal of Pacific History* for its lack of Indigenous authors, though the very criteria of her analysis (confined to the 2015–2020 period, and not including all sections of the journal) leave her analysis open to criticism. Moreover, the more fundamental question of whether the lack of Pacific voices is due to the journal rejecting Indigenous scholarship or to low numbers of submissions by Pacific Islanders (who might choose other publishing outlets, especially associated with Pacific Studies) is not considered. Marcia Leenen-Young, "'Guardians' of Signatures? Future Directions in Pacific History from a Pacific Early Career Academic in Aotearoa," *The Journal of New Zealand Studies*, no. NS33 (2021), https://doi.org/10.26686/jnzs.iNS33.7381.

81 Leenen-Young, "'Guardians' of Signatures?," 41.

82 This is the framework I adopted for my doctoral dissertation, to include in the historical narrative of Kerewo speakers' colonial past the various contemporary issues my interlocutors in the field were facing, trying to make sense of them precisely referring to the past. See Dario Di Rosa, "Frustrated Modernity: Kerewo Histories and Historical Consciousness, Gulf Province, Papua New Guinea" (PhD diss., Canberra, Australian National University, 2018).

in small countries". "There are places where 'people's history' is all very well, but a bigger question is who wrote the history, and from whose point of view".[83] Clearly there is no unitary "indigenous point of view" within a single national territory, let alone the whole region.

Perceptively, Meleisea and Schoeffel link postcolonial anxieties about identity to the diaspora, creating a dissonance about the perception of the past: "While Samoans have consciously or unconsciously embraced religious, economic, and social changes of the past 200 years, more recent changes resulting from emigration have provoked a particular fixation on cultural identity as well as fears about culture and language loss",[84] projecting onto their home country "a nostalgic utopian space (. . .) the site of authentic and properly enacted cultural knowledge".[85] What is left out from the picture painted by postcolonial (or nativist) scholars, is the very politico-economic structure that makes migration not quite a matter of free personal choice.

5.6 Conclusions

Has Pacific history ever been a form of history from below? In his 1966 article, Thompson wrote "the history of the 'common people' has always been something other than – and distinct from – English History Proper. (. . .) In *English* History Proper *the people of this island* (. . .) appear as one of the problems Government has had to handle", adding that "until recently, '*Labour History*' has been defined by its antagonism to this orthodoxy".[86] If we replace the italicised passages respectively with "imperial", "Pacific islanders", and "Pacific history", then we must answer in the affirmative. But approaching this question in this way, in my view, holds value at the historiographical level. Samuel was conscious that "People's history, whatever its particular subject matter, is shaped in the crucible of politics, and penetrated by the influence of ideology on all sides. In one version it is allied with Marxism, in another with democratic liberalism, in yet another with cultural nationalism, and (. . .) the Left can make no proprietorial claim to it".[87]

---

83 Malama Meleisea and Penelope Schoeffel, "Forty-Five Years of Pacific Island Studies: Some Reflections," *Oceania* 87, no. 3 (2017): 338.

84 Meleisea and Schoeffel, "Forty-Five Years of Pacific Island Studies," 339.

85 Ilana Gershon, *No Family Is an Island: Cultural Expertise among Samoans in Diaspora* (Ithaca/London: Cornell University Press, 2012), 17; cited in Meleisea and Schoeffel, "Forty-Five Years of Pacific Island Studies," 339.

86 Thompson, "History from Below," 279.

87 Samuel, "People's History," xx.

Pacific history – as an instance of history from below – was born out of democratic liberalism and soon coopted by, if not cultural nationalism, then by culturalism.[88] Indeed, as Durutalo noted almost four decades ago, "the majority of our people are taken in by the official commitment of all island countries to parliamentary democracy, despite the underlying reality of oligarchic privileges. (. . .) democracy in the islands is an illusion for the majority" and the "islanders who are resigned to misery must be given the reality – the economic reality of democracy".[89] This statement still rings true today. One of the main tenets of the socialist tradition of "history from below" was the notion that it is people who make history. It is here that the change in historiographical point of view intersects with an emancipatory project that goes beyond the university.

Can such perspectives be integrated into Pacific history? There is no way to answer that question on an ideal level but only through practice, by trial and error. I am convinced that while a Marxist approach (dare I say historical materialism?) could surely enrich Pacific historiography, I also believe that a serious and non-doctrinal engagement with the Pacific region's past and present is going to present a challenge to Marxist categories of analysis. From the standpoint of the two pillars of global capitalism, production and consumption, the Pacific constitutes a fairly limited basin. The very structure of the political-economy of the region has not allowed the formation of a significant working-class or peasantry. This, though, does not mean that class relations do not exist in the region, but simply that we need to craft heuristic tools to appreciate how capitalism has configured the region and how it impacted people's lives. A starting point to reckon with the complexity of the task at hand can be appreciated from Meleisea's autobiographical piece. It is worth quoting at length. After receiving his degree at the University of Papua New Guinea:

> I returned to my village and tried to see it through new eyes, through my new understanding. I looked for our emerging class system. [. . .] So where was the revolution to begin? I concluded that it had begun years before I acquired my analytical understanding and critical perspective. What was the nature of this revolution? Fundamentally *it was a revolution of aspirations*. People wanted [. . .] all the other things taken for granted in New Zealand and the United States. But they also wanted the certainties of *fa'a Samoa* [the Samoan way], its dignity, order and cohesion. The two sets of aspirations seemed to contradict each other.[90]

---

88 As I see it, postcolonialism has inherited one of the unresolved tensions within twentieth century Marxism, namely the relationship between "the national question" in colonial contexts and the internationalism of working class emancipatory politics.

89 Durutalo, "The Liberation of the Pacific Island Intellectual," 13.

90 Malama Meleisea, "Ideology in Pacific Studies: A Personal View," in *Class and Culture in the South Pacific*, ed. Antony Hooper (Auckland /Suva: Centre for Pacific Studies, University of Auckland, and Institute of Pacific Studies, University of the South Pacific, 1987), 146–47 (my italics).

This words strongly resonate with the preoccupations that Kerewo-speakers shared with me during my period of fieldwork, which I tried to capture with the expression "frustrated modernity".[91] People were seeking answers in their past to the question as to why the modernity sought by so many colonial projects, for which their ancestors underwent drastic social and cultural changes, has not brought about its promised fruits. If those concerns were expressed in culturally specific idioms, they also voiced a predicament known to all those who fall short of the promised riches of capitalism; indeed they capture key contradictions in capitalist ideology and structure. One of the chief lessons to be drawn from Thompson's socialist humanism is that indissoluble interplay between – to use terms now out of fashion – the ideal and the material that moves the very people who make history.

References

Appadurai, Arjun. "The Past as a Scarce Resource." *Man* 16, no. 2 (1981): 201–219.
Biersack, Aletta. "Local Knowledge, Local History: Geertz and Beyond." In *The New Cultural History*, edited by Lynn Hunt, 72–96. Berkeley – Los Angeles – London: University of California Press, 1989.
Brass, Tom. "Contextualizing Sugar Production in Nineteenth-century Queensland." *Slavery & Abolition* 15, no. 1 (1 April 1994): 100–117. https://doi.org/10.1080/01440399408575118.
Campbell, Ian C. "More Celebrated than Read: The Work of Norma McArthur." In *Texts and Contexts: Reflections in Pacific Islands Historiography*, edited by Doug Munro, and Brij V. Lal, 98–110. Honolulu: University of Hawaii Press, 2006.
Carrier, James C., ed. *History and Tradition in Melanesian Anthropology*. Berkeley – Los Angeles – Oxford: University of California Press, 1992.
Chappell, David A. "Active Agents versus Passive Victims: Decolonized Historiography or Problematic Paradigm?" *The Contemporary Pacific* 7 (1995): 303–326.
Cohn, Bernard S. "Toward a Rapprochement." *The Journal of Interdisciplinary History* 12, no. 2 (1981): 227–252.
Corris, Peter. *Passage, Port and Plantation: A History of Solomon Islands Labour Migration, 1870–1914*. Carlton: Melbourne University Press, 1973.
Crocombe, Ron. "Pacific History: Perceptions from Within." *Pacific History Association Newsletter*, no. 12 (1984): 1–9.
Davidson, J. W. "Problems of Pacific History." *The Journal of Pacific History* 1 (1966): 5–21.
Davidson, J. W. *The Study of Pacific History: An Inaugural Lecture Delivered at Canberra on 25 November 1954*. Canberra: Australian National University, 1955.

---

91 Di Rosa, „Frustrated Modernity: Kerewo Histories and Historical Consciousness, Gulf Province (Papua New Guinea" (PhD diss., Canberra: Australian National University, 2018).

Davidson, J. W. "Understanding Pacific History: The Participant as Historian." In *The History of Melanesia: Second Waigani Seminar*, edited by Research School of Pacific Studies, 1–15. Canberra/Port Moresby: Australian National University/The University of Papua New Guinea, 1969.

Daws, Gavan. "On Being a Historian of the Pacific." In *Historical Disciplines and Culture in Australasia: An Assessment*, edited by John A. Moses, 119–129. St Lucia: University Of Queensland Press, 1979.

Dening, Greg. *Islands and Beaches: Discourse on a Silent Land : Marquesas, 1774–1880*. Melbourne: Melbourne University Press, 1980.

Denoon, Donald. *People's History*. Inaugural Lecture. Boroko, P.N.G.: University of Papua New Guinea, 1973.

Denoon, Donald, Stewart Firth, Jocelyn Linnekin, Malama Meleisea, and Karen Nero, eds. *The Cambridge History of the Pacific Islanders*. Cambridge: Cambridge University Press, 1997.

Di Rosa, Dario. "Frustrated Modernity: Kerewo Histories and Historical Consciousness, Gulf Province, Papua New Guinea." PhD diss., Australian National University, 2018.

Di Rosa, Dario. "Microstoria, Pacific History, and the Question of Scale: Two or Three Things That We Should Know About Them." *The Journal of Pacific History* 53, no. 1 (2018): 25–43.

Dirks, Nicholas B. "Is Vice Versa? Historical Anthropologies and Anthropological Histories' Terence." In *The Historic Turn in the Human Sciences*, edited by J. McDonald, 17–51. Ann Arbor: The University of Michigan Press, 1996.

Douglas, Bronwen. "Doing Ethnographic History: Reflection on Practices and Practising." In *Pacific Islands History: Journeys and Transformations*, edited by Brij V. Lal, 92–106. Canberra: The Journal of Pacific History, 1992.

Durutalo, Simione. "Bucaneers and Chiefly Historians." *Journal of Pacific Studies* 11 (1985): 117–156.

Durutalo, Simione. "The Liberation of the Pacific Island Intellectual." *Review* 4, no. 10 (1983): 6–18.

Hobsbawm, Eric, and Terence Ranger, eds. *The Invention of Tradition*. Cambridge: Cambridge University Press, 1983.

Filer, Colin. "What is This Thing Called 'Bridgeprice'?" *Manikind* 15, no. 2 (1985): 163–183.

Filer, Colin. "Compensation, rent and power in Papua New Guinea." In *Compensation for Resource Development in Papua New Guinea*, edited by Susan Toft, 156–189. Boroko: Law Reform Commission, Monograph 6, Australian National University, National Centre for Development Studies, Pacific Policy Paper 24, Canberra.

Friedman, Jonathan. "Will The Real Hawaiian Pleas Stand: Anthropologists and Natives in the Global Struggle for Identity." *Bijdragen Tot de Taal-, Land- En Volkenkunde* 149, no. 4 (1993): 737–767.

Geertz, Clifford. "History and Anthropology." *New Literary History* 21, no. 2 (1990): 321–335. https://doi.org/10.2307/469255.

Geertz, Clifford. *The Interpretation of Cultures* (New York: Basic Books, 1973).

Geertz, Hildred. "An Anthropology of Religion and Magic, I." *The Journal of Interdisciplinary History* 6, no. 1 (1 July 1975): 71–89. https://doi.org/10.2307/202825.

Gershon, Ilana. *No Family Is an Island: Cultural Expertise among Samoans in Diaspora*. Ithaca – London: Cornell University Press, 2012.

Graves, Adrian. *Cane and Labour: The Political Economy of the Queensland Sugar Industry, 1862–1906*. Edinburgh: Edinburgh University Press, 1993.

Graves, Adrian. "Truck and Gifts: Melanesian Immigrants and the Trade Box System in Colonial Queensland." *Past & Present*, no. 101 (1983): 87–124.

Guha, Ranajit. "The Prose of Counter-Insurgency." In *Selected Subaltern Studies*, edited by Ranajit Guha and Gayatri Chakravorty Spivak, 45–86. New York – Oxford: Oxford University Press, 1988.

Hau'ofa, Epeli. "Epilogue: Pasts to Remember." In *Remembrance of Pacific Pasts: An Invitation to Remake History*, edited by Robert Borofsky, 453–471. Honolulu: University of Hawaii Press, 2000.

5 Indigenous History from Below? Problems and Perspectives from the Pacific —— **137**

Hempenstall, Peter. "Tasman Epiphanies: The 'Participant History' of Alan Ward." *Journal of New Zealand Studies* 4–5 (2006, 2005): 65–80.

Hobsbawm, E. J. "From Social History to the History of Society." *Daedalus* 100, no. 1 (1971): 20–45.

Howard, Michael C. "Vanuatu: The Myth of Melanesian Socialism." *Labour, Capital and Society / Travail, Capital et Société* 16, no. 2 (1983): 176–203.

Howe, Kerry R. *Where the Waves Fall: A New South Sea Islands History from First Settlement to Colonial Rule*. Pacific Islands Monograph Series, no. 2. Honolulu: University of Hawaii Press, 1984.

Howe, Kerry R. "Review Islands and Beaches. Discourse on a Silent Land: Marquesas 1774–1880 by Greg Dening." *New Zealand Journal of History* 15 (1981): 190–194.

Howe, Kerry R. "Pacific Islands History in the 1980s: New Directions or Monograph Myopia?" *Pacific Studies* 3, no. 1 (1 November 1979): 81–90.

Howe, Kerry R. "The Fate of the 'Savage' in Pacific Historiography." *The New Zealand Journal of History* 11, no. 2 (1977): 137–154.

Isaac, Rhys. "Ethnographic Methods in History: An Action Approach." *Historical Methods* 13, no. 1 (1980): 43–61.

Jolly, Margaret. "Specters of Inauthenticity." *The Contemporary Pacific* 4, no. 1 (1992): 49–72.

Keesing, Roger M. "Anthropology as Interpretive Quest [and Comments and Reply]." *Current Anthropology* 28, no. 2 (1987): 161–176.

Keesing, Roger M. "Class, Culture, Custom." In *Melanesian Modernities*, edited by Jonathan Friedman, and James G. Carrier, 162–182. Lund: Lund University Press, 1996.

Keesing, Roger M. "Colonial and Counter-Colonial Discourse in Melanesia." *Critique of Anthropology* 14, no. 1 (1 March 1994): 41–58. https://doi.org/10.1177/0308275X9401400103.

Keesing, Roger M. "Conventional Metaphors and Anthropological Metaphysics: The Problematic of Cultural Translation." *Journal of Anthropological Research* 41, no. 2 (1985): 201–217.

Keesing, Roger M. "Creating the Past: Custom and Identity in the Contemporary Pacific." *The Contemporary Pacific* 1, no. 1/2 (1989): 19–42.

Keesing, Roger M. "Politico-Religious Movements and Anticolonialism on Malaita: Maasina Rule in Historical Perspective." *Oceania* 48, no. 4 (1978): 241–261.

Keesing, Roger M. "Reply to Trask." *The Contemporary Pacific* 3, no. 1 (1991): 168–171.

Keesing, Roger M., and Robert Tonkinson, eds. "Reinventing Traditional Culture: The Politics of Kastom in Island Melanesia (Special Issue)." *Mankind* 13, no. 4 (1982).

Lal, Brij V. "From Across the Horizon: Reflections on a Sojourn in Hawai'i'." *The Journal of Pacific Studies* 20 (1996): 244–237.

Lal, Brij V., and Doug Munro. "The Text in Its Context: An Introduction." In *Texts and Contexts: Reflections in Pacific Islands Historiography*, edited by Doug Munro, and Brij V. Lal, 1–14. Honolulu: University of Hawaii Press, 2006.

Lawson, Stephanie. "'Melanesia': The History and Politics of an Idea." *The Journal of Pacific History* 48, no. 1 (2013): 1–22.

Lawson, Stephanie. "'The Pacific Way' as Postcolonial Discourse: Toward a Reassessment." *The Journal of Pacific History* 45, no. 3 (2010): 297–314.

Leckie, Jacqueline. "Crossing the Boundaries – Labour Migration in the Eastern Pacific." In *Messy Entanglements: The Papers of the 10th Pacific History Association Conference*, edited by Alaima Talu, and Max Quanchi, 141–147. Brisbane: Pacific History Association, 1995.

Leckie, Jacqueline. "Toward a Review of History in the South Pacific." *The Journal of Pacific Studies* 9 (1983): 9–69.

Leenen-Young, Marcia. "'Guardians' of Signatures? Future Directions in Pacific History from a Pacific Early Career Academic in Aotearoa." *The Journal of New Zealand Studies*, no. NS33 (14 December 2021). https://doi.org/10.26686/jnzs.iNS33.7381.

Macdonald, Berrie. "'Now an Island Is Too Big': Limits and Limitations of Pacific Islands History." *Pacific Studies* 20 (1996): 23–44.

Malinowski, Branislaw. *Argonauts of the Western Pacific: An Account of Native Enterprise and Adventure in the Archipelagoes of Melanesian New Guinea*. London: Routledge and Kegan Paul, 1922.

Maude, H. E. "The Swords of Gabriel: A Study in Participant History." *The Journal of Pacific History* 2 (1967): 113–136.

Meleisea, Malama. "Ideology in Pacific Studies: A Personal View." In *Class and Culture in the South Pacific*, edited by Antony Hooper, 140–152. Auckland – Suva: Centre for Pacific Studies, University of Auckland, and Institute of Pacific Studies, University of the South Pacific, 1987.

Meleisea, Malama, and Penelope Schoeffel. "Forty-Five Years of Pacific Island Studies: Some Reflections." *Oceania* 87, no. 3 (2017): 337–343. https://doi.org/10.1002/ocea.5166.

Monson, Rebecca. *Gender, Property and Politics in the Pacific: Who Speaks for Land?*. Cambridge: Cambridge University Press, 2023.

Moorehead, Alan. *The Fatal Impact: An Account of the Invasion of the South Pacific, 1767–1840*. [1st ed.]. New York: Harper & Row, 1966.

Munro, Doug. 'Labour Trade Studies: What and Where?' In *Messy Entanglements: The Papers of the 10th Pacific History Association Conference*, edited by Alaima Talu, and Max Quanchi, 131–139. Brisbane: Pacific History Association, 1995.

Munro, Doug. 'Review Article: Revisionism and Its Enemies: Debating the Queensland Labour Trade'. *The Journal of Pacific History* 30, no. 2 (1 December 1995): 240–249. https://doi.org/10.1080/00223349508572798.

Munro, Doug. *The Ivory Tower and Beyond: Participant Historians of the Pacific*. New Castle upon Tyne: Cambridge Scholars Publishing, 2009.

Munro, Doug. "The Labor Trade in Melanesians to Queensland: An Historiographic Essay". *Journal of Social History* 28, no. 3 (1995): 609–627.

Munro, Doug, and Brij V. Lal, eds. *Texts and Contexts: Reflections in Pacific Islands Historiography*. Honolulu: University of Hawaii Press, 2006.

Neumann, Klaus. *Not the Way It Really Was: Constructing the Tolai Past*. Honolulu: University of Hawaii Press, 1992.

Palmer, Bryan D. "Reasoning Rebellion: E.P. Thompson, British Marxist Historians, and the Making of Dissident Political Mobilization." *Labour/Le Travail* 50, no. Fall (2002): 187–216.

Philipp, June. "Traditional Historical Narrative and Action-Oriented (or Ethnographic) History." *Historical Studies* 20, no. 80 (1 April 1983): 339–352. https://doi.org/10.1080/10314618308682932.

Potts, David. "Two Modes of Writing History: The Poverty of Ethnography and the Potential of Narrative." *Australian Historical Association Bellettin* 66–67 (1991): 5–24.

Roseberry, William. "The Unbereable Lightness of Anthropology." *Radical History Review* 65, no. 5 (1996): 5–25.

Sahlins, Marshall. "L'apothéose Du Capitaine Cook." In *La Fonction Symbolique. Essais d'Anthropologie*, edited by Michel Izard and Pierre Smith, 307–39. Paris: Gallimard, 1979.

Sahlins, Marshall. *Historical Metaphors and Mythical Realities: Structure in the Early History of the Sandwich Islands Kingdom*. Ann Arbor: University of Michigan Press, 1981.

Sahlins, Marshall. "The Apotheosis of Captain Cook." In *Between Belief and Transgression: Structuralist Essays in Religion, History, and Myth*, edited by Michel Izard, and Pierre Smith, 73–102. Chicago: University of Chicago Press, 1982.

Sahlins, Marshall. *Islands of History*. Chicago and London: University of Chicago Press, 1985.

Samuel, Raphael. "People's History." In *People's History and Socialist Theory*, edited by Raphael Samuel, xv–xxxix. London: Routledge, 2016.

Saunders, Kay. *Workers in Bondage: The Origins and Bases of Unfree Labour in Queensland, 1824–1916*. St Lucia: University of Queensland Press, 1982.

Scarr, Deryck. "Recruits and Recruiters: A Portrait of the Pacific Islands Labour Trade." *The Journal of Pacific History* 2 (1967): 5–24.

Scarr, Deryck. "Secret Disharmonies and 'Scholarly Discourse': The Case of Nicholas Thomas." *Australian Historical Studies* 24, no. 97 (1 October 1991): 447–451. https://doi.org/10.1080/10314619108595860.

Shineberg, Dorothy. "The Early Years of Pacific History." *The Journal of Pacific Studies* 20 (1996): 1–16.

Stella, Sister Mary, Asesela Ravuvu, and Raymond Pillai. "Pacific History and National Integrity." *Pacific Perspective* 1, no. 2 (1973): 1–7.

Thomas, Keith. "An Anthropology of Religion and Magic, II." *The Journal of Interdisciplinary History* 6, no. 1 (1 July 1975): 91–109. https://doi.org/10.2307/202826.

Thomas, Nicholas. "Taking Sides: Fijian Dissent and Conservative History-writing." *Australian Historical Studies* 24, no. 95 (1 October 1990): 239–251. https://doi.org/10.1080/10314619008595844.

Thomas, Nicholas. *Marquesan Societies. Inequality and Policital Transformation in Eastern Polynesia* (Oxford: Clarendon Press, 1990).

Thomas, Nicholas, Allen Abramson, Ivan Brady, R. C. Green, Marshall Sahlins, Rebecca A. Stephenson, Friedrich Valjavec, and Ralph Gardner White. "The Force of Ethnology: Origins and Significance of the Melanesia/Polynesia Division [and Comments and Replies]." *Current Anthropology* 30, no. 1 (1989): 27–41.

Thompson, E. P. "Folklore, Anthropology and Social History." *Indian Historical Review* 3, no. 2 (1978): 247–266.

Thompson, E. P. "History from Below." *Times Literary Supplement*. 7 April 1966.

Trask, Haunani-Kay. "Natives and Anthropologists: The Colonial Struggle." *The Contemporary Pacific* 3, no. 1 (1991): 159–167.

Walters, Ronald G. "Signs of the Time: Clifford Geertz and the Historians." *Social Research* 47, no. 3 (1987): 537–556.

Ward, Alan. "Pacific History and Inter-Disicplinary Studies; Some Recent Trends." *Research in Melanesia* 1, no. 2 (1975): 22–30.

Wesley-Smith, Terence. "Historiography of the Pacific: The Case of The Cambridge History." *Race & Class* 41, no. 4 (2000): 101–117.

West, Francis James. "The Study of Colonial History." *Journal of Southeast Asian History* 2, no. 3 (1961): 70–82.

Olaf Kaltmeier

6 Horizontality and Decolonisation of Knowledge: Doing Oral History in Latin America

The indigenous and Afro-American mobilisations in the 1990s and 2000s shook the elitist and white-mestizo foundations of the self-image of Latin American societies and their history, which was based on European ideas of civilisation, progress and modernisation. In almost all countries, there were constitutional changes that defined the respective countries as pluricultural or even plurinational and thus in some cases – as in Bolivia and Ecuador – set in motion a profound decolonisation that was tantamount to a refounding of the nation. Indigenous and Afro-American movements, their organic intellectuals and increasingly critical social and cultural scientists also questioned the coloniality of knowledge in the process.[1]

One of the major overarching academic debates in this cultural-political context is related to the critique of the coloniality of knowledge.[2] Coloniality of knowledge is only one of the spheres that allow us to understand the dynamics of coloniality as a structuring axis of the social relations that have allowed the domination of the West over the rest of the world. In the Latin American debate, coloniality is basically seen as a longue durée-temporal layer that emerged with the European colonisation of the Americas. The early political independence and the emergence of a republic political system in Latin America in the first half of the 19th century is not conceived of as a post-colonial turn, but as a conjuncture of consolidation of political-cultural patterns of coloniality in other forms. This line of thought includes the epistemological critique that, especially in the 19th century, a specific local form of knowledge, modern-Western knowledge, claims universal validity. This leads to the dynamics of the imposition of Eurocentrism as the only way of knowing the world. Thus, other systems and ways of knowledge production have been and are devalued, and systematically, violently repressed and fought against. Portuguese sociologist Boaventura de Sousa Santos speaks in

---

1 Olaf Kaltmeier, "Politics of Indigeneity in the Andean Highlands. Indigenous Social Movements and the State in Ecuador, Bolivia, and Peru (1940–2014)," in *Indigeneity on the Move. Varying Manifestations of a Contested Concept*, eds. Eva Gerharz, Nasir Uddin, and Pradeep Chakkarath (Oxford: Berghahn, 2017), 172–198.
2 Walter D. Mignolo, *Local Histories/Global Designs. Coloniality, Subaltern Knowledges, and Border Thinking.* (Princeton: Princeton University Press, 2000).

https://doi.org/10.1515/9783111522180-006

this sense of a true epistemicide. The uni-versity can certainly be understood as one of the principal guardians of the uni-versality of (unitary) western thought.[3] Nevertheless, the university is no closed power apparatus, and critical Western scholars opposed this epistemicide, as did indigenous intellectuals who are familiar with the functioning of the academic field. Thus, at the beginning of the 21st century, an upsurge of indigenous methodologies can be observed in and beyond Latin America.[4] Maori scholar Linda Tuhiwai Smith locates this project of "researching back" in the same tradition of thought as the approaches of "writing back" or "talking back" that characterise post-colonial literary studies.[5]

In these approaches to renewing one's own knowledge traditions and decolonising hegemonic knowledge, oral history has a special function. For both indigenous researchers and other critical intellectuals, oral history is considered a central approach to interrupting the hegemonic narration of history oriented towards a Western-European imaginary, and to telling alternative stories. Central to this is the development of alternative, oral archives. In this, the Ecuadorian Kichwa intellectual Ariruma Kowii claims that "the elders as source of memory" took on a central role in the production of historical knowledge and that they could be understood as "our libraries".[6] But for critical scholars and indigenous intellectuals it is not sufficient to expand the archive, the patterns of knowledge production itself have to be decolonised. One fundamental critique is that the Global South is reduced in the research process to a "treasure trove of ethnographic 'cultural difference'",[7] while the general, supposedly universal theories are produced in the North. The asymmetry produced by this can be understood as an act of cultural imperialism similar to economic imperialism, because here, too, the periphery provides the resources, while the intellectual surplus value is realised in the centres. Given this epistemological violence of occidental, modern knowledge, it is a matter of decolonising and democratising the way knowledge is acquired in order to be able to criticise Western, universal narrations of History,

---

3 Olaf Kaltmeier, "De la universidad a la pluriversidad: Creatividad y crisis de la producción academica de conocimiento," in *Creatividad en conflicto. Perspectivas interdisciplinarias desde las Américas en contextos de crisis*, eds. Olaf Kaltmeier, Wilfried Raussert, and Matti Steinitz (Buenos Aires: Clacso, 2024), 69–82.
4 Linda Tuhiwai Smith, *Decolonizing Methodologies. Research and Indigenous Peoples* (London: Zed Books, 1999); Angela Waziyatawin Wilson, and Michael Yellow Bird, eds., *For Indigenous Eyes only. A Decolonization Handbook* (Santa Fe: School of American Research Press, 2005).
5 Smith, *Decolonizing*, 7.
6 Ariruma Kowii, "Memoria, identidad e interculturalidad de los pueblos del Abya Yala," in *Intelectuales indígenas piensan América Latina*, ed. Claudia Zapata (Quito: Abya Yala, 2007), 115.
7 Gayatri Chakravorty Spivak, *A Critique of Postcolonial Reason. Toward a History of the Vanishing Present* (Cambridge: Harvard University Press, 1999), 388.

with a capital "H", and to introduce other forms of narrating and conceptualising history. This is important, as not only the content but also the form and narrativity of historiography[8] is shaped by the Western discipline.

In this sense, writing history is an eminently political project that produces tensions between different forms and fields of knowledge production. This chapter explores the highly relevant tension between the rules of scholarly production in the academic field on the one hand, and the political demands and forms of knowledge production brought to the oral historian by social movements and communities on the other. Thereby the chapter focuses on oral history production around indigenous movements, communities and personalities. However, many of the conceptual and methodological aspects of oral history are applicable to other social and political fields in Latin America and beyond. First, we will have a look at the history of the reciprocal relationship between oral history and indigeneity. In view of the extension of the archive by oral sources, the significance of oral history but also that of autoethnographic texts will be elaborated. In a second step, possible contributions of oral history to a decolonisation of knowledge are explored. In doing so, it will be illuminated to what extent the entire oral history research process – from the project idea to the final publication – can be designed horizontally and reciprocally. This essay ends with a plea for a self-reflexive, intercultural, dialogical, co-constructed research process in oral history and beyond.

6.1 Oral History and Indigeneity

A privileged possibility to make the voices and concerns of subalternised, oppressed and/or colonised people audible and visible is to create conditions in which they can speak for themselves. The growing corpus of auto-ethnographic texts such as eyewitness accounts, diaries, testimonial literature, video and film productions, etc. are particularly significant for this enterprise. It is also possible to generate auto-ethnographic testimonies in the field research situation. In this context, oral history is highly relevant for the study of history.

However, oral history is also entangled with the emergent coloniality of knowledge from the beginning of the *conquista* and the invention of Latin America in the process of European expansion. The chronicles and the collections of indigenous testimonies that European priests and colonisers such as Bernadino de Sahagún in Mesoamerica or Pedro de Cieza de León in the Andes collected

---

8 Hayden White, *Metahistory. Die historische Einbildungskraft im 19. Jahrhundert in Europa* (Frankfurt am Main: Suhrkamp Verlag, 1991).

shaped the European image of Latin America and its people. But even this European dominance in the representation and imagination of Latin America was not unbroken as early as the 16th century, as indigenous intellectuals appropriated Western writing and formulated more or less resistant texts. In the Andean region, for example, the chronicles of Inca Garcilaso de la Vega and especially the autoethnographically conceived, well-illustrated work *Primer Nueva coronica y buen gobierno* of Guaman Poma de Ayala (1614) provided groundbreaking insights into indigenous everyday life in the Tahuantinsuyo, the Inca Empire, before the colonial rupture. Furthermore, it contained a well-sustained and detailed critique of the Spanish colonial regime from an indigenous point of view, including aspects of forced labour, (sexual) abuse, tax payments, ecological degradation, etc.[9] Another important aspect of this work is the self-reflexive way in which Guaman portrayed, in chapter 36 of the Nueva Coronica, his own political position as chronicler who wrote this text to present it to the Spanish king in order to denounce the existing colonial practices and to achieve a better colonial regime.[10]

When researching coloniality, understood as the persistence and renewal of colonial structures and discourses up to the present, the historian must face the problem of the "double foreignness" that results from the spatial and temporal distance. The foreign-cultural spatial distance requires an examination of cultural difference, as conducted by social and cultural anthropology. Parallel to this, a historical contextualisation must be undertaken that deals with historical difference.[11] In the combination of both experiences of difference, one's own cultural and historical location must be self-reflexively considered. Thus, it would be less a matter of grasping the historical or the foreign-cultural as a limited and distanced object, but rather of shaping the process of appropriation of the culturally and historically foreign by working in dialogue with both.

The integration of oral history methods into social history, especially into the British Labour History of the New Left of the 1960s, led to a shift in emphasis to-

---

9 Rolena Adorno, *Guaman Poma. Writing and Resistance in Colonial Peru* (Austin: University of Texas Press, 2000); Felipe Guaman Poma de Ayala, *Primer Nueva Corónica y Buen Gobierno*, ed. Rolena Adorno (Copenhagen: Royal Library of Denmark, 2006 [1614]).
10 Olaf Kaltmeier, *Politische Räume jenseits von Staat und Nation* (Göttingen: Wallstein, 2012), 81–86.
11 Christian Büschges, "Auf der Suche nach dem historischen Subjekt. Über die (Un-) Möglichkeit eine Geschichte von Indigenität und Staatsbürgerschaft im Andenraum des 18. und 19. Jahrhunderts zu schreiben," in *Methoden dekolonialisieren. Eine Werkzeugkiste zur Demokratisierung der Sozial- und Kulturwissenschaften*, ed. Olaf Kaltmeier, and Sarah Corona Berkin (Münster: Westfälisches Dampfboot, 2012), 232; Iris Gareis, *Die Geschichte der Anderen. Zur Ethnohistorie am Beispiel Perus 1532–1700* (Berlin: Reimer, 2003); Bernard S. Cohn, *An Anthropologist Among the Historians and Other Essays* (New Delhi: Oxford University Press, 1987), 18–49.

wards political issues. Many of the representatives of oral history, especially between the 1960s and the 1980s, made the democratising claim to set a "history from below" against the history of the "elite white men",[12] as it has been mostly reproduced in conventional historiographies. This brought ethnic minorities, the exploited and socially excluded, women and gender relations, and increasingly also migrants, as well as the neglected history of everyday life, into the focus of interest. And in Latin America, topics such as coping with and remembering the violence of the military dictatorships of the 1970s and 1980s as well as indigenous peoples and nations also came into focus.[13] In the Andean region, the reception of oral history occurred via and in parallel to the social history of the New Left, with reference to historians such as E.P. Thompson, Eric Hobsbawm, Christopher Hill.[14] While (US-American) ethnohistory was generally quite distanced from the approaches of oral history, which were considered established in the United States in areas of Afro-American anthropology and folk studies,[15] in the Andean region – as in Latin America as a whole – there was a surge of attention to oral history under the influence of the New Left and the neo-Marxist approaches of the 1970s, in which indigenous peasant groups became the focus of interest.[16] In the process, an academic dynamic unfolded in the Andean region that might be comparable to that of the Indian Subaltern Studies Group.[17] First and foremost, the *Taller de Historia Oral Andina* (THOA) was founded in La Paz in the early 1980s under the influence of the Aymara katarist movement. The katarist movement, named after the 18th-century indigenous leader Túpac Katari, emerged in the 1970s in Bolivia combining Marxist class analysis with ethnic-indigenous identity politics.

---

12 Rebecca Sharpless, "The History of Oral History," in *Thinking about Oral History. Theories and Applications*, ed. Thomas Lee Charlton, Lois E. Myers, and Rebecca Sharpless (Lanham: AltaMira Press, 2008), 14.

13 David Carey, *Oral History in Latin America. Unlocking the Spoken Archive* (New York: Routledge, 2017); Dora Schwarzstein, "La historia oral en América Latina," *Historia y Fuente Oral* 14 (1995).

14 Rosaleen Howard-Malverde, "Pautas teóricas y metodológicas para el estudio de la historia oral andina contemporánea," in *Tradición oral andina y amazónica. Métodos de análisis e interpretación de textos*, ed. Juan Carlos Godenzzi (Cuzco: Programa de Formacion en Educacion Intercultural Bilingue para los Paises Andinos, 1999), 340.

15 Michael E. Harkin, "Ethnohistory's Ethnohistory: Creating a Discipline from the Ground Up," *Social Science History* 34, no. 2 (2010); Shepard Krech, "The State of Ethnohistory," *Annual Review of Anthropology* 20 (1991): 345–375.

16 Segundo E. Moreno Yánez, "La Etnohistoria: anotaciones sobre su concepto y un examen de los aportes en el Ecuador," in *Contribución a la etnohistoria ecuatoriana*, ed. Segundo Moreno Yáñez, and Udo Oberem (Otavalo: IOA, 1981), 21–44; Carey, *Oral History*, 6–12.

17 Bustos, Guillermo, "Enfoque subalterno e historia latinoamericana: nación, subalternidad y escritura de la historia en el debate Mallon-Beverley," *Fronteras de la historia* (7. 2002): 253–276.

In historical terms, they claimed a structural continuity of aspects of colonialism into contemporary society. One of its later protagonists, the mestizo sociologist Silvia Rivera Cusicanqui Rivera, wrote the influential, socio-historically inspired study *Oprimidos, pero no vencidos* in 1984. This work is committed to the project of inscribing indigenous, subaltern history into national history and epistemologically contributed to fighting internal colonialism, the colonial practices and endeavours enfolded by the postcolonial republics within their national territories against indigenous peoples and other local communities.

Similar history workshops, in Spanish *tallers*, were also founded in other countries by indigenous and indigenous-oriented intellectuals and activists. In 1976, the *Taller Cultural Causanacunchic* was founded in the Ecuadorian stronghold of the indigenous movement Otavalo, which became a cadre for *dirigentes* and redefined culture and history with explicit recourse to oral history and testimonios, whereby the testimonios of the elders and sages in particular were seen as a source of cultural renewal.[18] In Chile, Mapuche intellectuals founded the *Centro de Estudios y Documentación Mapuche Liwen* in Temuco at the end of the 1980s – at the time of the transition from Pinochet's military dictatorship to democracy.[19] Currently, it is above all the *Comunidad de Historia Mapuche* that shapes the historiographical and political-cultural debate.

With these workshops, a democratisation and diffusion of oral history can be observed, which is being driven forward by indigenous activists and NGOs. In many places, oral histories are being created on their own, thus acquiring the character of auto-ethnographic texts. An example is the oral history *Movimiento Indígena y Campesino de Cotopaxi: Historia y proceso organisativo* by the indigenous intellectuals Lourdes Tibán Guala, Raúl Ilaquiche Licta and the non-indigenous author Eloy Alfaro Reyes from the Ecuadorian NGO Instituto de Estudios Ecuatorianos. Here, recourse to oral history is made for political-cultural reasons and not for academic considerations, as Chilean historian Claudia Zapata also emphasises: "Hence, the preference for these methodologies is neither random nor fashionable, but the most practical and logical way to implement the project of decolonisation in the field of knowledge production."[20] Indigenous knowledge workshops and methodologies are not to be understood as a new academic discipline following the logic of the academic field, but must be understood as part of a broad process of decolonisation. In indigenous methodologies, a fundamental epistemological change of perspective can be seen: indigenous people are now no longer

---

18 Claudia Zapata, *Intelectuales indígenas en Ecuador, Bolivia y Chile* (Quito: Abya Yala, 2013), 221–223.

19 Zapata, *Intelectuales indígenas*, 230–233.

20 Zapata, *Intelectuales indígenas*, 385.

objects of research, but they are its subjects. In this sense, indigenous research is part of the broad political-cultural project of empowerment with the goal of cultural self-determination.

These concrete practices and projects of "research back" in Oral History had also its repercussions in national debates on history, memory and historical justice. One example is the work of the *Comisión de Verdad Histórica y Nuevo Trato*, a truth commission on the relationship between the Chilean state and the Mapuche people, which completed its work in 2003.[21] This commission was formed by Chilean, Mapuche, and other indigenous intellectuals combining archival work, the revision of the national historiography, and oral history, in diverse thematic and regional workshops. In this commission, historical truth is not limited to the reconstruction of historical events but especially to the different and competing social imaginaries that connect the past with the present day political conflict between indigenous peoples and the Chilean state. The commission reflects on its role as follows:

> It is not easy, however, to judge history fairly, let alone reconstruct it with strict fidelity. The Commission is aware of these difficulties and is also aware of the inevitable relativity of historical narrative and reconstruction. We may know, in essence, what the events were, but we cannot aspire to reconstruct fully the meaning assigned to them by those who were involved in them at the time. Actions and events that we judge harshly today may have been seen differently by the actors themselves. History is not a set of simple facts devoid of any valuation. When the events take place, they are confused with the will and the inspiration of those who carry them out, and that will and that inspiration are sometimes lost forever. In reconstructing the history presented in these pages, the Commission – assisted by widely recognised experts – has made the effort to avoid mere reproach from centuries away, and instead to try to discern the value of these events in the light of the convictions of our society today, inspired by the democratic ideal. [. . .] Our duty is to shed light, as far as possible, on these facts which, whether we like it or not, constitute us.[22]

In addition to the main report, the Comisión published a bunch of documents and testimonials from the workshops and meeting.

The Colombian truth commission, established in 2016 after the peace agreement between the most influential guerrilla organisation, Fuerzas Armadas Revolucionarias de Colombia (FARC), and the Colombian state, had a similar approach,

---

21 Comisión de Verdad Histórica y Nuevo Trato, *Informe de la Comisión Verdad Histórica y Nuevo Trato con los Pueblos Indígenas*, (Comisionado Presidencial para Asuntos Indígenas: Santiago de Chile, 2008).
22 Comisión de Verdad Histórica y Nuevo Trato, *Informe*, 26–27.

but a broader scope, which ended up in the publication of 24 volumes.[23] Volume 6, *Cuándo los pájaraos no cantaban*, collects testimonies – also from indigenous communities – on the multiple experiences of violence in the civil war. But the state-run commission was not the only project related to the rewriting of national histories vis-à-vis profound cultural-political crises. A collaborative Oral History-project conducted by British and Colombian historians was engaged in creative constrictions of histories based on approaches of story-telling in everyday-contexts like cooking, music, re-enactments.[24] The reflections of these projects and commissions, more related to the field of memory studies, is an invitation to methodological reflections for the oral historian.

Methodological Reflections on Oral History

Within the framework of historiographical methodologies, two approaches to oral history can be distinguished.[25] On the one hand, there is an empiricist-reconstructive approach, which sees oral history as a "gap filler" to fill in the empty spaces of the written archive. The main aim here is to record facts and data in order to describe history in a positivistic way. A second approach is constructivist, and asks above all about the positioning and cultural location of the actors. This is primarily about the reconstruction of past political-cultural patterns of interpretation, but also about the question of how the view of history changes in the process of memory.[26] This approach thus focuses primarily on the appropriation of history, both historical and contemporaneous, in line with the reflections of the Chilean Comisión de Verdad Histórica y Nuevo Trato. In concrete research practice, both approaches can certainly be combined in such a way that historical facts are reconstructed from contemporary testimonies and supplemented and – in part – corrected by written sources. Oral history can expand the historical archive in an emancipatory way. This is in particular the case for cultural contexts characterised by orality. For example, in the Andean region, oral history takes up the orality that is predominant in the indigenous communities and valorises it in contrast to the written form that has otherwise been priv-

---

23 Comisión de la Verdad, *Hay futuro si hay verdad. Informe Final de la Comisión para el Esclarecimiento de la Verdad, la Convivencia y la No Repetición*, 24 vols (Bogotá: Comisión de la Verdad, 2022).
24 Matthew Brown, "History on the margins: truths, struggles and the bureaucratic research economy in Colombia. 2016–2023," *Rethinking History* 27, no. 2 (2023): 1–23.
25 Howard-Malverde, "Pautas teóricas y metodológicas," 342–343.
26 Alessandro Portelli, "What makes Oral History different," in *The Oral History Reader*, ed. Robert Perks, and Alistair Thomson (London: Routledge, 2006).

6 Horizontality and Decolonisation of Knowledge — **149**

ileged in the region since colonial times, which is in conformity with the rules and norms of the Spanish colonisers, and mostly also in their language.[27]

However, oral history practised by Western intellectuals in indigenous or other intercultural contexts has to face the problem of double foreignness, just like source-critical analysis. A special feature of oral history is that the problem of cultural difference manifests itself in the direct face-to-face communication described by anthropologists as the "situation in the field". In this sense, the historian must also leave the safe ethnographic "armchair" or the dusty familiarity of the archive and expose himself to direct experiences of foreignness. In this respect, it is also indispensable, from a historiographical perspective, to face up to the debate, conducted above all in social anthropology, about co-presence in the field, as well as author-ity (in the double sense of authority and authorship) and possible alienation of the spoken word during evaluation and textualisation.[28]

At the same time, the problem of historical distance arises. For the interpretation and appropriation of history by the historian, oral history is a double-edged sword. On the one hand, oral history has a historical range of up to 80 years,[29] so that the narrated and fixed memories still lie in the oral historian's own temporal space of experience, who basically shares memory traditions and everyday actions with the interview partners. On the other hand, this familiarity is also a major shortcoming of oral history, since here – if one disregards the archives for oral history that are currently being established – only contemporary history can be pursued, while deeper historical layers of time can no longer come into view.

A methodological problem with regard to dealing with historical difference is the change in perspective on historical events due to historical distance. Statements by contemporary witnesses are memories, and not contemporary remnants, and are therefore subject to changes through the cognitive process of remembering, which can be shaped both by individual personality changes and by the influence of social patterns of interpretation. Finally, changes can also occur

---

27 Walter D. Mignolo, "Afterword: Writing and Recorded Knowledge in Colonial and Postcolonial Situations," in *Writing Without Words. Alternative Literacies in Mesoamerica and the Andes*, ed. Elizabeth Hill Boone, and Walter D. Mignolo (Durham: Duke University Press, 1994), 292–312; Martin Lienhard, *La voz y su huella. Escritura y conflicto étnico-cultural en América Latina, 1492–1988* (Lima: Editorial Horizonte, 1992); Howard-Malverde, "Pautas teóricas y metodológicas," 340–342.

28 James Clifford and George E. Marcus, eds., *Writing Culture. The Poetics and Politics of Ethnography* (Berkeley: University of California Press, 1986); Eberhard Berg, and Martin Fuchs, eds., *Kultur, soziale Praxis, Text. Die Krise der ethnographischen Repräsentation* (Frankfurt am Main: Suhrkamp, 1995).

29 Jan Assmann, *Das kulturelle Gedächtnis. Schrift, Erinnerung und politische Identität in frühen Hochkulturen* (München: Verlag C. H. Beck, 2007), 51.

as a result of the communication situation in the interview. The status of these contemporary testimonies is weighted differently in the various academic disciplines. While qualitative surveys are fully established in social anthropology and qualitative social research, the contemporary witness has often been considered the "natural enemy of the historian". The "pitfalls of memory" are criticised above all, as well as the fact that the historian himself is involved in generating the sources here.

Two types of responses can be found to these criticisms. The first is to point to the limits of value-neutral collection of qualitative data. Both in social anthropology and in qualitative social research, there are a wide variety of approaches and methods for collecting data that are indisputably recognised in the academic field. A similar approach should therefore be possible in the field of academic history, since the problem here is not fundamentally different from other qualitatively oriented social sciences. This approach is thus focused on the production of factual knowledge. Here it is then a matter of matching data and events through different source locations in the sense of the triangulation already mentioned above. The Bolivian historian Estebán Ticona also argues in this direction:

"To remedy this negative claim, it is necessary to take into account other nonoral sources, such as written sources and graphic material (photographs), which are very important for the reconstruction of the facts. They also allow for oral corroboration, or accuracy of certain events not very well remembered".[30]

Various historians have recently been working with this mix of methods and sources, in which oral history is at the centre. Since the 2000s, the focus has increasingly been on expanding, correcting and/or questioning the (trans-)national historiography through local approaches. Examples include the work of Florencia Mallon on the land struggles in Mapuche-comunidad Nicolás Ailió in southern Chile[31] or my own work on dynamics of de- and recolonisation in Saquisilí, in the Ecuadorian Andean highlands.[32]

A second response to the question of the significance of oral testimonies is, conversely, to view all sources and testimonies as expressions of strategic positioning, in which the conditions for the construction of knowledge must always be re-

---

30 Estebán Ticona, *Memoria, política y antropología en los Andes bolivianos. Historia oral y sabers locales* (La Paz: AGRUCU, Universidad de la Cordillera, Plural Editores, 2005), 31.

31 Florencia Mallon, *Courage Tastes of Blood: The Mapuche Community of Nicolás Ailío and the Chilean State, 1906–2001* (Durham: Duke University Press, 2005).

32 Olaf Kaltmeier, *Jatarishun. Testimonios de la lucha indígena de Saquisilí (1930–2006)* (Quito: Universidad Andina Simón Bolívar Ecuador, 2008); Olaf Kaltmeier, *Resistencia indígena y formación del Estado. Saquisilí del siglo XVI al XXI* (Quito: Corporación Editora Nacional, 2021).

flected. This also includes the broad debate on the (post-)colonial construction of the archive and its silences.[33] Seen from such a starting point, the supposed disadvantage of oral history becomes an advantage. For it is precisely in the dialogical communication situation that further conclusions about the locus of enunciation of the interview partner can be drawn by asking questions, analysing tone of voice and intonation, observing facial expressions and gestures, and so on.

In this sense, one's own positioning as a privileged, white scholar must always be taken into account. For it is precisely the logics and fashions in the academic field that shape the production of knowledge.[34] This also applies to critical approaches. The anthropologist Michael Taussig has pointed to the circular argument that it is the "academic machine" itself, shaped by subaltern and postcolonial theoretical approaches, that produces the subaltern. The subaltern, on the other hand, is already well acquainted with the workings of the academic field through multiple "research contacts" and positions himself in postcolonial mimicry in such a way that the result desired by the researcher emerges in the process.[35] In his own oral history-based study of Argentina, the Argentinean-Mexican historian Mario Rufer describes the case of Don Efrén, known as a village chronicler, who by no means tells a locally perspectivised story, and in doing so not only repeats the national-state official historiography, but in an ironic manner, dictated into the microphone to the historian, who was still young at the time, what he would need for his university career. In short: he should not write that the villagers were simple, impoverished rural people, but that they were "indios" and lived "in burrows".[36] If these aspects do not fall out of the research as "unevaluable residue", it is precisely such subtexts that offer an approach on a meta-reflexive level to address the complex entanglement of the academic field in the production of knowledge.

Another advantage of the dialogical communication situation created in oral history is that the strict subject-object separation that emerged in colonial Western modernity can be at least partially undermined in the research process. In

---

33 Frida Gorbach and Mario Rufer, coord., *(In)disciplinar la investigación. Archivo, trabajo de campo y escritura* (México: Universidad Autónoma Metropolitana, 2016); Ann Laura Stoler, *Along the Archival Grain. Epistemic Anxieties and Colonial Common Sense* (Princeton: Princeton University Press, 2008).

34 Olaf Kaltmeier, "Hacia la descolonización de las metodologías: reciprocidad, horizontalidad y poder," in *En diálogo. Metodologías horizontales en ciencias sociales y culturales*, ed. Sarah Corona Berkin, and Olaf Kaltmeier (Barcelona: Gedisa, 2012a), 37–38, 54.

35 Michael Taussig, ed., *Un Gigante en convulsiones. El mundo humano como sistema nervioso en emergencia permanente* (Barcelona: Gedisa, 1998).

36 Mario Rufer, "El habla, la escucha y la escritura. Subalternidad y horizontalidad desde la crítica poscolonial," in *En diálogo. Metodologías horizontales en ciencias sociales y culturales*, ed. Sarah Corona Berkin, and Olaf Kaltmeier (Barcelona: Gedisa, 2012), 57–58.

oral history, we speak in this context of a "shared authority",[37] according to which researcher and interviewee alike control the process of producing knowledge. Especially in contexts marked by coloniality – understood as the persistence and continuous renewal of colonial elements, rather than a completed historical process or a specific period—a dialogical and horizontal production of knowledge would be elementary for the project of decolonising knowledge.[38] This includes an ability to hear the voice of the others on their own terms, and not to hear only those aspects that the researcher wants to hear for political or academic reasons. The art of listening is essential for doing oral history. Or, as the editors of the testimonio-volume of the Colombian truth commission state:

"we set out to listen to people on their 'own terms'. We want to understand the stories from the worlds in which they were told, from their own points of view, abysses and languages; from their chains of meanings. Every voice is the expression of an inner life and of a community. [. . .] The idea was not to put the arguments of a researcher into the voice of others."[39]

Autoethnographic Texts and Testimonios

Beyond the oral sources created through oral history itself, (other) autoethnographic texts and testimonios are of particular interest to historians. They can also be used to record deeper layers of time. A paradigmatic example of an autoethnographic text is the aforementioned *Primer Nueva coronica y buen gobierno* written by Felipe Guaman de Ayala at the turn from the 16th to the 17th century. Written in the narrative format par excellence of the colonisers – the chronicle – this text represents one of the harshest critiques of Spanish colonial rule. However, the text is not to be understood as a "pure" indigenous presence. Rather, it is a hybrid text that self-critically reflected the author's position "between worlds". Such texts can thus be understood as auto-ethnographic texts.[40] But

---

37 Michael H. Frisch, *A Shared Authority. Essays on the Craft and Meaning of Oral and Public History* (New York: State University of New York Press, 1990).
38 Sarah Corona Berkin, and Olaf Kaltmeier, eds., "En diálogo. Metodologías horizontales en Ciencias Sociales y Culturales," in *En diálogo. Metodologías horizontales en Ciencias Sociales y Culturales*, ed. Sarah Corona Berkin, and Olaf Kaltmeier (Barcelona: Gedisa, 2012).
39 Comisión de la Verdad, *Hay futuro si hay verdad. Informe Final de la Comisión para el Esclarecimiento de la Verdad, la Convivencia y la No Repetición*, vol. 6, *Cuando los pájaros no cantaban: historias del conflicto armado en Colombia, tomo testimonial* (Bogotá: Comisión de la Verdad, 2022), 32.
40 Heewon Chang, *Autoethnography as Method* (New York: Routledge, 2008); Carolyn Ellis, *The Ethnographic I. A Methodological Novel about Autoethnography* (Walnut Creek: AltaMira Press, 2004)

unlike the auto-ethnographic method in social anthropology, these are texts in which "the object of study" itself becomes the ethnographer. In this respect, the temptation to regard these texts as pure, uncontaminated expressions of the subaltern must be resisted. Rather, with Mary Louise Pratt's postcolonial twist on the concept of auto-ethnography, it should be emphasised that auto-ethnographies are texts in which

> people undertake to describe themselves in ways that engage with representations others have made of them. Thus, if ethnographic texts are those in which European metropolitan subjects represent to themselves their others (usually the conquered others), auto-ethnographic texts are representations that the so defined others construct *in response to* or in dialogue with those texts.[41]

From this definition, it can be deduced that auto-ethnographies are strategic and tactical positionings of subalterns that take place in given intercultural constellations characterised by power asymmetries. Under the conditions of cultural contact, such auto-ethnographic texts contain multiple intertextual references to other, often hegemonic, narratives and representations.

Such texts represent a unique source for the historian, as they express the perspective of indigenous actors in their concrete temporal-spatial contexts. However, in interpreting these texts, the historian must again face the double historical and cultural difference. From a historical and cultural perspective, such texts must be contextualised and placed in their communicative context so that the locus of enunciation of the speaker as well as its addressees can be recognised. As Gerardo Cham notes in his inter-American historical work on autobiographical testimonies of enslaved African-Americans, the genre of autobiography in Ibero-America was limited to the male, wealthy, white-mestizo upper class,

> which, from colonial privileges, did their best to keep indigenous people and people of African origin excluded from hegemonic cultural models. During the nineteenth century and much of the twentieth century, autobiographical textuality practically became the monopoly of those who claimed self-conferred rights of use with respect to Western values which, from their particular perspectives, should be preserved, exalted and disseminated by printed media.[42]

Testimonial literature is a special autoethnographic genre that is also highly relevant to historiography. Since the 1970s, there has been a veritable boom in testimonial literature in Latin America, which focuses on the life histories of indigenous people. One can think of the autobiography of Gregorio Condori Mamani and his

---

41 Mary Louise Pratt, "Arts in the Contact Zone," *Profession* (1991): 34.

42 Gerardo Cham, *Narrativas de exesclavizados afroamericanos. Conflictos de autoría* (Bielefeld: Bielefeld University Press, 2023), 10.

wife Asunta, which was recorded by Ricardo Valderrama Fernández and Carmen Escalante Gutierrez and published by the Centro de Estudios Rurales Bartolomé de las Casas in 1977. Worthy of mention is the testimonio of the miner and trade unionist Domitila Barrios de Chungara, also published in 1977 (1978 in English), which was recorded by the Brazilian feminist Moema Viezzer and received special attention through the foreword by Eduardo Galeano, as well as in the German edition by the German journalist Günter Wallraff. And finally, the testimonio of the later Nobel Peace Prize winner Rigoberta Menchú, published by the Venezuelan journalist Elizabeth Burgos-Debray in 1983, should be highlighted. The latter is of particular interest for the debate on oral sources in historiography, as various controversies were ignited by this book. I will deal with the debate on authorship in the testimonio later; here, the question of the truth and veracity of oral sources will be addressed. US-American anthropologist David Stoll questioned the accuracy of some of Menchú's statements, also on the basis of his own interviews.[43] For example, Menchú probably did not tell the truth about the death of her brother, and concealed her schooling. But Stoll's criticism went even further. He accused Menchú of deliberate manipulation to make her narrative compatible with the political orientation of the *Ejercito Guerillero de los Pobres,* an insurgent liberation army with which she sympathised. Thus, Stoll continues, the left historians are also to be criticised for finding this testimony true and ignoring other testimonies that were not politically convenient. All these points are highly relevant for dealing with testimonios. Yet a number of historians, foremost Greg Grandin, defended Menchú. On the one hand, the alternative voices that Stoll cited were questioned in terms of source criticism. More important, however, was the argument about the self-understanding of the testimonio. Menchú herself explicitly emphasised that she does not tell her life story in the bourgeois-occidental sense as an individual life story, but as the biography of a collective experience: "I'd like to stress that it's not only my life, it's also the testimony of my people."[44] In this sense, it is always necessary to ask what sort of understanding of the subject and thus also of biography the testimonados have, or to explore the "enunciative conflict between the narrating self and the author as the testimonial subject of what is narrated."[45]

In addition to the collection of testimonies, the development of oral sources that have already been collected is of particular interest to historians. The above-mentioned history workshops of indigenous historians are also increasingly turning to this area. Thus, Claudio Alvarado Lincopi and Enrique Antileo Baeza of the

---

43 David Stoll, *Rigoberta Menchú and the Story of All Poor Guatemalans* (London: Routledge, 1999).
44 Rigoberta Menchú, *I, Rigoberta Menchú,* trans. Elizabeth Burgos-Debray (London: Verso, 1984), 1.
45 Cham, *Narrativas,* 21.

Comunidad de Historia Mapuche published a volume in 2019 comprising articles published in Mapuche newspapers, most of which are autoethnographic. While the texts collected here already elaborated Mapuche contributions to the national public debate, the volume *Santiago waria mew* published by the same editorial duo gathers testimonios from Mapuche in the Chilean capital Santiago. This projects indigenous history into urban space and breaks open a colonial politics of location. Alvarado Lincopi and Antileo Baeza write self-confidently:

> 'Santiago Mapuche' is a reality that challenges. It confronts anthropology and history (if it could ever exist in the singular), it challenges urban and poverty studies, it confronts nationalism and essentialism. It shatters folklore, neoliberal multiculturalism, shamanic discourses and consumers of ethnicity, it puts indigenous policy technocrats and other champions of diversity fashion on the spot.[46]

In this way, they consciously avoid more identitarian attributions and classifications, unlike the oral histories and testimonios from the 1970s to the end of the 1990s, which aimed to form closed political ethnicities.

> It is very difficult for us to talk about being and not being Mapuche or about the characteristics that would constitute them/us. It is likely that labelling – regardless of whether it comes from the labelled or the 'white' scrutiniser who rates the condition of the other – is the most arrogant act that can be girded in people's histories. For us, the processes of identification and dis-identification are uncontainable, diffuse and often arise from brutal branding.[47]

6.2 Doing Oral History: Horizontal, Dialogical, and Reciprocal Production of Knowledge

Colonial extractivism, it has been noted, is also present in (oral) history, right down to the academic language. Colonial and imperial projects aim to open up sources for the process of accumulation and exploitation. Economically oriented Marxist approaches discuss "accumulation by dispossession"[48] and "neo-extractivism"[49] in

---

46 Claudio Alvarado Lincopi, and Enrique Antileo Baeza, eds., *Santiago waria mew. Memoria y fotografía de la migración mapuche* (Temuco: Ediciones Comunidad de Historia Mapuche, 2017), 211.
47 Alvarado Lincopi, and Antileo Baeza, *Santiago waria mew*, 211–212.
48 David Harvey, *The New Imperialism* (Oxford: Oxford University Press, 2003).
49 Eduardo Gudynas, "Diez tesis urgentes sobre el nuevo extractivismo. Contextos y demandas bajo el progresismo sudamericano actual," in *Extractivismo, política y sociedad,* ed. Centro Andino de Acción Popular, and Centro Latino Americano de Ecología Social (Quito: Fundación Rosa Luxemburgo Stiftung, 2009).

this context, with scholars taking a crucial role in identifying, categorising and exploiting sources. A very similar dynamic can be identified in the search for knowledge sources within the framework of cultural imperialism. The very term "source" as used in historical scholarship expresses a spirit of inequality and appropriation. It is the researcher-subject who must "seek" and "explore" the "sources" in order to make the knowledge dormant there bubble up so that it can then be quantified, classified and represented. Epistemological power is acknowledged to be concentrated in the researcher, while the voices present in the source are reduced to the status of object or passive informant. To mitigate this epistemological violence, it is necessary to come to a dialogical relationship with the source texts and the interactions and voices condensed in them.

This line of argument subjected the research process to a rigorous methodological critique, while in parallel, new, less utilitarian, collaborative approaches based on reciprocity were discussed interdisciplinarily. In this context, oral history was one of the points of reference in the debate – especially because of the dialogue-based and democratising approaches that had been developed in Latin America. An example of these interdisciplinary and intercultural platforms is the discussion on *Decolonising Native Histories* initiated by the historian Florencia Mallon. One of these platforms is the interdisciplinary network *Horizontal Methods*, comprising social scientists and historians working between Western Europe and Latin America, initiated by the Mexican communication scholar Sarah Corona Berkin and myself in 2008.[50] This network starts from the following premise: "horizontal and reciprocal exchange is the starting point for producing knowledge, the conditions of which must be permanently negotiated with others in the field".[51] In doing so, we were aware that horizontal exchange and reciprocity not only relates to the collection of testimonies, but profoundly encompasses all stages of the research process and thereby challenges the image of disciplined science cultivated in the Western academic field.

Defining the Topic

A research topic does not spring from the inward-looking inspiration of a researcher-subject, but is a product of social interaction. In the first place, the dy-

---

50 Corona Berkin, and Kaltmeier, "En diálogo"; Rebeca Pérez Daniel, and Stefano Sartorello, *Horizontalidad, diálogo y reciprocidad en los métodos de investigación social y cultural* (San Cristobál de Chiapas: CENEJUS Universidad Autónoma de Chiapas, 2012); Inés Cornejo, and Mario Rufer, eds., *Horizontalidad. Hacia una crítica de las metodologías* (Buenos Aires: Clacso, 2022).
51 Corona Berkin and Kaltmeier, "En diálogo," 12.

namics of the academic field, in which researchers are eager to position themselves with an innovative topic, flow into the search for a topic in most cases. For the researcher, the main issue is to navigate the waves of academic fashions from the linguistic to the spatial, to the visual, to the performative, to the affective turn, without falling into the trap of opportunism, which would devalue academic capital and prestige. In order to acquire academic capital, it is necessary to identify "research gaps" and thus gain reputation and prestige. The search for topics for research projects can thus be understood with Bourdieu as an anticipation of the possible reception of the said topic in the academic field.[52] This field-internal dynamic is increasingly reinforced by the need for project funding, which is increasingly subject to entrepreneurial criteria. The requirements set by public and private funding institutions as well as the corresponding forms of project evaluation structure research projects more sustainably than the dialogue with the "researched". This is exemplified in the much-invoked "research proposal prose", which is almost a genre of its own in academic literature, and which has the sole purpose of "selling" a project. These texts are full of imaginaries about the Other, produced on the basis of intertextual references to other academic works in the sense of an "armchair ethnology". In this way, the researcher enters the research field with a subject that emerges from the internal dynamics of the academic field, but not from the dialogue with the Other.

This starting point changes in the research process when the topic is redefined through the power of the Other. On the one hand, this is related to the power of encounter and dialogue in fieldwork – especially in cases where there is face-to-face contact with subaltern actors. Here the interest of the researcher meets the interests of the researched. According to the Mexican communication scholar Sarah Corona, a "generating conflict"[53] occurs in which the interests of the "researcher" and the "researched" are negotiated. This does not necessarily lead to convergences. For a topic of interest in academia does not necessarily interest the "researched", and vice versa. In this sense, the Colombian indigenous intellectual Abelardo Ramos Pacho also reflects on his exchange with the US anthropologist Joanne Rappaport:

> Despite the generosity of the participants, such a dialogue cannot but produce tensions. These may be due to the prejudices each member brings to the table, to the underlying sense of competition, and to the epistemological differences between them, whether academic or organisa-

---

52 Pierre Bourdieu, *Los usos sociales de la ciencia* (Buenos Aires: Ediciones Nueva Visión, 1997).
53 Sarah Corona Berkin, "Notas para producir metodologías horizontales," in *En diálogo. Metodologías horizontales en ciencias sociales y culturales*, ed. Sarah Corona Berkin, and Olaf Kaltmeier (Barcelona: Gedisa, 2012), 92–94.

tional epistemologies or those of the Native culture. Such conflict requires that participants act responsibly. Tensions can easily turn into nonnegotiable conflicts, or they can be fruitful. It is the responsibility of the participants to aim toward negotiation, not toward rupture.[54]

This conflict is already evident in the negotiation of the research topic, as I would like to explain using the example of an oral history project I conducted in 2006 and 2007 in Ecuador. This research project on the ethnicisation of the political was an integral part of the collaborative research project SFB 1288 "The Political as Communicative Space in History" at Bielefeld University. In order to be able to start working with the indigenous organisation Jatarishun in Saquisilí, I presented "my project" at the general assembly of the Jatarishun. And mediated by the support of an Ecuadorian NGO that has been working with the Jatarishun for a long time, I received formal permission to carry out the research. But de facto this did not change much, because I could hardly conduct interviews rich in content: The topic of my research on the gubernamentalisation of ethnic politics was of no interest to either the indigenous organisation or the indigenous smallholders. Instead, in various conversations with the spokespersons, *dirigentes*, of the Jatarishun and the *comunidades* it unites, the idea emerged to write a history of the organising process of the indigenous movement in the region.

Changing one's research topic is not insignificant for the self-positioning in the academic field. This is all the more true, if this change of topic does not take place according to the internal logic of the academic field, but is initiated by the intervention of the Other, from an "unscientific" standpoint outside the field. On the one hand, there could be a distancing of the research from the academic field. If the topic is then seen as too "populist" or too "ideologically" influenced by the orthodox gatekeepers of the field, a devaluation of both the symbolic-academic capital of the research and that of the researcher himself follows. On the other hand, it is also a requirement of the academic field, especially in the social and cultural sciences, that the researcher must listen to the other in order to produce new knowledge. This is especially true for those disciplines, such as social anthropology, whose logics of practice require the researcher to arrive at an "authentic" representation of the Other. To produce this academic authenticity, the voice of the Other must be present. In this respect, the determination of the research topic reveals a complicated web of negotiation processes that point beyond the dialogue in the field.

---

54 Abelardo Ramos Pacho, and Joanne Rappaport, "Collaboration and Historical Writing: Challenges for the Indigenous-Academic Dialogue," in *Decolonizing Native Histories: Collaboration, Knowledge, and Language in the Americas*, ed. Florencia Mallon (Durham: Duke University Press, 2012), 133.

Co-Presence and Reciprocity

In critical social anthropology, and especially in Latin American oral history, there is a broad consensus that research is neither a matter of speaking *about* the Other, nor of speaking *for* him in an advocatory way. Instead, the scientific-ethical ideal envisages a dialogue *with* the Other. Dialogue, exchange, is the starting point in the production of knowledge. Johannes Fabian has conceptualised this in the form of an "encounter", the conditions of which must be constantly negotiated in the field. Social anthropologist Dennis Tedlock emphasises that this is about the construction of a common basis of understanding.[55] The fundamental condition for the possibility of a common basis of understanding is based on the fact that there is a "co-presence"[56] between the researcher and the subaltern, that is, that both share the same space and time in the ethnographic situation. It is in this here and now that the difference of different orders of experience, each illuminating different aspects and silencing others, is negotiated.[57] In none of these conflicting orders can a higher degree of truth be discerned, for there is no external universal standard. Accordingly, the challenge lies precisely in cultural translation. This cannot be reduced to an instrumental act, since cultural orders of knowledge can be incommensurable. Therefore, translation is not about incorporating the foreign into one's own, but precisely about expanding the boundaries of one's own language and culture.

A common basis of understanding can be the foundation for a dialogical and horizontally structured process of knowledge production, as Ramos Pacho explains: "The process of co-theorising can be conceptualised in terms of local indigenous practice, through the application of the metaphor of the *minga* – collective work activities that benefit the community or a family – to the organisation as a whole".[58] Ramos Pacho's contribution to the discussion of methodology now lies primarily in the fact that research is reformulated here not only in the concepts and discourses of occidental social research, but in endemic indigenous concepts such as the *minga*, a form of collective work in the Andean region, which is trans-

---

55 Dennis Tedlock, "Fragen zur dialogischen Anthropologie," in *Kultur, soziale Praxis, Text. Die Krise der ethnographischen Repräsentation*, ed. Eberhard Berg, and Martin Fuchs (Frankfurt am Main: Suhrkamp Verlag, 1995).

56 Johannes Fabian, *Time and the Other. How Anthropology Makes Its Object* (New York: Columbia University Press, 1983); Johannes Fabian, "Präsenz und Repräsentation. Die Anderen und das anthropologische Schreiben," in *Kultur, soziale Praxis, Text. Die Krise der ethnographischen Repräsentation*, ed. Eberhard Berg, and Martin Fuchs (Frankfurt am Main: Suhrkamp Verlag, 1995).

57 Bernhard Waldenfels, *Ordnung im Zwielicht* (Frankfurt a.M.: Suhrkamp, 1987).

58 Ramos Pacho and Rappaport, "Collaboration and Historical Writing," 131.

ferred here to the field of intellectual work. The Ecuadorian-Swiss geographer Yvonne Riaño from the Horizontal Methods Network has also worked in this direction by taking up collective knowledge production in the *minga* and transferring it to her work with migrants in Switzerland.[59]

But the concept of dialogue should not be misunderstood to mean that it is about adopting everything else without reservation. It is not a matter of "going native", which can quickly become "going naïve" and thus no longer question the geopolitical hegemonies of knowledge. This attitude is explained by Spivak as follows: "By positioning themselves as 'outsiders', they downplay their complicity with North-South polities, and hide behind naïveté and lack of knowledge, while constantly congratulating themselves on being 'saviours of marginality'."[60] This approach has its implications for the coloniality of knowledge, as Ilan Kapoor confirms: "This inside/outside divide [. . .] shifts the obligation for change and engagement solely to the Third World subaltern (or to the indigenous informant as its agent)".[61] Therefore, we assume that contextualising research within a "shared history" shaped by colonial deep structures requires active and self-reflexive actors from both the South and the North in order to achieve a decolonisation of knowledge and to be able to produce new knowledge in a dialogical way.

However, intercultural exchange is not to be understood solely as a tête-à-tête between researcher and "researched". For with the reference to a constellation analysis already made, it was emphasised that research is a "contact zone"[62] in which different actors with different logics of practice and cognitive maps meet. In terms of a synchronic level of temporality, it is important to emphasise that each actor is shaped by their interactions with the others. In a diachronic perspective, it must be pointed out that the present logic of practice and discourses have emerged from prior historical interactions and struggles that refer to different "temporal layers".[63] The longue durée of colonial structures should be pointed out in this context, but also the interrupting moments of resistance.

Temporality, however, is also a problem in other, much more concrete respects with regard to co-presence in the field. During the fieldwork, the re-

---

59 Yvonne Riaño, "La producción de conocimientocomo 'minga'. Co-determinación y reciproci-daden la investigación con mujeres migrantes de América Latina, Medio oriente y Europa suroriental en Suiza," in *En diálogo. Metodologías horizontales en ciencias sociales y culturales*, ed. Sarah Corona Berkin, and Olaf Kaltmeier (Barcelona: Gedisa, 2012).

60 Gayatri Chakravorty Spivak, *Outside in the Teaching Machine* (London: Routledge, 1993), 61.

61 Ilan Kapoor, *The Postcolonial Politics of Development* (London: Routledge, 2008).

62 Pratt, "Arts in the Contact Zone".

63 Reinhart Koselleck, *Zeitschichten. Studien zur Historik* (Frankfurt am Main: Suhrkamp Verlag, 2000).

searcher participates in the everyday life of the communities, which is marked by festivals, (communal) work, gatherings, etc. He is thus involved in the long cycles of reciprocity as expressed in friendships, gifts and counter-gifts, ritual kinship (*padrinazgo*) as well as offices and community services. However, the researcher has a different time rhythm than that of the community member, because research as a project has a beginning and an end. In most cases, the end of the research project also represents the termination of reciprocity relations. And yet, especially in North-South contexts, the question of ongoing reciprocity arises. Daphne Patai, following her oral history project in Brazil, reflected on which of the sixty women she interviewed she could stay in contact with, denying the fundamental question of the possibility of perfect and transparent ethical research.[64] However, as Cornelia Giebeler and Marina Meneses' comments on give and take in the research process in Juchitán, Mexico, show, it is also entirely possible to maintain reciprocal relationships for many years.[65] I myself am still involved in patronal relationships almost twenty years after completing my research in Ecuador, which no longer serve any academic purpose for me. Some oral historians also shift their centre of life to the *comunidad*, so that the research project becomes a life project. In the majority of cases, however, the end of co-presence in the field also means the end of reciprocity relationships and the end of dialogue in research, which creates an ethical dilemma regarding the permanence of reciprocity relationships.

Methodologically too, the end of dialogue poses a major problem for the project of decolonising knowledge. While the phase of data collection was dialogue-based, the phase of analysis and interpretation becomes a monologue. If viewed slightly cynically, dialogue and participation in the field could be seen as a co-optation strategy of the researcher to "rob" data in a knowledge-piracy-way. Despite all the reflexive attempts at self-justification by researchers, this argument cannot be quickly dismissed. Dialogue, participation and self-activation of the population can certainly be understood as instruments of post-colonial appropriation of knowledge. Therefore, it is important to also include the phase after data collection in a critical reflection on research methods and methodologies.

---

64 Daphne Patai, "U.S. academics and third-world women: Is ethical research possible?," in *Women's Words. The Feminist Practice of Oral History,* ed. Sherna Berger Gluck, and Daphne Patai (New York: Routledge, 1991), 137, 149.

65 Cornelia Giebeler, and Marina Meneses, "Geben und Nehmen im Forschungsprozess," in *Methoden dekolonialisieren. Eine Werkzeugkiste zur Demokratisierung der Sozial- und Kulturwissenschaften,* ed. Olaf Kaltmeier, and Sarah Corona Berkin (Münster: Westfälisches Dampfboot, 2012), 145–169.

Author-ity and Narration

After the phase of co-presence, the stage of mono-presence of the researcher usually sets in, in which he or she is the authority and translates the social interactions into textual representations. In this way, the balance of power is transformed – from a meeting in which power is negotiated between subjects to representation in the text in which the Other becomes an object. For the researcher, writing ethnography or oral history is also an act of "purification". As the anthropologist Vincent Crapanzano bitingly puts it, it is about "exorcising" the Other[66] in order to reintegrate into one's own society after a stay in a foreign culture – beyond the "normal" order. Although this exorcism may be beneficial for the psychological hygiene of the researcher, its consequences for the entanglement of power and knowledge must nevertheless be considered. For with the change of location from the field to the desk, the balance of power also changes. While research is still negotiated in a dialogue between subjects when they meet in the field, the Other becomes an object when represented by the researcher, which is fixed in the text in an act of epistemological violence. A critical approach therefore requires a self-reflection of the researcher's author-ity – understood in the double connotation of "author" and "authority".

Within the existing geopolitics of knowledge and the structure of the academic field, I think it is hardly possible to achieve a state of research free of domination. But to conclude from this that all (foreign) representations of the Other are to be avoided is hardly a solution, since this only reproduces the existing conditions of subaltern speechlessness and invisibility. Non-representation is thus also an act of epistemological violence.

For further critical reflection, it seems to me that an examination of the concept of "author" is important. Despite all post-structuralist deconstructions of the author as a central figure of modernity the idea remains that the author is the sole creator of the text. This idea is anchored in the book markets and their forms of marketing as well as in the academic field with the logic of the practice that academic capital and prestige is accumulated through the researcher's publications and their reception in the academic field.

Despite this often-unquestioned notion of the author as creator-subject, there are some ways to limit his authority. One form of limiting authorship that is genuinely found in oral history and life stories, but is also quite contradictory, is mediation. Basically, oral history produces texts that are the result of mediation. This

---

66 Vincent Crapanzano, "On the Writing of Ethnography," *Dialectical Anthropology* 2, no. 1 (1977): 69–73.

6 Horizontality and Decolonisation of Knowledge — **163**

is how Claudia Zapata defines it: "It is a heterogeneous text in which the voices of the legal mediator – however much he may hide or renounce his protagonism – coexist with those of the *testimoniante* [witness]."[67] Peruvian cultural theorist Antonio Cornejo Polar has poetically illustrated the special interweaving of orality and textuality, of word and writing, with the concept of "writing in the air".[68] The mediator is a subject position, that "chooses the witness, who collects, transcribes, translates, edits, and publishes".[69] Estebán Ticona identifies "this transition between the oral and the written" as the neuralgic point of oral history, since a "transposition of languages" takes place here. Accordingly, he calls for this process not to be left to the mediator alone, but to be shaped dialogically.[70] Ticona places the mediator of oral history on a comparable level to the *escribano*,[71] a mestizo social figure who wrote down the concerns of illiterate indigenous people for a fee in the late colonial period and the Republic. In doing so, the *escribano*, or *tinterillo*, always interpreted and translated culturally into legal terminology. This is where the problem of ventriloquism arose, according to which only the *escribano* actually speaks.[72]

One strategy to limit ventriloquism is to make polyphony explicit and limit author-ity to the role of moderation. In *Jatarishun. Testimonios de la lucha indígena en Saquisilí*, I have chosen this very role, which had the task of guiding the conversation of the different voices virtually present in the text, the point being precisely to allow all voices to have their say. Each chapter begins with a brief historical contextualisation written by me to explain the issues raised in the chapter to the reader. After that, I limited my role to making connections between the interview fragments and arranging them in such a way as to create the impression of a dialogue among the interviewees. But even this approach fails to overcome authority. I was in control of the text at every moment. I chose the narrative form, selected the interview fragments printed and arranged them in such a way that a new context of meaning emerged. Another way of limiting author-ity is the technique of "writing with two hands" developed by Sarah Corona in exchange

---

67 Zapata, *Intelectuales indígenas*, 386.

68 Antonio Cornejo Polar, *Escribir en el aire. Ensayo sobre la heterogenidad socio-cultural en la literaturas andinas* (Lima: Editorial Horizonte, 1994).

69 Zapata, *Intelectuales indígenas*, 385.

70 Ticona, *Memoria*, 9.

71 Ticona, *Memoria*, 32.

72 Andrés Guerrero, "El proceso de identificación: sentido común ciudadano, ventriloquía y transescritura," in *Etnicidades*, ed. Andrés Guerrero (Quito: Facultad Latinoamericana de Ciencias Sociales, 2000).

with wixáritari teachers in the highlands of Jalisco.[73] Here, the text of the other is juxtaposed with the text of the researcher, without the former's narrative being evaluated or devalued by the latter. The questions of author-ity and mediation transcend the complex interconnections inherited from colonialism and are also fundamentally faced by indigenous intellectuals who practice oral history.[74] However, here the political control of the *testimonio* remains mostly in the historical community – even though there may be different, even contradictory opinions internally.

The question of knowledge, especially in a globalised knowledge society, is not only an issue of representation, but also one of ownership in the material sense. Based on the debates about intellectual property, the theft of knowledge in connection with medicinal plants or gene piracy, the importance of appropriating knowledge and know-how in the current phase of capitalism becomes obvious. The question of intellectual property is mainly discussed in the academic field in relation to plagiarism, but this would also and especially have to be done with regard to interviewees and "informants". For it is they who provide knowledge and information and their voices are present in academic texts. But the academic field ignores this contribution and demands that authorship, with all its attendant intellectual rights, belongs to the researcher alone. The subalterns are not only represented by occidental others, but they are also dispossessed of their intellectual rights. This is exemplified in the Menchú debate. In the early 1990s, the conflict over the authority of life history *I, Rigoberta Menchú*, began, as Menchú questioned the sole authorship of Elizabeth Burgos-Debray. In 1993, Menchu then asked Burgos-Debray to transfer authorship rights to her as well. Burgos-Debray refused and instructed the publisher to stop paying royalties to Menchú.[75] Legally, Elizabeth Burgos-Debray is thus considered the sole author. To address the problem of authorship, Sarah Corona has given "Sarah Corona Berkin y otras voces" as authors in her cross-cultural study. My solution to the dilemma of authorship was also not fundamental, but tactical. Thus, although I stand as the author, I have added the words "with the support of Arturo Ashca, Mario Castro and Carmen Cofre" to the cover page and citation, so that the indigenous researchers are explicitly and prominently mentioned. However, this is not a solution to the problem. A real recognition of the intellectual rights of co-authors would have to take the polyphony of the texts seriously. In terms of property rights, this would go in

---

73 Corona Berkin, Sarah et al., *Entre voces. Fragmentos de educacción entrecultural* (Guadalajara: Universidad de Guadalajara, 2007).

74 Zapata, *Intelectuales indígenas*, 386–397.

75 Carey, *Oral History*, 81.

the direction of deprivatisation or better communalisation of rights or towards knowledge-commons.

Nevertheless, the complex, bewitched configuration of textuality cannot be resolved solely through the question of authority. The question arises of the narrative forms and established discourses that regulate what can be said. In the field of historical narration, the discourse of national heritage, which was deeply anchored in many Latin and Central American countries after early independence at the beginning of the 19th century, is particularly noteworthy. Accordingly, the historian Mario Rufer points to the difficulty of subaltern narratives that are repeatedly overlaid by national narratives, here for example heritage discourses: "Even when it pretends to be spoken from "the others" (the subaltern groups, the community, the locality), heritage functions as an origin with a mythical foundation and a libretto that draws the universe of the possible".[76]

However, the sub-categorisation and categorisation is not without disruptions. Carolina Crespo, who does research with Mapuche communities in Argentina, argues that an "ethnographic analysis crossed by historical dimensions" can put a stop to hasty classification into hegemonic discourse orders and differentiate history. Such an approach "emphasises less the object and the rule, than the contending practices and relationships, before, during, and after the formulation of these policies",[77] and thus "de-naturalizing and contextualizing norms, discourses, practices, and programmes" can be made visible.[78]

On the other hand, there is always the danger of uncritical adoption of the testimonio. This is true even for indigenous intellectuals who conduct oral histories in their communities. The Bolivian historian Estebán Ticona vividly describes this permanent danger of manipulation as follows: "Manipulation acts like a ghost, and honesty like daylight, permanently haunting the mind of the researcher; its conjuration has to do with the degree of ideological commitment of the witnessed".[79]

---

76 Mario Rufer, "No vamos a traducir. Instalar un secreto, negar la dádiva, redefinir el juego," in *Horizontalidad. Hacia una crítica de las metodologías*, ed. Inés Cornejo, and Mario Rufer (Buenos Aires: Clacso, 2020), 277.

77 Carolina Crespo, "Processes of heritagiziation of indigenous cultural manifestations: lines of debate, analytical axis, and methodological approaches," in *Entangled Heritages. Postcolonial Perspectives on the Uses of the Past in Latin America*, ed. Olaf Kaltmeier, and Mario Rufer (New York: Routledge, 2017), 166.

78 Crespo, "Processes of heritagiziation," 167.

79 Ticona, *Memoria*, 30.

Publics and Publications

Every text is addressed to an imagined public. In the case of oral history, these are always, in the first place, academic studies addressed to an expert audience in the academic field. The logic of the field's practice obliges researchers to use an apparatus of academic rhetoric. This includes certain narrative forms, inter-textual references to important academic works, and language appropriate to the academic environment, usually English. In the majority of cases, the audience addressed is not the 'researched' subaltern community or group. Aiming the reception of a publication at this audience would mean using a different writing style and structuring the work differently.

In this way, the rupture between co-presence and textual representation is extended and deepened to the reception of the texts produced. This is also largely due to the – often internalised and habitualised – rules of the academic field, in which the number and quality of published texts – preferably published in peer-reviewed US journals – is one of the most important indicators for the accumulation of academic capital. In line with this, the Uruguayan literary theorist Hugo Achugar has emphasised the power of the mediator in terms of the circulation of the testimonial text as well as the charging of the text with authority (by a prestigious publisher, by academic institutions, etc.) as much as translation – broadly understood as cultural translation – for a wider audience.[80] At the same time, the indigenous history workshops in particular are concerned with finding a hearing in the majority society as well, in order to change the previous historiography. The book published in 2006 by the *Comunidad de Historia Mapuche* makes this approach abundantly clear with the following imperative call in the title: *¡Escucha Winka!* (Listen no-Mapuche!).

However, the concept of the public sphere can hardly be used homogeneously and comprehensively any more, given the increasing fragmentation of society. In this respect, the indigenous history workshops and critical works of oral history also form their own public spheres. The influence of the *Taller de Historia Oral* in Bolivia went so far that Stephenson recently argued in retrospect that an "indigenous counterpublic sphere"[81] was established. However, this public sphere is about much more than the mere accumulation of scientific knowledge, as it has a dimension

---

80 Hugo Achugar, "La Voz del Otro: Testimonio, Subalternidad y Verdad Narrativa," Revista de Crítica Literaria Latinoamericana 18, no. 36 (1992): 56–63.
81 Marcia Stephenson, "Forging an Indigenous Counterpublic Sphere. The Taller de Historia Oral Andina in Bolivia," *Latin America Research Review* 37, no. 2 (2002): 99.

linked to social work and pedagogy. This is particularly expressed in connection with aspects of healing, spiritual decolonisation and overcoming colonial trauma.[82]

For non-Indigenous researchers working with oral history, this indigenous counterpublic sphere raises the question of what content and formats they should use to approach the public. Many researchers dare to walk the tightrope between two very different public spheres such as the academic world and the indigenous communities. For example, oral historian David Carey published a Mayan-language book in Guatemala in 2004, alongside his academic publication, which was intended for educational work. In my research, I too have produced a monograph for the academic field[83] and another monograph for political education in the *comunidades*.[84] Even though there has been an appropriation of the book by the indigenous organisation here, the reception has its limits. It is questionable whether a book is the appropriate format for transmitting knowledge in an oral culture. Other formats such as a radio broadcast (some *testimonios* were broadcast on Radio Latacunga, the radio station of the indigenous movement in Cotopaxi) or an autoethnographic documentary would have been more accessible to the indigenous peasants, although these would have been even less in line with standard academic formats. In this sense, this monograph has certain weaknesses with regard to both public spheres – the academic and the community-indigenous. My 300-page non-academic book does not conform to academic conventions. It lacks citations or other references to the relevant secondary literature. The extensive use of interview excerpts is just as problematic as the choice of Spanish, which occupies a marginal position in the academic field in Germany, where I work. Moreover, the book lacks overarching theoretical reflections and analytical comments by the researcher. It was published by an Ecuadorian publishing house, which is internationally marginal. There, it appeared in a series that deals with the social history of Ecuador and is aimed at a politically interested, and above all, non-academic audience. Although the back cover of the book bears the emblems of the Universidad Andina Simón Bolívar (Quito) and Bielefeld University, which situates the book in an academic context, the book's value in accumulating academic capital is low, as it is not recognised as a monograph. The reception in the indigenous communities has been better. A certain number of the books were distributed free of charge in

---

82 Smith, *Decolonizing Methodologies*, 117; Olaf Kaltmeier, "Heritage Cities and the Trauma of Coloniality. Postcolonial Conflicts about Space, Identity, and Memory in Historic City Centers in the Americas," in *Remembering and Forgetting: Memory in Images and Texts*, ed. Wilfried Raussert et al. (Bielefeld: Aisthesis Verlag, 2010).
83 Olaf Kaltmeier, *Resistencia indígena y formación del Estado. Saquisilí del siglo XVI al XXI* (Quito: Corporación Editora Nacional, 2021).
84 Kaltmeier, *Jatarishun*.

168 —— Olaf Kaltmeier

the region's intercultural schools and among indigenous organisations – especially the Jatarishun and the provincial organisation Movimiento Indígena-Campesino de Cotopaxi (MICC) – and were used in indigenous movement workshops. In this sense, the "indigenous counterpublic sphere" is not only produced by indigenous intellectuals but also by mestizo scholars and foreign academics, including myself. It relies on interethnic collaborations as well as on interchanges between different social fields and cultural worlds; and indigeneity can be defined as "a relational field of governance, subjectivities, and knowledges that involve us all—indigenous and non-indigenous—in the making and remaking of its structures of power and imagination."[85]

6.3 Oral History in the Geopolitics of Knowledge

At the end of this essay, Western intellectuals might ask themselves, why should I still be doing oral history in Latin America at all? Indigenous and Afro-American researchers, who often have privileged access to the communities, have long since established themselves academically, despite all the racist restrictions on access. The "research-back" approach has not only made knowledge and history more polyphonic, but has also contributed to decolonising Western one-size-fits-all thinking. Nevertheless, I believe there are a number of reasons why oral history projects carried out horizontally and reciprocally by Western researchers together with indigenous researchers are helpful, especially for power-theoretical, decolonising motives. Colonial expansion and the formation of the coloniality of knowledge have led to a shared history.[86] On the one hand, it is a shared history with variable interactions and, on the other, a history of asymmetrical power relations, exploitation and social inequality, i.e. a separate history. It is precisely this shared, bequeathed, historical web that can hardly be dissolved by a "pure" subaltern or indigenous knowledge production. In view of this shared history, shared methodologies and a shared authority are necessary. In this sense, as Latin-American thinkers such as Silvia Rivera Cusicanqui and Walter Mignolo suggest, concepts such as interconnectedness, translation, transculturality or

---

85 Marisol de la Cadena and Orin Starn, *Indigenous Experience Today* (New York: Berg 2007), 3.
86 Sebastian Conrad, Shalini Randeria, and Regina Römhild, eds., *Jenseits des Eurozentrismus. Postkoloniale Perspektiven in den Geschichts- und Kulturwissenschaften* (Frankfurt am Main: Campus Verlag, 2002), 17.

ch'ixi must be placed at the centre.[87] In methodological terms, this means developing horizontal methodologies based on reciprocity and dialogue in order to build a shared foundation of understanding to overcome one history and multiply history from different perspectives.

References

Achugar, Hugo. "La Voz del Otro: Testimonio, Subalternidad y Verdad Narrativa." *Revista de Crítica Literaria Latinoamericana* 18, no. 36 (1992): 51–73.

Adorno, Rolena. *Guaman Poma. Writing and Resistance in Colonial Peru*. Austin: University of Texas Press, 2000.

Alvarado Lincopi, Claudio, and Enrique Antileo Baeza, eds. *Diarios Mapuche 1935–1966*. Temuco: Ediciones Comunidad de Historia Mapuche, 2019.

Alvarado Lincopi, Claudio, and Enrique Antileo Baeza, eds. *Santiago waria mew. Memoria y fotografía de la migración mapuche*. Temuco: Ediciones Comunidad de Historia Mapuche, 2017.

Assmann, Jan. *Das kulturelle Gedächtnis. Schrift, Erinnerung und politische Identität in frühen Hochkulturen*. München: Verlag C. H. Beck, 2007.

Barrios de Chungara, Domitila with Moema Viezzer. *Let me speak: Testimonio of Domitila, a Woman of the Bolivian Mines*. New York: Monthy Review Press, 1978.

Barrios de Chungara, Domitila with Moema Viezzer. *Wenn man mir erlaubt zu sprechen . . . Zeugnis der Domitila, einer Frau aus den Minen Boliviens*. Göttingen: Lamuv Verlag, 1985

Berg, Eberhard, and Martin Fuchs, eds. *Kultur, soziale Praxis, Text. Die Krise der ethnographischen Repräsentation*. Frankfurt am Main: Suhrkamp Verlag, 1995.

Bourdieu, Pierre. *Los usos sociales de la ciencia*. Buenos Aires: Ediciones Nueva Visión, 1997.

Brown, Matthew, Andrei Gómez-Suarez, Diana Valencia Duarte, Laura Acosta Hankin, Fabio López de la Roche, Julia Paulson, Maca Gómez Gutiérrez, Mary Ryder, María Teresa Pinto Ocampo, Martín Suarez, and Goya Wilson Vásquez. "History on the margins: truths, struggles and the bureaucratic research economy in Colombia. 2016–2023." *Rethinking History* 27, no. 2 (2023): 1–23.

Büschges, Christian. "Auf der Suche nach dem historischen Subjekt. Über die (Un-) Möglichkeit eine Geschichte von Indigenität und Staatsbürgerschaft im Andenraum des 18. und 19. Jahrhunderts zu schreiben." In *Methoden dekolonialisieren. Eine Werkzeugkiste zur Demokratisierung der Sozial- und Kulturwissenschaften*, edited by Olaf Kaltmeier, and Sarah Corona Berkin, 227–242. Münster: Westfälisches Dampfboot, 2012.

Bustos, Guillermo. "Enfoque subalterno e historia latinoamericana: nación, subalternidad y escritura de la historia en el debate Mallon-Beverley." *Fronteras de la historia* 7 (2002): 253–276.

Carey, David. *Oral History in Latin America. Unlocking the Spoken Archive*. New York: Routledge, 2017

Castro Gómez, Santiago. "Decolonizar la Universidad. La hybris del punto cero y el diálogo de saberes." In *Des/decolonizar la universidad*, edited by Zulma Palermo, 79–91. Buenos Aires: Del Signo, 2014.

---

87 Silvia Rivera Cusicanqui, *Un mundo ch'ixi es posible. Ensayos desde un presente en crisis* (Buenos Aires: Tinta Limón, 2018); Mignolo, *Local Histories/Global Designs*.

Cham, Gerardo. *Narrativas de exesclavizados afroamericanos. Conflictos de autoría*. Bielefeld: Bielefeld University Press, 2023

Chang, Heewon. *Autoethnography as Method*. New York: Routledge, 2008.

Clifford, James, and George E. Marcus, eds. *Writing Culture. The Poetics and Politics of Ethnography*. Berkeley: University of California Press, 1986.

Cohn, Bernard S. *An Anthropologist Among the Historians and Other Essays*. New Delhi: Oxford University Press, 1987.

Comisión de Verdad Histórica y Nuevo Trato. *Informe de la Comisión Verdad Histórica y Nuevo Trato con los Pueblos Indígenas*. Comisionado Presidencial para Asuntos Indígenas: Santiago de Chile, 2008. https://www.memoriachilena.gob.cl/602/articles-122901_recurso_2.pdf, accessed November 09, 2024.

Comisión de la Verdad. *Hay futuro si hay verdad. Informe Final de la Comisión para el Esclarecimiento de la Verdad, la Convivencia y la No Repetición*. 24 vols. Bogotá: -Comisión de la Verdad, 2022.

Comisión de la Verdad. *Hay futuro si hay verdad. Informe Final de la Comisión para el Esclarecimiento de la Verdad, la Convivencia y la No Repetición*, vol. 6. *Cuando los pájaros no cantaban: historias del conflicto armado en Colombia, tomo testimonial*. Bogotá: Comisión de la Verdad, 2022.

Condori Mamani, Greogorio. *Autobiografía*. Cuzco: Centro de Estudios Rurales Andinos Bartolomé de las Casas, 1978.

Conrad, Sebastian, Shalini Randeria, and Regina Römhild, eds. *Jenseits des Eurozentrismus. Postkoloniale Perspektiven in den Geschichts- und Kulturwissenschaften*. Frankfurt am Main: Campus Verlag, 2002.

Cornejo Polar, Antonio. *Escribir en el aire. Ensayo sobre la heterogeneidad socio-cultural en la literaturas andinas*. Lima: Editorial Horizonte, 1994.

Cornejo, Inés, and Mario Rufer, eds. *Horizontalidad. Hacia una crítica de las metodologías*. Buenos Aires: Clacso, 2022.

Corona Berkin, Sarah, Zeyda Rodríguez Morales, Elisa Cárdenas Ayala, Francisco Hernández Lomelí, Rebeca Pérez Daniel, Evelyn Diez-Martínez Day, Feliciano Díaz Sotero, Agustín Salvado Martínez, Viviana Ortiz Enrique, Graciela Ortiz Sotero, Eduardo Madera de la Cruz, Everardo de la Cruz Ramírez, Carlos Salvador Díaz, Fermín Santibáñez Madera, Apolonia de la Cruz Ramírez, and Ceferino Carrillo Díaz. *Entre voces. Fragmentos de educacción entrecultural*. Guadalajara: Universidad de Guadalajara, 2007.

Corona Berkin, Sarah, and Olaf Kaltmeier. "En diálogo. Metodologías horizontales en Ciencias Sociales y Culturales." In *En diálogo. Metodologías horizontales en Ciencias Sociales y Culturales*, edited by Sarah Corona Berkin, and Olaf Kaltmeier, 11–24. Barcelona: Gedisa, 2012.

Corona Berkin, Sarah, and Olaf Kaltmeier, eds. *En diálogo. Metodologías horizontales en Ciencias Sociales y Culturales*. Barcelona: Gedisa, 2012.

Corona Berkin, Sarah. "Notas para producir metodologías horizontales." In *En diálogo. Metodologías horizontales en Ciencias Sociales y Culturales*, edited by Sarah Corona Berkin, and Olaf Kaltmeier, 85–110. Barcelona: Gedisa, 2012.

Crapanzano, Vincent. "On the Writing of Etnography." *Dialectical Anthropology* 2, no. 1 (1977): 69–73.

Crespo, Carolina. "Processes of heritagiziation of indigenous cultural manifestations: lines of debate, analytical axis, and methodological approaches." In *Entangled Heritages. Postcolonial Perspectives on the Uses of the Past in Latin America*, edited by Olaf Kaltmeier, and Mario Rufer, 153–174. New York: Routledge, 2017.

de la Cadena, Marisol, and Orin Starn. *Indigenous Experience Today*. New York: Berg, 2007.

Ellis, Carolyn. *The Ethnographic I. A Methodological Novel about Autoethnography*. Walnut Creek: AltaMira Press, 2004.

Fabian, Johannes. *Time and the Other. How Anthropology Makes Its Object*. New York: Columbia University Press, 1983.

Fabian, Johannes. "Präsenz und Repräsentation. Die Anderen und das anthropologische Schreiben." In *Kultur, soziale Praxis, Text. Die Krise der ethnographischen Repräsentation*, edited by Eberhard Berg and Martin Fuchs, 335–364. Frankfurt am Main: Suhrkamp Verlag, 1995.

Frisch, Michael H. *A Shared Authority. Essays on the Craft and Meaning of Oral and Public History*. New York: State University of New York Press, 1990.

Gareis, Iris. *Die Geschichte der Anderen. Zur Ethnohistorie am Beispiel Perus 1532–1700*. Berlin: Reimer, 2003.

Giebeler, Cornelia, and Marina Meneses. "Geben und Nehmen im Forschungsprozess." In *Methoden dekolonialisieren. Eine Werkzeugkiste zur Demokratisierung der Sozial- und Kulturwissenschaften*, edited by Olaf Kaltmeier, and Sarah Corona Berkin, 145–169. Münster: Westfälisches Dampfboot, 2012.

Gorbach, Frida, and Mario Rufer, coord. *(In)disciplinar la investigación. Archivo, trabajo de campo y escritura*. México: Universidad Autónoma Metropolitana, 2016.

Guaman Poma de Ayala, Felipe. *Primer Nueva Corónica y Buen Gobierno*, edited by Rolena Adorno. Copenhagen: Royal Library of Denmark, 2006 [1614]. http://www.kb.dk/permalink/2006/poma/1/es/text/?open=id3083606, accessed November 09, 2024.

Gudynas, Eduardo. "Diez tesis urgentes sobre el nuevo extractivismo. Contextos y demandas bajo el progresismo sudamericano actual." In *Extractivismo, política y sociedad*, edited by Centro Andino de Acción Popular and Centro Latino Americano de Ecología Social, 187–225. Quito: Fundación Rosa Luxemburgo, 2009.

Guerrero, Andrés. "El proceso de identificación: sentido común ciudadano, ventriloquía y transescritura." In *Etnicidades*, edited by Andrés Guerrero, 9–60. Quito: Facultad Latinoamericana de Ciencias Sociales, 2000.

Harkin, Michael E. "Ethnohistory's Ethnohistory: Creating a Discipline from the Ground Up." *Social Science History* 34, no. 2 (2010): 113–128.

Harvey, David. *The New Imperialism*. Oxford: Oxford University Press, 2003.

Howard-Malverde, Rosaleen. "Pautas teóricas y metodológicas para el estudio de la historia oral andina contemporánea." In *Tradición oral andina y amazónica. Métodos de análisis e interpretación de textos*, edited by Juan Carlos Godenzzi. Cuzco: Programa de Formación en Educación Intercultural Bilingüe para los Países Andinos, 1999.

Kaltmeier, Olaf. "De la universidad a la pluriversidad: Creatividad y crisis de la producción académica de conocimiento." In *Creatividad en conflicto. Perspectivas interdisciplinarias desde las Américas en contextos de crisis*, edited by Olaf Kaltmeier, Wilfried Raussert, and Matti Steinitz. Buenos Aires: Clacso, 2024.

Kaltmeier, Olaf. *Resistencia indígena y formación del Estado. Saquisilí del siglo XVI al XXI*. Quito: Corporación Editora Nacional, 2021.

Kaltmeier, Olaf. "Politics of Indigeneity in the Andean Highlands. Indigenous Social Movements and the State in Ecuador, Bolivia, and Peru (1940–2014)." In *Indigeneity on the Move. Varying Manifestations of a Contested Concept*, edited by Eva Gerharz, Nasir Uddin, and Pradeep Chakkarath, 172–198. Oxford: Berghahn, 2017.

Kaltmeier, Olaf. "Hacia la descolonización de las metodologías: reciprocidad, horizontalidad y poder." In *En diálogo. Metodologías horizontales en Ciencias Sociales y Culturales*, edited by Sarah Corona Berkin, and Olaf Kaltmeier, 25–54. Barcelona: Gedisa, 2012.

Kaltmeier, Olaf. *Politische Räume jenseits von Staat und Nation*. Göttingen: Wallstein, 2012.

Kaltmeier, Olaf. "Heritage Cities and the Trauma of Coloniality. Postcolonial Conflicts about Space, Identity, and Memory in Historic City Centers in the Americas." In *Remembering and Forgetting: Memory in Images and Texts*, edited by Wilfried Raussert et al. Bielefeld: Aisthesis, 2010.

Kaltmeier, Olaf. *Jatarishun. Testimonios de la lucha indígena de Saquisilí (1930–2006)*. Quito: Universidad Andina Simón Bolívar Ecuador, 2008.

Kapoor, Ilan. *The Postcolonial Politics of Development*. London: Routledge, 2008.

Koselleck, Reinhart. *Zeitschichten. Studien zur Historik*. Frankfurt am Main: Suhrkamp Verlag, 2000.

Kowii, Ariruma. "Memoria, identidad e interculturalidad de los pueblos del Abya Yala." In *Intelectuales indígenas piensan América Latina*, edited by Claudia Zapata, 113–125. Quito: Abya Yala, 2007.

Krech, Shepard. "The State of Ethnohistory." *Annual Review of Anthropology* 20 (1991): 345–375.

Lienhard, Martin. *La voz y su huella. Escritura y conflicto étnico-cultural en América Latina, 1492–1988*. Lima: Editorial Horizonte, 1992.

Mallon, Florencia. *Courage Tastes of Blood: The Mapuche Community of Nicolás Ailío and the Chilean State, 1906–2001*. Durham: Duke University Press, 2005.

Menchú, Rigoberta. *I, Rigoberta Menchú*. Translated by Elizabeth Burgos-Debray. London: Verso, 1984.

Mignolo, Walter D. "Afterword: Writing and Recorded Knowledge in Colonial and Postcolonial Situations." In *Writing without words. Alternative Literacies in Mesoamerica and the Andes*, edited by Elizabeth Hill Boone, and Walter D. Mignolo, 292–312. Durham: Duke University Press, 1994.

Mignolo, Walter D. *Local Histories/Global Designs. Coloniality, Subaltern Knowledges, and Border Thinking*. Princeton: Princenton University Press, 2000.

Millalén Paillal, José, Pablo Marimán Quemenado, Sergio Caniuqueo Huircapán, and Rodrigo Levil Chicahual. *¡. . . Escucha, winka . . .! : cuatro ensayos de historia nacional mapuche y un epílogo sobre el futuro*. Santiago de Chile: LOM, 2006.

Moreno Yánez, Segundo E. "La Etnohistoria: anotaciones sobre su concepto y un examen de los aportes en el Ecuador." In *Contribución a la etnohistoria ecuatoriana*, edited by Segundo Moreno Yáñez, and Udo Oberem, 21–44. Otavalo: IOA, 1981.

Patai, Daphne. "U.S. academics and *third-world women*: Is ethical research possible?" In *Women's Words. The Feminist Practice of Oral History*, edited by Sherna Berger Gluck, and Daphne Patai, 137–154. New York: Routledge, 1991.

Pérez Daniel, Rebeca, and Stefano Sartorello. *Horizontalidad, diálogo y reciprocidad en los métodos de investigación social y cultural*. San Cristobál de Chiapas: CENEJUS Universidad Autónoma de Chiapas, 2012.

Portelli, Alessandro. "What makes Oral History different." In *The Oral History Reader*, edited by Robert Perks, and Alistair Thomson. London: Routledge, 2006.

Pratt, Mary Louise. "Arts in the Contact Zone." *Profession* (1991): 33–40.

Ramos Pacho, Abelardo, and Joanne Rappaport. "Collaboration and Historical Writing: Challenges for the Indigenous-Academic Dialogue." In *Decolonizing Native Histories: Collaboration, Knowledge, and Language in the Americas*, edited by Florencia Mallon, 122–143. Durham: Duke University Press, 2012.

Riaño, Yvonne. "La producción de conocimiento como "minga". Co-determinación y reciprocidaden la investigación con mujeres migrantes de América Latina, Medio oriente y Europa suroriental en Suiza." In *En diálogo. Metodologías horizontales en Ciencias Sociales y Culturales*, edited by Sarah Corona Berkin, and Olaf Kaltmeier, 137–160 Barcelona: Editorial Gedisa, 2012.

Rivera Cusicanqui, Silvia. *Un mundo ch'ixi es posible. Ensayos desde un presente en crisis*. Buenos Aires: Tinta Limón, 2018.

Rivera Cusicanqui, Silvia, and Luis H. Antezana. *Oppressed but not defeated. Peasant Struggles among the Aymara and Qhechwa in Bolivia 1900–1980*. Geneva: United Nations Research Institute for Social Development, 1987.

Rufer, Mario. "El habla, la escucha y la escritura. Subalternidad y horizontalidad desde la crítica poscolonial." In *En diálogo. Metodologías horizontales en Ciencias Sociales y Culturales*, edited by Sarah Corona Berkin, and Olaf Kaltmeier, 55–84. Barcelona: Gedisa, 2012.

Rufer, Mario. "No vamos a traducir. Instalar un secreto, negar la dádiva, redefinir el juego." In *Horizontalidad. Hacia una crítica de las metodologías*, edited by Inés Cornejo, and Mario Rufer, 277–302. Buenos Aires: Clacso, 2020.

Schwarzstein, Dora. "La historia oral en América Latina." *Historia y Fuente Oral* 14 (1995): 39–50.

Sharpless, Rebecca. "The History of Oral History." In *Thinking about Oral History. Theories and Applications*, edited by Thomas Lee Charlton, Lois E. Myers, and Rebecca Sharpless. Lanham: AltaMira Press, 2008.

Smith, Linda Tuhiwai. *Decolonizing Methodologies. Research and Indigenous Peoples*. London: Zed Books, 1999.

Sousa Santos, Boaventura. *Epistemologies of the South: Justice against Epistemicide*. Boulder: Paradigm Publishers, 2014.

Spivak, Gayatri Chakravorty. *Outside in the Teaching Machine*. London: Routledge, 1993.

Spivak, Gayatri Chakravorty. *A Critique of Postcolonial Reason. Toward a History of the Vanishing Present*. Cambridge: Harvard University Press, 1999.

Stephenson, Marcia. "Forging an Indigenous Counterpublic Sphere. The Taller de Historia Oral Andina in Bolivia." *Latin America Research Review* 37, no. 2 (2002): 99–118.

Stoler, Ann Laura. *Along the Archival Grain. Epistemic Anxieties and Colonial Common Sense*. Princeton: Princeton University Press, 2008.

Stoll, David. *Rigoberta Menchú and the Story of All Poor Guatemalans*. London: Routledge, 1999.

Taussig, Michael, ed. *Un Gigante en convulsiones. El mundo humano como sistema nervioso en emergencia permanente*. Barcelona: Gedisa, 1998.

Tedlock, Dennis. "Fragen zur dialogischen Anthropologie." In *Kultur, soziale Praxis, Text. Die Krise der ethnographischen Repräsentation*, edited by Eberhard Berg, and Martin Fuchs, 269–287. Frankfurt am Main: Suhrkamp Verlag, 1995.

Ticona, Esteban. *Memoria, política y antropología en los Andes bolivianos. Historia oral y sabers locales*. La Paz: AGRUCU, Universidad de la Cordillera, Plural Editores, 2005.

Tibán, Lourdes, Raúl Ilaquiche, and Eloy Alfaro. *Movimiento indígena y campesino de Cotopaxi (MICC). Historia y proceso organizativo*. Latacunga: Movimiento Indígena y Campesino de Cotopaxi, 2003.

Waldenfels, Bernhard. *Ordnung im Zwielicht*. Frankfurt a.M.: Suhrkamp, 1987.

White, Hayden. *Metahistory. Die historische Einbildungskraft im 19. Jahrhundert in Europa*. Frankfurt am Main: Suhrkamp, 1991.

Wilson, Angela Waziyatawin, and Michael Yellow Bird, eds. *For Indigenous Eyes only. A Decolonization Handbook*. Santa Fe: School of American Research Press, 2005.

Zapata, Claudia. *Intelectuales indígenas en Ecuador, Bolivia y Chile*. Quito: Abya Yala, 2013.

Part Three: **Case Studies**

Menachem Klein

7 Jerusalem's History from Below – a History of Personal and Historiographical Transitions

7.1 Introduction

> Muslim women respected Jewish religious customs. Their Jewish neighbors would ask them not to draw water from the communal well in the courtyard on the Sabbath, so as not to dirty the yard that the Jewish women had worked so hard to clean the day before. The Muslim women acceded to the request of their Jewish neighbors and drew the water they needed for their households before the Sabbath began.[1]

In the following pages, I explain the historical significance of this and similar primary sources regarding late 19th and early 20th century Jerusalem, why conservative historians underestimated them and how I came to put them in the centre of a book. More generally, through the case study of modern Jerusalem I present a case for the difference history from below makes.

The city of Jerusalem's long and rich history and exalted religious status has produced countless top-down historical studies. However, it is only recently that historians of modern Jerusalem have begun to study the city from its residents' perspective. In the first part of this chapter, I summarise the findings and gains from those studies. It should be noted that studying modern Jerusalem, i.e. from late 19th century up to the 1948 war, from its average citizens' perspective, produces a congruence of subject-matter shared across all Middle Eastern societies: Arab-Jewish identity, endorsing modernisation, developing national identities, and resisting colonialism. In the second part, I turn from discussing subjects to methods and sources. I bring to the fore problems that students of Jerusalem's history, and of related Israeli-Palestinian subjects, face when dealing with Israeli archives' regulations, and in the absence of a Palestinian state archive or an independent Palestinian Jerusalem archive. Following this, I suggest a few methods to overcome these problems.

In both parts of this chapter, I integrate into the narrative my own personal double shifts: from political and cultural history to bottom-up history, and from far-off societies' history to the history of my place of living. My experience, I hope, illustrates the main subjects I discuss.

---

1 Ya'acov Ela'zar, *Hatzerot Beyerushalayim Ha'atikah [Courtyards in Jerusalem's Old City]* (Jerusalem: Yad Larishonim, 1980), 227.

https://doi.org/10.1515/9783111522180-007

7.2 Lately My Research meets My City

I was not born in Jerusalem, but have lived there most of my life. Even though the city attracts plenty of researchers in a variety of fields, I started studying Jerusalem quite late in my academic career. My city experience did not meet my academic interests. Middle East studies' methodology brought me to separate my everyday urban experience from my academic interests. Middle East and Islamic studies at the Hebrew University where I studied, as in all Israeli universities, has a philological-linguistic base. According to the German Jews who founded the Oriental Science Institute at the young Hebrew University (1924–1925), Arabic was the key factor in forming departmental boundaries, leaving Hebrew-based Israel and Jewish studies outside.[2]

Seeing Jerusalem as a Jewish and Israeli city became common in Biblical, Jewish history, and Geography departments, but not in mine. Moreover, Middle East history and Islam departments in the 1970s and 80s did not share the same school with European, American, and Jewish departments of history. Thus, non-linguistic or philological methodologies that shaped Western historical studies were rarely endorsed by Orientalists. The short distance between humanities and social science faculty buildings was rarely bridged methodologically. In addition, Middle East studies leaned heavily on archival documents and printed materials. Oral history's reliability was doubted, and interviews and participant observation were left to sociologists and anthropologists. Current events, i.e. post World War II matters, were considered relatively thin International Relations subjects that bordered on journalism and were lacking in a solid historical base. Unfortunately, my life experience in the city remained outside my academic boundaries. Consequently, I lacked critical thinking on Jerusalem.

Like most of my Israeli Jewish compatriots, after the 1967 War I viewed Jerusalem's Palestinians as a collection of religious factions very different from mine. Israelis perceived the Old City as an "open museum," merely the setting for a series of Jewish archaeological and historical sites from the time of King David and the Second Temple, in which the Palestinians were part of the set-up, an echo of the past, friendly, charming strangers. At that time, I was not aware that this is a

---

2 Amit Levy, "The Archive as Storyteller: Refractions of German-Jewish Oriental Studies Migration in Personal Archives," *JBDI* 17 (2018): 425–446. Amit Levi, "Conflicting German Orientalism: Zionist Arabists and Arab Scholars 1926–1938," *British Journal of Middle Eastern Studies* 49 (2022): 2, https://www.tandfonline.com/doi/full/10.1080/13530194.2022.2064819, accessed July 10, 2024; Yonatan Mandel, *The Creation of Israeli Arabic: Security and Politics in Arabic Studies in Israel* (Hampshire: Palgrave 2014).

7 Jerusalem's History from Below — **179**

typical colonialist-orientalist perspective. Their apparent passivity gave rise to the notion that they accepted Israeli sovereignty. The 1987 Intifada changed my mind.

I started researching Jerusalem as an ex-academia think-tank member simultaneously to preparing my PhD on Egypt's intellectuals in the 1950s. Following the 1993 Oslo agreement in which Israel and the Palestinian Liberation Organisation (PLO) agreed to decide the future of East Jerusalem within five years, the Jerusalem Institute for Israel Studies established a team of academics to collate data and compose policy papers for the future negotiations. Following my publications on the PLO, I was asked to join that team. Then, the myth of "united Jerusalem the eternal capital of Israel" ruled over the Israeli public and state agencies. The political leadership did not delegate its agencies to look into the urban reality that showed clearly that the city is deeply divided between Jews and Arabs. At the Camp David 2000 summit, the Israeli delegation's proposals to divide Jerusalem were based on the Jerusalem Institute drafts. Besides, in 1999–2000 I advised the Israeli Prime Minister and the Minister of Foreign Affairs.

The Jerusalem Institute team met regularly with their Palestinian counterpart team operating in the Orient House, the Palestinian headquarters in Jerusalem. The Orient House founder, Faisal Husseini, established it to introduce the city to the PLO leadership that lived outside Jerusalem, and up to 1994 outside Palestine. I learned a lot from those Palestinian experts. Thus, from 1994 to 2000, I gradually moved my academic interest to the socio-political division of Jerusalem.[3] Yet, contemporary and future Jerusalem dominated my attention, not the city's history.

I reoriented my interest around 2010 when it became clear that no political breakthrough could be expected in the near future. In that period, I participated in an Israeli-Palestinian intellectual exercise, organised by the Bruno Kreisky Forum for International Dialogue in Vienna, on discovering alternatives to the Oslo model of land partition. This approach goes against the common wisdom. In addition to security considerations supporting the building of a hard border between Israel and Palestine, a hidden hypothesis exists behind the Oslo partition and separation model: that Israel is an island of advanced Westerners surrounded by underdeveloped oriental Arabs. Contrary to that hypothesis, we acknowledged that historically

---

3 Menachem Klein, *Jerusalem: The Contested City* (New York: New York University Press and London: C. Hurst, 2001); Menachem Klein, "Jerusalem without East-Jerusalemites? The Palestinians as the 'Other' in Jerusalem," *Journal of Israeli History* 23, no. 2 (2004): 174–199. Menachem Klein, "Old and New Walls in Jerusalem," *Political Geography* 24, no. 1 (2005): 53–76. Menachem Klein, "Jerusalem as an island Israeli Problem – a Review of Forty Years of Israeli Rule Over Arab Jerusalem," *Israel Studies* 13, no. 2 (2008): 54–72.

Jews were an integral part of the region and its history, and we suggested guiding principles for a Jewish Israeli-Palestinian partnership.[4] Intellectually, I was ready to consider sharing Jerusalem rather than dividing it with a physical barrier.

7.3 Subjects

Palestine's Native Jews

Zionism was established outside Palestine in the late 19th century. From then, and into the early 20th century, Zionists debated the movement's end goal. The views moved from establishing Jewish cultural or national autonomy somewhere in Europe, maybe in more than one location, through building a centre of spiritual identity in Palestine, to socio-political self-determination in Palestine. Once the majority opted for the latter against the flow of Jewish immigrants to America, financial and political sponsors were needed to persuade Jews to immigrate to a Palestine that was neither empty nor ungoverned. It is reasonable to assume that without rich Jews' donations to the Zionist immigrants, and Great Britain's political patronage, this form of Zionism would have remain unfulfilled. Conservative studies are interested in the development of the Zionist enterprise but much less in the attitudes and living conditions of native Palestinians. Only recently have they been examined. The "new portrait of the early years of the Zionist-Arab encounter", Jonathan Gribetz demonstrates, "is much richer, more nuanced, and in many respects more interesting than that of the conventional accounts".[5]

Today the term "Arab Jew" sounds bizarre and contradictory. Jews descending from Arab countries prefer to call themselves oriental Jews. However, before nationalism brutally separated the two words and required Middle East inhabitants to count themselves as one or the other, there were people who thought of themselves as Arab Jews just as today there are American or British Jews. This identity was more a fact of life encountered daily than an ideology expressed theoretically in books and articles. Middle East Jews spoke Arabic, consumed Arab culture, and, as modernisation reached the region, integrated into the majority

---

4 Yehouda Shenhav, *Beyond the Two States Solution – A Jewish Political Essay* (Cambridge: Polity Press, 2012). Bashir Bashir and Azar Dakwar, eds., *Rethinking the Politics of Israel/Palestine, Partition and its Alternatives* (Vienna: Bruno Kreisky Forum for International Dialogue, 2014), https://issuu.com/brunokreiskyforum/docs/rethinking_-_the_politics_of_israel, accessed July 10, 2024.
5 Jonathan M. Gribetz, *Defining Neighbors Religion Race and the Early Zionist-Arab Encounter* (Princeton: Princeton University Press, 2014), 4.

society. Led by scholars located outside Israel, far from where conservative Zionism dominated researchers' agenda, the history of Arab Jews in the modern Middle East has developed in the last three decades. Palestine's Arab Jews, however, have only recently been studied at all by critical historians. Jerusalem with its Arab Jews stands at the center of those studies.[6]

It is widely assumed that Albert Memmi[7] coined the term "Arab Jew" in 1975. Nevertheless, it was not an Arab Jew from Algiers who invented the term in the late 20th century. It was an outsider observer – a traveler, an Ashkenazi Jew, Abraham Shmuel Hirschberg, who wrote in 1910 that Sephardi Jews in Jerusalem "are characteristics of the people among whom they settle. They are Arab Jews – having good manners on the exterior but uncivilized internally".[8] For Hirschberg, shared language, culture, or customs are not sufficient to define those Jews as Arab Jews. Hirschberg looked beyond these external expressions. According to him, Jews and Arabs share the same character and manner. Moreover, due to the impact of their Sephardi compatriots, Hirschberg added, in Jerusalem, Ashkenazi men and women form a hybrid type of Ashkenazi-Sephardi-Arab-Jew personality.[9] Primary sources show that not only an external observer like Hirschberg used the name Arab Jew. Palestinians publishing in the late 19th and early 20th centuries, or reflecting back on these early times, write on *al-yahud al-'arab* (Arab Jews), *yahud awlad 'arab* (native Arab Jews), *al-yahud al muwalidun fi Filastin* (Palestine-born Jews), *al-yahud al-'asliin* (original Jews) and *abna al-balad* (local Jews).[10] Since the late 19th century, Jews were the majority in Jerusalem, and the city was heavily mixed. Big Jewish communities existed also in Jaffa, Hebron, Safed and Tiberius. In the mid-1920s between 700 and 800 Jews lived in the Arab towns of Gaza, Be'er Sheva, Nazareth,

---

6 Menachem Klein, "Arab Jews in Palestine," *Israel Studies* 19, no. 3 (2014): 134–135.

7 Memmi Albert, *Who Is an Arab Jew?* (Jerusalem: Israel Academic Committee on the Middle East, 1975), also in "harissa," http://www.harissa.com/eng/whoisanarabjew.htm, accessed July 10, 2024.

8 Abraham Hirshberg, *In the Orient Land* (Vilnius 1910), 393–94 [in Hebrew].

9 Hirshberg, *Orient*, 393–94.

10 Abigail Jacobson and Moshe Naor, *Oriental Neighbors – Middle Eastern Jews and Arabs in Mandatory Palestine* (Waltham Massachusetts: Brandeis University Press, 2016), 8. Menachem Klein, *Lives in Common: Arabs and Jews in Jerusalem, Jaffa and Hebron* (London: Hurst and NY: Oxford University Press, 2014), 21; Yuval Evri and Hillel Cohen, "Between Shared Homeland to to National Home, the Balfour Declaration from a Native Sephardic Perspective," in *The Arab and Jewish Questions, Geographies of Engagements in Palestine and Beyond*, ed. Bashir Bashir and Leila Farsakh (New York: Columbia University Press, 2020), 148–172.

Bissan-Beit Shean, Ramleh Acer, Jericho, Jenin or Sameh in addition to the big Jewish communities in Jerusalem, Jaffa, Hebron, Safed, and Tiberius.[11]

Zachary Lockman's pioneering social history on blue-collar workers' relations between 1906 and 1948, and his method of relational history,[12] opened the door for urban and social historians like Jacobson and Naor, Wallach, Tamari, Lemir, LeVine [see below] and myself to revise the dominant school's approach and conclusions.

Studies written from the perspective of a central authority conclude that local patriotism did not exist in Palestine in the late 19th to the early 20th century, or was the weakest identity compared with two vertical belongings: Arab nationalism and Ottoman loyalty.[13] Bottom up studies, however, lead to the conclusion that indigenous Jews and Arabs shared a strong local identity, i.e. an identity belonging to a region and people much larger than one's extended family and religious denomination. That local patriotism did not replace religious identity and belonging. Yet, it lowered the barriers that earlier sharply divided Jews, Muslims and Christians.[14] Indeed, only with the establishment of the British Mandate in 1922 did Palestine become a distinct administrative and political unit. Nevertheless, it was not that unit that created the Palestinian identity, but rather the other way around. Local identity had already developed prior to World War I in urban centres, first and foremost in Jerusalem, where natives encountered growing numbers of Western visitors, exchanged ideas, established modern schools, or enjoyed modern medical treatment. The main cities in Palestine went through significant modernisation processes, which gradually changed everything, from the physical environment, transportation and the appearance of the residential neighborhoods and streets, through patterns of education, the economy and intel-

---

11 Jacobson and Naor, *Oriental Neighbors*. Klein, *Lives in Common*; Reuven Gafni, *A Hebrew Presence in Bein Shean: A Jewish Community in an Arab City in the British Mandate Period* (Jerusalem: Magness, 2018) [in Hebrew].

12 Zachary Lockman, *Comrades and Enemies. Arab and Jewish Workers in Palestine 1906–1948* (Berkeley: University of California Press, 1966).

13 Mishelle Campos, *Ottoman Brothers, Muslim Christian and Jews in early twentieth-century Palestine* (Stanford: Stanford University Press, 2011); Yehoshoua Porath, *The Emergence of the Palestinian-Arab National Movement 1918–29* (London: Frank Cass, 1974); Muhammad Muslih, *The Origins of Palestinian Nationalism* (New York: Columbia University Press, 1989); Rashid Khalidi, *Palestinian Identity – The Construction of Modern National Consciousness* (New York: Columbia University Press, 1997).

14 Menachem Klein, "Joint Jewish and Muslim Holy Places, Religious Believes and Festivals in Jerusalem between the late 19th Century and 1948," *Religion* 9, no. 7 (2018): 220, http://www.mdpi. com/journal/religions/special_issues/jewish-muslim, accessed July 10, 2024. Published as special issue on Remembering Jewish – Muslim Encounters Challenges and Cooperation.

lectual life, to self-definition in terms of nationalism.[15] Modernity, therefore, was not an exclusive Jewish-Zionist enterprise as Zionists claim, echoing colonial arguments on its civilising mission. The escalating Zionist-Palestinian conflict in the 1930s, however, divided the Arab Jewish identity. Each national movement claimed a powerfully exclusive patriotism, and shaped its collective memory via textbooks, ceremonies, and mythical heroes. The process reached its peak in the 1948 war. Until recently, Arab Jewish identity remained confined to the memories of the few who experienced it.

The move to write Jerusalem's history from its citizens' perspective brought about new conclusions on four subjects: first, it suggested an alternative periodisation not necessarily dominated by wars and confrontations, but by the city-dwellers' encounters before and after violent clashes. Second, instead of a binary approach, bottom-up history portrays the Arab Jew as a hybrid identity expressed in everyday life, in joint public spaces, shared holy sites, and religious festivals. Third, new historical studies expose roads that mainstream actors preferred not to take, roads that the top-down method leaves uncharted. Palestine's Arab Jews published political programme that went against the Zionist claim for establishing an exclusive Jewish national homeland in Palestine. Similar to their Palestinian Arab compatriots, in 1921 Haim Ben Kiki and Yosef Haim Castel opposed the Balfour Declaration and the Zionist leadership's collaboration with Britain. Ben Kiki saw the Declaration as a clear expression of Western colonialisms. Castel suggested rewriting the Balfour Declaration to recognise the national rights of the Palestinian (Arab Muslim and Arab Christian) majority alongside the national rights of the Jews. Palestine, he argued, is also the homeland of local Arabs.[16] In November 1929, following August riots, David Avissar, the chairperson of the Association of the Pioneers of the East, criticised the Zionist leadership for not considering the Arabs' rights. Instead, he suggested, "a single, joint homeland for Jews and Arabs should be established in Palestine ... both peoples would enjoy national self-determination through the egalitarian allocation of governmental powers and the autonomy of each people to nurture its own life".[17] In December 1927, Eliyahu Sasson, a Syrian born Jew who joined the Arab nationalist movement, argued: "the Palestinian country will not gain its freedom and independence unless all forces – Jews, Christians and Muslims – unite to free it from foreign powers".[18] In other words, he opposed the Zionist political strategy to rely

---

15 Klein, *Lives in Common*; Yair Wallach, *A City in Fragments. Urban Text in Modern Jerusalem* (Stanford: Stanford University Press, 2020).

16 Evry and Cohen, *Between Shared Homeland*.

17 Jacobson and Naor, *Oriental Neighbors*, 30.

18 Jacobson and Naor, *Oriental Neighbors*, 101–102.

exclusively on Britain. Later, Sasson and his contemporaries transformed from sharp critics of Zionist political strategy to political operators serving the Zionist-Ashkenazi establishment and its pro-British policy. Sasson accepted Zionist hegemony both in policy making and determining social status hierarchies. Thus, during the Mandatory years, Arab Jews' role changed from loyal opposition to subordinated operators in the service of the Zionist elite.

Fourth, bottom-up history locates modernisation, enlightenment and local-patriotism in the Middle East, not just in Europe. In other words, Middle Eastern intellectuals were agents of enlightenment, not just subjects of the encounter with the West. Everyday life history disproves the Orientalist-Zionist dichotomy between modern Zionist immigrants and British administration on the one hand, and Arab city and Ottoman regime backwardness on the other hand.[19] Based on new Ottoman archives, maps drawn by Jerusalemites, old photographs, and the first documentary films produced, Lemir describes Jerusalem of the late 19th century as a vivid city with new energies.[20] Tamari gives voice and historical presence to the Palestinian partners in the local identity. His work is extremely important because many Palestinian primary sources were lost in the 1948 war or still remain unpublished.[21]

Conclusion: History from Below: Perspective and Methodology

Historians of elite groups, political historians, and those interested in the Arab-Israeli conflict move from one violent clash to the next. Interested in the escalation and in the development of conflict, they do not ask in what ways everyday life was reestablished when urban violence ended. Conflict studies use mostly top-down methods. They are interested in elite groups, powerful ruling institutions, fights or revolts against them, religious movements and their authorities, top-down planning and zoning, ethnic demography, and social infrastructure. Their political and military narratives on the Israeli-Palestinian conflict are mainly deterministic and teleological: the first conflict at any given year zero started a chain of tragic bloodshed, during which each conflict paved the way for

---

19 Mark LeVine, *Overlooking Geography – Jaffa Tel Aviv and the Struggle for Palestine 1880–1948* (Berkeley: University of California Press, 2005).

20 Vincent Lemir, *Jerusalem 1900 The Holy City in the Age of Possibilities* (Chicago: Chicago University Press 2017).

21 Salim Tamari, *Mountain against the Sea – Essays on Palestinian Society and Culture* (Berkeley: University of California Press 2009).

the next one.[22] Whereas the mainstream historiography sees Zionist-Palestinian clashes only as nation building events, either Jewish-Israeli or Palestinian, new critical historians[23] consider them also as destructive events. Inter-communal violence destroyed local patriotism, the identity that Jews and Arabs shared.

Recently, scholars have moved from the history of clashes and elite groups to human encounter; and from dramatic events to prosaic everyday life, including the impact of those clashes on everyday life in between rounds of violence.[24] Unlike the previous school, urban bottom-up history puts the city dweller in the center. These histories reject the conclusion that Jews and Arabs in Palestine interacted only in a very limited way. Those who endorse this conclusion, they claim, read late 19th to early 20th century events from the perspective of the later conflict. Instead of using binary categories, they suggest studying forms of encounters between Jews and Arabs across the social spectrum.[25] In other words, not all local ethno-national communities shared their leadership's exclusive perspective of an unavoidable all-out conflict.

Whereas the conflict-based school looks into Zionist-British relations and compares Mandatory Palestine to British colonial methods elsewhere, relational historians remain in the Arab region. They can show that, based on a shared identity and culture, Palestine Arab Jews maintained close relations with Arab-Jews in the Levant and Egypt.[26] Yet, more comparative studies across the Middle East and North Africa are needed to explore further what Arab Jews have in common and what constitute their unique local identity.

---

22 Hillel Cohen, *1929 Year Zero of the Arab – Israeli Conflict* (Waltham Massachusetts: Brandeis University Press 2016). Baruch Kimmerling and Yoel s. Migdal, *The Palestinian People. A History* (Cambridge: Harvard University Press, 2003). Simon Sebag Montefiore, *Jerusalem the Biography* (New York: Vintage, 2011).
23 Menachem Klein, "The 21st Century New Critical Historians," *Israel Studies Review* 32, no. 2, (2017): 146–163.
24 Klein, *Lives in Common*; Jacobson and Naor, *Oriental Neighbors*; Campos Mishelle, *Ottoman Brothers, Muslim Christian and Jews in early twentieth-century Palestine* (Stanford: Stanford University Press, 2011); Gafni Reuven, *A Hebrew Presence in Bein Shean: A Jewish Community in an Arab City in the British Mandate Period* (Jerusalem: Magness Press, 2018) [in Hebrew]; Lemir, *Jerusalem 1900*; Tamari, *Mountain against the Sea*; Yair Wallach, *A City in Fragments*.
25 Deborah Bernstein, *Constructing Boundaries: Jewish and Arab Workers in Mandatory Palestine* (Albany: SUNY Press, 2000).
26 Jacobson and Naor, *Oriental Neighbors*, 95–106.

7.4 Sources

The Challenge of Sources

Historians turning from hegemonic institutions to average citizens' history often face the challenge of finding the right sources. "Open Jerusalem" is a web directory and catalogue of archives aiming to help historians write bottom-up studies on the city between the years 1840–1940.[27] The rich collection links to different archives: municipalities, the Waqf (Islamic endowment), consulates, patriarchates, and associations that store documents on Jerusalem for that period. The Open Jerusalem website catalogue also includes a section on personal documents held in those archives. However, "Open Jerusalem" does not include documents still in the possession of private persons.

The project has an accompaying book in which scholars extract from those archives different aspects of Jerusalem's everyday life.[28] The volume's fundamental research question is "in the face of religious barriers and projections of national identities, how do residents proceed to 'make a city' anyway?"[29] In other words, how is local identity developed and maintained. Yasemin Avci, Vincent Lemir and Falestin Naili, show the benefits that can be derived from Jerusalem's Ottoman municipality archive. Since 1967, these documents are part of the Historical Archive of Jerusalem Municipality. In the 1967 war, Israel expropriated the Jordanian municipality documents, including the Ottoman archive that the Jordanians inherited from the British Mandate authority (see below for more on the municipal archive). The Ottoman archive, the three authors write, "offer a unique perspective into the urban development of Jerusalem and the workings of the administration in the last decades of the Ottoman rule".[30] The documents include "routine administrative procedures . . . public bids for civil administration and army needs . . . public sales of tax farming rights . . . and nomination of municipal staff. The municipality owned a large number of stores and several hotels", and therefore income-generating activities "occupy an important place in the municipal minutes".[31]

---

27 "Open Jerusalem," http://www.openjerusalem.org/, accessed July 10, 2024.

28 Angelos Dalachanis and Vincent Lemire, eds., *Ordinary Jerusalem 1840–1940, Opening New Archives Revisiting a Global City* (Leiden: Brill 2018).

29 Angelos Dalachanis and Vincent Lemire, "Introduction: Opening Ordinary Jerusalem," in *Ordinary Jerusalem*: 7.

30 Yasemin Avci, Vincent Lemir and Falestin Naili, "Publishing Jerusalem's Ottoman Municipal Archives (1892 – 1917): A Turning Point for the City Historiography," *The Jerusalem Quarterly*, 60 (2015): 111, https://www.palestine-studies.org/sites/default/files/jq-articles/JQ_60_Publishing_Jerusalem_0.pdf, accessed July 10, 2024.

31 Avci, Lemir, and Naili, "Publishing Jerusalem's Ottoman," 114.

The Challenge of the Consequences of War

History sources of all kinds are also wars' victims. In the 1948 war, for instance, the Jaffa municipality documents, and the city residents' private papers and libraries were lost forever. West Jerusalem Palestinian refugees left behind rich collections of books. When the fires went out in those areas, a team of the Israeli National Library collected abandoned books from houses with open doors and integrated them into the library collection.[32] In addition, the Palestinian defeat in 1948, the catastrophe (Nakba in Arabic), destroyed Palestinians' attention to writing their history. The first Nakba generation was busy in surviving socially and economically, against circumstances of occupation, geographical division, and the fate of becoming refugees. In addition, many felt ashamed by their leadership's failures, and chose silence. Whereas the Zionist movement claimed its origins in Jewish enlightenment and in scientific inquiry into Jewish history, the Palestinian national movement, reestablished in the 1960s, based itself on armed struggle, resistance, and national liberation ideologies. Developing national history and restoring collective memory were not part of the Palestinian renaissance. Until late in the 20th century, only a few Palestinian academics in Western countries collected and published on their nation's modern history.[33]

To the deficit in Palestinian primary sources, we have to add the winner's interest in shaping history according to its ideology. Besides publishing documents supporting its own narrative, Israeli authorities keep classified documents that disprove the official historiography or damage the state image as the pure victim side in the bloody conflict. Although the Israeli law is clear on the period that the state is allowed to keep documents classified, the Israeli State Archive is very slow in declassifying files. In 2019, 300,000 files were still closed, including more than 100 files of the 1800s, and 125 files from the 19th century.[34] In addition, in spring 2016, the archive closed its reading room where students could read paper files. Instead, it offers to send, upon request, digitised files. However, the Israeli authorities consider any scanned and sent-out digitised files to be a "publication", unlike reading paper files in the Archive. Therefore, each digitised file

---

32 Gish Amit, "Salvage or Plunder? Israel's 'Collection' of Private Palestinian Libraries in West Jerusalem," *Journal of Palestine Studies* 40, no. 4 (2011), https://www.palestine-studies.org/en/node/42473, accessed July 10, 2024.

33 "Vimeo," *Conversation between Beshara Doumani Issam Nassar and Salim Tamari* in https://vimeo.com/127736799, accessed July 10, 2024.

34 Asaf Shalev, "More than 100 Files from the 1800s are still classified in Israel's Archives," *+972 Magazine* February 15 (2019), https://www.972mag.com/israel-archives-1800s-classified/, accessed July 10, 2024.

deemed to relate to security matters will be sent first to the Military Censor for review.[35] Moreover, in 2020–2021, a team on behalf of the Military Censor and the Director of Security of the Defence Establishment visited various archives to collect and reclassify documents that opened after fifty years, among them those that historians published or used to base their critical studies.[36] In general, Israel understands security in a very broad sense. Instead of declassifying all files after 30 or 50 years, with few sheer security exceptions, the Israeli archive's rule is the opposite. Therefore, for instance, Arab consulate documents captured in the 1948 war, and most Jordanian files appropriated in 1967, are still closed. However, Israeli Jewish academic researchers serving in the military intelligence or in the occupation administration have used the Jordanian security reports.[37] But when the Jerusalemite-Palestinian historian Musa Budeiri asked to read the same files, the Director of the State Archive rejected his request, arguing that those files were under the military authority. Budeiri was forced to go back and forth between different offices until he was permitted to see only some of those Jordanian files. Frequently, he received "lost", "non-existent", "closed" or "misplaced" answers to his files orders.[38] Worse, in August 2001, under the pretext of security, Israeli police looted the Arab Studies Society library and photography collections located in the Orient House, the Palestinian headquarter in the city that Israel or-

---

35 Haggai Matar, "The End of History at Israel's State Archives?," *+972 Magazine* April 12 (2016), https://www.972mag.com/the-end-of-history-at-israels-state-archives/, accessed July 10, 2024.

36 *These Matters Are Unpleasant*, Akevot report October 2021 in https://www.akevot.org.il/en/news-item/these-matters-are-unpleasant-a-new-report-by-akevot/, accessed July 10, 2024; *Silencing DSDE's Concealment of Documents in Archives*, Akevot report July 2019 in https://www.akevot.org.il/en/news-item/akevots-report-reveals-dsdes-unlawful-concealment-of-files-in-archives/, accessed July 10, 2024. Ofer Aderet, "State Archive Error Shows Israeli Censorship Guided by Concerns Over National Image," *Haaretz* January 5 (2022), https://www.haaretz.com/israel-news/.premium. HIGHLIGHT.MAGAZINE-state-archive-error-shows-israeli-censorship-guided-by-concerns-over-national-image-1.10517841, accessed July 10, 2024. "Israel State Archivist Demand All State-related Documents be Handed," *The Jerusalem Post* May 31 (2020), https://www.jpost.com/israel-news/israels-state-archives-demand-all-state-related-documents-be-handed-in-629789, accessed July 10, 2024.

37 Eldad Ben Aharon and Itay Mack, "Israeli Archives Censorship Regulations and Oral History," *The Jerusalem Post* August 22 (2022), https://www.jpost.com/opinion/israeli-archives-censorship-regulations-and-oral-history-639569, accessed July 10, 2024; Amnon Cohen, *Political Parties in the West Bank under the Jordanian Regime 1949–1967* (Ithaca/London: Cornel University Press, 1982); Avraham Sela, *The Palestinian Ba'ath the Arab Socialist Ba'ath Party in the West Bank Under Jordan, 1948–1967* (Jerusalem: The Hebrew University, 1984), [in Hebrew].

38 Musa K Budeiri, "Controlling the Archive: Captured Jordanian Security Files in the Israeli State Archive," *Jerusalem Quarterly* 66 (Sumer 2016), https://www.palestine-studies.org/en/node/202343, accessed July 10, 2024.

dered to close down. The collections included the private papers of the prominent Palestinian leader Musa al-Alami (1897–1984), approximately 17,000 books and 70 periodicals, the press archive, maps, manuscripts, oral history records, and photographs recording Jerusalemites' ethnographic relations since the 19th century.[39] All efforts to find out where the appropriated collections are stored and if they are kept in the right storage conditions, have so far failed.

In addition to the state-made regulations limiting accessibility to primary source in all Israeli archives, there are those that historians of modern Jerusalem face in the municipal archive. Most of Israeli documents on Jerusalem are divided between the State Archive and the Jerusalem Municipality Historical Archive. A few are available in small local archives such as Yad Ben Zvi and David Citadel Museum. The Jordanian documents that Israel captured in the 1967 war are kept in hundreds of boxes. The State Archive holds Jerusalem District Governor files and the Municipal Archive stores the Jordanian Municipality files.

Preparations to open a Jerusalem Municipal Archive started in 1959, but it was only in 1963 that it opened its doors. It never gained high priority in Mayors' agenda and budget allocation, nor did it become a cultural and educational institution. The neglected municipal archive in the basement of the big modern municipality building stores documents from the foundation of the Ottoman municipality in 1867 up to today. Its historical importance is spread far beyond local institutions or the State of Israel's history. According to unofficial data that I was able to get, the archive stores about 100,000 boxes, out of which 35,000 boxes contain historical documents. Only 7000 boxes are located in the municipality building; the rest are stored in a West Bank settlement. Its rich historical collections include educational and religious institutions' papers, NGOs archives, neighbourhood committee's reports, ethnic association committees' papers, and dignitaries' private archives. Despite its first-class historical treasures, the archive suffers from many years of neglect by the municipality authorities. Mayors and state leaders that proudly raise statements on Jerusalem's history, do nearly nothing to preserve it. With its dysfunctional website, and an undetailed and inappropriate catalogue, it ensures that researchers face serious problems knowing what the collection exactly contains, and what to order. Open three days a week for only three hours, it offers a tiny reading room. Most of the staff serving there are not professional archivists, neither do they have a wide historical knowledge on the city and the region. Lack of a budget and a qualified work force make the big photograph collection unavailable for users and unca-

---

39 Nur Masalaha, *The Palestinian Nakba, Decolonizing History Narrating the Subaltern Reclaiming Memory* (London: Zed Books, 2012), 145–147.

talogued even by the archive's already low standards. Concerning the Jordanian documents, none of the employees read Arabic. Therefore, no information is available on the boxes' contents except their title. In principle, they are closed. When I asked to get them to complete my study on Jerusalem 1949–1967, I was told that the archive must receive legal permission. After many months, I was allowed to read eight boxes containing 19 heavy volumes of the Jordanian City Council minutes. These volumes are invaluable sources for the study of the Jordanian municipality administration, issuing building permits, the development of water and electricity infrastructure systems, the city's sanitation, its street maintenance, and the city's physical development. Through these volumes, not only can researchers benefit, but also Palestinian Jerusalemites can reclaim their history. However, I did not get permission to see other boxes nor to know their subjects. I was told that they are in Arabic [surprise, indeed] and that they contain "security issues". I assume that those files include the confidential debates the Municipality council had had since December 1963.[40]

The State Archive deals much better with the Jordanian District files. It enjoys better financial resources and professionally qualified personnel. Their files are fully catalogued, but it takes several months until the Archive team can declassify a requested file. The Archive's review of files once classified is irregular and very selective. Moreover, according to the new regulations, the ministry or agency that deposited a file 30 or 50 years ago should declassify it upon request. Nevertheless, this is not included in the priority list of those administrations, nor have they qualified personnel for that job. It should be noted that Jordanian documents concerning its rule in Jerusalem are unavailable and unpreserved in the Amman archives, apart from a very few.[41] History writing has either to wait, find a few of those classified documents elsewhere in small archives or private collections, or move to history from below where state archives are less necessary. Ethnographic sources, instead, are essential in exploring Jerusalem's history from below.

The Alternative: Ethnographic Sources

State agencies' documents have an impersonal, dry style. They are written in formal language, with a bureaucratic and hierarchical approach built in. History of

---

40 Lemire Vincent and Rioli Msris Chiara, "Archives and Potentiality in Jordanian Jerusalem (1948–67)," *Jerusalem Quarterly* 92 (2022): 146, https://www.palestine-studies.org/sites/default/files/jq-articles/Archives%20and%20Potentiality%20in%20Jordanian%20Jerusalem%20%281948%E2%80%9367%29.pdf, accessed July 10, 2024.
41 Lemire and Rioli Msris, "Archives and Potentiality," 146.

everyday life in general and ethnographic ones in particular, for instance the Hebrew volumes of Ya'acov Yehoshua's memoirs (see below), are colourful. They express not only facts but also the unique spirit of their time, place, and the author's personality. Here are two examples:

"[Meir] Hefetz's wife remembers the Muslim infant Shihab whom she raised for nine months with her own son after the death of his mother. When he grew up he did not forget them and he was like a member of the family," Yehoshua related, quoting the woman: "'He ate of my bread and drank my milk. I not only gave him my breast but I also cared for him like a mother cares for her child. I washed him and diapered him. His father came each day to see how his son Shihab was growing and developing.'" Hefetz himself related: "'I remember Dib Nimer, a Muslim who was circumcised on the eighth day by Hakham Elazar Mizrahi because several of his brothers had died before him and his father decided that being circumcised on the eighth day by a Jewish *mohel* [ritual circumciser] would mark him for long life. When he grew up he was given the additional name of Ben Zion, a name he used among us, the Jews.'"[42]

According to the Bible, Moses never crossed the Jordan and his burial site is unknown. Jerusalem Jews, nevertheless, found a place for popular Muslim tradition in their own lives, and to a large extent identified with it, making it part of their common experience with their Muslim neighbours. Jerusalem's Jews felt a special tie to the Muslim pilgrims from Hebron attending Nabi Mussa festival. "We imagined," Yehoshua wrote, "that the inhabitants of Hebron and its surrounding villages, who, according to legend, were the descendants of the Jews who had remained in the Holy Land after the destruction of the Second Temple, were making their pilgrimage to the Temple in Jerusalem."[43]

In both cases, the close relationship between neighbours crossed religious barriers. In the first case, a Jewish name that is an identity indication, was added to the Muslim person. In the second case, the writer was not a passive spectator. He transformed the image of the celebrating Muslims to his own religion's rituals. In the context of present Muslim-Jewish relations in Palestine / Israel, it is hard to believe that such close relations between Jews and Arab Muslims indeed existed. Consequently, I decided to transfer these and other ethnographic texts' qualities to my book *Lives in Common*, putting aside the impersonal, abstract and remote common academic style. I hoped the reader would feel Jerusalem's everyday life as much as it can be done in a text. Nevertheless, I acknowledge that not every scholar let himself / herself ignore

---

42 Yaakov Yehoshua, *Yaldut Beyerushalayim Hayeshanah [Childhood in Old Jerusalem]* (Jerusalem: Mass, 1979), 215–216 [in Hebrew].

43 Yaakov Yehoshua, *Yerushalayim Tmol Shilshom* (Jerusalem: Mass, 1977), 24.

Conclusion: Ex-archival Sources

Unlike diplomatic history where state archives are unavoidable and provide comprehensive collections of primary sources on a given subject, these archives are short of serving the needs of bottom-up history. If the Ottoman Municipality minutes are taken as a "starting point", Avci, Lemir and Naili conclude, "they give rise to questions that can probably be answered by consulting other primary sources".[44] This applies also to court registries documenting crisis events, disputes, and crimes that the court is asked to settle or publish its verdict on. In these types of sources about irregular events, the legal logic and discourse hide ordinary life events, if not leave them unnoticed.

Bottom-up history, therefore, calls upon us to use ex-archival primary sources, such as ethnographic reports and popular customs. Documents on folklore, popular festivals, or private and family papers that conservative historians neglect, classify as unreliable, or see as individual cases that do not support general conclusions, are invaluable primary sources for social historians alongside memoirs and photograph collections. The rapidly developing social media landscape is also a place where individuals or ad-hoc groups upload private papers, short memoirs, and photographs.[45] Relational historians trust oral history more than conservative political historians do, and do not hesitate to conduct interviews.

This method is intertwined with new approaches in urban geography. The city, accordingly, is described as a hybrid place, an arena where people and identities mix and divide simultaneously. Henri Lefebvre[46] and Michel de Certeau[47] argue that space production is a comprehensive social product. Indeed, to ensure continuity and cohesion or to realise elite members' goals and translate grand visions into central planning through professional knowledge, ruling authorities impose spatial order. Accordingly, the municipality directs central planning, publishes regulations and at certain times meets neo-liberal economic interests. However, argue Lefebvre and de Certeau, citizens' everyday practices contribute to

---

44 Yaakov, *Yerushalayim Tmol Shilshom*, 115.

45 "Life in pre-1948 Jerusalem," *This Week in Palestine* 288 (May 2022), https://thisweekinpalestine.com/288-april-2022/, accessed July 10, 2024.

46 Henri Lefebvre, *The Production of Space* (Oxford: Blackwell, 1991), 1–67.

47 Michel de Certeau, *The Practice of Everyday Life* (Berkeley: University of California Press, 1984), I–XV, 20–30.

the production and re-production of space. They decode the top-down order and reproduce space through their different lived practices and structures of social relations. In other words, Jerusalemites' everyday life and customs shaped the city no less than its ruling class.

Working with this type of sources call upon us to use different search skills and information management practices than the ones exercised in preparing a top-down study. Unlike state archive files that are often well catalogued with cross references or even fully digitised, indexed annually, per subject, and according to administration branches, ex-archival sources for history from below are spread out in many volumes, on websites, and in private papers, or have not been published but are remembered and transmitted orally. In most cases, the researcher has to pick up anecdotes or individual events. He or she has to connect them to other pieces found earlier in order to compose an argument or reconstruct a historical reality. In short, the craft of political and institutional history is usually about selecting and judging between conflicting interests and narratives, and deciding on causes and consequences in the relations of given events. History from below, however, is like puzzle or mosaic tiles put together. Care and sensitivity to social customs are needed, besides an awareness that nostalgia might colour a historical record.

References

Aderet Ofer. "Israel State Archivist Demand All State-related Documents be Handed." *The Jerusalem Post* May 31 (2020). https://www.jpost.com/israel-news/israels-state-archives-demand-all-state-related-documents-be-handed-in-629789, accessed July 10, 2024.

Aderet Ofer. "State Archive Error Shows Israeli Censorship Guided by Concerns Over National Image." *Haaretz* January 5 (2022). https://www.haaretz.com/israel-news/.premium.HIGHLIGHT. MAGAZINE-state-archive-error-shows-israeli-censorship-guided-by-concerns-over-national-image-1.10517841, accessed July 10, 2024.

Akevot report. *Silencing DSDE's Concealment of Documents in Archives*, July 2019 in https://www.akevot. org.il/en/news-item/akevots-report-reveals-dsdes-unlawful-concealment-of-files-in-archives/, accessed July 10, 2024.

Akevot report. *These Matters Are Unpleasant*, October 2021 in https://www.akevot.org.il/en/news-item/these-matters-are-unpleasant-a-new-report-by-akevot/, accessed July 10, 2024.

Avci Yasemin, Lemire Vincent, and Naili Falestin. "Publishing Jerusalem's Ottoman Municipal Archives (1892 – 1917): A Turning Point for the City Historiography." *The Jerusalem Quarterly* 60 (2015): 110–119. https://www.palestine-studies.org/sites/default/files/jq-articles/JQ_60_Publishing_Jerusalem_0.pdf, accessed July 10, 2024.

Angelos Dalachanis, and Vincent Lemire, eds. *Ordinary Jerusalem 1840–1940, Opening New Archives Revisiting a Global City* (Leiden: Brill, 2018).

Bashir, Bashir, and Azar Dakwar, eds. *Rethinking the Politics of Israel/Palestine, Partition and its Alternatives*, Bruno Kreisky Forum for International Dialogue 2014 in https://issuu.com/brunok reiskyforum/docs/rethinking_-_the_politics_of_israel, accessed July 10, 2024.

Ben Aharon Eldal, and Mack Itay. "Israeli Archives Censorship Regulations and Oral History." *The Jerusalem Post* August 22, 2022. https://www.jpost.com/opinion/israeli-archives-censorship-regulations-and-oral-history-639569, accessed July 10, 2024.

Bernstein, Deborah. *Constructing Boundaries: Jewish and Arab Workers in Mandatory Palestine*. Albany: SUNY Press, 2000.

Budeiri, Musa K. "Controlling the Archive: Captured Jordanian Security Files in the Israeli State Archive." *Jerusalem Quarterly* 66 (Sumer 2016). https://www.palestine-studies.org/en/node/202343, accessed July 10, 2024.

Campos, Mishelle. *Ottoman Brothers, Muslim Christian and Jews in early twentieth-century Palestine*. Stanford: Stanford University Press, 2011.

Cohen, Amnon. *Political Parties in the West Bank under the Jordanian Regime 1949–1967*. Ithaca: Cornel University Press, 1982.

Dalachanis, Angelos, and Lemire Vincent. "Introduction: Opening Ordinary Jerusalem." In *Ordinary Jerusalem*, edited by Angelos Dalachanis, and Vincent Lemire, 1–10. Leiden: Brill, 2018.

De Certeau, Michele. *The Practice of Everyday Life*. Berkeley: University of California Press, 1984.

Ela'zar, Ya'acov. *Hatzerot Beyerushalayim Ha'atikah [Courtyards in Jerusalem's Old City]*. Jerusalem: Yad Larishonim, 1980.

Evri, Yuval, and Cohen Hillel. "Between Shared Homeland to National Home, the Balfour Declaration from a Native Sephardic Perspective." In *The Arab and Jewish Questions, Geographies of Engagements in Palestine and Beyond*, edited by Bashir, Bashir, and Leila Farsakh, 148–172. New York: Columbia University Press, 2020.

Gafni, Reuven. *A Hebrew Presence in Bein Shean: A Jewish Community in an Arab City in the British Mandate Period*. Jerusalem: Magness, 2018 [in Hebrew].

Gish, Amit. "Salvage or Plunder? Israel's 'Collection' of Privet Palestinian Libraries in West Jerusalem." *Journal of Palestine Studies* 40, no. 4 (2011). https://www.palestine-studies.org/en/node/42473, accessed July 10, 2024.

Gribetz, Jonathan M. *Defining Neighbors Religion Race and the Early Zionist-Arab Encounter*. Princeton: Princeton University Press, 2014.

Hirshberg, Abraham. *In the Orient Land*. Vilnius, 1910 [in Hebrew].

Jacobson, Abigail, and Naor Moshe. *Oriental Neighbors – Middle Eastern Jews and Arabs in Mandatory Palestine*. Waltham Massachusetts: Brandeis University Press, 2016.

Khalidi, Rashid. *Palestinian Identity – The Construction of Modern National Consciousness*. New York: Columbia University Press, 1997.

Kimmerling, Baruch, and Yoel S. Migdal. *The Palestinian People, A History*. Cambridge: Harvard University Press, 2003.

Klein Menachem. *Jerusalem: The Contested City*. New York: New York University Press and London: C. Hurst, 2001.

Klein, Menachem. "Jerusalem without East-Jerusalemites? The Palestinians as the 'Other' in Jerusalem." *Journal of Israeli History* 23, no. 2 (2004): 174–199.

Klein, Menachem. "Old and New Walls in Jerusalem." *Political Geography* 24, no. 1 (January 2005): 53–76.

Klein, Menachem. "Jerusalem as an Israeli Problem – a Review of Forty Years of Israeli Rule over Arab Jerusalem." *Israel Studies* 13, no. 2 (Summer 2008): 54–72.

Klein, Menachem. *Lives in Common Arabs and Jews in Jerusalem Jaffa and Hebron*. London: Oxford University Press, 2014.

Klein, Menachem. "Arab Jews in Palestine." *Israel Studies* 19, no. 3 (2014): 134–135.

Klein, Menachem. "The 21st Century New Critical Historians." *Israel Studies Review* 32, no. 2 (2017): 146–163.

Klein, Menachem. "Joint Jewish and Muslim Holy Places, Religious Believes and Festivals in Jerusalem between the late 19th Century and 1948." *Religion* 9, no. 7 (2018): 220, http://www.mdpi.com/journal/religions/special_issues/jewish-muslim, accessed July 10, 2024. Published as special issue on Remembering Jewish – Muslim Encounters Challenges and Cooperation.

Lefebvre, Henri. *The Production of Space*. Oxford: Blackwell, 1991.

Lemir, Vincent. *Jerusalem 1900 The Holy City in the Age of Possibilities*. Chicago: Chicago University Press, 2017.

Lemire, Vincent, and Chiara Rioli Msris. "Archives and Potentiality in Jordanian Jerusalem (1948–67)." *Jerusalem Quarterly* 92 (2022): 143–153. https://www.palestine-studies.org/sites/default/files/jq-articles/Archives%20and%20Potentiality%20in%20Jordanian%20Jerusalem%20%281948%E2%80%9367%29.pdf, accessed July 10, 2024.

LeVine, Mark. *Overlooking Geography – Jaffa Tel Aviv and the Struggle for Palestine 1880–1948*. Berkeley: University of California, 2005.

Levy, Amit. "The Archive as Storyteller: Refractions of German-Jewish Oriental Studies Migration in Personal Archives." *JBDI* 17 (2018): 425–446.

Levi, Amit. "Conflicting German Orientalism: Zionist Arabists and Arab Scholars 1926–1938." *British Journal of Middle Eastern Studies* 49, no. 2 (2022). https://doi.org/10.1080/13530194.2022.2064819.

Lockman, Zachary. *Comrades and Enemies, Arab and Jewish Workers in Palestine 1906–1948*. Berkeley: University of California Press, 1966.

Mandel, Yonatan. *The Creation of Israeli Arabic: Security and Politics in Arabic Studies in Israel*. London: Palgrave, 2014.

Masalaha, Nur. *The Palestinian Nakba, Decolonizing History Narrating the Subaltern Reclaiming Memory*. London: Zed Books, 2012.

Matar, Haggai. "The End of History at Israel's State Archives?" *+972 Magazine* April 12, 2016. https://www.972mag.com/the-end-of-history-at-israels-state-archives/, accessed July 10, 2024.

Memmi, Albert. *Who Is an Arab Jew*? Jerusalem: Israel Academic Committee on the Middle East, 1975. http://www.harissa.com/eng/whoisanarabjew.htm, accessed July 10, 2024.

Muslih, Muhammad. *The Origins of Palestinian Nationalism*. New York: Columbia University Press, 1989.

Open Jerusalem, http://www.openjerusalem.org/, accessed July 10, 2024.

Porath, Yehoshoua. *The Emergence of the Palestinian-Arab National Movement 1918–29*. London: Franck Cass, 1974.

Sebag, Montefiore Simon. *Jerusalem the Biography*. New York: Vintage, 2011.

Sela, Avraham. *The Palestinian Ba'ath the Arab Socialist Ba'ath Party in the West Bank Under Jordan, 1948–1967*. (Jerusalem: The Hebrew University, 1984) [in Hebrew].

Shalev, Afaf. "More than 100 Files from the 1800s are still classified in Israel's Archives," *+972 Magazine* February 15, 2019. https://www.972mag.com/israel-archives-1800s-classified/, accessed July 10, 2024.

Shenhav, Yehouda. *Beyond the Two States Solution – A Jewish Political Essay*. Cambridge: Polity Press, 2012.

Tamari Salim. *Mountain against the Sea – Essays on Palestinian Society and Culture*. Berkeley: University of California Press, 2009.

Wallach Yair. *A City in Fragments, Urban Text in Modern Jerusalem*. Stanford: Stanford University, 2020.

Yehoshua, Yaakov. *Yerushalayim Tmol Shilshom [Jerusalem of Yesterday]*. Jerusalem: Mass, 1977 [in Hebrew].

Yehoshua, Yaakov. *Yaldut Beyerushalayim Hayeshanah [Childhood in Old Jerusalem]*. Jerusalem: Mass, 1979 [in Hebrew].

"Vimeo," Conversation between Beshara Doumani Issam Nassar, and Salim Tamari in, https://vimeo.com/127736799, accessed July 10, 2024.

Irit Carmon Popper

8 Art "from Below": Activating Socially Engaged Art at a Site-in-Conflict – the Israeli-Palestinian Case

[. . .] more than 'New Historians' [. . .] we need as always, artists. (Larry Abramson)[1]

8.1 Introduction

This paper is concerned with the "Common Views: Sourcing Water" art intervention (2019–2020) by the *Common Views* art collective in the Israeli Negev (Arabic: Naqab) desert region of southern Israel in 2019–2020, as a model of collaborative and socially engaged art at a site-in-conflict. In their art actions, they reflect upon a conflictual area, highlighting the spatial injustices and civic inequalities between Bedouin and Jewish communities sharing a common desert vista. By employing site-specific and socially engaged practices, the collective aims to reawaken and revitalise traditional local heritage of water harvesting and enact sustainable practices as a mutually fertile ground for both communities. This partakes of a wider global art phenomenon, converging the artistic with the social, yet it challenges the conventional genealogy of the genre by calling for action while seeking to intertwine the civic and political with the environmental. This case study thus delves into aspects of the complex circumstances of the Israeli-Palestinian conflict, with a focus on promoting social justice and equality. The artists follow a 'from below' approach, which aims to elevate the voices, experiences, and perspectives of marginalised communities. They challenge traditional power structures and hierarchical narratives using their artistic toolbox to face complex situations while navigating between civic and institutional forces.

"Common Views: Sourcing Water" was a durational socially engaged art intervention, initiated by the *Common Views* art collective, led by artists David Behar-Perahia and Dan Farberoff. Their ongoing practice is based on participatory and socially-led art in collaboration with residents; who in this case were the local inhabitants of the Israeli desert region—those of the Jewish town of Arad and the nearby Bedouin of the settlements in Al Baqi'a Valley. The diverse, multicultural communities share a common view—the common desert vista – but

---

1 Larry Abramson, "We Are All Felix Nussbaum," *Studio Art Magazine*, 133 (2002): 69 [Hebrew].

https://doi.org/10.1515/9783111522180-008

nevertheless, between them lies a disparity and an inequity, especially in the allotment of and access to natural resources.

In the context of a binary division between Jews and Bedouins, the artists have directed their attention toward contemplating the distributive imbalance in water utilisation and supply. This choice underscores the significance of water as the most valuable resource in a desert environment. Not only the Bedouins who live in the desert today and practice desert traditions, but also ancient Hebrews, who were desert dwellers themselves, have also practiced them in the past. All inhabitants of the desert used these methods, which the artists are working to revive. The artists have collaborated with local commons and their representatives to revitalise and awaken an interest in the local heritage of the tradition of rainwater harvesting, and to enact sustainable practices as a mutually fertile ground for both desert communities. These actions served to trigger conversation and public discourse, to suggest a solution for future collaboration, and to provide a possible sustainable future. The artwork combines the sustainable and the communal, an approach referred to by the art collective as "Environmental Reconciliation". (Fig.1)

The artistic strategies used are part of the contemporary phenomenon of participatory and socially engaged art interventions worldwide, touching upon political and civic issues. These practices broaden the artistic toolbox to include a collaborative dimension of social experiences of everyday life, and to involve forms of engagement with social groups of both art and non-art communities in the creative process. The rejection of the idea of art as an object, and its progression toward cooperative spatial intervention, releases the artistic creative process from individual authorship, steering it to collective production. Artists who adopt strategies of social involvement seek to contribute to a society where other social agents have failed, using their unique cultural capital. West Coast scholars distinguish them as an art genre of collectives that propose alternative models for social activity through joint continuous site-specific works.[2]

Both disciplines of this paper, art history and geopolitical Israeli historiography, adopt the perspective "from below". On the one hand, I draw on contemporary art discourse that has been characterised since the 1990s by socially led and participatory practices, emphasising the crucial role of creative agents within local communities concerning institutional apparatus. The significant attempts to rethink the role of artists in society can be traced back to the 19th century with

---

2 Claire Bishop, "Participation and Spectacle: Where Are We Now?" lecture for *Creative Time's Living as Form*, 2011; Robert Atkins et al., eds., *The Art of Participation: 1950 to Now*, exhibition catalogue (San Francisco: San Francisco Museum of Modern Art, 2008).

Fig. 1: *Adama Nekuva* (Pierced Land) site specific performance, led by artist Iris Nais, part of *Common Views: Sourcing Water* exhibition opening event, Bir Umm al Atin Cistern, June 5, 2020. Photograph: Dan Farberoff.

movements reflecting the rise of socialism, and are rooted in the avant-garde movements of the early 20th century, which later evolved in the art movements of the 1960s and 1970s, and became institutionalised in the 1990s. In this context, reference is made to the development of the concept of "from below", which often follows a similar social claim and deals with similar values and ideas regarding community-led agenda reclaiming and bottom-up activities.

On the other hand, I lean on the local research platform designed by the New Historians of 1980s Israel, characterised by the tendency to write the history of the unheard people, focusing the research on the Bedouin minority in Israel. I will discuss the historiographic framework of the Bedouin as an integral part of the Palestinian communities in Israel, employing the research context on the Israel-Palestinian conflict, using *Common Views* intervention in Israel as an example. The geo-political circumstances of this case study are suited to the "history from below" values in describing the lives, ideas, and experiences of those who lay below dominant historical narratives. The concept of "history from below" was developed at the same time, as an expression of a broader shift at work within the British Left in the 1970s and 1980s, focused on the marginalised ethnic, religious, and sexual minorities.[3] Although emerging from a political economy point of view, with workers and their unions at the center of the historical agenda, and not from an ethnic point of view in particular, both are encompassed within the same overarching framework. A Bedouin minority in Israel is included within the explicit aim of the artists to give voice to lower-income strata of mainstream society as lower-income groups in political, social, and cultural status, based on E.P. Thompson's concept of "history from below."[4] When artists take a "from below" perspective, they often explore issues of oppression such as race, gender, and class. This approach calls for social transformation. Moreover, in the endeavor to recount the narrations of those systematically excluded from the historical record, the artists engage in a collaborative effort to rewrite the history of the Bedouins from their own lived perspective.

8.2 The Negev Bedouins in Israel: Action "from Below" and Inherent Conflict

The timeframe of the study case discussed in this paper refers to recent contemporary history and relates to current geo-political contexts in Israel, yet the worldviews are rooted in the 1948 war as the most prominent event in the country's recent history. The war, as the key event in the conflict, is the most transformative of the country's physical and human landscape, which culminated in the establishment of the State of Israel and representing both the independence of the Jews in Israel and the Palestinian *Nakba* (Catastrophe in Arabic), simultaneously. It involved the depopulation, destruction, and displacement of most of the Arab population and completely transformed the landscape by dotting it with hundreds of deserted and ruined sites of Arab settlements. This huge grab involved the creation of a series of bodies and regulations to take formal control of refugee property, initially referred to as "abandoned lands", and to govern its usage into the 1950s and beyond.[5]

---

3 Andy Wood, "History from Below and Early Modern Social History," in: *The Many-Headed Monster: The History of 'The Unruly Sort of Clowns' and other Early Modern Peculiarities*, https://manyheadedmonster.com/2013/08/21/andy-wood-history-from-below-and-early-modern-social-history/, accessed November 09, 2024.
4 Edward Palmer Thompson, *The Making of the English Working Class* (England: Penguin Books, 2013).
5 Michael R. Fischbach, *Records of Dispossession: Palestinian Refugee Property and the Arab-Israeli Conflict* (New York: Columbia University Press, 2003), 14–15.

The Israeli Bedouin case is particularly pertinent since it has seen intensive activities seeking on the one hand, the formation of a local Jewish identity in respect to the question of their historical link to their ancestral home, and on the other hand, that of the local Bedouin traditions, narratives and identity, its recognition, and its civic rights as a minority in Israel. This significant social binary, fluctuating between Jewish and non-Jewish, renders the inquiry about the past within Israeli culture, fertile ground for investigation of hybrid, complex, and stratified local identities. In this framework, since Israel has dedicated major efforts to secure their control over the land, Bedouin citizens have been entangled in a protracted legal and territorial battle over traditional tribal land in the Negev region.[6] The State's spatial policy toward the Bedouins reflects diverging directions, as both sides are trapped within their respective ideologies of control and resistance.

Bedouin tribes throughout the Middle East have lived in the desert and followed a nomadic lifestyle that has gradually changed in the last centuries with urbanisation and modernisation processes, yet maintain some ancient norms and traditional values to this day. The first Bedouin tribes are believed to have migrated into the Negev from the Arabian Peninsula at the beginning of Arab rule in the region, in the 7th century AD. This movement was accelerated during the Ottoman period (1517–1917) and continued during the subsequent British Mandatory period (1917–1948), during which the Bedouin transitioned from a nomadic lifestyle to a predominantly semi-nomadic one. Under British rule, the Bedouins were granted special conditions that recognised and respected their traditional customs including their grazing and water rights.[7]

Within contemporary Israel, the Bedouin constitute an indigenous Arab-Muslim ethnic minority, and still constitute the majority population in the Negev region of southern Israel.[8] In 1948, most of the tribes were either expelled or left, seeking refuge in surrounding Arab countries and territories. In 1951, many tribes

---

6 Alexander Kedar, Ahmad Amara, and Oren Yiftachel, *Emptied Lands: A Legal Geography of Bedouin Rights in the Negev* (Stanford: Stanford University Press, 2018), 13.

7 Ilana Meallem, *The Management of Solid Waste in Recognized and Unrecognized Bedouin Villages of the Negev: Social Context, Impacts and Recommendations* (Sedeh Boker, Israel: Albert Katz International School for Desert Research, 2006), 11–17.

8 Muhammad Youssef Suwaed, "Bedouin-Jewish Relations in the Negev 1943–1948," *Middle Eastern Studies* 51:5 (2015): 774.

Although Negev is the standard geographic term used in the study of southern Israel/Palestine, it has not been constituted as a defined geographic unit or as a separate administrative unit under any of the last three regimes that exercised power over the area (Ottoman, British, and Israeli). Negev is a biblical term that refers to a smaller area of land than what is considered the Negev region today. Further, in its earlier English version, the "Negeb" (with a b) used to refer

were relocated into the Siyag (Hebrew for 'confinement') – a special area located in the Northeastern Negev, known for its low agricultural fertility. The relocation included restricted access to essential resource use such as cultivating lands, migrating with herds, and using traditional wells and cisterns. As part of the State procedure during the years of military rule over the Arab population (1948–66), a national strategic plan was established, from which the Bedouins in the Siyag were excluded.[9]

Since then, they have been a dense population dispersed in tribes, villages, and rural settlements, most of which are officially classified as "unrecognised" and "illegal", their inhabitants considered "trespassers" on State land. The heart of this land dispute lies in opposing conceptualisations of ownership, possession, and land use. On the one hand, the Bedouins claim land rights based on customary and official laws, possession, and cultivation of the land for generations, and tax payments to previous regimes, which, in their views, should provide proof of ownership and be integrated into contemporary land laws from Ottoman and British statutes. On the other hand, Israel, drawing on a highly formalist approach, views many of the Bedouins as illegal trespassers invading State property.[10]

In 1962, the Jewish city of Arad (pop. 2017~26,000) was established to settle and develop the Negev frontier. Arad serves as the main urban center of the area and provides various services to all communities, Jewish and Bedouin alike.[11] While the Jewish residents enjoy a water-rich town, with paved roads, leafy gardens, and sanitation facilities, the actual realities of the neighboring Bedouins, especially those of the unrecognised villages surrounding the town, are completely different. Nowadays the Bedouin Arab population in the Negev is over 250,000, of which about 25%-40% live in 35 unrecognised villages (the smallest village has a population of 400, and the largest has over 10,000 inhabitants). The residents exist without basic infrastructure and municipal services such as water, electricity, roads, and garbage removal, and without proper access to education, social and medical services. Moreover, due to the lack of land ownership arrangements, the state refuses to develop their residential areas and to issue building permits and infrastructure. Therefore, the temporary living structures in the unrecog-

---

mainly to a climatic unit of a desert region and not to a geographic or politically defined territory (Kedar, Amara, Oren, *Emptied Lands*, 16).

9 Meallem, *The Management of Solid Waste.*

10 Kedar, Amara, Oren, *Emptied Lands*, 5.

11 Avinoam Meir, Arnon Ben Israel, Batya Roded, Ibrahim Abu-Ajaj, "Taming the Road, Tamed by the Road: Sense of Road as Place among Indigenous Bedouin in an Ethnic Frontier in Israel," *Mobilities*, 14:2 (2019): 250–266, https://doi.org/10.1080/17450101.2019.1567987.

nised villages, which include tin-shacks, cabins, and tents, are defined as unauthorised and are in constant danger of demolition, and indeed continue to be destroyed periodically, to this day.[12]

Under those circumstances, the Khamisa and Khawamasha Bedouin families from the Genbiv tribe and a family from the Abu Jawid tribe, members of the Dulam headquarters, were transferred to the Al Baqi'a valley. Since then, they have been spread out in scattered residential complexes (rural, small family settlements), isolated from one another. Each settlement is based on one male ancestor and his descendants. They own herds of sheep, camels, donkeys, and horses, but are also employed in state academies and institutions, including local tourist sites. As their settlements are considered illegal and therefore temporary, their living conditions are harsh, with inadequate transportation infrastructure such as unpaved roads, the absence of basic facilities such as water and power supply, and cellular phone reception.

The significance of stability in the water supply is an essential part of desert living conditions, despite the romantic myth attached to water and cisterns from ancient times. Cisterns and dug water tanks are an ancient phenomenon that has provided desert dwellers for millennia. Archaeological research indicates that since the Iron Age, in this area of the Judean Desert, storing water near the settlements was common, mainly due to the limestone found there, which is suitable for quarrying water and preventing infiltration. Water cisterns located at the bottom of the slope collect rainwater which reaches them through channels that stretch from the top of the slopes to the bottom.[13] The Bedouin inhabitants of Al Baqi'a Valley used to rely on rainwater harvesting for all their needs. Some carried water on camels and donkeys, which were later replaced with modern tractors and tankers up until the laying of a national water pipeline from the city of Arad to Mount Masada in the 1960s, to which fixed taps were added at the *Kfar Nokdim* tourist site near-by. From this site, the Bedouin replaced the cisterns with plastic water tanks and an unauthorised network of self-laid, sun-beaten agricultural black PVC plastic irrigation pipes that wind their way for miles, bringing precious water from the official pipeline to the isolated settlements. (Fig. 2)

Since the State prevents its water supply system from becoming permanent by not allowing an iron pipeline or the burial of a pipeline in the ground, the Bedouin solution for their water supply has become a community self-care system.

---

12 "The Unrecognized Bedouin Villages in the Negev - Facts and Figures," The Association for Civil Rights in Israel, https://www.acri.org.il/post/_341, accessed June 30, 2022.

13 Seffi Ben Joseph, *The New Israel Guide: The Judean Desert and the Dead Sea Valley* (Tel Aviv: Ktav Publishing House: 2001), 59, 168 [Hebrew]; Zvika Tzuk, "To the Waterholes," in *Beshvil Haaretz (On the Path of the Land),* ed. The Israel Nature and Parks Authority (2005), 29–30 [Hebrew].

Fig. 2: Self-laid sun-beaten black agricultural PVC irrigation pipes in Al Baqi'a valley, 2020. Photograph: Dan Farberoff.

The head of one of the extended families receives the water bill from the local water corporation and lists it according to the count of each family based on their respective independent water clocks. The amounts are collected from the families and the bill is paid by the representative. This has gradually led to the Bedouin deserting their traditional use and maintenance of the cisterns, and these were abandoned and subsequently filled with alluvium so that they could no longer fulfill their purpose, rendering them unusable by the early 2000s.

Despite the challenging living conditions, many inhabitants of Al Baqia settlements, particularly the elderly, desire to remain in their villages and uphold their traditional way of life. Faced with this existential situation, the Bedouin inhabitants of Al Baqi'a Valley as part of a larger group of "unrecognised" villages continue to face challenges in obtaining state recognition and permanent housing permits. Efforts to address this issue involve collaborating with social and environmental organisations to advocate for the acceptance of professional norms and principles within the Israeli planning apparatus. One of the approaches seeks the recognition and development of Bedouin villages as distinct types of localities, that preserve the existing social and spatial arrangements, including allocating land for livelihood and agriculture, aiming for agricultural-tourist villages initiatives. This initiative not only promotes equality and justice, and bridges significant gaps between the Bedouin and Jewish populations in the area, but also supports sustainable land use by and envisioned a contribution to the ecosystem rehabilitation of the desert.[14]

8.3 The Historiographical Perspective: Local History "from Up and Below"

The field of Euro-American social historians in the late twentieth century drew heavily upon the influence of postwar British Marxist historians and social science methodology and theory. As a result, a distinct emphasis on materialism emerged. However, the new social history successfully reconstructed and analyzed the collective experiences of various social groups such as research communities, social movements, unions, crowds, and the everyday lives of common people. This emphasis on collective experiences served to highlight their significance for broader historical narratives.[15] During the early 1970s, historiography underwent a significant transformation. A discernible left-wing orientation, predominantly Marxist or quasi-Marxist, became apparent in the approach of historians to their tasks and the people involved. These changes were primarily linked to social history, even when referred to as "history from below." In all this historiographical upheaval, one central element of continuity remained: new subjects of history might be revealed. From the middle of the decade, its insight was absorbed into the historiographical mainstream.[16]

---

14 Oren Yiftachel et al., *Alternative Master Plan for the Unrecognized Bedouin Villages in the Negev*, BIMKOM: Planners for Planning Rights, RCUV: The Regional Council for the Unrecognized Villages in the Negev, SIDREH: The Bedouin Arab Women's Organization of the Negev, Abridged version 2012; Daniel E. Orenstein, Alon Tal, and Char Miller, eds., *Between Ruin and Restoration: An Environmental History of Israel* (University of Pittsburgh Press, 2013); Tomer Kahana, *Social Survey – The Bedouins of Al-Baki'a Valley*, December 2015, without specifying page numbers [Hebrew].
15 James R. Barrett, *History from the Bottom Up and the Inside Out: Ethnicity, Race, and Identity in Working-Class History* (Durham and London: Duke University Press, 2017), 5–2.
16 William Thompson, *What Happened to History?* (London: Sterling, Va, Pluto Press, 2000), 49–50.

The monolithic, uniform, and solid story of the ruling Israeli historiography was told from the beginning of Zionism and with the establishment of the state of Israel, yet the 1970s marked the turning point in which additional voices testifying to a heterogeneous society entered the supposedly homogenous culture. The dominant narrative of Israeli modernism was being challenged not because of new information, but rather due to the rediscovery, sharing, and integration of forgotten facts and memories. This undermined official Zionist narratives, leading to a shift in historical discussion from a consensus-based approach to one that was full of contrasts and conflicts.[17]

Since the establishment of the State of Israel, many of the Negev Bedouin have experienced profound transitions due to the processes of forced displacement and induced urbanisation. These transitions and processes have been extensively studied from economic, social, and spatial perspectives and were mostly framed within the broader context of nation-state vs. indigenous politics, during the military rule in the region till mid-1960.[18] After the 1967 war, mainly Arab scholars dealt with the Nakba, relying on Palestinian oral history. They aimed to create a broad picture of the narrative of the Arab villages and neighborhoods in the Israeli Independence War and its aftermath.

Since the late 1980s, we have witnessed the emergence of an anti-hegemonic intellectual phenomenon that revisited various notable chapters in Israeli history, whose protagonists were soon dubbed the "New Historians." They challenged the Zionist narrative, the Israeli establishment, accusing its agents and mechanisms of discrimination and appropriation of Palestinian property, large-scale demolition, and failure to deal with the Palestinian refugee problem. Numerous Jewish historiographers have been instrumental in producing an array of books and articles with radical criticism on the subject. These publications have provided significant insights into the subject and have been widely circulated since their inception.[19] This anti-hegemonic intellectual phenomenon includes not only historians, but social scientists, sociologists, anthropologists, and geographers,

---

17 Uri Ram, "Memory and Identity: Sociology of the Historians' Debate in Israel," *Theory and Criticism* 8, (1996): 9–32, https://theory-and-criticism.vanleer.org.il/, accessed September 30, 2024.
18 Ahmad H. Sa'di and Lila Abu-Lughod, eds., *Nakba: Palestine, 1948, and the Claims of Memory* (New York: Columbia University Press, 2007), Nakba Archive website, since 2002, https://www. nakba-archive.org/new/, accessed September 30, 2024.
19 Benny Morris, *The Birth of the Palestinian Refugee Problem Revisited* (Cambridge: Cambridge University Press, 2004); Benny Morris, *1948: The First Arab-Israeli War* (New Haven and London: Yale UP, 2008); Sharif Kanaana and Bassam Al-Ka'bi, *Destroyed Palestinian Villages Series* (Ramallah: Bir Zeit University Documentation Center, 1987);. Walid Khalidi, ed., *All That Remains – The Palestinian Villages Occupied and Depopulated by Israel in 1948* (Beirut: Institute for Palestinian Studies, 1992).

who revisited various notable chapters in Israeli history. They exposed and challenged the agents, the acts, and the causes of the Zionist establishment, by referring to the 1948 ethnic cleansing of Palestine.[20] The new social historians of the 1970s and 1980s understood power as located in social structure: if they were hesitant in applying class-based categories, there was continuous attention to issues of structural inequalities of wealth and power. This was a social history with a grittily materialist sense of economics. The political sympathies of most of these social historians lie with the Left,[21] and they therefore examine a range of often overlooked practices employed by non-elite Palestinians attempting to safeguard their rights as they defined them. Those researchers, both Palestinians and Jews, were using the "from below" agenda as a resistance strategy, acting as a bottom-up criticism of the leading national historical narratives. In the last two decades, research has begun to explore critical social theories that focus on human agency as a venue for the analysis of Bedouin spatiality and their reciprocal relations with social practices, constructed identities, and sense of place.[22]

Moreover, research has begun to focus on the political and ethnic aspects of the Bedouin community and issues of civil and land rights in general. This line of discourse has highlighted the lack of home, as a metaphorical concept in the Bedouin community—their need for culturally appropriate spaces. More specifically, it supports their demand for a land-territory-place nexus emanating from their indigeneity and their economic and social marginality. A recent byproduct of the vivid discussion on the conflict and its implications is the question of the Bedouin place. This rather new line of research has dredged up an array of distorted Bedouin interactions with space, manifested in a negative sense of place, along with prevalent emotions of alienation. These include their nomadic heritage as a state of mind, landlessness as war refugees and uprooted populations, being a cultural ethnic-religious-national minority in Israel, economic and social weakness, unequal development policy by the State, and lack of diversified settlement options and residential opportunities. Several factors have been suggested to be responsible for this distortion. As these studies refer to the connection between the Bedouin and the place, the art collective as well commences from the same point, in

---

20 Ilan Greilsammer, "The New Historians of Israel and Their Political Involvement," *Bulletin Du Centre de Recherche Français à Jérusalem* 23 (2012), http://journals.openedition.org/bcrfj/6868, accessed September 30, 2024.

21 Wood, *Ibid.*

22 Yuval Karplus and Avinoam Meir, "Past and Present in the Discourse of Naqab/Negev Bedouin Geography and Space: A Critical Review," in *The Naqab Bedouin and Colonialism: New Perspectives*, ed. Mansour Nasasra et al. (New York: Routledge, 2019).

which a place is a place in the sense of shared interests of Bedouin and Jew alike, from an ecological perspective.[23]

Yet, in practice, the movement of local or civil society and non-governmental organisations (NGOs) has recently emerged for purposes of public representation and welfare support in local communities. Only as late as 2012 was a district dedicated to Palestinian minority communities' sector within the Council for the Preservation of Israel's Heritage Sites established, to deal with locating and preserving Palestinian heritage sites. The present Zeitgeist motivates NGOs and private agencies to include social, communal, and cultural values in the context of intangible Palestinian heritage. For example, BIMKOM – Planners for Planning Rights, established in 1999 by architects and planners, offers alternative professional research-based work to develop a practice concentrating on strengthening the weakened and silenced social layers.[24]

8.4 The Participatory Turn and Socially Engaged Art Practices

The perspective "from below" in art has evolved and has found its way into various stages of artistic development. This perspective is rooted in a desire to represent and amplify the voices, experiences, and struggles of marginalised or oppressed groups within society. Therefore, the roots of the perspective "from below" can be traced back to the 19th century with movements like Realism reflecting the commitment to represent ordinary people, to investigate the lives of marginalised groups and individuals, and to reinterpret the old ones, and they did that by depicting the harsh realities of industrialisation and poverty. A second moment in the development of the "below" perspective can be traced to the avant-garde movements dur-

---

23 Aref Abu Rabia, "Negev Bedouin: Displacement, Forced Settlement and Conservation," in *Conservation and Mobile Indigenous Peoples, Displacement, Forced Settlement, and Sustainable Development*, ed. Dawn Chatty, and Marcus Colchester (Oxford and New York: Berghahn Books, 2002); Oren Yiftachel, "Bedouin Arabs and the Israeli Settler State: Land Policies and Indigenous Resistance," in *The Future of Indigenous Peoples: Strategies for Survival and Development*, ed. Duane Champagne, and Ismael Abu-Saad (Los Angeles: UCLA American, 2005); Arnon Ben-Israel, "The Bedouin Formation of Place: Space and Landscape Construction by Urbanized Pastoral-Nomads, the Case of the Bedouin of Hura-YA'tir" (PhD diss., Ben Gurion University of the Negev, 2009) [Hebrew].
24 "Bimkom," https://bimkom.org/eng/home-mobile/, accessed September 30, 2024.

ing the 20th Century, which challenged traditional artistic norms and the relationship of artists to social power.[25]

The first moment in the historical avant-garde that anticipated the emergence of the contemporary socially engaged art with a fraught relationship to political context refers to the early modern art movements of the 1920s–1930s, as Futurism, Russian constructivism, Dadaism, that shared an interest in the individual, and in the centrality of the relationship between art and the spectator (the public). The second moment is linked to the art movements post World War II to include the public art of social realism and happenings of the 1950s, followed by performance art, minimalism and land art of the 1960s–70s. All delt with the significant change of the art object and the spatial reality of its display and the immediate physical experience of the participant.[26] The 1990s marked the third historical shift following the decline of collective political ideologies after the collapse of communism, as argued by Clair Bishop. During this period, site-specific art as a methodology gained institutional recognition, based on the significance of the artwork as it derives from the spatial and temporal consumption conditions of a given site, subsequently evolving into community-specificity as a platform for dialogue and interpretation of a given community, as noted by Miwon Kwon.[27] Moreover, Giusy Checola borrowed the geographical term "place-specificity," to argue for a parallel process in the 1990s of institutionalisation of site-specificity and of the new geographical tendency to treat places as "special signs." The landscape is perceived not merely as territory but as a place in our consciousness, which is embedded with values and meanings by local communities.[28]

Since the 1990s, artists and collectives have striven toward social and collective processes that include spectatorship as participation as integral to the art-

---

25 Avant-garde is originally a French term, that appeared regarding art in France at the first half of the 19th century. Avant-garde art can be said to begin in the 1850s with the realism of Gustave Courbet, who was strongly influenced by early socialist ideas. This was followed by the successive movements of modern art. Matei Calinescu, *Five Faces of Modernity: Modernism, Avant-Garde, Decadence, Kitsch, Postmodernism* (NC: Duke University Press Books, 1987).

26 Claire Bishop, *Artificial Hells: Participatory Art and the Politics of Spectatorship* (New York: Verso, 2012), 190–91; Gustaf Almenberg, *Notes on Participatory Art: Toward a Manifesto Differentiating It from Open Work, Interactive Art and Relational Art* (UK: Author House, 2010), 44; Ilana Tenenbaum, "Eleven Notes on Political Art in the 1990s," in *Social Realism in the 1950s, Political Art in the 1990s*, ed. Yael Lotan (Haifa: The Haifa Museum of Art, 1998), 177–78.

27 Miwon Kwon, "One Place after Another: Notes on Site-Specificity," *October Magazine* 80 (1997): 86, 91.

28 Giusy Checola, "The Imaginary Institution of Place: Art, Locality and Territory in the Biella Region," in *Understanding Territoriality: Identity, Place and Possession*, ed. Understanding Territoriality Project (Brighton: Fabrica, 2017), 25–26.

work. These tendencies have replaced artistic representations with interventionist action grounded in interpersonal collaborative relationships in a specific place. It has theoretically grounded various types of art practices, such as participatory art, community-based art, socially engaged projects, and political activism. The practices broaden the artistic toolbox to include a collaborative dimension to social experience, to involve forms of social engagement with participants – social groups and art and non-art communities – to promote social-political issues with their artistic toolbox.[29]

Curator and theoretician Nicolas Bourriaud recognised the artist generation of the 1990s in Europe as belonging to a relational era based theoretically on human interaction and social context, and sociologically on the birth of a global urban culture. He coined the term *esthétique rélationnelle* – relational esthetics or relational art – referring to the tendency of artworks that "highlight social methods of exchange, interactivity with the onlooker within the esthetic experience proposed to him/her, and communication processes, in their tangible dimension as tools for linking human beings and groups to one another."[30] Relational practices have attracted ensuing theoretical debates that have questioned the social-political perspective of the notion, as curator Nato Thompson for example argues that "symbolic gestures can be powerful and effective methods for change."[31] In contrary, Bishop pointed to the gap in Bourriaud's theory between the symbolic and substantive values of the artwork and therefore its minor emphasis on social change and activism. She raised moral doubts regarding the democratisation of art and suggests the term *relational antagonism* as a criticism of the lack of essential prerequisites that prevent artwork from becoming a political action.[32]

The widespread adoption of socially engaged agenda during times of political change is indicative of internal conflicts within each historical period, as participatory art challenged various artistic and sociopolitical conventions, thereby as-

---

29 Bishop, "Participation and Spectacle: Where Are We Now?"; Atkins et al., eds., *The Art of Participation: 1950 to Now*.

30 Nicolas Bourriaud, *Relational Aesthetics* (Dijon: Les presses du réel, 1998), 160.; Bourriaud, "Traffic: Space-Times of the Exchange," trans. Simon Pleasance and Fronza Woods, *May Quarterly Journal* (2012), http://www.mayrevue.com/en/traffic-espaces-temps-de-lechange, accessed September 30, 2024.

31 Nato Thompson, *Living as Form: Socially Engaged Art from 1991 –2011* (Cambridge: MIT Press, 2012), 18; Hal Foster, "Chat Rooms," in *Participation: Documents on Participatory Art*, ed. Claire Bishop (London and Cambridge, Massachusetts: Whitechapel, The MIT Press, 2004), 190–95.

32 Claire Bishop, "Antagonism and Relational Aesthetics," *October Magazine* 110 (2004): 51–79. Bishop refers to the concept of Antagonism as explained by Ernesto Laclau and Chantal Mouffet in *Hegemony and Socialist Strategy, Towards a Radical Democratic Politics* (London and New York: Verso, 2001).

suming different forms.[33] These attempts are parallel to the stages of development of "History from Below": the concept of bottom-up history introduces a personal dimension to the phenomenon that a purely political analysis might have overlooked.[34]

Hal Foster recognises the role of the artist as an ethnographer. He claims that artists can be seen as having undertaken an ethnographic role in their modes of intervention in communities and present pseudo-documentary materials. This sheds light on the instrumental use of art to create a one-sided and heavily politicised narrative and raises the problematic characterisation of the *Other* as an inferior object, whose image serves the hegemonic gaze. By identifying the role of the artist as an observer and participant Foster points to a contradictory situation in which the observation includes appropriation of the community he observes, and the participation involves the act of preserving the community's cultural heritage. The artist observes and studies the community and reflects on it, and in this way, he appropriates it. As a participant, he takes part in the community's actions as if he belongs to it, and through the mutual actions he contributes to preserving its materialistic values.[35]

Beyond the ethnographic perception of the role of art, there is also an emerging understanding from the 1980s onward that the artist is involved with histories and archives, and, as emphasised by Mark Godfrey, engaged in historical research and representation: artworks invite the viewers to "think about the past; make connections between events, characters, and objects; join together in memory; and to reconsider how the past is represented."[36] Godfrey follows Foster's notion of art practices dealing with archives, in describing their outcome in the form of the physical (intangible) presence of lost or displaced data.[37]

I argue, for the case that we are examining here, that by turning to the modus operandi of art practices, the artists have managed to fathom the multilayered history of the sites and offer alternatives to the hegemonic historicisations, and that their set of actions mark a shift from the critique of power relations to interventions in the processes through which history is remembered and narrated. In this manner, their activities in the local Israeli arena explore the role of art as a form of rewriting local history. Socially engaged artists such as the *Common Views* art collective are involved in the re-writing of local histories, and

---

33 Bishop, *Artificial Hells*, 190–91.; Bishop, *Participation and Spectacle*.

34 Barrett, *History from the Bottom Up and the Inside Out*, xi, 34.

35 Hal Foster, "The Artist as Ethnographer," in *The Return of the Real*, ed. Hal Foster (Cambridge: MIT Press, 1996), 302–9.

36 Mark Godfrey, "The Artist as Historian," *October Magazine* 120 (2007): 143.

37 Hal Foster, "An Archival Impulse," *October Magazine* 110 (2004): 4.

share with "history from below", and the "New Historians" in particular, the attempt to make history-writing broad-based. The artists' strategies are based on the participation of the local disadvantaged communities in rewriting their history and negotiating their interests with the dominant authorities as well. In this way, they are able to meet the aspiration to democratising the project of writing history, by enabling citizens to research their histories, and connecting these histories to current political dialogue.[38]

A reflexive ethnographic stance, in which the process has developed throughout the research process, acknowledges my own position as an art curator and academic researcher, who has been engaged in both projects as a creative agent and participant. I was an active participant at all stages of the intervention. One of my major contributions was in the dialogue with women participants, and I curated the exhibition project. My close involvement in the projects, and the personal acquaintances I established with the participants, the various agencies, and the stakeholders, allowed me to accompany all stages of the project, including the collection of materials in the preliminary research, and the formation of participatory actions.

In this manner, I overcame the obstacle of the ethnographic role played by artists in their modes of intervention in communities and the danger of presenting pseudo-documentary materials, thus creating a one-sided narrative.[39] My writing can be regarded as reflexive writing, done after a period that allowed for questioning, observation, and reviewing of the events that took place within the historiographical and theoretical contexts. The art collective sought my involvement due to my research specialisation in the disciplines that characterise these areas of research, and include practices of contemporary art, heritage preservation, and Israeli-Palestinian sites-in-conflict.[40]

8.5 Art Project "from Below": Activating Socially Engaged Practice at a Site-in-Conflict

The *Common Views* art collective is acquainted with the issue of the living conditions of the Bedouins in the valley, their political-civic situation, the illegality, the communities, and their association with their environmental and natural resour-

---

38 Jennifer L. Allen, *Sustainable Utopias: The Art and Politics of Hope in Germany* (Cambridge, MA: Harward University Press, 2012), 70.
39 Foster, *The Artist as Ethnographer.*
40 Irit Carmon Popper, "Art as Preservation: Interventions in Sites-in-Conflict, Israel, 1948–2008" (PhD diss., Technion Israel Institute of Technology, 2019), 36–37.

ces. Under their leading concept of *environmental reconciliation,* they treated this subject through the question of water as the desert inhabitants' most precious and essential natural resource. The topic of water in the desert as a central theme was used by the art collective in the art project "Common Views: Sourcing Water" to reflect on its imbalanced distribution between the Bedouin of Al Baqi'a Valley and Jewish city dwellers of the town of Arad, as well as on the relationship between communities and their environments, and sustainability in a broader context. The solution that was marked by the art collective was to engage with traditional rainwater harvesting, including the water cisterns that until only a few decades ago had served as their principal water source, but are now deserted, neglected, and unused. The water cisterns were subjected to actions of enclosure by the State, which designated them as archeological sites, effectively precluding their maintenance. The Bedouins view the many cisterns dotting the area as representations of their connection to the land and as an important part of their cultural landscape.[41] (Fig. 3)

As a central aspect of the project, the artists initiated special actions to revive existing cisterns in the area, with the participation of local inhabitants and participants from further afield, employing site-specific, and community-engaged, participatory practices to touch upon the native desert tradition of water harvesting and the current distributive inequity. These actions served as a trigger for sparking conversation and public discourse, pointing to the possibility of a sustainable future for the region's desert habitation. The project is associated with 'commoning' (using political and social traditions of sharing and mutual aid in general, and as a form of social organisation in particular),[42] which induces interaction and participation as part of the artistic toolbox held by the art collective. These actions are aimed at engendering a sense of mutual responsibility and empathy with each other, Jews and Bedouins, and with the environment (the common desert vista) and serve as catalysts for potential transformation.

This long-duration art project consists of several levels or steps on a chronological line, all driven by the specific site and its environmental and communal characteristics. The first essential step is to form ideas in a theoretical manner that will underline the art vision and the modes of action based on a process of historical and archival research for visual and textual documentation in formal

---

41 David Behar Perahia and Dan Farberoff, "Commoning: Environmental Reconciliation in the Work of Common Views," *Oncurating* 54 (2022–2023).

42 Peter Linebaugh, *Stop, Thief!: The Commons, Enclosures and Resistance* (Oakland: PM Press, 2014).

Valérie Fournier, "Commoning: on the Social Organisation of the Commons," *M@n@gement* 16 (2013/4): 433–453, doi: 10.3917/mana.164.0433, https://www.cairn.info/revue-management-2013-4-page-433.htm, accessed September 30, 2024.

Fig. 3: One of many water cisterns found in the area of the Negev, 2019. Photograph: Dan Farberoff.

and informal local agencies. Another step is to reach out to active agents such as officials, activists, community leaders, educators, and researchers, some of whom are already engaged and can offer insight into the relevant local issues. As part of this initial preliminary site research, a fertile dialogue was held with Bedouin community leaders in the valley who drive the struggle against their uncertain existential situation, with their settlements constantly under the threat of eviction. On behalf of the art practice, the focus of the negotiation was on listening, establishing trust, and forging solidarity that invites mutual exploration, and leads to an agents' network, which expands into an intricate web, encompassing various individuals and organisations, some of which are controversial.

The site chosen for the project was Bir Umm al Atin cistern, located close to the Hamai'sa family's unrecognised settlement. The cistern, dated likely to the Late Ottoman period,[43] includes a settling pond at its entrance and canals to

---

[43] Interview Hamai'sa family by artists Behar Perahia and Farberoff, 2019 [Hebrew].

which surface runoff flows along the mountainous topography.[44] Nowadays, since the cistern has not been used for years, it has lost its original ability to store water for both human and animal use. Its interior was filled with alluvial soil, and the water-carrying canals have been eroded, preventing the accumulation of water in the short wintertime. (Fig. 4) The first action at the site (December 2019) was dedicated to the cleaning and evacuation of the channels for runoff water to accumulate in the cistern, based on voluntary collaboration with the Jewish and Bedouin communities and other volunteers, using excavation tools such as hoes and buckets, while working side by side for the sake of common future use of the site. (Fig. 5) The second action (February 2020) was dedicated to a comprehensive cleaning of the cistern in collaboration with the Israel Antiquities Authority (IAA), under the community-educational practice of "adopting a site." The action was

Fig. 4: Bir Umm al Atin Cistern, Negev. Source: Topographic maps © Israel Mapping Center. Urban maps only: © OpenStreetMap contributors, CC-BY-SA. PEF maps: Courtesy of Dan Jordani. Satellite photo: Google.

---

44 Menachem Markus, *The Southern Judean Desert: A Survey of Landscapes and Itineraries Including an Introduction on the Judean Desert* (Israel: Nature Reserves Authority Pub, 1984) [Hebrew].

Fig. 5: First intervention at Bir Umm al Atin Cistern engaged with cleaning and excavating channels for runoff water, December 2019. Photograph: Dan Farberoff.

based on preliminary negotiations with archeologists and representatives of the IAA, to engage in a unique activity that combines field trips and indoor study, to be carried out at various locations of cisterns in Israel, in collaboration with school pupils as part of an environmental studies programme.

However, due to the Israeli Antiquities Law, under which archaeology was the old justification regarding artifacts found underground until the 17th century, digging in the cistern is forbidden. Since archeology is seen as significant in nation-building, and embraced in other places around the world, it has developed as a field of research in tandem with the emergence of nationalism dealing with destruction and conservation of cultural property. Israeli archaeological practices created the place for the Jewish national home and established the connection between the ancient Jewish nation and the new nation-state in the same territory as a scientific fact. Thus, it rephrased political, geographical, historical, and epistemological truths.[45]

---

[45] Carmon Popper, *Art as Preservation*; Nadia Abu El-Haj, *Facts on the Ground: Archaeological Practice and Territorial Self-Fashioning in Israeli Society* (Chicago: Chicago University Press, 2001); Michael Feige and Zvi Shiloni, *Archaeology and Nationalism in Eretz-Israel* (Beer-Sheva: Ben-Gurion University of the Negev, 2008) [Hebrew]; Raz Kletter, *Just Past?: The Making of Israeli Archaeology* (London: Routledge, 2005).

The final goal of preparing the cistern for functional use was not achieved due to disagreements between the archaeologists and the Bedouin concerning the modes of intervention in the old cistern, such as excavation using modern mechanical instruments. (Fig. 6). Representatives of the Bedouin community aspired to significant intervention at the site in order to establish an active cistern that would collect runoff water during the winter. The act on-site included a collaboration between the pupils of a nearby Bedouin school and an archaeologist, a representative of IAA, in which they had no other recourse, due to the restrictions on mechanical intervention, but to undertake manual excavation of the edge of the cistern. This created a state of action that was more symbolic of an open dialogue and of a study of local traditions and desert life, rather than a dynamic act of changing the status of the site.

Fig. 6: Second intervention at Bir Umm al Atin Cistern engaged with Schoolchildren and IAA archeologist clearing buildup of earth, February 2020. Photograph: Dan Farberoff.

The third action was implemented at the art exhibition I curated "Common Views: Sourcing Water" at the Arad Contemporary Art Center (ACAC) in 2019–2020. Documentation from the above actions was embedded into artworks presented at the gallery 'white cube', serving as a spatial experience in which there was a translation of actions and processes into mediating objects and presentations, to allow for engagement with a wider audience. The participatory work applied a creative process to facilitate the development of a series of artworks that served as mediating elements for such issues as ownership, inequity, and exploitation, to be displayed in an art exhibit. The engagement also included educational tours of the exhibition for schoolchildren, public visits to cisterns and nearby Bedouin settlements for the wider public, and academic seminars (Fig. 7).

Fig. 7: Third intervention: *Common Views: Sourcing Water* exhibition at the ACAC, 2020. Curated by: Irit Carmon Popper. Photograph: Doron Orgil.

The exhibition combined digital and sculptural installations, some of which are site-specific new artworks, as well as a special place at the heart of the exhibition dedicated to the presentation of research materials. The collected raw materials are transformed and translated by the artists into site-specific, formalistic structures, parts of which extend out into the public space inside and outside the gallery building. The artworks include sculpture, video, and sound installations, drawings, and photographic works. All artworks touch on the topics of water in the desert, control and distribution of resources, conservation, and relationships between humans and the landscape. The various artworks throughout the space alternate, turning on and off, to create a holistic composition that draws the audience's attention and guides them through the space. The exhibition is designed so that the sound from the various installations combines with spatial sound into a unified, orchestrated soundscape.

To demonstrate the current Bedouin challenges of water sourcing to a wider, largely unaware public, a network of water tanks and black pipes, scavenged from the desert, was set up as the main visual symbolic art intervention in the gallery, spilling out into the street below (Fig. 8). This was accompanied by a series of sculptures of a *"Rujum"* – the desert way marker traditionally made of piled-up stones, as a practical and symbolic object that became a minimalist sculpture, in the form of a pyramid-shaped metal grid draped in colorful knitted surfaces, created by the women of Arad and the nearby Bedouin settlements. The participatory knitting action was based on a series of colored palettes conceived by the art collective, matching the different countries of origin of the various women, and selected by personal preference according to their traditional cultural style. The series of *"Rujums"* displayed at the exhibition portrays the future trail, emphasising forming a link between the gallery and the outdoors, between art and life – between the communities sharing a common landscape and looking out onto a common view (Fig. 9).

Fig. 8: Common Views Collective, main installation made of black plastic water tank and pipes, *Common Views: Sourcing Water* exhibition, ACAC, 2020. Curated by: Irit Carmon Popper. Photograph: Doron Orgil.

The next future action based on *Common Views* collectives' vision to revitalise and reawaken the native tradition of water harvesting, proposes the creation of a cistern trail linking the town of Arad with the Bedouin settlements in the Al Baqi'a valley and running past several existing cisterns along the way. The first landmark on which a *Rujum* will be erected will be a convergence of the Desert Threshold Promenade – a future promenade circumducting the perimeter of the city of Arad, emanating from a collaboration between the art collective and the Promenade

Fig. 9: Common View collective In collaboration with the Arad knitting women society and Tel Arad women, *Rujm – marking the cisterns trail*, 2020, Steel, stone, embroidery and wool knitting, "Common Views: Sourcing Water" Exhibition, ACAC, Arad, 2020. Curated by: Irit Carmon Popper. Photographed by Dan Farberoff.

Planning Team, as part of a public participant planning initiative in which the diverse human landscape of Arad and the Bedouin communities takes part.

The act of placement stems from a direct affinity between the body and space that will be expressed in a ceremonial action on site. The meaning of human presence is exposed to political and cultural coverage and is directly linked to nature and the essential connection between the desert environment and the water cycle that passes through it. The act of erecting the first *Rujum* will be the beginning of an annual ritual of renewing and "draping" the *Rujum* cyclically each year. This will be followed by future operations in the other cisterns along the trail. It should be noted that the idea of a desert road in general and the creation of a walking path in particular stemmed from an artistic point of view, but in practice it does not necessarily correspond with the local concept of the Bedouins of orientation in the desert, which is based on the lack of marked paths.

The marking of the water cistern trail is designed to present a tourist trip in the public desert space, and to initiate through it a process of mutual sharing between urban and scenic communities, and Jewish and Bedouin ethnicities. The occupation with the theme of "Water as a Scarce Resource" and how it reflects on the equitability and sustainability of resource use, eventually evolved in discussion with several environmental researchers, into a vision for a potential commons trajectory in the area. The vision has vastly expanded from a dormant proposal by local activists for a biosphere reserve that would balance the needs of the Bedouin and the desert environment at Al Baqi'a, to encompass the entire region surrounding the town of Arad, including its urban center, villages, and nature reserves. This conceptual, regional plan for a social-ecological commons that brings the needs of all inhabitants and lifeforms into consideration, was presented at the exhibition.

The Bir Umm al Atin cistern served as the site for a series of mediating actions which included an introductory tour, an action to renew the rainwater harvesting channels leading to the cistern, an action to renew the cistern sedimentation pool, and finally a performance at the site. These actions served as points of mediation for the wider Bedouin community and the Jewish community from the nearby town and further afield. This resulted in a continuous conversation among them, which engendered solidarity, and thus formed a for-purpose community. This successful bringing together of Bedouin and Jewish children, religious nationalists with liberals, the disenfranchised, independent women, and conservative patriarchs, to work together and collaborate meaningfully, should not be underestimated considering the region's entrenched divisions. The cistern served as a common ground, bringing together the different interests of those with a love of nature, of "The Land", of history, archeology, ecology, culture, and of tradition while aligning their various needs with those of the environment.

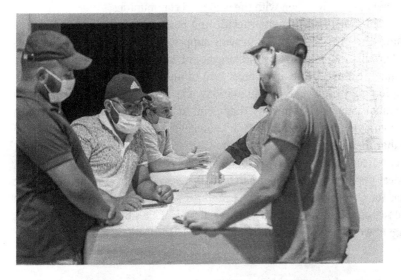

Fig. 10: Dreaming Room, *Common Views: Sourcing Water* Exhibition, ACAC, Arad, 2020. Curated by: Irit Carmon Popper. Photographed by Doron Orgil.

From the curatorial, conceptual, and practical process, recognising the need to distinguish between the works, the archival material, and the future vision of the exhibition, an intimate space was defined at the heart of the exhibition, where the audience was invited to sit, view the documentation, and review professional literature. As an integral part of this space called "The Dreaming Room", strategically placed nylon maps of the area allowed the public to mark the route they thought appropriate for the water cistern trail. (Fig. 10)

8.6 Conclusions

The case study of "Common Views: Sourcing Water" presents the instruments, techniques, and practices utilised, drawing on the use of socially engaged art practices which include participation, action, and reaction to a specific space and its communities. It demonstrates how the *Common Views* collective, using its unfolding network with community members and official agents, was able by spatial and communal intervention to bring into focus civic and political issues, and by doing so, offer a programme for environmental preservation and re-use. The tools utilised by the artists are not fixed but rather relative, lucid, part of an ongoing process of negotiation with various agencies, through which discriminated and appropriated narratives become visible and recognisable as they manage to re-write them in collaboration with the contested communities.

Social-led practices using site-specific and participatory art can lead to the unearthing of repressed histories, provide support for greater visibility of marginalised groups, and initiate the re(dis)covery of 'minor' places so far ignored by the dominant culture.[46] The art actions help in understanding how to deal with the historiography of the site, and in marking it as a necessary step for a forward move, symbolically and practically. They point to the preliminary steps in which the site's complex historiography is acknowledged and its layers are engaged with, rather than silenced. In this way, transforming divergences into encounter, dialogue, reflection, and finally, reconciliation may be an alternative approach. The critical perspective thereby created challenges and subverts the hegemonic one, aims for change, and thus can be examined as a tool for indirect civic action or social resistance. It can influence the reclaiming of sites by allowing awareness of divergent worldviews, community-based approaches, and sustainability.[47]

---

46 Kwon, "One place after Another," 105.

47 Heghnar Watenpaugh, "Preserving the Medieval City of Ani: Cultural Heritage Between Contest and Reconciliation," *Journal of the Society of Architectural Historians* 73:4 (2014): 555.

The *Common Views* art collective aims to amplify the voices, local knowledge, and experiences of the Al-Baqia Bedouin community. They have implemented an approach that focuses on activating "from below" strategies. The community members' voices and perspectives were integrated at every stage of the art project, involving consultation and brainstorming with the art team, conducting interviews with various local agents using ethnographic methods and semi-structured interviews, and collaborating with skilled women from the Jewish and Bedouin communities in traditional knitting and weaving techniques. All the materials gathered were incorporated into the artworks presented at the exhibition. The main site-specific installation, made from black plastic water pipes, symbolised the unjust situation of the Al Baqia water sourcing, and was spread throughout the exhibition space. In addition, documented materials such as recorded interviews, maps, scholarly and academic materials were available for exploration in the dreaming space at the heart of the exhibition.

Common Views art collective can be seen as a civic guardian of repressed cultural heritage, acting against the restrictive policy of the establishment. Yet, the case in question reveals an inherent impasse, such that the art collective, representative of the dominant Jewish community, is acting to preserve the material culture of the minority group, and thereby defending its civil rights in Israel. This predicament leads to the complexity of reading art interventions in the context of an intractable national conflict. Against this background, artists of various periods exercise similar spatially and socially driven modes of action that can be read as counter-hegemonic, creative-performative models of cultural negotiation. Given the complexity of the case, the challenge was to demonstrate how the art action could serve as an example of a leading strategy, which promoted collaboration between contested communities, sharing a common view, to formulate an oppositional ideology and implement it within the dominant apparatus. As the collective guides all efforts toward the environment with the climate crisis in focus, we identify it as an act of solidarity, and view it as such. Concerning the reuse of material remains of the traditional desert cultural heritage, they succeed in excluding citizenship and property rights from the equation.

Theoretical debates have accompanied the flourishing of the genre, questioning the efficacy of artistic influence to generate socio-political change and the gap between the symbolic and substantive values of these artworks. Moreover, the theories on the artist's power to induce and motivate socio-political moves – developed in France, the UK, and the US – have specifically failed to deal with more conflictual areas. Critical dilemmas are intensified when discussing artists in political spaces of conflict and war, such as the Israeli-Palestinian conflict, concerning the non-participation of the Palestinian community in the art actions conducted on their lands by Jewish artists. This unique perspective presents a solution that moves through the environment and leads to the communal and social realms.

Activist art aspires to create change not from within the art field, but rather from reality by way of art, as a response to the failures of the modern welfare state, and in our context, of the military and planning agencies, in dealing with civil issues. Groys discusses the voices that criticise the quality of activist art, claiming that the aestheticisation of the act makes it a spectacle and neutralises its practical influence. Moreover, the futility attributed to the art field condemns artistic activism to predetermined failure.[48] At the same time, art is perceived as an aestheticisation of an existing state, and therefore ostensibly contains resistance to change.

I adopt an attitude closer to Bishop, discussed above, and argue that, unlike Groys' pessimistic view, art is not abandoned, but rather remains an active factor in social and political struggles, especially in sites-in-conflict. This art practice contains healing values for Palestinian/Israeli wounds and sites in conflict worldwide. As the first step to promoting such healing, we must not merely recognise the value of civilian forces in preserving repressed communities whose voices are not heard, using contemporary art practices. However, the self-critical look at the political dilemmas and contradictions arises when artists aim to trigger social change while navigating the complexities of their own role as avant-garde, which is historically associated with pushing artistic boundaries and challenging societal norms.

In essence, artists who persist as avant-garde figures on the fringes bolster their distinct perspectives without compromising their artistic integrity. Nevertheless, when engaging with established institutions, a certain degree of negotiation becomes imperative. This necessitates a delicate balance, acknowledging objections to while recognising the potential benefits of advancing a project that addresses the concerns of marginalised communities. The negotiation process featured prominently in our endeavors. Specifically, our collaboration with the Bedouins aimed at promoting recognition for unrecognised settlements, aligning with our sustainability goals. Despite the challenges and the lack of immediate success, the initiative laid a foundation, involving citizens, and institutions, and fostering heightened awareness. Although the venture may not have yielded immediate results, it signifies a meaningful beginning, and the seeds sown may yet bear fruit in future endeavors.

---

48 Boris Groys, "A Genealogy Participatory Art," 20–24.

References

Abu El-Haj, Nadia. *Facts on the Ground: Archaeological Practice and Territorial Self-Fashioning in Israeli Society*. Chicago: Chicago University Press, 2001.

Atkins Robert, Rudolf Frieling, Boris Groys, and Manovich Lev, eds. *The Art of Participation: 1950 to Now*. Exhibition catalogue. San Francisco Museum of Modern Art, 2008.

Barrett, James R. *History from the Bottom Up and the Inside Out: Ethnicity, Race, and Identity in Working-Class History*. Durham and London: Duke University Press, 2017.

Behar Perahia, David, and Dan Farberoff. "Commoning: Environmental Reconciliation in the Work of Common Views" *Oncurating* 54 (2022–2023).

Bishop, Claire. "Antagonism and Relational Aesthetics." *October Magazine* 110 (2004): 51–79.

Bishop, Claire. *Artificial Hells: Participatory Art and the Politics of Spectatorship*. New York: Verso, 2012.

Bishop Claire, ed. *Participation: Documents on Participatory Art*. London and Cambridge, Massachusetts: Whitechapel, The MIT Press, 2004.

Bourriaud, Nicolas. *Relational Aesthetics*. Dijon: Les presses du réel, 1998.

Carmon Popper Irit "Art as Preservation: Interventions in Sites-in-Conflict, Israel, 1948–2008." PhD diss., Haifa: Technion IIT, 2019.

Foster, Hal, ed. *The Return of the Real*. Cambridge: MIT Press, 1996.

Godfrey, Mark. "The Artist as Historian." *October Magazine* 120 (2007): 140–172.

Kahana, Tomer. *Social Survey – The Bedouins of Al-Baki'a Valley*. December 2015, Research paper [Hebrew].

Kedar, Alexander, Ahmad Amara, and Oren Yiftachel. *Emptied Lands: A Legal Geography of Bedouin Rights in the Negev*. Stanford: Stanford University Press, 2018.

Khalidi, Walid, ed. *All That Remains – The Palestinian Villages Occupied and Depopulated by Israel in 1948*. Beirut: Institute for Palestinian Studies, 1992.

Kwon, Miwon. *One Place after Another: Site-Specific Art and Locational Identity*. Cambridge: MIT Press, 2004.

Morris, Benny. *The Birth of the Palestinian Refugee Problem Revisited*. Cambridge: Cambridge University Press, 2004.

Nasasra, Mansour, Sophie Richter-Devroe, Sarab Abu-Rabia-Queder, and Richard Ratcliffe, eds. *The Naqab Bedouin and Colonialism: New Perspectives*. New York: Routledge, 2019.

Ram, Uri. "Memory and Identity: Sociology of the Historians' Debate in Israel." *Theory and Criticism* 8 (1996): 9–32 [Hebrew].

Suwaed, Muhammad Youssef. "Bedouin-Jewish Relations in the Negev 1943–1948." *Middle Eastern Studies* 51:5 (2015): 767–788.

Thompson, William. *What Happened to History?* London: Sterling, Va, Pluto Press, 2000.

Yiftachel, Oren, Nili Baruch, Said Abu Sammur, Nava Sheer, and Ronen Ben Arie, *Alternative Master Plan for the Unrecognized Bedouin Villages in the Negev*, BIMKOM: Planners for Planning Rights, Abridged version 2012. https://bimkom.org/eng/wp-content/uploads/Bedouin-Negev-Alternative-Master-Plan.pdf, accessed September 30, 2024.

Yiftachel, Oren. "Bedouin Arabs and the Israeli Settler State: Land Policies and Indigenous Resistance." In *The Future of Indigenous Peoples: Strategies for Survival and Development*, edited by Duane Champagne, and Ismael Abu-Saad, 21–47. Los Angeles: UCLA American, 2005.

Wood, Andy. "History from Below and Early Modern Social History." In *The Many-Headed Monster: The History of 'The Unruly Sort of Clowns' and other Early Modern Peculiarities*. https://manyheadedmonster.com/2013/08/21/andy-wood-history-from-below-and-early-modern-social-history/, accessed September 9, 2023

Yannick Lengkeek

9 Regimes at Play: Rethinking Games, Agency, and Power Relations under the Portuguese Estado Novo

The observation that play and games are a powerful form of agency in their own right, has been made repeatedly over the last two centuries. The observers in question, however, were for the most part novelists, and not academics. For instance, in the words of Mrs Battle, the protagonist of a short story written by Charles Lamb, "cards are war, in disguise of a sport."[1] The list of insightful references could be expanded ad libitum, including titles like Dostoevsky's *The Gambler* (1866) or Walter Tevis' *The Hustler* (1959) and *The Queen's Gambit* (1983). These literary explorations of play highlight how literary production and discourses surrounding games were closely intertwined, with a spotlight on the complexities of human agency.[2] Academic research on play in the humanities and social sciences, on the other hand, has traditionally portrayed play from a top-down perspective. From Johan Huizinga's seminal *Homo Ludens*, which introduced the idea that play precedes and shapes culture,[3] to Clifford Geertz's influential essay on Balinese cockfights as a playful representation of how power was renegotiated within the specific context of rural communities in Bali,[4] we can observe a strong culturalist bias, which has only been reinforced by the so-called cultural turn.[5]

In a recent article that explores arcades and the game of pinball in mid-twentieth-century London through materials from the British Mass Observation Archive, Benjamin Litherland, reiterating a position voiced by Aphra Kerr in

---

1 Charles Lamb, "Mrs. Battle's Opinions on Whist," in *The Works of Charles and Mary Lamb Vol. 2: Elia and the Last Essays of Elia*, ed. Charles Lamb, and E.V. Lucas, (*Project Gutenberg*, 2003), http://www.gutenberg.org/ebooks/10343, accessed September 30, 2024.
2 For a fruitful theoretical exploration of the historical cross-fertilisation of games and literature, see Douglas Guerra, *Slantwise Moves: Games, Literature, and Social Invention in Nineteenth Century America* (Philadelphia: University of Pennsylvania Press, 2018), 1–25.
3 Johan Huizinga, *Homo Ludens: A Study of the Play-Element in Culture* (London: Routledge, [1944] 1949), 46. For a helpful historical contextualisation of Huizinga's ideas and how they fit into academic debates from the 1940s until the 1970s, see Robert Anchor, "History and Play: Johan Huizinga and his Critics," *History & Theory* 17, 1 (1978).
4 Clifford Geertz, "Deep Play: Notes on the Balinese Cockfight," in idem, *The Interpretation of Cultures: Selected Essays* (New York: Basic Books, 1973).
5 See the critique presented in Thomas M. Malaby, "Anthropology and Play: The Contours of Playful Experience," *New Literary History* 40, 1 (2009): 207–10.

https://doi.org/10.1515/9783111522180-009

2006, has pleaded for a shift away from this strong culturalist bias towards an approach that is more in line with E.P. Thompson's idea of 'history from below.'[6] What is often overlooked, however, is that Thompson's work, like the kindred traditions of Italian *microstoria* or German *Alltagsgeschichte*, already implicitly formulated a viable set of conceptual frameworks to locate play and games in the stunningly diverse landscapes of everyday life. In his 1967 essay *Time, Work-Discipline, and Industrial Capitalism*, Thompson highlighted how "the leisured classes began to discover the 'problem' [. . .] of the leisure of the masses"[7] and discussed contemporary critiques of 'jocularity', idleness, and gaming during the early Victorian period, which were seen as "non-productivity, compounded with impertinence."[8] In Germany, Alf Lüdtke's close study of coffee breaks, time-wasting, and horseplay in German factories at the turn of the twentieth century made a case for a more serious engagement with idleness and spontaneous efforts to pass time. Like E.P. Thompson before him, he studied these seemingly trivial activities as tactics employed by 'ordinary' citizens to resist the pervasive schedules and calendars imposed from above by managers, bureaucrats, and other representatives of the social elite.[9] Looking at an entirely different setting – the French Pyrenees around the turn of the fourteenth century – Emmanuel Le Roy Ladurie, while not explicitly presenting play and idleness as forms of protest, showcased the centrality of dice and board games even amidst the tumultuous religious and political conflicts between Catharism and the Church. In Ladurie's narrative, games appear as a welcome distraction in people's lives, to find some relief from the struggles they became embroiled in.[10]

Building on Jim Sharpe's argument about a gradual convergence of different national traditions of writing history 'from the bottom up',[11] this chapter explores play and games as a prism through which historians can explore questions of

---

6 Benjamin Litherland, "Ludosity, Radical Contextualism, and a New Games History: Pleasure, Truth, and Deception in the Mid-20th-Century London Arcade," *Games and Culture* 16, 2 (2021): 143; Aphra Kerr, *The Business and Culture of Digital Games: Gamework and Gameplay* (London: Sage, 2006), 20.

7 E.P. Thompson, "Time, Work-Discipline, and Industrial Capitalism," *Past & Present* 38 (1967): 90.

8 Ibid.

9 Alf Lüdtke, "Cash, Coffee-Breaks, Horseplay: Eigensinn and Politics among Factory Workers in Germany circa 1900," in *Confrontation, Class Consciousness, and the Labor Process: Studies in Proletarian Class Formation*, ed. Michael Hanagan and Charles Stephenson (Westport: Greenwood Press, 1986), 65–95.

10 Emmanuel Le Roy Ladurie, *Montaillou: Cathars and Catholics in a French Village, 1294–1324*, trans. Barbara Bray (Harmondsworth: Penguin: [1978] 1980), 259 and 263–64.

11 Jim Sharpe, "History from Below," in *New Perspectives on Historical Writing*, ed. Peter Burke (Cambridge: Politi, 1991).

9 Regimes at Play — **229**

agency, lived experiences of escapism, and the social and cultural dynamics behind the stigmatisation of certain forms of play. Arguing from a distinctly Thompsonian perspective, James Francis Warren described the experiences of rickshaw drivers in colonial Singapore, many of whom regularly squandered their entire earnings in gambling dens, in the following words:

> "What motivated rickshawmen to gamble? What kept them going even when they lost their hard-earned cash and had to pawn their few possessions? Many pullers who gambled were optimistic about winning next time, hoping to recoup their losses and make enough to go home to China in some style and comfort. A pipe-dream for most, perhaps, but they knew the odds were against them living much beyond the age of forty. They were prepared to stake everything against the eventuality of a premature death."[12]

Warren's rich account of the daily lives of rickshaw drivers is saturated with instances of gambling, sometimes with tragic consequences.

Contrasting the social history of illegal gambling in unlicensed venues with the history of billiards, a game that trickled down from the ballrooms of the aristocracy and emerging bourgeois gentleman's clubs all the way to the taverns and bars frequented by the working classes, this chapter seeks to locate play and games in the wider panorama of history from below. It makes a case for reconsidering play as a central – or, at the very least, certainly not a peripheral – category for scholars aiming to get a better grasp of what mattered to people in their daily lives, and how these priorities conflicted with an emerging culture of moral paternalism (both secular and religious) across Europe and beyond. To illustrate this argument, this chapter looks at António de Oliveira Salazar's so-called Estado Novo ('New State') in Portugal, a regime known for its exceptional longevity, and its firm control of citizens, institutions, and public opinion over a period of almost fifty years. This case study is particularly interesting because it forms an excellent backdrop against which we can examine play and games at the grassroots level over a period of almost half a century, allowing us to gain important insights into how leisure and idleness were monitored and contested under dictatorial rule. As Alf Lüdtke wrote in the introduction to his edited volume, *Everyday Life in Mass Dictatorship* (2016), dictatorships provide a particularly fertile environment to study the dynamics of collusion and evasion, as the potential for clashes and friction between individuals and the state were drastically increased in heavily regu-

---

12 James Francis Warren, *Rickshaw Coolie: A People's History of Singapore 1880–1940* (Singapore: Singapore University Press, 2003), 253.

lated and policed societies,[13] including not only examples like Salazarism, National Socialism, or Stalinism, but also many colonial regimes. These regimes all had a tendency to produce large amounts of files and police records on the activities and whereabouts of their citizens, which historians with an interest in everyday life perspectives and experiences 'from below' can use to reconstruct oft-neglected aspects of daily life, including various forms of 'self-willed' behaviour (*Eigensinn*),[14] or, in the words of James Scott, 'weapons of the weak' and means of passive resistance.[15]

This chapter will proceed in three steps. First, it will situate play in the broader field of everyday life and question monolithic ideas of what everyday life is and is not. Building on these considerations, it will present games as an alternative way to bring agency 'from below' back into a field that is, ever since everyday life history started to become something of an umbrella term for different traditions and iterations of Thompson's approach and its mainland European counterparts,[16] increasingly dominated by an unconscious bias of 'everydayness.' Secondly, Portugal will be introduced as a case study of a country that was not only subject to dictatorial rule for an exceptional amount of time but also sported a pioneering casino and gambling culture (for the upper classes) that was unparalleled anywhere else in Europe, with the exception of the French Riviera. Third, and finally, the chapter will look at billiards as a game that was appropriated from above as well as from below, making it a fascinating example that showcases how the right to play was tied to powerful cultural tropes surrounding class, space,[17] and intergenerational conflict. Taken together, the research presented in the following pages aspires to breathe new life into stale narratives

---

13 Alf Lüdtke, "Introductory notes," in *Everyday Life in Mass Dictatorship: Collusion and Evasion*, ed. Alf Lüdtke (New York: Palgrave Macmillan, 2016), 8–11.

14 Alf Lüdtke, *Eigen-Sinn. Fabrikalltag, Arbeitererfahrungen und Politik vom Kaiserreich bis in den Faschismus* (Hamburg: Ergebnisse Verlag, 1993).

15 James C. Scott, *Weapons of the Weak: Everyday Forms of Peasant Resistance* (New Haven: Yale University Press, 1985).

16 Paul Steege et al., "The History of Everyday Life: A Second Chapter," *The Journal of Modern History* 80, 2 (2008): 358–362.

17 In the work of E.P. Thompson, a similar theme emerges in *Whigs and Hunters*, where the relationship between poachers, their aristocratic overlords, and those caught in between was deeply enmeshed in ideas and discourses about power and ownership. While the increase in poaching and various raids that culminated in passing the notorious Black Act in the British parliament in 1723 was largely caused by economic disruptions at the time, the fundamental issue at the heart of these draconian measures was to protect the privileges of the landed gentry and ensure that landowners could go about pursuing their favourite pastimes, such as hunting, undisturbed. For a closer analysis of these inter-class dynamics, see E.P. Thompson, *Whigs and Hunters: The Origin of the Black Act* (London: Allen Lane, 1975), 219–69.

about how non-elite citizens experienced their daily lives in the shadow of repressive governments, and how they played the hand they had been dealt, both literally and metaphorically, to better their circumstances.

9.1 Situating Play in the Landscape of Everyday Life

The conceptual dichotomy between play and everyday life is not just rooted in an overly abstract and normative understanding of play in the tradition of Johan Huizinga, but also in an equally abstract and normative image of everyday life. In his influential *Critique of Everyday Life*, Henri Lefebvre, building on previous generations of Marxist thinkers, portrayed everyday life as a distinctly modern phenomenon, as well as a reflection of capitalist power relations in industrialised societies.[18] Within this framework, Lefebvre identified monotony and repetition as central aspects of everyday life and lamented the resulting sense of passivity, which, as he claimed, limits human agency to the point where it becomes a mere reaction to a steady stream of events.[19] In contrast to this bleak image of the everyday, he defined leisure and entertainment as their necessary counterpart. In Lefebvre's words, "the worker craves a sharp break with his work, a compensation. He looks for this in leisure seen as entertainment or distraction. In this way, leisure appears as the non-everyday in the everyday."[20]

Aiming to move beyond this rigid Marxist image of everyday life as a reality dictated 'from above', Michel de Certeau's *Practice of Everyday Life*, published more than three decades after Lefebvre's *Critique of Everyday Life*, explored everyday life as a creative process 'from below'. Furthermore, De Certeau thought of his work as a necessary counterpart to Michel Foucault's discourse-centred and somewhat monolithic ideas surrounding discipline and *dispositifs*, where resistance could only result from challenging discourses, institutions, and overarching power structures.[21] His primary concern was to "make explicit the systems of operational combination (*les combinatoires d'opérations*) which also compose a

---

18 Henri Lefebvre, *Critique of Everyday Life*, 3 Vol. (London: Verso, 1991).

19 Henri Lefebvre and Christine Levich, "The Everyday and Everydayness," *Yale French Studies* 73 (1987): 10.

20 Henri Lefebvre, *Critique of Everyday Life*, Vol. 1 (London: Verso [1947] 1991), 40.

21 Michel de Certeau, *The Practice of Everyday Life*, trans. Steven Rendall (Berkeley: University of California Press, 1984), xiv.

'culture'",[22] thus highlighting how "[e]veryday life invents itself by poaching in countless ways on the property of others."[23] Of course, we may raise the question, as Norbert Elias did in 1978,[24] of whether everyday life warrants all the special attention as an allegedly distinct category. Surveying the most important theoretical contributions surrounding everyday life as a separate category, Rita Felski conceded that everyday life defies any attempts at neat categorisation and is generally either invested with "enormous symbolic weight" or portrayed as "the realm of ultimate alienation and dehumanization."[25] Hence, there is hardly any consensus on what exactly constitutes everyday life, nor is it possible to exactly define the constituent parts of everyday life: 'ordinary' people who live through it,[26] the popular culture that gives voice to the seemingly 'mundane',[27] or the spaces it takes place in.[28] Finally, we need to acknowledge that "the social space we call everyday life will have already been made meaningful by powerful forces over which we have little control,"[29] meaning that individuals have limited power over the contexts and environments they find themselves in, and incomplete knowledge of the world around them.

Henri Lefebvre's observation that the separation of play and leisure from the rhythms of daily working life was a product of industrialisation was also shared by E.P. Thompson in *The Making of the English Working Class*, where he noted

---

22 Ibid, xi.

23 Ibid, xii.

24 Norbert Elias, "Zum Begriff des Alltags," in *Materialien zur Soziologie des Alltags: Kölner Zeitschrift für Soziologie und Sozialpsychologie, Sonderheft 20*, ed. Kurt Hammerich, and Michael Klein (Leverkusen: Opladen, 1978).

25 Rita Felski, "The Invention of Everyday Life," *New Formations* 39 (2000): 31.

26 Claire Langhamer, "Who the Hell are Ordinary People? Ordinariness as a Category of Historical Analysis," *Transactions of the Royal Historical Society* 28 (2018).

27 Without delving too deep into this rich and controversial topic, it is worth noting that popular culture is neither entirely synonymous with a top-down capitalist culture industry (as coined by Adorno and Horkheimer in their *Dialectic of Enlightenment*), nor simply the same as folk culture. On the problems of defining folk culture as a distinct category 'from below,' see the reflections in Carlo Ginzburg, *The Cheese and the Worms: The Cosmos of a Sixteenth-century Miller* (Baltimore: John Hopkins University Press, 1980), xix. The problem is also amply discussed in Jim Sharpe, "History from Below," in *New Perspectives on Historical Writing*, ed. Peter Burke (Cambridge: Polity, 1991). Peter Burke's well-known contribution to the debate, which stated that popular culture should be seen as a distinctly modern phenomenon that builds on, but is not equivalent to folk culture, is presented in Peter Burke, "Popular Culture Reconsidered," *Storia della Storiografia* 17 (1990).

28 For a case study of one such 'everyday space,' see Kate Ferris, "Bars," in *Doing Spatial History*, ed. Riccardo Bavaj, Konrad Lawson, and Bernhard Struck (Abingdon, Oxon: Routledge, 2021).

29 John Storey, *From Popular Culture to Everyday Life* (Abingdon, Oxon: Routledge, 2014), 135.

that there "was a conscious resistance to the passing of an old way of life, and it was frequently associated with political Radicalism. As important in this passing as the simple physical loss of commons and 'playgrounds,' was the loss of leisure in which to play and the repression of playful impulses."[30] Bars and taverns, where the working classes met to drink, chat, and play various games either for money or simply for fun, were notorious hotbeds of the kind of resistance described by Thompson. In Nazi Germany and Stalinist Russia, the bonds forged between individuals in these recreational environments often ran parallel to the ties of allegiance that were encouraged by the regimes of Hitler and Stalin.[31] Likewise, bars in Italy,[32] Spain,[33] and Portugal all proved to be remarkably resistant to the intrusions of the state, despite being targeted by regime agents. Portuguese bars and taverns in rural areas drew their resilience from deep patronage networks, and the fact that the Portuguese gendarmerie in the countryside – the *Guarda Nacional Republicana* – was deeply entrenched in rural society, and often neither able nor willing to properly enforce the agenda of the central government in Lisbon,[34] which was seen as distant and elusive.

However, the adult diversions that took place in these pockets of idleness rarely become the subject of serious analysis, and certainly do not feature prominently in contemporary social history and histories of everyday life. Unlike children's play,[35] which is considered essential for healthy child development, and sports, which are perceived as productive outlets for competitive ambitions and practical lessons in fair play,[36] adult games of chance or skill that do not take place in an 'athletic' environment hardly ever receive the same attention. The fact that sports history has managed to garner far more attention than research on other games can be traced back to two factors. First, sports fit into larger nar-

---

30 E.P. Thompson, *The Making of the English Working Class* (New York: Penguin, [1963] 1970), 448.

31 Sheila Fitzpatrick and Alf Lüdtke, "Energizing the Everyday: On the Making and Breaking of Social Bonds in Nazism and Stalinism," in *Beyond Totalitarianism: Stalinism and Nazism Compared*, ed. Michael Geyer, and Sheila Fitzpatrick (Cambridge: Cambridge University Press, 2009), 292–95.

32 Kate Ferris, "Bars," 143–50.

33 David D. Gilmore, "The Role of the Bar in Andalusian Rural Society: Observations on Political Culture under Franco," *Journal of Anthropological Research*, 41: 3 (1985): 268–74.

34 Joaquim Pais de Brito, "A taberna: lugar e revelador da aldeia," in *Lugares de aqui: Actas do seminário "Terrenos Portugueses"*, ed. Brian Juan O'Neill, and Joaquim Pais de Brito (Lisbon, 1991), particularly 185–98.

35 For an excellent discussion of childhood play and games from a historical perspective, see Mary Clare Martin, "The state of play: historical perspectives," *International Journal of Play* 5, 3 (2016).

36 Roger Caillois, *Man, Play and Games*, trans. Meyer Barash (Chicago: University of Illinois Press, [1961] 2001), 15.

ratives about nationalism and discourses of power and representation more easily than other games[37] – a fact that has been observed by illustrious academics, including Clifford Geertz and Brian Sutton-Smith.[38] Secondly, organised sports as a global phenomenon can only be understood in conjunction with the emergence of mass media coverage of sporting events,[39] whereas other games, due to their more private or morally contested nature (as in the case of gambling), marginalised themselves to a certain extent. Moreover, as parties of board or card games in private settings were generally not recorded for posterity, the task of locating the player remains a major challenge for game historians.[40]

As for children's play, game historians face a similar set of problems, albeit of a more paradigmatic nature. First of all, in historical scholarship on the subject, there is the problematic idea, rarely made explicit, that the purpose of play fundamentally shifts from learning and growth during childhood and youth towards leisure, distraction, and escapism in adulthood.[41]

What makes adult play in the form of casual gaming and gambling particularly interesting is precisely this aura of apoliticism and detachment from ordinary affairs. As Johan Huizinga, Roger Caillois, and other theorists of play believed, play is autotelic, that is, a self-contained activity that people partake in for its own sake. Without getting too much into the theoretical minutiae behind the concept of autotelicity, suffice it to say that those who argue in favour of play as an essentially autotelic activity tend to be more interested in games as objects of study, and less in gamers or players as active subjects.[42] For scholars with a particular interest in gamers rather than games themselves, examining the thin line

---

37 For an analysis of the ongoing intellectual conversation between theories of nationalism and sports history, see Matti Goksøyr, "Nationalism," in *Routledge Companion to Sports History*, ed. S.W. Pope, and John Nauright (Abingdon, Oxon: Routledge, 2010).

38 Brian Sutton-Smith, *The Ambiguity of Play* (Cambridge, MA: Harvard University Press, 1997), 85–90; Geertz, "Deep Play," 417.

39 For an excellent overview of the theoretical implications of this convergence between sports and mass media, see for instance Garry Whannel, *Culture, Politics and Sport: Blowing the Whistle, Revisited* (Abingdon, Oxon: Routledge, 2008).

40 Regarding board games, see also the remarks in Holly Nielsen, "'The British Empire Would Gain New Strength from Nursery Floors': Depictions of Travel and Place in Nineteenth-Century British Board Games," in *Historia Ludens: The Playing Historian*, ed. Alexander von Lünen, Katherine J. Lewis, Benjamin Litherland, and Pat Callum (Abingdon, Oxon: Routledge, 2020), 31.

41 Moreover, the question of how children exercised agency through play and how games created a space for reciprocal influencing between adults and children still provides a fertile ground for debates among historians. See also Martin, "The state of play," 330.

42 Roger Caillois even goes as far as to describe extrinsic motivations for play as 'corruption,' thus reinforcing the conceptual barrier between play and ordinary life. See Caillois, *Man, Play and Games*, 43–56.

between extrinsic motivations (such as advancing one's social status or making money) and intrinsic ones (autotelicity) becomes an important aspect of their research, calling the rigid categorisation of play as an entirely self-contained activity into question.[43] As Michel de Certeau observed in *The Practice of Everyday Life*, games "formulate (and already formalise) rules organising moves and constitute [. . .] a memory (a storage and a classification) of schemas of actions articulating replies with respect to circumstances."[44] In short, games are used by individuals to reflect on their day-to-day lives, giving them a safe space to rethink their actions and, speaking in the language of De Certeau, 'tactics.' However, the relationship between games and everyday life does not stop here. As De Certeau emphasises, it is very much a reciprocal relationship, with ludic experiences frequently seeping into everyday interactions. As he puts it, "people tell each other about the hand they had to play the night before, or the slam they made the previous week."[45] Finally, everyday experiences of gambling and succumbing to blind fate, which revolved around surrendering control to higher powers such as god, a pantheon of deities, or destiny, always had a religious and spiritual dimension to them throughout most of human history.[46]

Yet, it appears that the implicit assumption of play being primarily autotelic – beyond the repercussions in academic debates discussed above – has contributed to the notion that playing games is a marginal, self-contained activity, rather than a serious area of historical enquiry. In democratic societies, play appears like a projection screen for larger moral and cultural debates, such as fears about play exerting a corrupting influence on younger generations. The debates about pool in the United States, which became a symbol of the moral degradation of youth from the 1950s onwards, can be interpreted in terms of moral scapegoating in US society throughout the Cold War.[47] However, if we consider that the vast majority of the American pool players who rose to some degree of national fame hailed from exceptionally poor and unstable family backgrounds and started their careers as 'pool sharks', playing for money in dingy bars,[48] we have to acknowledge

---

43 See the excellent criticisms raised in Stephen E. Schmid, "Beyond Autotelic Play," *Journal of the Philosophy of Sport* 38, 2 (2011).

44 De Certeau, *Practice of Everyday Life*, 22.

45 De Certeau, *Practice of Everyday Life*, 22.

46 Bjørn Thomassen, *Liminality and the Modern: Living through the In-Between* (Farnham: Ashgate, 2014), 144.

47 Ned Polsky, "Of Pool Playing and Poolrooms," in idem, *Hustlers, Beats, and Others* (Chicago: Aldine Publishing 1967).

48 Famous pop-cultural adaptations of the pool shark motif can be found in the novel *The Hustler* (1959), written by Walter Tevis, as well as the well-known broadway musical *The Music Man* (1957) by Meredith Wilson.

that simple narratives about moral projection cannot accommodate the full complexity of play. The history of so-called numbers games and illegal lotteries organised by residents of poor African American neighbourhoods in downtown Chicago and New York (among other big cities) is another case in point, highlighting how play was just as much about control as it was about freedom.[49]

Hence, it is puzzling to see that play in dictatorial regimes has received even less attention than play in democracies. Landmark publications on everyday life and the history of organised leisure activities in various regimes have significantly broadened our understanding of leisure under dictatorial rule.[50] On the exceedingly rare occasion when adult play is mentioned in passing, it is framed in terms of escapism, unmasking implicit assumptions about games being played for their own sake, with no political intent. Yet, as Miguel Sicart puts it, "it is precisely the autotelic nature of play that makes it political action. Like carnival, play has a particular status in its relation to reality that allows political action while being relatively immune to the actions of power."[51] Therefore, it is plausible to assume that play was instrumentalised, or, in some cases, used as an excuse for unsanctioned gatherings, similar to the way alcohol was used in Fascist Italy as a pretext for expressing dissent.[52]

To illustrate how play and games can serve as an analytical lens that allows us to rethink everyday sociability and the contestation of power from below, this article will zoom in on the Portuguese Estado Novo regime, the longest-lived dictatorship in the history of Western Europe. The question of how exactly the regime survived for such a long time amidst the many social and cultural changes that rocked Portuguese society between 1933 and 1974 keeps sparking debates among experts on Portuguese history and dictatorship more broadly.[53] Many of

---

49 Matthew Vaz, *Running the Numbers: Race, Police, and the History of Urban Gambling* (Chicago: University of Chicago Press, 2020); LaShawn Harris, *Sex Workers, Psychics, and Numbers Runners: Black Women in New York City's Underground Economy* (Urbana: University of Illinois Press, 2016), 54–122.

50 This list includes, but is not limited to, titles such as Antonio Cazorla Sánchez, *Fear and Progress: Ordinary Lives in Franco's Spain 1939–1975* (Chichester: Wiley-Blackwell, 2010); Sheila Fitzpatrick, *Everyday Stalinism: Ordinary Life in Extraordinary Times. Soviet Russia in the 1930s* (Oxford: Oxford University Press, 2010); Andrew Stuart Bergerson, *Ordinary Germans in Extraordinary Times: The Nazi Revolution in Hildesheim* (Bloomington: Indianapolis University Press, 2004); Victoria de Grazia, *The Culture of Consent: Mass Organizations of Leisure in Fascist Italy* (Cambridge, UK: Cambridge University Press, 1981).

51 Miguel Sicart, *Play Matters* (Cambridge, MA: MIT Press, 2014), 75.

52 Kate Ferris, "Everyday Spaces: Bars, Alcohol and the Spatial Framing of Everyday Political Practice and Interaction in Fascist Italy," *European History Quarterly* 52, 2 (2022): 152–157.

53 In a review essay published in 2002, Filipe Ribeiro de Meneses provides a solid overview of historiographical strands aiming to explain the foundations of Salazar's rule. Meneses repeatedly emphasises the regime's mixed messaging and contradictions, reminding readers that Salazarism

the typologies put forward by well-known historians of the period, such as Fernando Rosas,[54] while certainly thought-provoking, tend to ignore the bottom-up agency of ordinary citizens. More recent scholarship on the regime's control apparatus, particularly the Estado Novo's secret police PIDE (*Polícia Internacional e de Defesa do Estado*) has challenged unidirectional narratives about the control of citizens through ubiquitous policing by emphasising the role of informers. The findings of these studies show that policing under the Salazar regime relied on members of civil society to a far larger extent than previously assumed.[55] At the same time, recently published research on the activities of the secret police in the Azores, far from the direct control of the central authorities in Lisbon, reminds us of the unpredictability of civilian actors, who could be just as willing to assist the police as they were ready to undermine authority if circumstances required it.[56]

The two distinct case studies of play, casual gambling and billiards, which this article uses to rethink everyday experiences of dictatorial rule under Salazar, worked along similar lines. Without wanting to engage too much with debates surrounding terms like fascism, totalitarianism, or authoritarianism,[57] one particular point made by Juan J. Linz deserves closer scrutiny. Linz argues that a key difference between authoritarian and totalitarian regimes lies in their diametrically opposed attitudes towards mass mobilisation. In his view, authoritarian regimes, which would include the Estado Novo as a prime example, rely more on demobilisation, working tirelessly to create a sense of apathy, inertia, and helplessness among their populations.[58] With regard to the Portuguese case, Joyce Firstenberg Riegelhaupt, an anthropologist, made a similar argument as early as 1979, giving various examples to substantiate her claim that ordinary citizens, es-

---

was a political framework rather than a fully developed and coherent ideology. See Filipe Ribeiro de Meneses, "The Origins and Nature of Authoritarian Rule in Portugal, 1919–1945," *Contemporary European History* 11, 1 (2002), 153–163.

54 Fernando Rosas, *Salazar e o Poder: A Arte de Saber Durar* (Lisbon: Tinta-da-China, 2012).

55 Irene Flunser Pimentel, *Informadores da PIDE: Uma Tragédia Portuguesa* (Lisbon: Temas e Debates, 2022); Duncan Simpson, "Approaching the PIDE 'From Below': Petitions, Spontaneous Applications and Denunciation Letters to Salazar's Secret Police in 1964," *Contemporary European History* 30 (2021): 398–413.

56 Beatriz Valverde Contreras, and Alexander Keese, "Living at the Margins of Repression: Everyday Life and Hidden Challenges in the Azores' Central Group, 1954–1960," *European History Quarterly* 52, 2 (2022): 221–244.

57 On the problems of interpreting Salazarism purely in terms of fascism, to the exclusion of other categories, see António Costa Pinto, *Salazar's Dictatorship and European Fascism: Problems of Interpretation* (New York: Columbia University Press, 1995).

58 Juan J. Linz, *Totalitarian and Authoritarian Regimes* (Boulder: Lynne Rienner, 2000), 54 and 159.

pecially in rural areas, were systematically cut off from politics and discouraged from seeking out opportunities for participation in public life.[59]

Yet, this view on authoritarian regimes 'from above' is slowly shifting, with historians of Spain and Italy, such as Peter Anderson,[60] Claudio Hernández Burgos,[61] Kate Ferris,[62] and Paul Corner advocating for a more critical engagement with consensus as a two-way-street,[63] where citizens tried to use the state to advance their own agendas – some of them, sadly, just as authoritarian as the regimes in question. With this change of perspective comes a renewed interest in what Paul Steege and his co-authors called the technique of 'dwelling', that is, the practice of reading seemingly marginal sources on isolated events or situations closely.[64] The research presented in this chapter relies on similar methods. Instances of illegal gambling and issues surrounding games were rarely compiled in explicitly game-related files and are often dispersed across various police and civil administration archives. Moreover, the Portuguese government usually delegated the policing of games to local authorities, who – as we will see during the course of the argument – had diverse views on adult gaming practices, ranging from negligence and cautious laissez-faire to pre-emptive measures designed to curb the playing of games, particularly among the poorer strata of society. Therefore, thinking of archives not so much as an institutional and governmental 'product' but rather as a process, can help us to understand why games were grouped together with files on nightlife and social problems and not seen as an issue of their own.[65]

This chapter argues that games were a focal point in the contestation of autonomy and individual agency, both from above and from below. Through policies, (police) interventions, and its social and cultural agenda, the Estado Novo intended to weaponise play as an additional barrier to curtail social mobility and

---

59 Joyce Firstenberg Riegelhaupt, "Os camponeses e a política no Portugal de Salazar – o Estado Corporativo e o "apoliticismo" nas aldeias," *Análise Social* 15, 59 (1979).

60 Peter Anderson, *The Francoist Military Trials: Terror and Complicity, 1939–1945* (New York: Routledge, 2010), particularly 63–122.

61 Claudio Hernández Burgos, "The Triumph of 'Normality', Social Attitudes, Popular Opinion and the Construction of the Franco Regime in Post-War Rural Spain (1936–1952)," *European History Quarterly* 46, 2 (2016): 291–310.

62 Kate Ferris, *Everyday Life in Fascist Venice, 1929–40* (New York: Palgrave Macmillan, 2012).

63 Paul Corner, "Dictatorship revisited: consensus, coercion, and strategies of survival," *Modern Italy* 22, 4 (2017): 435–444.

64 Steege, Bergerson, Healy and Swett, "History of Everyday Life," 375–76.

65 On this distinction between product and process in archival research, see the reflections on colonial archival practices in Ann Laura Stoler, *Along the Archival Grain: Thinking through Colonial Ontologies* (Princeton, 2009), 20.

squash dissent under the pretext of preserving national harmony.[66] At the same time, games were exploited by citizens to navigate daily experiences under dictatorial rule, assert their autonomy vis-à-vis the regime and other social groups, and pursue self-expression and personal ambitions under a government that aspired to predefine and fix their lot in life from the cradle to the grave.[67] Ultimately, the research presented in the following pages endeavours to show that the writing of histories 'from below' benefits from a thorough engagement with games and the reasons why people enjoyed, despised, and instrumentalised them.

9.2 Gambling, Segregation, and the Making of a New Portuguese Leisure Class under Salazar

Unlike in Spain, where gambling remained illegal throughout the entire duration of the Franco regime, based on a law already promulgated in 1928 under the government of Primo de Rivera,[68] Portugal boasted Europe's most thriving cluster of regime-approved casinos from 1927 onward. After Salazar consolidated his grip on power and proclaimed the Estado Novo in 1933, this network of licensed gambling venues, including illustrious places like Estoril, Figueira da Foz, and Póvoa de Varzim, but also casinos in Funchal (Madeira) and on the coast of the Algarve, became a trademark of Salazar's new order.[69] Overall, the Estado Novo easily pursued the most liberal approach towards casino gambling, compared to Nazi Germany,[70] Fascist Italy, or even democracies like the United States or Canada – a

---

66 See also the arguments put forward in Fernando Rosas, "O salazarismo e o homem novo: ensaio sobre o Estado Novo e a questão do totalitarismo," *Análise Social* 25, 157 (2001): 1042–54.

67 On the idea of citizens being confined to fixed roles, see also the arguments laid out in Rita Almeida de Carvalho and António Costa Pinto, "The Everyman of the Portuguese New State during the Fascist Era," in *The New Man in Radical Right Ideology and Practice, 1919–1945*, ed. Matthew Feldman, Jorge Dagnino, and Paul Stocker (London: Bloomsbury, 2018).

68 José Ignacio Cases, "La transformación de las políticas públicas de juego de azar en España," *GAPP: Revista de Gestión y Análisis de Políticas Públicas 6* (2011): 80.

69 For the original wording of the laws, see Diário do Govêrno n. ° 267/1927, Série I de 1927–12–03; Diário do Govêrno n.° 134/1928, Série I de 1928–06–13; Diário do Govêrno n.° 56/1958, Série I de 1958–03–18.

70 The confusing, and, in colloquial terms, hypocritical gambling policies of the Nazis are explored by Robert Jarvis in a recent monograph. While the book presents a range of interesting cases for consideration, it, unfortunately, does not integrate these findings into larger debates about the Nazi regime as a whole and only rarely moves beyond a top-down perspective. See Robert M. Jarvis, *Gambling under the Swastika: Casinos, Horse Racing, Lotteries, and other Forms of Betting in Nazi Germany* (Durham, NC: Carolina Academic Press, 2019).

point that will be demonstrated throughout the further course of the argument. Portugal's vibrant casino gambling culture was firmly rooted in a tradition of domestic upper-class tourism, and Portuguese casinos, such as the *Grande Casino Peninsular* in Figueira da Foz, appealed to international high society and successfully attracted a great number of foreign guests, particularly (but not exclusively) during the Second World War.[71] As a result of an obligatory dress code, state-imposed identity and background checks, and other social filtering mechanisms, casinos remained the exclusive domain of the wealthy.[72] Moreover, certain professional groups, such as civil servants in charge of financial matters, bankers, as well as students, and, from 1958 onwards, married women,[73] were categorically barred from entering.

The history of casino gambling in Portugal, while hardly a booming field of research, has received a modicum of attention over the last two decades.[74] The experiences of non-elite gamblers in Portugal, on the other hand, have not been explored so far. While Portugal did indeed appear remarkably progressive through its legalisation of casino gambling, the flipside of the gambling laws was the criminalisation of any form of gambling happening *outside* the casinos. Since casinos were exclusive spaces situated along the Atlantic coast, most Portuguese citizens had no access at all to gambling, making it a considerable privilege. Moreover, the prosecution of illicit gambling was not handled lightly: elaborate systems were put in place to root out gambling among the middle and lower classes.

These systems addressed different layers of Portugal's non-elite gambling culture. Apart from the ubiquitous threat of fines and arrests, the targeting of spaces frequented by non-elite citizens, such as taverns and cafés, became a key method for rooting out everyday gambling. To give an example, a regulation drafted by the civil governor of Évora, the regional capital of the Alentejo, restricted the right to allow card games in combination with alcoholic beverages depending on "reputation of the respective owners, managers and clients",[75] granting the police the final say on the matter. Moreover, the Estado Novo relied on existing patterns

---

71 Irene Vaquinhas, *O Casino da Figueira: sua evolução histórica desde o Teatro-Circo à actualidade, 1884–1978* (Coimbra: Palimage, 2012), particularly 177–79 and 224–28.

72 Irene Vaquinhas, "Casinos," in *Dicionário de História da I República e do Republicanismo*, Vol. I, ed. Maria Fernanda Rollo (Lisbon: Assembleia da República, 2013), 578.

73 Diário do Govêrno n.º 56/1958, Série I de 1958–03–18.

74 João Gomes, "'A banca é o meu palco!': Jogadores e Dealers num casino em Portugal," *Vivência: Revista de Antropologia* 56, 1 (2020); Filipe Paulo Natos do Nascimento, "O Casino de Espinho: Jogo e Lazer, 1905–2005" (Master's Thesis, Universidade do Porto, 2016); Vaquinhas, *O Casino*.

75 Regulamento de Jogos, 29 November 1962, PT/TT/MI-DGAPC/D/2/1250, Ministério do Interior, Direcção Geral da Administração Política e Civil, NT 1194 (Inc. 2002), Arquivo Nacional Torre do Tombo (ANTT).

of social control and created additional incentives to encourage citizens to report suspicious behaviour. For example, in a letter sent to the government in 1945, a woman from Évora alerted the government that illegal gambling was supposedly taking place in a nearby café.[76] Needless to say, we cannot rule out the possibility that her act of denunciation was motivated by genuine disapproval and a heart-felt conviction that gambling posed a serious threat to society. Yet, we have every reason to believe that her motivation for acting on her disapproval received a healthy boost from the government's promise that "any person who denounces the existence of gambling venues outside the casinos where it is permitted – if a gambling session is effectively intercepted or gambling paraphernalia are confis-cated – will receive [. . .] a sum of no less than 5,000 [escudos], paid by the trans-gressors."[77]

Hence, we can so far discern three strategies the regime deployed to curb ille-gal gambling: the threat of considerable punishment, the targeting of non-elite spaces, and gathering information 'from below' through informants. However, a fourth strategy – the deliberate blurring of categories – played an equally impor-tant role. While the Ministry of the Interior consistently tried to classify and re-classify games in terms of their potential for abuse as gambling modalities, ulti-mately, it was often up to local authorities to decide what games were worthy of surveillance. For instance, in Porto during the 1940s, police had to take a stance on whether the game *loba*, a South American card game similar to bridge, quali-fied as a form of gambling. Given the game's rising popularity amongst the gen-eral population, the final verdict was that "as relatively large amounts [of money] are used that can cause heavy [financial] losses, given the way the game is played, [. . .] it can be considered a game of chance or luck and, as such, it is illicit."[78] Yet, Porto police also investigated cases that did not involve monetary rewards, such as the case of a slot machine that was confiscated in the centre of Porto. While the machine naturally only accepted coins, prizes came in the form of candies, chocolates, and cigarettes.[79] The Estado Novo's aim, therefore, was not necessarily to prevent gamblers from ruining themselves and their families financially. It

---

76 Report to Ministry of the Interior by Head of Presidency of the Council (*Presidência do Con-celho*) José Manuel da Costa, 19 December 1945, PT/TT/SGPCM-GPC/0938/000007, Secretaria-Geral da Presidência do Conselho de Ministros, Gabinete do Presidente, cx. 119, proc. 938/71, n.º 7, ANTT.

77 Decreto n.º 16 416 de 22-1-929, in *Jogo de Fortuna e Azar: Dec. n.º 16 416 e 48 912 e ainda outras disposições legais*, ed. J. Alcino Cordeiro, 4th ed. (Póvoa de Varzim: Empresa Norte Editora, 1969), 8.

78 Cópia da participação nº 4457 da 13a esquadra, 10 June 1947, PT/ADPRT/AC/GCPRT/F/138/0001/00010, Governo Civil do Porto, C/19/1/1–5.10, Arquivo Distrital do Porto (ADPRT).

79 Cópia da participação nº 4144 da 13a esquadra, 10 June 1947, PT/ADPRT/AC/GCPRT/F/138/0001/00010, Governo Civil do Porto, C/19/1/1-5.10, ADPRT.

was a crusade against the gambler's mindset, based on the assumption that lower-class citizens, unlike their wealthier compatriots, were not capable of gambling in moderation.

The basic ideas and prejudices behind this approach were not specifically Portuguese. The notion that gambling among poor and marginalised communities was particularly dangerous was just as prevalent in democracies like the United Kingdom[80] and the United States.[81] Equally, the idea that gambling did not necessarily have to be about cash prizes was also discussed outside Portugal. In the United States, two cases from the 1920s, *State v. Ellis* (1925) and *State v. Striggles* (1926),[82] settled a dispute between the state of Iowa and two manufacturers of slot machines, dispensing peppermints instead of cash prizes. Ultimately, the court decided that peppermints were just as illegal as cash prizes, as they encouraged the same patterns of behaviour. Nevertheless, there is a stark difference between prohibition-era America and the Estado Novo regime. While the United States only legalised the first casinos in Nevada from 1931 onwards,[83] Portugal was home to a highly visible network of casinos. Therefore, how Salazar's regime handled the issue highlights not so much the Estado Novo's disdain for gambling per se, but rather the contempt it showed towards lower-class gamblers. It was not so much the games themselves that mattered, but rather the people who played them. The regime turned these blatant double standards into official state policies, targeting

---

80 Reproducing the full range of these debates goes beyond the scope of this analysis. For a concise introduction to the main issues, see the discussion in Keith Laybourn, *Going to the Dogs: A History of Greyhound Racing in Britain, 1926–2017* (Manchester: Manchester University Press, 2019), 6–10.

81 Over the last few years, a number of excellent publications have brought the role of gambling as a means of subverting and contesting public spaces into sharp relief. On the case of poor African American communities in New York and the thin line between gambling as a criminal act and gambling as an expression of dissent, see Douglas J. Flowe, *Uncontrollable Blackness: African American Men and Criminality in Jim Crow New York* (Chapel Hill: University of North Carolina Press, 2020), 26–93. On gambling in more protected, white middle-class spaces, see Seth S. Tannenbaum, "'The Ever-Watchful Eye of the Magnate' – Policing and Ballpark Gambling in the Twentieth Century," in *All In: The Spread of Gambling in Twentieth-Century United States*, ed. Jonathan D. Cohen and David G. Schwartz (Reno/Las Vegas: University of Nevada Press, 2018).

82 *State v. Ellis*, 206 N.W. 105 (Iowa 1925), https://casetext.com/case/state-v-ellis-147, accessed January 08, 2023; *State v. Striggles*, 210 N.W. 782 (Iowa 1927) https://casetext.com/case/state-v-striggles, accessed January 08, 2023.

83 For a brief and general overview, see David G. Schwartz, *Roll the Bones: The History of Gambling* (New York: Gotham, 2007), 351–368. A more detailed exploration of the 'making' of Las Vegas and its integration into a shifting urban culture is provided in David G. Schwartz, *Suburban Xanadu: The Casino Resort on the Las Vegas Strip and Beyond* (Abingdon, Oxon: Routledge, 2003).

working-class gamblers and forcing members of certain professions, such as doctors or civil servants, underground, to gamble clandestinely.[84]

The only viable alternative for those who could not enter a casino was to play games under the supervision of the state, without any money being involved. In rural areas, the so-called *Casas do Povo* (People's houses), a network of institutions set up under the regime to 'educate' the rural working classes, provided 'legal games' such as chequers, dominoes, and billiards.[85] For the urban population, a small number of clubs and associations provided a space for games, but always under the watchful eye of the regime. The *Sociedade Harmonia Eborense* (SHE), a gentleman's club based in Évora with a history going back to the nineteenth century, is a good case in point. As the regime dissolved and absorbed a considerable number of clubs and associations to get leisure activities under tighter control,[86] the SHE was in a fortunate position to still exist and be able to continue its activities with relative independence. However, this did not grant the SHE immunity from state interventions. In 1947, the *Conselho de Administração de Jogos*, a unit of the Ministry of the Interior tasked with monitoring games and gambling, issued the following directive to all local authorities across the country:

> Given the rise of certain games in which the skill, dexterity, mathematical aptitude, or intelligence of players has very little impact and keeping in mind the social and economic conditions of the majority of people who partake in these games, we recognise the necessity to adopt repressive measures when these games take place in locations accessible to everyone. [. . .] [This prohibition] will extend to recreational associations, sports clubs, and any other clubs, where, according to their statutes, only the respective members have access, once it is confirmed that the losses, in the games mentioned, reach an unacceptable or overall inconvenient level for the people playing there.[87]

Naturally, the question as to whether financial losses could be deemed acceptable or not created plenty of leeway for interpretation. In a surprisingly bold move, the directorate of the SHE defended the right of its members to play these games

---

84 See the vivid account of Tito Livio de Freitas, a man from a respectable family and himself a victim of these new laws, Exposição de Tito Livio de Freitas Garcia relativa a um diploma legal sobre os jogos de fortuna e azar, PT/TT/SGPCM-GPC/0709/00002, Secretaria-Geral da Presidência do Conselho de Ministros, Gabinete do Presidente, cx. 93, proc. 709/53, n.° 2, ANTT.

85 Daniel Melo, *Salazarismo e Cultura Popular 1933–1958* (Lisbon: Imprensa de Ciências Sociais, 2001), 128–131.

86 Ibid, 326–74.

87 Circular do Conselho de Administração de Jogos, Proc. 32, L° 16, 8 November 1947, PT/ADEVR/ ASS/SHE/F/006–003/0006, Sociedade Harmonia Eborense, Secção:F – Actividades Culturais, lúdicas e desportivas, Série:006- Actividades desportivas e lúdicas, Subsérie:003- Documentação sobre jogos; Cx.72, Ui: 6, Arquivo Distrital de Évora (ADEVR).

for small sums of money, claiming that the total amounts of money that changed hands were negligible.[88] Nevertheless, since the police claimed that their investigation had come to the opposite conclusion, the SHE was forced to circulate an announcement among its members proclaiming that card games like poker, *loba* and others were to be ceased with immediate effect.[89]

The initial sense of absolute confidence displayed by the SHE shows remarkable similarities to Canada in the 1930s, where gentleman's clubs exploited legal loopholes to organise illegal gambling events behind closed doors, which garnered considerable attention in the press and forced lawmakers to act in 1938.[90] However, it bears repeating that gambling in Canada was generally illegal until 1969, whereas Portugal adopted a unique model of radical class segregation. At the same time, the archival record reveals that monitoring gambling across the entire population proved to be a difficult task for the regime. While intimidation and harsh penalties were powerful weapons, denunciation and moral stigma among the general population proved to be equally valuable tools. Even so, the power of the regime was intertwined with the agency and moral judgment of local authorities, and their assessments sometimes clashed. The case of billiards in Portugal, particularly in Porto, the country's second-largest city, is an excellent case in point. It reveals that the Estado Novo's moralistic politics of segregation did not simply radiate outward from Lisbon but sprang from multifocal debates about vice and leisure.

9.3 Guilt by Association: the Portuguese Billiards Scene and the Struggle for Recognition

In an article published in 1962 in a Portuguese billiards journal, French billiards champion Jean Albert was quoted, defending billiards as "a form of exercise. Would you like a brief example? Two individuals, one of whom happily smokes a cigar and plays a little bit of bridge, and another one who plays his party [of bil-

---

88 SHE to the Commander of PSP Évora, 24 May 1949, PT/ADEVR/ASS/SHE/F/006–003/0006, Sociedade Harmonia Eborense, Secção:F – Actividades Culturais, lúdicas e desportivas, Série:006- Actividades desportivas e lúdicas, Subsérie:003- Documentação sobre jogos; Cx.72, Ui: 6, ADEVR.
89 Jogos proibidos, 15 May 1949, PT/ADEVR/ASS/SHE/F/006–003/0006, Sociedade Harmonia Eborense, Secção:F – Actividades Culturais, lúdicas e desportivas, Série:006- Actividades desportivas e lúdicas, Subsérie:003- Documentação sobre jogos; Cx.72, Ui: 6, ADEVR.
90 Suzanne Morton, *At Odds: Gambling and Canadians, 1919–1969* (Toronto: University of Toronto Press, 2003), 48.

liards] with 400 strikes; would the latter not be exercising?"[91] This defence of billiards as a sport reverberates until this very day, as cue sports enthusiasts still fight to have their game acknowledged as a sport. What is especially interesting about this quote is not so much the argument that billiards is a sport, but rather the counterexample: smoking a cigar and playing bridge, a card game frequently played for money.

In the first two decades of the regime, throughout the 1930s and 1940s, billiards was in fact a very respected game in Portugal, with Alfredo Ferraz becoming the first Portuguese world champion in any game or sport after his victory at the world championship in Lausanne, Switzerland, in 1939. In the words of the journal *Bilhar Desportivo*, "it was billiards that gave Portugal its first world champion."[92] Ferraz became a widely celebrated figure and was awarded a medal for special contributions to sportsmanship by the regime.[93] After he passed away 1960, the Ministry of Education's *Direcção Geral dos Desportos* (General Directorate for Sports) publicly mourned his passing.[94] Why, then, did billiards players in the early 1960s feel the need to juxtapose their game to bad habits such as smoking and gambling? In fact, even before the Portuguese billiards scene lost its greatest public figure in 1960, articles stressing that billiards was all about skill and not about luck were published, with one anonymous author describing billiards in flowery prose as a "fight against blind luck, which has to be dominated [by the player]."[95]

To better understand the defensive attitude of Portuguese billiards players, a look at a case study from Porto in the 1960s will shed some more light on this issue. In the summer of 1962, a series of puzzling exchanges of letters took place between the civil governor of Porto, João de Brito e Cunha, and the Director of Political and Civic Administration of the Ministry of the Interior, António Pedrosa Pires de Lima. The subject of their animated discussion was the case of an unnamed young man below the age of eighteen, who had been caught playing billiards in a local bar. According to district law, minors below the age of 18 were not allowed to play games in bars and cafés, with the notable exception of table soccer. However, a different article of the exact same regulation (article 83) declared that billiards and table soccer were in a similar category, thus creating

---

91 Jean Albert, "A paixão pelo jogo de bilhar," *Jornal de Bilhar* 2, 9 (1962): 2.

92 "A abrir," *Bilhar Desportivo: Revista Bimestral de Divulgação do Bilhar*, 1 (May 1955): 3.

93 Câmara Municipal de Lisboa, *Alfredo Ferraz: Campeão do Mundo em Bilhar 1901–1960* (Lisbon: Imprensa Municipal, 1996), 9.

94 "Alfredo Ferraz," *Boletim Informativo da A.B.P.* 2 (July 1960). On the Ministry of Education and its loose ties to the Federação Portuguesa de Bilhar, see "Noticiário," *Bilhar Desportivo: Revista Bimestral de Divulgação do Bilhar*, 5 (July 1956), 43.

95 "O bilhar é um desporto," *Boletim Informativo da A.B.P.* 2 (July 1960).

ample confusion.[96] To add to the confusion, the bar in question had a valid licence for billiards, dominoes, chequers, and chess. The civil governor of Porto, however, argued that *partida livre* (straight rail), a well-known variety of billiards that was also featured in contemporary games manuals in Portugal,[97] should be treated separately. Refusing to admit any erratic behaviour on the part of the local authorities, the civil governor instead raised the minimum age for both billiards *and* table soccer to 21, putting them in the same age category as casino gambling. Moreover, he held on to his arbitrary distinction between straight rail billiards and other formats, arguing that the former was, for some inexplicable reason, more dangerous to young men.

The Ministry of the Interior, failing to understand what all the commotion was about, referred to laws passed by the government in the previous year and stated that "billiards is billiards, plain and simple, and is therefore not to be prohibited."[98] In the following year, after more puzzling claims from the district governor of Porto and the submission of a draft legal proposal to the Ministry of the Interior, the Director of Political and Civic Administration reiterated his previous message and commented on the proposal, noting that "in the revised version of the article, it looks like the practice of billiards will be prohibited to minors [. . .] below the age of 21, even in restaurants with a billiards room. It seems inconvenient to go that far for a game that is becoming an object of championships. It is, therefore, suggested that the Civil Government [of Porto] reflect on the matter."[99] As a result, the civil governor of Porto hesitantly accepted the demand to lower the minimum age for *all* forms of billiards to eighteen but took the liberty to put in place modifications to banish the game from certain quarters. As the new regulation declared, "to protect students, as we frequently receive information from the police and complaints from parents as well as the heads of different educational institutions, [billiards] will be confined to locations at least 200 meters from the respective buildings and at least 100 meters from the city centre of Porto."[100]

---

96 Transgressão – Jogo de "bilhar livre" por um menor de 17 anos, 28 June 1962, PT/ADPRT/AC/GCPRT/F/137/0471, PT/ADPRT/AC/GCPRT/F/137/0471, Governo Civil do Porto, C/19/10/2–7.2, ADPRT.

97 *Manual de Jogos* (Lisbon: Edição do G.D.L.P, 1958), 30–32.

98 Director-General António Pedrosa Pires de Lima to João de Brito e Cunha, Regulamento de jogos, 22 October 1962, PT/ADPRT/AC/GCPRT/F/137/0471, Governo Civil do Porto, C/19/10/2–7.2, ADPRT.

99 Director-General António Pedrosa Pires de Lima to João de Brito e Cunha, Regulamento de jogos, 8 February 1963, PT/ADPRT/AC/GCPRT/F/137/0471, Governo Civil do Porto, C/19/10/2–7.2, ADPRT.

100 District Governor João de Brito e Cunha to António Pedrosa Pires de Lima, Regulamento de jogos, 25 February 1963, PT/ADPRT/AC/GCPRT/F/137/0471, Governo Civil do Porto, C/19/10/2–7.2, ADPRT.

Ironically, this new regulation clashed with the needs and priorities of established institutions, including Catholic organisations that offered recreational facilities and programmes for young people. In July 1963, the head of the municipal government of Gondomar, a small town south-east of Porto, submitted a request raising questions about the feasibility of article 11 of the new regulation, which set up the guidelines for maintaining a 'safety radius' for billiards. In his words:

> It happens that, with the authorisation of parents and teachers, some associations are frequented by minors, and, with their permission, can play billiards, ping-pong, chess, and chequers, but never cards. [. . .] Since they are authorised to play by their own parents, but only to play billiards, ping-pong, chess, and chequers, it does not seem problematic to me. [. . .] Moreover, if I interpret article 11 correctly, this will force us to shut down several organisations, especially the *Ala dos Legionários de Nun' Alvares*, a Catholic organisation run by the Church, which is very popular among the youth.[101]

In a somewhat brusque reply, the civil governor of Porto brushed off these concerns, adding that children still had the option of "playing games in their private and family environment, at the exclusive responsibility of their parents."[102] This banishment of billiards from the public sphere exceeded the guidelines of the regime, showing that the regime was, in some cases, more pragmatic and less culturally conservative than some of its overzealous local representatives. This feeds into important debates about the role of local actors in sustaining and radicalising dictatorial rule. But it also highlights that adult play was just one of many arenas in which the Estado Novo tried to assert its ideology of purity, modesty, and self-sacrifice. Small-scale gambling presented an ideal target since the benefits of the regime fashioning itself as a moral authority in the everyday sphere far outweighed the negatives of missing out on relatively meagre earnings, at least compared to the high profits generated through casino gambling.

By virtue of its transnational ties and strong competitive spirit, the game of billiards did not lend itself to the exact same stigmatisation. As early as 1932, one year before Salazar tightened his grip on power, the general secretary of Lisbon's civil government, after looking at reports about Lisbon's rising billiards scene at the time, noted that it is "a game of skill, not of chance."[103] Thirty years later, the case from Porto described above painted a different picture, evoking

---

101 Padre Crispim Gomes Leite to João de Brito e Cunha, Regulamento sobre jogos, 1 July 1963, PT/ADPRT/AC/GCPRT/F/137/0471, Governo Civil do Porto, C/19/10/2–7.2, ADPRT.
102 District Governor João de Brito e Cunha to Padre Crispim Gomes Leite, Regulamento sobre jogos, 9 July 1963, PT/ADPRT/AC/GCPRT/F/137/0471, Governo Civil do Porto, C/19/10/2–7.2, ADPRT.
103 Civil Governor of Lisbon to Ministry of the Interior, 12 October 1932, PT/TT/MI-GM/4–38/52, Ministério do Interior, Gabinete do Ministro, Mç. 457, [pt. 17/17], ANTT.

stereotypes about billiards as an alcohol-fuelled pastime taking place in smoky bars. Granted, after the heyday of billiards under Alfredo Ferraz, the regime's financial support for the game dwindled, which made life more difficult for associations in the 1960s and 70s.[104] However, if we trust the material published by the billiards associations and analyse their rhetoric, we can identify another crucial factor for the game's rapid decline: a sense of classism and exclusivity that was not imposed by the state – as in the case of gambling – but enacted 'from below' by the members of the billiards associations themselves. While associations eventually tried to attract more people,[105] the stain of elitism and previous decades of openly displayed neglect for amateur billiards and associations in the provinces, were hard to erase. For example, in a letter to the editors of *Bilhar Desportivo* from August 1955, a man from Porto asked "why only players from Lisbon go to international championships? Are there no players in other cities that could represent national billiards?"[106] Tellingly, the answer was a short and sober no, and while the editors did acknowledge the possibility of hidden talent in the far provinces, it was hardly a recurring subject in contemporary billiards journals and bulletins.

As Pierre Bourdieu noted, sports and games that relied heavily on space and resources, celebrated individual achievement, and allowed for flexible schedules (as opposed to team sports, which imposed a communal schedule), were particularly appealing to the educated middle class, making them markers of social distinction and tools for bourgeois self-fashioning.[107] Furthermore, as Thomas S. Henricks points out, the overall increase in leisure time in industrialised societies throughout the twentieth century made 'hobbies',[108] including playful ones, just as important as work in defining one's place in society and developing a public persona worthy of respect.[109] Seen from that perspective, billiards was a perfect choice. Not only did the game perpetuate ideals of the 'gentlemanly' leisure

---

104 Henrique Marques, *De 1959 a 1989: Trinta Anos de História do Bilhar Português* (Lisbon: Federação Portuguesa de Bilhar, 1990), particularly 6–9.

105 See for instance "Torneio popular de Lisboa: um êxito sem procedentes no meio bilharístico da capital," *Bilhar Desportivo: Revista Bimestral de Divulgação do Bilhar*, 4 (November-December 1955): 5–8.

106 Letter from J. Antunes to editors, *Bilhar Desportivo: Revista Bimestral de Divulgação do Bilhar*, 2 (June-August 1955), 47.

107 Pierre Bourdieu, *Distinction: A Social Critique of the Judgement of Taste*, trans. Richard Nice (Cambridge, Mass.: Harvard University Press, 1984), 215.

108 On the evolution of the concept of hobbies in Western societies (particularly the United States) during the twentieth century from a historical perspective, see Steven M. Gelber, *Hobbies: Leisure and the Culture of Work in America* (New York: Columbia University Press, 1999).

109 Thomas S. Henricks, "Play Studies: A Brief History," *American Journal of Play* 12, 2 (2020): 147.

throughout the entire duration of Salazar's rule,[110] but it encouraged the neat segregation – as observed in the case of gambling – between elite venues (casinos, clubs, and certain types of associations) and non-elite spaces. Resistance towards making billiards more accessible to wider strata of society did not only come 'from above' in the form of regime interventions,[111] but more importantly 'from below' as a resistance to change, inclusion, and social permeability.[112] Hence, billiards associations under the Salazar regime can be seen as victims of a 'guilt by association' which caused them to be viewed with suspicion by the authorities and concerned citizens. This fear is mirrored in publicly expressed concerns about minors playing billiards, as we have seen in the case of a young man playing in Porto. Seeing how much commotion the sight of a 17-year-old caused in Porto, it is not hard to imagine the reactions to children playing cue sports, and billiards associations bemoaned that fact youngsters had no public access to the game, which restricted the pool of young talent to those few children who were fortunate enough to be raised in a household with a private billiards table.[113] This convenient excuse allowed associations to put a part of the blame for their recruitment issues on the Portuguese state and its strict policies on public games. At the same time, a condescending attitude towards amateurs who played recreationally was frequently expressed in major billiards magazines like *Bilhar Desportivo*, where Rego Chaves, a well-respected player in the 1950s, urged those who played casually to "not tell those who practice professionally [. . .] and who, day after day, in their exacting and passionate practice, discover new and major challenges to overcome, that 'you know how to do it.'"[114]

---

110 Billiards journals attempted to unmask the heavily male-centred nature of billiards associations as nothing but a stereotype. However, photos and tournament lists published throughout the decades did not contain a single female face or name. For some rather unconvincing attempts made by publishers to rectify this heavily gendered image, see "As senhoras também jogam . . .," *Bilhar Desportivo: Revista Bimestral de Divulgação do Bilhar*, 1 (May 1955), 15; "Uma rainha de beleza," *Bilhar Desportivo: Revista Bimestral de Divulgação do Bilhar*, 3 (September-October 1955), 25.
111 On the regime targeting associations, see Daniel Melo, "O associativismo popular na resistência cultural ao salazarismo: A Federação Portuguesa das Colectividades de Cultura e Recreio," *Penélope* 21 (1999): 95–130.
112 On these patterns of resistance towards working-class culture in associations and clubs in Portugal more generally, see also Elísio Estanque, "O Lazer e a Cultura Popular, entre a Regulação e a Transgressão: Um estudo de caso," *Revista Crítica de Ciências Sociais* 43 (1995): 138.
113 "Meninos prodígios," *Bilhar Desportivo: Revista Bimestral de Divulgação do Bilhar*, 3 (September-October 1955): 43.
114 Rego Chaves, "Rebatendo falsos conceitos," *Bilhar Desportivo: Revista Bimestral de Divulgação do Bilhar* 1 (1955): 17.

As we can see, the billiards scene held on to a dated image of gentlemanly leisure, hoping that this exclusive air would protect it from stigmatisation. However, this brief exploration of billiards shows that this only exacerbated the problem of marginalisation, cutting the scene off from the rest of society and creating an aura of secrecy and self-involvement that did very little to make cue sports more accepted as a serious pursuit in the eyes of the authorities. While players and organisers never openly blamed the regime for the game's sudden decline in popularity, there was a prevalent sense of nostalgia for the 'golden days' under Alfredo Ferraz and a lingering sense that the regime owed the billiards scene some form of gratitude for providing the nation with its first world champion in a competitive game.[115] What they ignored, however, was their own role in the Estado Novo's social system, and the privileges they enjoyed while other associations were systematically destroyed by the regime. In essence, the history of Portuguese billiards as a history from below shows above all else how the role of the pariah and the underdog needs to be critically examined not only when it is assigned by historians to certain social groups – something that E.P. Thompson was (sometimes overly) fond of[116] – but also when historical actors assumed this role in the past, be it out of a wounded sense of pride or for practical reasons, such as securing state funding or public support.

9.4 Conclusion

Play, understood as a distinct form of agency, can serve as a fruitful prism to unveil previously neglected layers of social life across different socio-cultural and geographical settings. In industrialised Western societies, the general perception of play as an apolitical activity has made it a textbook example of 'manoeuvring', as coined by Alf Lüdtke.[117] Under the pretence of simply having a good time, people met up to make a statement, break with social conventions, and position themselves vis-à-vis their governments and fellow citizens. This applies to casual

---

115 Marques, *De 1959 a 1989*, 16.

116 In 1978, British social historian Harold Perkin, who hailed from a working-class background, discussed Thompson's mission of rescuing working people from the 'enormous condescension of posterity' and answered that "it is no criticism of that great, rugged, sprawling, big-hearted book to say that what the English working class most needs to be rescued from is the enormous condescension of middle-class intellectuals." See Harold Perkin, "'The Condescension of Posterity:' The Recent Historiography of the English Working Class," *Social Science History* 3, 1 (1978): 87.

117 Lüdtke describes manoeuvring as a means for people to claim and create space for themselves in their day to day lives. See Lüdtke, "Ordinary People," 29.

games and gambling alike. The latter, due to its rich history of dubious moral connotations, has traditionally been treated separately from other games, at least as far as policymaking, monitoring, and policing are concerned. However, early academic theories of play regarded gambling as just one particular manifestation of play. In short, there often has been a historical disconnect between theoretical perspectives on gambling as a form of play, and hands-on approaches to gambling in the public sphere. This is mirrored in many historical case studies, where normative top-down perspectives clashed with the complex subjectivities of gamblers or the perceptions of those who approached the subject with genuine curiosity, including academics across various disciplines. Therefore, as Xavier Paulès rightly points out in a study of Chinese gambling in the early twentieth century, historians should not conflate the perspective of bureaucratic elites throughout history, who thought about gambling primarily in terms of risk management, with the lived experiences of the people who indulged in it.[118] Besides, other games were exposed to the same top-down scrutiny, ranging from billiards to arcade halls from the 1980s onwards.[119]

The example of the Estado Novo, one of the most tenacious dictatorial regimes in the Western world, reveals that the relationship between play and power, be it political, cultural, or economic, was hardly as straightforward as idealistic play theories in the spirit of Johan Huizinga or Clifford Geertz would have us believe. Nor was that relationship merely one of top-down control, as the Estado Novo frequently stressed. Salazar himself, in a speech he delivered shortly after his rise to power in the 1930s, proclaimed that it was his government's mission to "to preserve Portugal at all costs from the wave that is falling all over the world, [. . .] to preserve the simplicity of life, the purity of morals, the sweetness of the feelings, the balance of social relations, that familiar look, modest but worthy, of Portuguese life."[120] The traditional balance of social relations, however, which was enshrined in the regime's notion of *viver habitualmente* ('living as usual'),[121] did in practice include elements that were not easily compatible with the Estado Novo's agenda and Salazar's desire for control. Even in rural Portugal,

---

118 Xavier Paulès, "Gambling in China Reconsidered: Fantan in South China during the Early Twentieth Century," *International Journal of Asian Studies* 7, 2 (2010): 196.

119 Michael Ryan Skolnik, and Steven Conway, "Tusslers, Beatdowns, and Brothers: A Sociohistorical Overview of Video Game Arcades and the Street Fighter Community," *Games and Culture* 14, 7–8 (2017): 1–21.

120 António de Oliveira Salazar, "A Embaixada da Colónia Portuguesa no Brasil e a nossa Política Externa," in *Discursos e Notas Políticas II: 1935–1937*, 2nd ed. (Coimbra: Coimbra Editora, 1945), 276.

121 Rosas, "O salazarismo," 1034.

which Salazar idealised and made into a cornerstone of his ideology,[122] gambling was just as firmly entrenched as Catholicism and traditional family values.[123] One explanation for this propensity of rural populations in Portugal can be drawn from George Foster's work on peasant communities in Tzintzuntzan, Mexico. Given the widespread scarcity mindset in rural societies, where goods are imagined and, more often than not, experienced as limited, gambling and seeking refuge in the idea of luck appears like "a realistic approach to the near-hopeless problem of making significant individual progress."[124] In urban areas, similar arguments have been made by social historians researching the gambling habits of the working classes. For instance, British historian Ross McKibbin argued that "[m]ass betting was the most successful example of working-class self-help in the modern era."[125] In a social environment where options to improve one's opportunities for climbing the social ladder and planning for a better future appeared bleak and unpredictable, this perception can seem plausible. However, as has been pointed out above, the perspectives of gamblers and those in charge of regulating were oftentimes diametrically opposed, and under the Estado Novo, this tension was aggravated by the blatant hypocrisy of a system that was at the forefront of legalising large-scale gambling whilst simultaneously policing the same games in everyday settings.

In the case of other games, like billiards, the situation was quite different. The regime could not ignore the transnational entanglements and global visibility of the Portuguese billiards scene, especially after Alfredo Ferraz rose to international fame. Hence, Salazar's government simply tolerated the game, sharing in the achievements of professional players whenever it was suitable, while simultaneously giving local authorities some freedom to mitigate the alleged social harm caused by cue sports in lower-class environments. Ultimately, the billiards scene itself, despite the attempts made by organisers to grow the game's audience, was complicit in this exclusion, only realising too late that the gentlemanly identity

---

122 The regime's search for the 'most Portuguese village in Portugal' (*a aldeia mais Portuguesa de Portugal*), a contest organised in 1938 by the Estado Novo's *Secretariado de Propaganda Nacional* (SPN), is just one of countless examples for this obsession with uncovering the allegedly authentic spirit of the Portuguese nation. For a wide range of case studies related to the Estado Novo's ideological mission to reinvent tradition, see the excellent contributions and commentary provided in *Vozes do Povo: A folclorização em Portugal*, ed. Salwa El-Shawan Castelo-Branco and Jorge Freitas Branco (Lisbon: Etnográfica Press, 2003).

123 Jorge Dias, *Rio de Onor: Comunitarismo Agro-Pastoril* (Porto: Centro de Estudos de Etnologia Peninsular, 1953), 557–61.

124 George Foster, "Peasant Society and the Image of Limited Good," *American Anthropologist* 67, 2 (1965): 308.

125 Ross McKibbin, "Working-class gambling in Britain, 1880–1939," *Past & Present* 82 (1979): 172.

they held on to was a relic of the past. As the regime slipped into a turbulent decade throughout the 1960s, ushering in a period of imperialist warfare amidst a wave of decolonisation movements across most of the country's colonial territories, the relative calm of the 1950s came to an end, paving the way for a counter-cultural backlash and open criticisms of Salazar's government.

Interestingly, the decline of billiards in Portugal, despite being tied to a self-contained microcosm of middle-class players, mirrors some of the reasons for the regime's steady decline throughout the 1960s and early 1970s. The publications of the Portuguese billiards scene tell the story of a small elite group that lost contact with larger social developments and upheavals. Like in the United States, where the working-class takeover of pool sparked an immense controversy that found its way into popular culture, cue sports in Portugal were appropriated by social classes that were deemed poorly suited to the game by those in a more privileged position. However, from a *longue durée* perspective, the game itself was hardly in decline. Instead, it was simply going back to its roots. As Everton Clive put it in his book on the history of British billiards and snooker, "in its early days, billiards was either a gambling activity, as most games were, or a leisurely relaxation for the gentry. The twin traditions of billiards were epitomised by the country mansion and the tavern or public room. The gentry were often great patrons of the game, but the best players invariably came from much lower down the social scale."[126] The struggles of 'ordinary people', whoever they may be, to reclaim their right to play frivolously and in their own familiar spaces, are reflected in the larger, equally meaningful fights of citizens to regain their other civil liberties. With a history of repressive rule spanning more than four decades, the Portuguese Estado Novo provides ample material to illustrate the contestation and ceaseless renegotiation of power through different actions and mediums, including play and games.

References

Anchor, Robert. "History and Play: Johan Huizinga and his Critics." *History & Theory* 17, 1 (1978): 63–93.
Anderson, Peter. *The Francoist Military Trials: Terror and Complicity 1939–1945*. London: Routledge, 2010.
Bergerson, Andrew Stuart. *Ordinary Germans in Extraordinary Times: The Nazi Revolution in Hildesheim*. Bloomington, IN: Indianapolis University Press, 2004.
Bourdieu, Pierre. *Distinction: A Social Critique of the Judgement of Taste*. Translated by Richard Nice. Cambridge, MA.: Harvard University Press, 1984.

---

126 Clive Everton, *The History of Snooker and Billiards* (Haywards Heath: Partridge Press, 1986), 12.

Brito, Joaquim Pais de. "A taberna: lugar e revelador da aldeia." In *Lugares de aqui: Actas do seminário «Terrenos Portugueses»*, edited by Brian Juan O'Neill, and Joaquim Pais de Brito, 167–200. Lisbon: Dom Quixote, 1991.

Burgos, Claudio Hernández. "The Triumph of 'Normality', Social Attitudes, Popular Opinion and the Construction of the Franco Regime in Post-War Rural Spain (1936–1952)." *European History Quarterly* 46, 2 (2016): 291–310.

Burke, Peter. "Popular Culture Reconsidered." *Storia della Storiografia* 17 (1990): 40–49.

Caillois, Roger. *Man, Play and Games*. Translated by Meyer Barash. Chicago: University of Illinois Press, [1961] 2001.

Cases, José Ignacio. "La transformación de las políticas públicas de juego de azar en España." *GAPP: Revista de Gestión y Análisis de Políticas Públicas 6* (2011): 75–103.

Carvalho, Rita Almeida de, and António Costa Pinto. "The Everyman of the Portuguese New State during the Fascist Era." In *The New Man in Radical Right Ideology and Practice, 1919-1945*, edited by Matthew Feldman, Jorge Dagnino, and Paul Stocker, 131–50. London: Bloomsbury, 2018.

Castelo-Branco, Salwa El-Shawan, and Jorge Freitas Branco, eds. *Vozes do Povo: A folclorização em Portugal*. Lisbon: Etnográfica Press, 2003.

Certeau, Michel de. *The Practice of Everyday Life*. Translated by Steven Rendall. Berkeley: University of California Press, 1984.

Chapman, Adam. *Digital Games as History: How Videogames Represent the Past and Offer Access to Historical Practice*. London: Routledge, 2016.

Contreras, Beatriz Valverde, and Alexander Keese. "Living at the Margins of Repression: Everyday Life and Hidden Challenges in the Azores' Central Group, 1954–1960." *European History Quarterly* 52, 2 (2022): 221–44.

Corner, Paul. "Dictatorship revisited: consensus, coercion, and strategies of survival." *Modern Italy* 22, 4 (2017): 435–44.

De Grazia, Victoria. *The Culture of Consent: Mass Organizations of Leisure in Fascist Italy*. Cambridge, UK: Cambridge University Press, 1981.

Dias, Jorge. *Rio de Onor: Comunitarismo Agro-Pastoril*. Porto: Centro de Estudos de Etnologia Peninsular, 1953.

Elias, Norbert. "Zum Begriff des Alltags." In *Materialien zur Soziologie des Alltags: Kölner Zeitschrift für Soziologie und Sozialpsychologie, Sonderheft 20*, edited by Kurt Hammerich, and Michael Klein, 22–29. Leverkusen: Opladen, 1978.

Estanque, Elísio. "O Lazer e a Cultura Popular, entre a Regulação e a Transgressão: Um estudo de caso." *Revista Crítica de Ciências Sociais* 43 (1995): 123–45.

Everton, Clive. *The History of Snooker and Billiards*. Haywards Heath: Partridge Press, 1986.

Ferris, Kate. "Everyday Spaces: Bars, Alcohol and the Spatial Framing of Everyday Political Practice and Interaction in Fascist Italy." *European History Quarterly* 52, 2 (2022): 136–59.

Ferris, Kate. "Bars." In *Doing Spatial History*, edited by Riccardo Bavaj, Konrad Lawson, and Bernhard Struck, 139–53. London: Routledge, 2021.

Ferris, Kate. *Everyday Life in Fascist Venice, 1929-40*. London: Palgrave Macmillan, 2012.

Felski, Rita. "The Invention of Everyday Life." *New Formations* 39 (2000): 15–31.

Fitzpatrick, Sheila, and Alf Lüdtke. "Energizing the Everyday: On the Making and Breaking of Social Bonds in Nazism and Stalinism." In *Beyond Totalitarianism: Stalinism and Nazism Compared*, edited by Michael Geyer, and Sheila Fitzpatrick, 266–301. Cambridge: Cambridge University Press, 2009.

Fitzpatrick, Sheila, and Alf Lüdtke. *Everyday Stalinism: Ordinary Life in Extraordinary Times. Soviet Russia in the 1930s*. Oxford: Oxford University Press, 2010.

Flowe, Douglas J. *Uncontrollable Blackness: African American Men and Criminality in Jim Crow New York*. Chapel Hill: University of North Carolina Press, 2020.

Foster, George. "Peasant Society and the Image of Limited Good." *American Anthropologist* 67, 2 (1965): 293–315.

Gilmore, David D. "The Role of the Bar in Andalusian Rural Society: Observations on Political Culture under Franco." *Journal of Anthropological Research*, 41: 3 (1985): 263–77.

Geertz, Clifford. *The Interpretation of Cultures: Selected Essays*. New York: Basic Books, 1973.

Gelber, Steven M. *Hobbies: Leisure and the Culture of Work in America*. New York: Columbia University Press, 1999.

Ginzburg, Carlo. *The Cheese and the Worms: The Cosmos of a Sixteenth-century Miller*. Baltimore: John Hopkins University Press, 1980.

Goksøyr, Matti. "Nationalism." In *Routledge Companion to Sports History*, edited by S.W. Pope, and John Nauright, 268–94. Abingdon, Oxon: Routledge, 2010.

Gomes, João. "'A banca é o meu palco!': Jogadores e Dealers num casino em Portugal." *Vivência: Revista de Antropologia* 56, 1 (2020): 224–51.

Guerra, Douglas. *Slantwise Moves: Games, Literature, and Social Invention in Nineteenth-Century America*. Philadelphia: University of Pennsylvania Press, 2018.

Harris, LaShawn. *Sex Workers, Psychics, and Numbers Runners: Black Women in New York City's Underground Economy*. Urbana: University of Illinois Press, 2016.

Henricks, Thomas S. "Play Studies: A Brief History." *American Journal of Play* 12, 2 (2020): 117–55.

Huizinga, Johan. *Homo Ludens: A Study of the Play-Element in Culture*. London: Routledge, [1944] 1949.

Jarvis, Robert M. *Gambling under the Swastika: Casinos, Horse Racing, Lotteries, and other Forms of Betting in Nazi Germany*. Durham, NC: Carolina Academic Press, 2019.

Kerr, Aphra. *The Business and Culture of Digital Games: Gamework and Gameplay*. London: Sage, 2006.

Ladurie, Emmanuel Le Roy. *Montaillou: Cathars and Catholics in a French Village, 1294–1324*. Translated by Barbara Bray. Harmondsworth: Penguin, [1978] 1980.

Lamb, Charles. "Mrs. Battle's Opinions on Whist." In *The Works of Charles and Mary Lamb Vol. 2: Elia and the Last Essays of Elia*, edited by E.V. Lucas, http://www.gutenberg.org/ebooks/10343. *Project Gutenberg*: 2003.

Langhamer, Claire. "Who the Hell are Ordinary People? Ordinariness as a Category of Historical Analysis." *Transactions of the Royal Historical Society* 28 (2018): 175–95.

Laybourn, Keith. *Going to the Dogs: A History of Greyhound Racing in Britain, 1926–2017*. Manchester: Manchester University Press, 2019.

Lefebvre, Henri. *Critique of Everyday Life*. 3 Volumes. London: Verso, 1991.

Lefebvre, Henri, and Christine Levich. "The Everyday and Everydayness." *Yale French Studies* 73 (1987): 7–11.

Linz, Juan J. *Totalitarian and Authoritarian Regimes*. Boulder: Lynne Rienner, 2000.

Litherland, Benjamin. "Ludosity, Radical Contextualism, and a New Games History: Pleasure, Truth, and Deception in the Mid-20th-Century London Arcade." *Games and Culture* 16, 2 (2021): 139–159.

Lüdtke, Alf. "Introductory notes." In *Everyday Life in Mass Dictatorship: Collusion and Evasion*, edited by Alf Lüdtke, 3–12. New York: Palgrave Macmillan, 2016.

Lüdtke, Alf. "Ordinary People, Self-Energising, and Room for Manoeuvering: Examples from 20th Century Europe." In *Everyday Life in Mass Dictatorship: Collusion and Evasion*, edited by Alf Lüdtke, 13–36. New York: Palgrave Macmillan, 2016.

Lüdtke, Alf. *Eigen-Sinn. Fabrikalltag, Arbeitererfahrungen und Politik vom Kaiserreich bis in den Faschismus*. Hamburg: Ergebnisse Verlag, 1993.

Lüdtke, Alf. "Wo blieb die ‚rote Glut?' Arbeitererfahrungen und deutscher Faschismus." In *Alltagsgeschichte: Zur Rekonstruktion historischer Erfahrungen und Lebensweisen*, edited by Alf Lüdtke, 224–82. Frankfurt: Campus Verlag, 1989.

Lüdtke, Alf. "Cash, Coffee-Breaks, Horseplay: Eigensinn and Politics among Factory Workers in Germany circa 1900." In *Confrontation, Class Consciousness, and the Labor Process: Studies in Proletarian Class Formation*, edited by Michael Hanagan, and Charles Stephenson, 65–95. Westport: Greenwood Press, 1986.

Malaby, Thomas M. "Anthropology and Play: The Contours of Playful Experience." *New Literary History* 40, 1 (2009): 205–18.

Marques, Henrique. *De 1959 a 1989: Trinta Anos de História do Bilhar Português*. Lisbon: Federação Portuguesa de Bilhar, 1990.

Martin, Mary Clare. "The state of play: historical perspectives." *International Journal of Play* 5, 3 (2016): 329–39.

McKibbin, Ross. "Working-class gambling in Britain, 1880–1939." *Past & Present* 82 (1979): 147–78.

Melo, Daniel. *Salazarismo e Cultura Popular 1933-1958*. Lisbon: Imprensa de Ciências Sociais, 2001.

Melo, Daniel. "O associativismo popular na resistência cultural ao salazarismo: A Federação Portuguesa das Colectividades de Cultura e Recreio." *Penélope* 21 (1999): 95–130.

Meneses, Filipe Ribeiro. "The Origins and Nature of Authoritarian Rule in Portugal, 1919–1945." *Contemporary European History* 11, 1 (2002): 153–63.

Morton, Suzanne. *At Odds: Gambling and Canadians, 1919–1969*. Toronto: University of Toronto Press, 2003.

Nascimento, Filipe Paulo Natos do. "O Casino de Espinho: Jogo e Lazer, 1905–2005." MA Thesis, Universidade do Porto, 2016.

Nielsen, Holly. "'The British Empire Would Gain New Strength from Nursery Floors': Depictions of Travel and Place in Nineteenth-Century British Board Games." In *Historia Ludens: The Playing Historian*, edited by Alexander von Lünen, Katherine J. Lewis, Benjamin Litherland, and Pat Callum, 20–34. Abingdon, Oxon: Routledge, 2020.

Paulès, Xavier. "Gambling in China Reconsidered: Fantan in South China during the Early Twentieth Century." *International Journal of Asian Studies* 7, 2 (2010): 179–200.

Perkin, Harold. "'The Condescension of Posterity:' The Recent Historiography of the English Working Class." *Social Science History* 3, 1 (1978): 87–101.

Pimentel, Irene Flunser. *Informadores da PIDE: Uma Tragédia Portuguesa*. Lisbon: Temas e Debates, 2022.

Pinto, António Costa. *Salazar's Dictatorship and European Fascism: Problems of Interpretation*. New York: Columbia University Press, 1995.

Polsky, Ned. *Hustlers, Beats, and Others*. Chicago: Aldine Publishing 1967.

Riegelhaupt, Joyce Firstenberg. "Os camponeses e a política no Portugal de Salazar – o Estado Corporativo e o 'apoliticismo' nas aldeias." *Análise Social* 15, 59 (1979): 505–23.

Rosas, Fernando. *Salazar e o Poder: A Arte de Saber Durar*. Lisbon: Tinta-da-China, 2012.

Rosas, Fernando. "O salazarismo e o homem novo: ensaio sobre o Estado Novo e a questão do totalitarismo." *Análise Social* 25, 157 (2001): 1031–54.

Sánchez, Antonio Cazorla. *Fear and Progress: Ordinary Lives in Franco's Spain 1939–1975*. Chichester: Wiley-Blackwell, 2010.

Schmid, Stephen E. "Beyond Autotelic Play." *Journal of the Philosophy of Sport* 38, 2 (2011): 149–66.

Schwartz, David G. *Roll the Bones: The History of Gambling*. New York: Gotham, 2007.

Schwartz, David G. *Suburban Xanadu: The Casino Resort on the Las Vegas Strip and Beyond*. Abingdon, Oxon: Routledge, 2003.

Scott, James C. *Weapons of the Weak: Everyday Forms of Peasant Resistance*. New Haven: Yale University Press, 1985.

Sharpe, Jim. "History from Below." In *New Perspectives on Historical Writing*, edited by Peter Burke, 24–41. Cambridge: Politi, 1991.

Sicart, Miguel. *Play Matters*. Cambridge, MA: MIT Press, 2014.

Simpson, Duncan. "Approaching the PIDE 'From Below': Petitions, Spontaneous Applications and Denunciation Letters to Salazar's Secret Police in 1964." *Contemporary European History* 30 (2021): 398–413.

Skolnik, Michael Ryan, and Steven Conway. "Tusslers, Beatdowns, and Brothers: A Sociohistorical Overview of Video Game Arcades and the Street Fighter Community." *Games and Culture* 14, 7–8 (2017): 1–21.

Steege, Paul, Bergerson, Andrew Stuart, Healy, Maureen, and Swett, Pamela E. "The History of Everyday Life: A Second Chapter." *The Journal of Modern History* 80, 2 (2008): 358–78.

Stoler, Ann Laura. *Along the Archival Grain: Thinking through Colonial Ontologies*. Princeton: Princeton University Press, 2009.

Storey, John. *From Popular Culture to Everyday Life*. Abingdon, Oxon: Routledge, 2014.

Sutton-Smith, Brian. *The Ambiguity of Play*. Cambridge, MA: Harvard University Press, 1997.

Tannenbaum, Seth S. "'The Ever Watchful Eye of the Magnate' – Policing and Ballpark Gambling in the Twentieth Century." In *All In: The Spread of Gambling in Twentieth-Century United States*, edited by Jonathan D. Cohen, and David G. Schwartz, 44–72. Reno: University of Nevada Press, 2018.

Thomassen, Bjørn. *Liminality and the Modern: Living through the In-Between*. Farnham: Ashgate, 2014.

Thompson, E.P. *Whigs and Hunters: The Origin of the Black Act*. London: Allen Lane, 1975.

Thompson, E.P. *The Making of the English Working Class*. New York: Penguin, [1963] 1970.

Thompson, E.P. "Time, Work-Discipline, and Industrial Capitalism." *Past & Present* 38 (1967): 56–97.

Vaquinhas, Irene. "Casinos." In *Dicionário de História da I República e do Republicanismo*, Vol. I, edited by Maria Fernanda Rollo, 576–79. Lisbon: Assembleia da República, 2013.

Vaquinhas, Irene. *O Casino da Figueira: sua evolução histórica desde o Teatro-Circo à actualidade, 1884–1978*. Coimbra: Palimage, 2012.

Vaz, Matthew. *Running the Numbers: Race, Police, and the History of Urban Gambling*. Chicago: University of Chicago Press, 2020.

Warren, James Francis. *Rickshaw Coolie: A People's History of Singapore 1880–1940*. Singapore: Singapore University Press, 2003.

Whannel, Garry. *Culture, Politics and Sport: Blowing the Whistle, Revisited*. Abingdon, Oxon: Routledge, 2008.

Franziska Rueedi

10 Violence during the Transition "From Below" in South Africa

10.1 Introduction

The release of political prisoners from the late 1980s and the unbanning of liberation movements in 1990 gave rise to widespread hope among South Africa's black[1] majority that political change was imminent. However, as the end of white minority rule was in sight, collective violence escalated. Two regions of the country – KwaZulu and Natal[2] and the urban townships in the greater Johannesburg region (the Pretoria – Witwatersrand – Vereeniging, PWV complex) experienced an intensification of the scope and nature of violence that plunged these regions into a state of civil war. The death toll was severe and was estimated at close to 20,000 people.[3] Most of this violence was perpetrated in the name of Inkatha,[4] a Zulu nationalist movement under the leadership of Mangosuthu Buthelezi, which had its strongest support base in the Zulu-speaking regions of KwaZulu and Natal. On the other side of the divide were urbanised township communities loosely aligned to the progressive forces of the African National Congress (ANC). Furthermore, allegations were rife of a covert 'third force': different outfits of the South African security forces accused of stoking the fires of the conflict to destabilise and disrupt the political negotiations, and to aid Inkatha in its struggle for power.[5]

---

1 I use the term 'black' in its political sense, to refer to South Africans who were discriminated against due to their assigned racial classification. In the apartheid system of classification, those who were not assigned the status of 'white' were subdivided into the categories 'coloured', 'Indian', and 'black'; but those who were politically mobilised used the term 'black' as self-description.
2 Natal was part of 'white' South Africa; KwaZulu was a bantustan or 'homeland' designated to the Zulu-speaking population as part of apartheid's 'separate development'.
3 Jason Hickel, *Democracy as Death: The Moral Order of Anti-Liberal Politics in South Africa* (Oakland: University of California Press, 2015), 2. Other estimates are lower.
4 David Everatt, "Analysing Political Violence on the Reef, 1990-1994," in *The Role of Political Violence in South Africa's Democratisation*, ed. Ran Greestein (Johannesburg: Community Agency for Social Enquiry, 2003).
5 Piers Pigou, "The Apartheid State and Violence: What has the Truth and Reconciliation Commission Found?" *Politikon* 28/2 (2001): 207–233, doi: 10.1080/02589340120091664; Stephen Ellis, "The Historical Significance of South Africa's Third Force," *Journal of Southern African Studies* 24/2 (1998): 261–299, doi: 10.1080/03057079808708577. The history, role and composition of the third force, and its relation to the state, remains under-researched.

https://doi.org/10.1515/9783111522180-010

Much of the extant literature has focused on elite pact-making and macro-level politics, as well as the left critique of the emergent political and economic order.[6] We know less about how people experienced and shaped the transition from below and the visions they held. Furthermore, the violence of the transition era has largely been explored in terms of its roots and causes; the social consequences of violence, and the ways in which people responded to, participated in, and resisted violence has received less attention. An important exception is Vanessa Barolsky's detailed research on violence in the Kathorus region (comprising the townships of Katlehong, Thokoza and Vosloorus), and its entanglement with power and subjectivity.[7] In many instances, the population that lived through the horrors of the transition violence "appear only as fleeing refugees, or as injured at the hospital, or finally as more bodies in the veld", as the victim support group Khulumani has noted.[8] Yet experiences of violence played a significant role in destroying communal solidarity and further undermining the rule of law.

The centring of "ordinary"[9] people's agency in relation to broader structures and processes, and the ways in which they constructed their social worlds has a long tradition in South African historiography. At the forefront of South African history from below was the History Workshop (HW), established at the University of the Witwatersrand in 1977. From the outset, this was a "history in and for 'struggle'" that celebrated the agency, resilience, and creative ways in which the black majority resisted political domination and economic exploitation.[10] It was both a commitment to producing "counter-hegemonic" histories and foregrounding black people's "agency in the making of their own histories".[11] The HW's

---

6 This scholarship is vast. A prominent example is Allister Sparks, *Tomorrow Is Another Country: The Inside Story of South Africa's Road to Change* (New York: Hill and Wang, 1995). For a left critique of the transition, see Patrick Bond, *Elite Transition – Revised and Expanded Edition: From Apartheid to Neoliberalism in South Africa* (London: Pluto Press, 2014).

7 Vanessa Barolsky, *Transitioning out of Violence: Snapshots from Kathorus* (Johannesburg: Centre for the Study of Violence and Reconciliation, 2005). Other exceptions include Mxolisi Mchunu, *Violence and Solace: The Natal Civil War in Late-Apartheid South Africa* (Charlottesville and London: University of Virginia Press, 2020); Khulumani Support Group, *Katorus Stories* (Johannesburg: Khulumani, 2007); Gary Kynoch, *Township Violence and the End of Apartheid: War on the Reef* (Woodbridge: James Currey, 2018) and Deborah Bonnin, "Space, Place and Identity: Political Violence in Mpumalanga Township, KwaZulu-Natal, 1987–1993" (PhD diss., University of the Witwatersrand, 2008).

8 Khulumani Support Group, *Katorus Stories*, 2.

9 The term "ordinary" is problematic but in certain contexts difficult to replace. See Yannick Lengeek's chapter in this volume.

10 Deborah Posel, "Social History and the Wits History Workshop," *African Studies* 69/1 (2010): 33, doi: 10.1080/00020181003647165.

11 Arianna Lissoni, Noor Nieftagodien and Shireen Ally, "'Life after Thirty' – A Critical Celebration," *African Studies* 69/1 (2010): 3,4, doi: 10.1080/00020181003647082.

brand of history from below was therefore largely a "history of below", with the contours of the "below" overlapping with the broader emancipatory project.[12] Left worker movements, community organisations, women's groups and progressive student organisations certainly received more attention than those complicit in upholding apartheid power – such as black policemen and councillors, or bantustan leaders for example – and groups espousing narrow ethno-nationalist politics such as Inkatha.[13] Hence, the question of who constituted the 'below' was a politicised one.

With the beginning of political negotiations in 1990, the HW – and South African history from below more broadly – underwent a period of reorientation, as its overarching goal of "speaking back to power" had lost its main purpose.[14] Much of the HW's scholarship turned to new topics such as memory, museums, or the global HIV epidemic.[15] At the same time, a new triumphalist and teleological form of public history emerged, grounded in the imperatives of state formation and reconciliation.[16] At the centre of this public history were political elites and their role in hammering out a new democratic dispensation. In contrast to the HW's history from below of the 1980s, which foregrounded popular politics and the agency of grassroots non-elites in the making of a new political order, the history of the transition era has, to a significant extent, been written as a history 'from above'.

This is at least partly related to the "sudden evaporation [. . .] of the moral and epistemological certainties of the apartheid era"[17]: if it had been clear prior to the transition who the perpetrators and who the victims were, the now-escalating violence complicated these categories and the boundaries between the below and the above became blurred. Who was below during this period, whose voices and concerns were marginalised, and what role did "ordinary" people play in shaping the political transformation? What agency did they have within a context of rapid political change? These questions became particularly complicated in relation to violence. What role did individuals and communities play in contesting or curbing violence? How did violence – both as experience and threat – shape everyday life?

---

12 Posel, "Social History and the Wits History Workshop," 31.
13 The HW's intellectual project was far more expansive than grassroots resistance and popular politics. Themes explored also included, for example, the history of liquor and sports, gender, and migration. See Noor Nieftagodien, "The Place of 'The Local' in History Workshop's Local History," *African Studies* 69/1 (2010): 45, doi: 10.1080/00020181003647181.
14 Posel, "Social History and the Wits History Workshop," 33.
15 Ibid., 38.
16 Nieftagodien, "The Place of 'The Local' in History Workshop's Local History," 48.
17 T. Nuttall and J. Wright, "Exploring beyond History with a Capital 'H'," *Current Writing: Text and Reception in Southern Africa* 10/2 (1998): 40, doi: 10.1080/1013929X.1998.9678042.

And what about perpetrators of violence? To what extent did they pursue their own agendas and how did these overlap with broader ideological, political, and economic concerns?[18] In other words, how might a focus on violence at the grassroots level provide new insights into South Africa's transition to democracy?

This chapter expands on the HW's rich intellectual tradition and on Barolsky's research and approach by foregrounding the lived experiences of violence from below in the war-torn townships of the PWV. It explores how violence manifested itself in three different spheres: the production of space, forms of communication, and social relationships. Focusing on the view from below brings into relief the complicated relationships between direct physical violence and the insidious and pervasive ways in which violence impinged upon everyday life. The violence of the transition era was not merely epiphenomenal to political negotiations at the national level but central to the ways in which the transition in this region was experienced, contested, and ultimately remembered.

10.2 *Udlame*: The Changing Nature of Violence

To understand the effects of violence on everyday life, it is necessary first to trace its changing nature during this period. South Africa's history has been shaped by the violence of colonial conquest, political oppression, and economic exploitation.[19] During the tumultuous 1980s, as thousands of youths across the country revolted against the apartheid regime, political violence as a strategy became more widespread.[20] During the same period, a significant shift occurred. With the escalation of conflict between Inkatha and ANC-aligned groups in the Natal Midlands, violence turned inwards, reconstituting who was perceived or suspected to be an enemy.[21] The changing nature and scope of violence is captured in the isiZulu term *udlame*, which refers to a "brutal savagery that destroys social relationships".[22]

---

18 It is beyond the scope of this chapter to explore the motivations of perpetrators in detail. But see, for example, Kynoch, *Township Violence and the End of Apartheid.*

19 William Beinart, "Introduction: Political and Collective Violence in Southern African Historiography," *Journal of Southern African Studies,* 18/3 (1992): 455–486, doi: 10.1080/03057079208708324.

20 Franziska Rueedi, *The Vaal Uprising of 1984 & the Struggle for Freedom in South Africa* (Woodbridge: James Currey, 2021).

21 For a recent analysis of the civil war see Mchunu, *Violence and Solace*; Jill Kelly, *To Swim with Crocodiles: Land, Violence and Belonging in South Africa, 1880–1996* (East Lansing: Michigan State University Press, 2018).

22 Timothy Gibbs, "Inkatha's Young Militants: Reconsidering Political Violence in South Africa," *Africa* 87/2 (2017): 364, doi:10.1017/S0001972016001005.

Similar patterns of collective violence emerged in the urban townships of the PWV in 1990. After the unbanning of the liberation movements Inkatha, which until then had been predominantly a cultural movement, reinvented itself as a political party, the Inkatha Freedom Party (IFP). To strengthen its support base, it launched an aggressive recruitment campaign among the Zulu-speaking population of the Johannesburg region. It founds its greatest support among migrant workers from KwaZulu and Natal, who were residing in migrant worker hostels at the edge of the townships. These hostels were mostly built after the Second World War to accommodate male migrant workers from rural areas, who sought employment in the gold mines and the manufacturing industry around Johannesburg.[23]

Until the late 1980s, relations between hostels and neighbouring township communities were largely amicable, marked by social and economic exchange. Friendships, romantic relationships, church gatherings, or cultural events brought hostel dwellers and township residents together.[24] However, from the late 1980s, relations between hostel dwellers and township communities began to deteriorate. The reasons for this are complex and beyond the scope of this chapter. Struggles over resources and territories,[25] the marginalisation of migrant workers,[26] threats to the lifestyle of migrant workers,[27] competing visions of nationalism[28] and the new political order, cultural sensitivities and fears of losing one's way of life[29] all contributed to growing hostility. The nefarious role of the security forces and the significance of gangs in exploiting the breakdown of social order have also been explored.[30]

---

23 See for example Noor Nieftagodien, "Life in South Africa's Hostels: Carceral Spaces and Places of Refuge," *Comparatives Studies of South Asia, Africa and the Middle East* 37/3 (2017): 428, doi: 10.1215/1089201x-4279128.

24 Lauren Segal, "The Human Face of Violence: Hostel Dwellers Speak," *Journal of Southern African Studies* 18/1 (1992): 198, doi: 10.1080/03057079208708311.

25 Philip Bonner and Noor Nieftagodien, "The Truth and Reconciliation Commission and the Pursuit of 'Social Truth': The Case of Kathorus," in *Commissioning the Past. Understanding South Africa's Truth and Reconciliation Commission*, ed. Deborah Posel, and Graeme Simpson (Johannesburg: Wits University Press. 2002), 173–203.

26 Ari Sitas, "The New Tribalism: Hostels and Violence," *Journal of Southern African Studies* 22/2 (1996): 235–248, doi: 10.1080/03057079608708489.

27 Philip Bonner, and Vusi Ndima, "The Roots of Violence and Martial Zuluness on the East Rand," in *Zulu Identities. Being Zulu, Past and Present*, ed. Benedict Carton, John Laband, and Jabulani Sithole (Scottsville: UKZN Press, 2008), 363–382.

28 Ivor Chipkin, "Nationalism as Such: Violence during South Africa's Political Transition," *Public Culture* 16/2 (2004): 325–326, doi: 10.1215/08992363-16-2-315.

29 Hickel, *Democracy as Death*.

30 Kynoch, *Township Violence and the End of Apartheid*.

The first significant incident of violence by IFP-supporting hostel residents in the Johannesburg region occurred on 22 July 1990 in the township of Sebokeng in the Vaal Triangle.[31] On this day, a large IFP gathering escalated when crowds of hostel residents and IFP supporters attacked the township, leaving 27 dead and many more wounded. In response, hostel dwellers expelled all those suspected of being in support of the IFP from Sebokeng hostel. News of the expulsion from Sebokeng hostel travelled across the region and triggered violent responses by hostel dwellers elsewhere. In Thokoza to the east of Johannesburg, Zulu-speaking hostel dwellers asserted their power when they purged Khalanyoni hostel of non-Zulu-speaking hostel dwellers, who eventually fled to Phola Park, an informal settlement nearby. Cycles of violence and counter-violence ensued between Thokoza's Zulu-speaking hostel dwellers and Phola Park residents, with the security forces further exacerbating the violence.[32]

Before the 1990s, Inkatha had minimal influence over the migrant population; this changed when migrant workers' interests were increasingly threatened. Many joined not for overtly political reasons but to guard their interests.[33] The role of the IFP in this early mobilisation for violence in the hostels is therefore complex and warrants further research. What is clear is the critical role the Sebokeng violence played in politicising the hostels and paving the ground for the IFP's growing influence.

10.3 The Spatiality of Violence

One of the most visible manifestations of escalating violence was the re-spatialisation of black urban township spaces. This was particularly acute in the Kathorus region. Urban townships built during the apartheid era were structured like a grid, with the main road leading in and out of the township. Endless rows of four-roomed houses, widely known as "matchbox houses" for their small size, were built to accommodate nuclear families.[34] They were geared towards social and political control, yet their spatiality also produced specific forms of street politics and sociality: houses were in close proximity to one another and much of everyday life occurred in the street.[35]

---

31 Franziska Rueedi, "The Hostel Wars in Apartheid South Africa: Rumour, Violence and the Politics of Belonging," *Social Identities* 26/6 (2020): 756–773, doi: 10.1080/13504630.2020.1814235.
32 For a detailed overview of the violence, see Kynoch, *Township Violence and the End of Apartheid.*
33 Chipkin, "Nationalism as Such," 215.
34 The standard four-roomed house in urban townships was type NE51/6. It was approximately 50m^2 in size, with an asbestos roof and an outside toilet.
35 See Rueedi, *The Vaal Uprising of 1984 & the Struggle for Freedom in South Africa.*

Hostels, on the other hand, were built to house (mostly male) migrant workers. They were originally single-sex, though they became increasingly mixed from the late 1980s when women and children moved into these spaces.[36]

During the early phase of the violence in Kathorus, the informal settlement of Phola Park was at the centre of the conflict. This is not surprising, as many of those who had fled the hostels had fled to Phola Park. Significantly, the informal settlements housed the most impoverished and disadvantaged sections of township societies, as well as migrant workers from different parts of the country, who directly competed for resources with hostel inhabitants.[37] Yet, as violence spiraled, it engulfed other sections of the more formal townships.

By late 1990, many hostels had become semi-closed-off spaces. Like many other hostels across the PWV, Thokoza's hostels were soon under the control of the IFP, which considered this area to be central in its struggle for political power. Noor Nieftagodien has described the architecture of these hostels as "carceral", inspired by prison technology and geared towards surveillance and control.[38] Strict systems of traditional authority and the architecture of these hostels – with hundreds of men sharing overcrowded dormitories and communal spaces – facilitated collective mobilisation and promoted a siege mentality. Key to this system were the *izinduna* (headmen) loyal to the IFP, who connected the urban hostels in the PWV with the rural power base of the *amakhosi* (chiefs) in KwaZulu and Natal.[39] The layout of the townships, with only one main road connecting them with the towns, facilitated violent controls of transport routes and made certain sections particularly vulnerable to violent attacks. This was particularly acute in Thokoza, where three hostels under the control of the IFP were situated along Khumalo Street, Thokoza's main road.

Young men set up Self Defense Units (SDUs) to protect township communities against this escalating violence. They were loosely aligned to the ANC but never under its direct control. During the early phase of the conflict, the areas adjacent to the hostels remained politically, ethnically, and socially heterogeneous. Many families had lived there for decades and were unwilling to bend to the IFP's campaign of violence. Khumalo Street soon became notorious as anyone walking past

---

36 Glen S. Elder, "Malevolent Traditions: Hostel Violence and the Procreational Geography of Apartheid," *Journal of Southern African Studies* 29/4 (2003): 921–35, doi: 10.1080/0305707032000135897.

37 Hilary Sapire, "Politics and Protest in Shack Settlements of the Pretoria–Witwatersrand–Vereeniging Region, South Africa, 1980-1990," *Journal of Southern African Studies* 18/3 (1992): 670–97, doi: 10.1080/03057079208708331; Kynoch, *Township Violence and the End of Apartheid*; Bonner and Nieftagodien, "The Truth and Reconciliation Commission and the Pursuit of 'Social Truth'".

38 Nieftagodien, "Life in South Africa's Hostels," 428.

39 *Izinduna* (sg: induna) are representatives of *amakhosi*, Zulu royalty (and traditional authorities more broadly). I use the term preferred by *izinduna* themselves, instead of the English translation "headmen".

the hostels could face violent assault and death. But for most people living nearby, it was nearly impossible to avoid Khumalo Street entirely, as it was part of the main transport route. Instead, commuters and residents attempted to mitigate the threat by alerting each other if there were shooting incidents. Physical barriers aimed to prevent large crowds of hostel dwellers from attacking the township: "Sometimes the street was simply barricaded making progress impossible. The residents had rolled the boulders onto the street to make it impassible [sic], thus reducing the vulnerability of families in the vicinity to attack from hostel dwellers."[40] These measures hardly prevented attacks; but they highlight the coping strategies communities employed to curb violence and to protect their lives.

It is important to note that violence was cyclical and uneven; even Thokoza and Katlehong, the two townships that bore the brunt of the violence, experienced periods of relative stability.[41] This had much to do with localised patterns of conflict and triggers, as the view from below reveals. Incidents of political violence dropped in the first quarter of 1993 to an all-time low since 1989.[42] But in May 1993, violence flared up again, heralding a new phase of the conflict. In Thokoza, this new cycle of violence was triggered by a march organised by Phola Park residents along Khumalo street. Ignoring warnings, some marchers allegedly "surged forward" towards one of the hostels where they were shot at.[43] At the national level, another moment of intense violence threatened political stability: on 10 April 1993, popular Communist leader Chris Hani was assassinated by a member of the white ultra-right. Hani's murder threatened to derail the negotiations as tensions were mounting. To diffuse these tensions, and to prevent a further escalation of violence, the election date was set for 27 April 1994.[44] The setting of the election date appeased more radical sections of the liberation movements. But in its aftermath, the far-right accelerated its mobilisation to halt the negotiations, and sections of the white right strengthened its alliance with the IFP.[45] Key to this alliance was a shared vision of a federal system, that would protect the regional power of different groups.

---

40 Padraig O'Malley, "A Thokoza Family: Theo's Dream," https://omalley.nelsonmandela.org/omalley/index.php/site/q/03lv01508/04lv01513/05lv01514/06lv01515.htm, accessed August 01, 2022.
41 Bonner and Nieftagodien, "The Truth and Reconciliation Commission and the Pursuit of 'Social Truth': The Case of Kathorus," 196–197.
42 Ibid.
43 Ibid.
44 Adrian Guelke, "Political Violence and the South African Transition," *Irish Studies in International Affairs* 4 (1993): 59–68.
45 Evidence of this is scattered across different archives. To my knowledge, no comprehensive analysis exists to this day on the relationships between the white right-wing and the IFP. For an overview, see Jason Robinson, "Fragments of the Past: Homeland Politics and the South African Transition," *Journal of Southern African Studies* 41/5 (2015): 953–967, doi: 10.1080/03057070.2015.1064297.

10 Violence during the Transition "From Below" in South Africa — 267

In Kathorus, the intensification of political power struggles led to the increasing territorialisation of the conflict that parceled up the townships into mutually antagonistic camps. This led to the violent purging of entire sections along 'ethnic' and political lines.[46] In Thokoza, hostel leaders launched a campaign to force Zulu-speaking men to join the IFP and its paramilitary units, the Self Protection Units (SPUs). The worst affected section was Phenduka section, adjacent to Khumalo Street and the hostels. The intensification of the IFP's violent recruitment changed gender dynamics in this area: many men left to evade being recruited. Others attempted to disguise their sex by dressing as women. Children as young as nine were abducted and taken to the hostels; many never returned.[47] As men resisted recruitment, hostel leaders directed their attention to recruiting women, ordering them over megaphones and loudhailers to attend meetings.[48]

By July 1993, eviction notices were pushed under people's doors, ordering them to vacate their houses. Some notes simply read, "Can we have your house?"[49] In other instances, residents were told in no uncertain terms, "Because you are ANC you are not needed in this area. We have IFPs who are in need of that house."[50] By then, Thokoza's hostel population included a few hundred unemployed men who were "bored, frustrated and often hungry" and therefore more readily mobilised into violence.[51] Reports suggest that the forceful occupation of township houses was not only reflective of territorial struggles and broader political concerns but also due to material interests: in contrast to the overcrowded, degrading, and bleak dormitories of the hostels, township family housing offered higher living standards.[52]

For many township residents, the continuous threats and violence became unbearable. By September 1993, approximately 200 families had fled Phenduka section, leaving it a virtual "ghost town".[53] A woman living in Buthelezi Street,

---

46 Deborah Bonnin's PhD thesis is the most comprehensive analysis of how space became politicised in the Natal Midlands. See Bonnin, "Space, Place and Identity."

47 Historical Papers Research Archive, University of the Witwatersrand (henceforth ZA HPRA) AG2515 L2.5.1, Reports to Peace Action, Germiston/Alberton Area: Katlehong/Tokoza [sic], telephone monitoring forms: July and August 1993.

48 ZA HPRA AG2543 2.2.3–2.3.5, "Before we were Good Friends: An Account and Analysis of Displacement in the East Rand Townships of Thokoza and Katlehong," April 1994, 9.

49 Ibid., 13.

50 Ibid.

51 ZA HPRA AG2515 K10, KwaZulu Government Service: Report on the Visit to East Rand Hostels, September 22, 1993.

52 ZA HPRA AG2543 2.2.3–2.3.5, "Before we were Good Friends," 14.

53 Ibid., 8.

which marked the border between the sections controlled by the IFP and the ANC, used similar words:

> My street was like a ghost town. Almost all my neighbours had gone away. We could not sleep because of shots fired throughout the night. They would climb on top of my house and shoot. During the day, we had to lock our doors and stay inside. We tried to arrange for transport, but people were to [sic] afraid to enter our area.[54]

During the conflict in Kathorus, thousands of people were displaced and became internal refugees. They often lost all their material possessions as they fled for their lives. Most had to be escorted by soldiers of the South African Defence Force stationed nearby. Those who remained in embattled areas were at constant risk: their houses were burnt down, and attacks on families accused of siding with or being loyal to the ANC increased.[55] Access to necessities and medical care became scarce, as ambulances rarely entered, and many people struggled to navigate safely through the danger zones.[56] For those who needed to cross through no-go areas to go to work, the financial toll of having to pay protection money became severe.

Vacated houses were soon occupied by IFP supporters, while areas around the hostels became no-go areas, separated by strips of deserted land and burnt-out houses.[57] In Katlehong, adjacent to Thokoza, territorial struggles intensified during the same period. The streets of sections close to the hostel were "soon crisscrossed with barricades and deep trenches. Neighbourhoods were patrolled by members of the local Self-Defense Units (SDUs)", and the sound of gunshots was heard throughout the night.[58]

> Burnt out houses and empty streets bear testimony to the devastation which the violence has wrought on the community. The danger of sniper fire from gunmen hiding in the ruins means that only the security forces driving around in armoured vehicles are willing to cross this area.[59]

Two double-storey buildings became notorious hotspots for sniping, forcing people to avoid these areas at all cost.[60] Surviving the violence, therefore, required

---

54 Ibid., 15.

55 CB, SDU commander Thokoza, interview with author, Germiston, December 14, 2018.

56 Khulumani Support Group, *Kathorus Stories*, 35.

57 ZA HPRA AG2543-2–2.3–2.3.5, "Before we were Good Friends," 2.

58 Anthony Minnaar, "East Rand Townships under Siege," *Indicator SA* 10/4 (1993): 68, https://hdl.handle.net/10520/AJA0259188X187, accessed August 20, 2022.

59 ZA HPRA AG2543 2.2.3–2.3.5, "Before we were Good Friends," 2.

60 Khulumani Support Group, *Katorus Stories*, 29; AC, ANC official Thokoza, interview with author, Pretoria, December 10, 2018.

10 Violence during the Transition "From Below" in South Africa — 269

spatial knowledge that was often only available to insiders who were residents in the area. The renaming of different sections reflected struggles over territorial control. Areas under the control of the IFP came to be known as 'Ulundi' after the capital of the KwaZulu bantustan, and SDUs renamed Phenduka 'Slovo' and 'Tambo' sections to honour the ANC's leadership.[61]

Conversely, SDUs forced those suspected of being IFP supporters out of the sections under their control. SDU attacks on Zulu-speaking migrant workers and others accused of sympathising with the IFP increased. Among the displaced were some of the most marginalised sections of society: impoverished women who had migrated to the urban areas to seek employment and were, based on their place of origin, accused of being IFP supporters. By mid-1993, a few hundred women sought protection with their children inside Kwesine hostel in Katlehong.[62] Living conditions deteriorated rapidly, as the arrival of these refugees placed great strain on the infrastructure. A report summarising the dire situation noted that

[a]s many as 50 families share two hot plates to prepare meals. One sink is used for washing clothes, dishes and bathing. Conditions are squalid and extremely unhygienic. Such overcrowding has put a serious strain on the inhabitants' health. Children are the most vulnerable.[63]

The situation worsened after armed units aligned to the ANC disrupted the railway line to Kwesine hostel and sabotaged water and sanitation pipes.[64] Like other hostels, Kwesine hostel was placed under a blockade, with no regular access to food, water, and medical care. Many adults lost their jobs as commuting to work became too dangerous, and communication with the outside world was severely curtailed: the telephone was often out of order, and two-way radios became the only means of communication among hostel leaders.[65] Relief agencies struggled to deliver food parcels, as they feared being shot at in the vicinity of the hostels.[66] Inside the hostels, high levels of violence were therefore compounded by hunger and disease. Women had to give birth without the support

---

61 Kynoch, *Township Violence and the End of Apartheid*, 212.

62 BG, female hostel resident Katlehong, interview with author, Katlehong, March 29, 2019; Bonner and Ndima, "The Roots of Violence and Martial Zuluness on the East Rand," 377; Kynoch, *Township Violence and the End of Apartheid*, 215.

63 ZA HPRA AG2543 2.2.3–2.3.5, "Before we were Good Friends, 35.

64 ZA HPRA A3079 I-I1, Robert McBride, interview with Gary Kynoch, Johannesburg, June 21, 2006.

65 BG, female hostel resident Katlehong, interview with author, Katlehong, March 29, 2019.

66 ZA HPRA AG2515 K10, KwaZulu Government Service: Report on the Visit to East Rand Hostels, 22 September 1993, 4; Minnaar, "East Rand Townships under Siege," 70.

of midwives and nurses, and most struggled to access the necessities to care for their infants after birth. Across the divide, women and children suffered greatly.[67]

The rigid spatial division disrupted social networks, curtailed freedom of movement, and tore apart families, who could no longer visit each other. The violence also severed old networks of trust and friendship, as one woman explained: "Most of them I grew up with, and I don't know why they thought I was IFP."[68] To remain politically neutral became impossible. Alleged political allegiance was determined based on one's place of origin, physical markers (such as scarification), language and cadence, and choice of clothing.[69] Anyone speaking 'deep' Zulu (indicating they had migrated from Natal or KwaZulu) was alleged to support the IFP. At the same time, urbanised township residents were considered supporters of the ANC and its allies.

Contrary to macro-level analyses that have foregrounded ideology and politics from above, the view from below highlights the complex ways in which identities were forged through experiences of violence and persecution, and their embeddedness in the shifting spatiality of the townships.

In some instances, interpersonal relationships that cut across the divide persisted. Individuals showed great courage and compassion in attempting to contain the violence and were at the forefront of peace initiatives. Evidence suggests that some landlords protected their tenants at significant risk, and hostel dwellers alerted residents of impending attacks. These ongoing relationships between hostel residents and township communities were usually built on a history of personal engagement and trust.[70]

For township women, IFP-controlled hostels came to be feared not only for their role as a springboard for large-scale attacks but also as sites of sexual violence. One mother explained: "They [IFP-aligned hostel residents] came back late at night and when I ask, they say I must shut up, they want these girls. I know what they want. We just keep quite [sic] when they come to fetch the girls."[71] Eyewitness testimonies found in the archives are harrowing and confirm that many women knew that abduction into a hostel was often a death sentence. In 1993, hostel dwellers diverted a minibus taxi full of women and children into one of Thokoza's notorious hostels. One of the women who man-

---

67 Gary Kynoch explores this to some extent. See Kynoch, *Township Violence and the End of Apartheid*. See also Barolsky, "Childhood in the Shadow of Violence."
68 ZA HPRA AG2543 2.2.3–2.3.5, "Before we were Good Friends," 18.
69 Bonner and Ndima, "The Roots of Violence and Martial Zuluness on the East Rand."
70 ZA HPRA AG2543 2.2.3, "Fortresses of Fear: Hostels and Reef Violence," 29.
71 ZA HPRA AG2543 2.2.3–2.3.5, "Before we were Good Friends," 10.

aged to escape recounted, "a woman who knew me grabbed my hand and told me to say goodbye to her family for her. She was not crying she was just sad."[72] The threat of sexual violence was not confined to the hostels. Members of the security forces were alleged to rape and assault with impunity, and some SDUs were accused of sexual violence.[73]

If women endured horrific acts of violence against their children and themselves, they also became active in ending the violence. On 27 October 1993, a crowd of approximately a thousand women staged a march to the regional offices of the ANC. They demanded the party increase its efforts to end the violence and called for the removal of the police' notorious Internal Stability Unit (ISU), which had been heavily implicated in the violence across the region.[74] If local *izinduna*, police, and leaders of SPUs and SDUs, gangs and loose groups of men were key in initiating cycles of violence, grassroots initiatives emerged to end them. On the ground, violence was therefore both initiated and contested by diverse groups, whose motivations often had more to do with localised concerns and their lived experiences, than with ideological concerns.

10.4 (Un)making the Everyday

In contrast to earlier periods of violence in recent memory, this violence was intra-communal and intimate: entire communities became the target of attacks with little consideration for age or gender. Hit-and-run forms of violence emerged that "were aimed at the heart of community life and instilled a psychosis of fear and mistrust in the community".[75] The pervasive threat of violence impacted daily routines and affected both private and public spaces. The familiar became uncertain: everyday activities, such as going to school or work, watching television in the evening, or drinking a beer at a tavern, could lead to violence and death. The excessive and arbitrary violence – and the threat thereof – "unmade" the everyday, as Vanessa Barolsky has argued: "The everyday as we assume it appears to fall away, to retreat, to develop irrelevance. There is a radical disordering of the social world and a displacement of the "ordinary" [. . .]."[76]

---

72 "Women take a Stand," *Speak*, February 1994, 27.
73 Khulumani Support Group, *Katorus Stories*, 10.
74 "Women take a Stand," *Speak*, February 1994, 26.
75 ZA HPRA AG2543 2.3.5.01, "Before we were Good Friends", 5.
76 Vanessa Barolski, "Childhood in the Shadow of Violence," in *Violence and Non-Violence in Africa*, ed. Pahl Ahluwahlia, Louise Bethlehem, and Ruth Ginio (London and New York: Routledge, 2007), 179.

People's mobility was curtailed not only due to territorial struggles in townships but also to risks associated with using public transport. Violent attacks on train commuters turned the daily commute to work into a severely risky act. On 24 July 1990, two days after the beginning of violence in the PWV, alleged IFP supporters attacked train passengers commuting to Johannesburg. Warnings of impending attacks had been circulating for days, and the regional commissioner of police had been alerted, but failed to respond.[77] During the first eighteen months of the violence, 48 attacks on trains were recorded, with dozens of people murdered.[78] Eyewitness testimonies alleged time and again that the perpetrators were seen escaping into the hostels in the aftermath of attacks.[79]

If attacks on trains threatened commuting adults' lives and livelihoods, schools became sites of violence for children. In Thokoza, an attack on a school led to the death of one pupil and the subsequent closure of the school.[80] In Alexandra in the north of Johannesburg, where violence escalated in 1992, snipers, allegedly based at the hostel, opened fire on primary school children on their way to school on more than one occasion.[81] Consequently, many schools had to close, and children lived in a constant state of fear. The attacks on schools affected children across the divide. Children who fled to the hostels at the height of the violence in 1993 became trapped inside the hostels, with no schooling, daycare facilities or infrastructure to rely on.[82] The effect violence had on children and youth was devastating.[83] George Ndlozi, a peace monitor, explained:

> Whether you were involved in defence or not, the violence affected you. It was not unknown for children attending nursery school or creches to find a body near their jungle gym or swing. Hostel inmates and SDUs took potshots at each other across school yards. Children were not spared the horror. Schooling in the area came to a standstill. Children barely reaching their teens left schools to defend life and property.[84]

---

77 ZA HPRA AG2543 C20, Letter by Cheadle, Thompson, and Haysom to the General Secretary, re threats of Violence: Inkatha, dated July 18, 1990.

78 ZA HPRA AG2543 A3, "Blood on the Tracks: A Special Report on Train Attacks by the Independent Board of Inquiry".

79 ZA HPRA AG2543 A3, Train Violence, Statement Ephriam [sic] Mogale. Allegations surfaced early on that the third force was involved in the train attacks.

80 ZA HPRA AG2515 L2.1., Telephone monitoring form (M121), Thokoza, May 18, 1992.

81 ZA HPRA AG2543 2.2.3, "Fortresses of Fear: Hostels and Reef Violence", Appendix 1: Alexandra, 4.

82 ZA HPRA AG2515 K10, KwaZulu Government Service, Report on the Visit to East Rand Hostels, September 22, 1993.

83 Barolsky, "Childhood in the Shadow of Violence."

84 Truth and Reconciliation Commission, Johannesburg Children's Hearing, June 12, 1997, George Ndlozi, https://www.justice.gov.za/trc/special/children/ndlozi.htm, accessed August 1, 2022.

10 Violence during the Transition "From Below" in South Africa — **273**

As Ndlozi's narrative shows, children and youth were not only the targets of violence but soon became actively involved.[85] By the early 1990s, children as young as twelve joined SDUs and armed themselves with automatic rifles and home-made zip guns, known as *qwashu*, to counter the violence meted out by hostel residents. CB, who was sixteen years old by the time he became a commander of one of Thokoza's SDUs, recalls how his daily routine changed when he joined an SDU:

> We would move at night and go to do whatever operation that needed to be done. And then we will come back early in the morning, and we will wake up like everybody else, and wear our [school] uniform and even our parents didn't know what we were doing, what we were involved with.[86]

CB's explanations point towards the culture of secrecy that permeated generational relations. Initially, he and his comrades[87] maintained the daily routine of school children during the day. At night, in contrast, generational hierarchies were upended as they assumed the role of protecting communities. Their perceived role as defenders of the community also led to open disobedience of parental authority:

> Then we began not to listen to parents because they would say don't go out, don't do that, we'd say mama if I don't go out I'll be betraying my people. They are out there, we need to go and fight. Then they were afraid if we would die. We were prepared to die.[88]

SDU members were expected to show courage, bravery and toughness, which was at the core of a "militarised masculinity".[89] This militarisation also seeped into constructions of their social world, as symbols of war replaced the mundane objects of everyday life. Guns were always present, as a group of SDU members recalled: "An AK47, it's your baby you sleep with it. [. . .] We even happened to have a song which we composed, and it was our love song: *AK47 s'thandwa sam'* [AK47 my love]."[90] Fewer women joined the SDUs, and among those that did, even though they were often involved in combat, they were also required to take

---

85 Barolsky, "Transitioning out of Violence," 69. On the role of youth, see Monique Marks, *Young Warriors. Youth Politics, Identity and Violence in South Africa* (Johannesburg: Wits University Press, 2001).
86 CB, SDU commander Thokoza, interview with author, Germiston, December 14, 2018.
87 The term 'comrade' was widely used to refer to ANC-aligned activists.
88 SDU member, quoted in Sasha Naidoo, "Exploring the Challenges Facing Former Combatants in Post-Apartheid South Africa" (MA thesis, University of the Witwatersrand, 2007), 33.
89 Naidoo, "Exploring the Challenges Facing Former Combatants in Post-Apartheid South Africa," 38.
90 SDU members Thokoza, group interview with author, Thokoza, February 23, 2019.

over domestic duties such as cooking.[91] With the intensification of territorial struggles in 1993, CB's group moved out of their parental homes and into vacant houses, which became their bases. They slept and ate in turns while others patrolled the streets.

One of the SDUs' main tasks centred on the protection of homes, which became a "central battle target" during this period.[92] In black urban townships, the home had long been politicised. For decades, it was the site of frequent intrusions by the state; experiences of being woken up in the middle of the night during the infamous pass raids[93] were widespread. With the escalation of violence, the safety of domestic spaces was further eroded. Township residents were told by IFP supporters "to keep their doors and garden gates unlocked for easy access and escape routes".[94] Homes were invaded, material goods looted, telephones used, and food taken.[95] Among the culprits were hostel residents but also members of security forces, who gained a track record of assaulting people in their homes.[96]

However, private homes were also spaces of contestation, used to subvert the control of the apartheid state: Those on the run from apartheid police had long utilised domestic spaces to hide themselves, weapons, illegal pamphlets, and banned literature.[97] As attacks on households increased during the early 1990s, this knowledge was utilised by wider communities. The home was, therefore, "reconstituted in war: its drainage, its ceilings, its gates, the family car, the refrigerator, now hiding places for weapons."[98]

Violence was both embedded in the everyday and the *everynight*. Many attacks on homes occurred at night and surprised people in their sleep. Some of the most ordinary aspects of everyday life, such as sleep, came to constitute a risk that some families attempted to mitigate by staying awake.[99] Consequently, the rhythms and routines were upended: "[O]rdinary times and spaces of the

---

91 On gender during the liberation struggle, see Emily Bridger, *Young Women against Apartheid: Gender, Youth and South Africa's Liberation Struggle* (Woodbridge: James Currey, 2021).

92 Beinart, "Introduction," 485.

93 Under the Natives (Abolition of Passes and Co-ordination of Documents) Act, Act No. 67 of 1952 (popularly referred to as the Pass Laws), the black population over the age of 16 had to carry a reference book to confirm the right to reside in the urban areas.

94 ZA HPRA AG2543 2.3.5.01, "Before we were Good Friends," 12.

95 Ibid.

96 "Women take a Stand," *Speak,* February 1994, 28.

97 Franziska Rueedi, "'Our Bushes are the Houses': People's War and the Underground during the Insurrectionary Period in the Vaal Triangle, South Africa," *Journal of Southern African Studies* 46/6 (2020): 615–633, doi: 10.1080/03057070.2020.1771072.

98 Barolsky, "Childhood in the Shadow of Violence," 180.

99 ZA HPRA AG2515 E1, Peace Action Report for July 1993, 6.

childhood day", Barolsky noted, became imbued with "fear and horror".[100] The scarcity of streetlights in some areas provided attackers with the cover of darkness: "Nights were bad", CB recalled, "it was better in the day [. . .] at night you don't see".[101] During the initial phase of the violence, patrolling SDUs would shout *tshwe*, a township slang alerting people of impending danger and calling on them to seek safety. Switching off the TV and lights and lying down on the floor provided a modest degree of protection against targeted attacks and stray bullets.[102] In Soweto, the area around Mzimhlophe hostel came under attack in 1992. Violence monitors visiting the area described their experience: "As we were talking, we heard gunfire, then all the lights went off, and everyone hit the floor. Children in the house all sleep on the floor".[103] Some families also tried to protect themselves by avoiding rooms facing the street; others left their homes to hide in a nearby river at night.[104] The meaning of different spaces therefore changed: outside spaces such as rivers became spaces of refuge, while the home came to signify a "space for war".[105]

The violence also affected religious rites and sacred spaces. Cemeteries became part of the territorial struggles, as families could not bury their loved ones in cemeteries on 'enemy' territory.[106] The lengthy funeral rites, which usually lasted for days, were often dangerous to undertake, as mourners came under attack in their homes and in the cemeteries. During the height of violence in Thokoza and Katlehong in July and August 1993, corpses rotting in the streets and piling up in the morgues showed the extent of the violence. Many remained unidentified and were buried in pauper graves. Implementing the proper rites was hampered by the disappearance of bodies, risks associated with large gatherings, and logistical challenges. "We had to discuss with the forensic team to say rather than just put people into a grave, let's use other methods of identification. [. . .] And then we ordered the police to stop with mass burials", a clergyman recalls.[107] Tensions during some of the funerals ran high when alleged IFP members were among the victims to be buried:

---

100 Barolsky, "Transitioning out of Violence," 66.

101 CB, SDU commander Thokoza, interview with author, Germiston, December 14, 2018.

102 Ibid.

103 ZA HPRA AG2515 L2.2.4, Field monitoring – Mzimhlophe, March 25, 1992.

104 Ibid.; Naidoo, "Exploring the Challenges Facing Former Combatants in Post-Apartheid South Africa," 43.

105 Barolsky, "Transitioning out of Violence," 64.

106 Andreas Mapheto, "The South African War. The Violence: A View from the Ground," *Work in Progress* 69 (September 1990): 6.

107 AB, clergyman, interview with author, Vereeniging, November 12, 2018.

The understanding is that these are the enemies of the community. When we arrived at the cemetery, the coffins were lined up, and I remember I asked Reverend S[. . .], who was a senior, and I said: "Reverend, will you lead us in prayer", because no one wanted to do it, and at every grave, there was a pastor. No one wanted to pray. They were scared, and I was not aware because I was not looking around, and comrades were lining up in front of us with AK47s, brand new AK47s. [. . .] And fortunately, by the grace of God, no one died.[108]

Death became depersonalised in newspaper reports and police statistics. Bodies were counted in numbers, evacuated of meaning or subjectivity. The extent and forms of violence were "often extreme in the bodily mutilations it delivered", as Barolsky has noted.[109] Burying the body according to proper cultural customs constituted one way of reclaiming the dignity and personhood of the deceased and allowing them to transition into the realm of their ancestors,[110] and this was often not possible.

10.5 Uncertainty and Rumours

As violence was raging in the Kathorus region, another region severely affected was the Vaal Triangle to the south of Johannesburg. At the centre of this reign of terror was the IFP-controlled KwaMadala hostel outside Boipatong township. One of the first massacres occurred on the night of 12 January 1991, when a gang of armed men attacked mourners attending a night vigil for Christopher Nangalembe, leaving 45 people dead and many more wounded. Nangalembe, a local youth activist aligned to ANC structures, had been kidnapped and murdered a week earlier by a local gang. Church leaders who visited the Nangalembe family the day before the vigil recounted that "the family expressed their dreadful fear" after the gang had threatened that the vigil would be attacked, and they "kept their house under surveillance".[111] The police failed to adequately respond to the warnings, despite promises to send protection. Khetisi Kheswa, whose gang had

---

108 Ibid.

109 Barolsky, *Transitioning out of Violence*, 46. See Mchunu, *Violence and Solace* for a discussion of mutilations in KwaZulu and Natal.

110 Best described as "living dead", ancestors, known as *amadlozi* in isiZulu and *izinyanya* in isiXhosa connect the spiritual realm with the world of the living. See Dineo Skosana on the significance of burials. Dineo Skosana, "Grave Matters: Dispossession and the Desecration of Ancestral Graves by Mining Corporations in South Africa," *Journal of Contemporary African Studies* 40/1 (2022): 57–58, doi: 10.1080/02589001.2021.1926937. On the impact of violence, see also Mchunu, *Violence and Solace*, 194.

111 ZA HPRA AG2543 C20, Fax Vaal Council of Churches.

allegedly perpetrated the massacre, became one of the region's most feared and hated people. Together with other members of his gang, he fled to KwaMadala hostel, where he joined the IFP.

During the next three years, drive-by shootings and attacks on public spaces such as taverns terrorised local communities. In some instances, activists aligned to the ANC were directly targeted; in other cases, assailants driving around in cars opened fire on pedestrians. "Whole families are wiped out by unknown gunmen, people drinking in shebeens die without warning in a hail of bullets [. . .]. Residents risk their lives every time they gather together", a report noted in 1993.[112] Community relations were riddled with suspicions and fears, as the report further stated: "[T]he chances of a society maintaining any coherence or stability are minimal. Paranoia and fear become endemic. People begin to turn inwards in the absence of an identifiable enemy. Ultimately, the community begins to destroy itself." Ibid.

Within this context of uncertainty and ambiguity, alternative modes of communication and knowing emerged. Rumours – broadly defined as information with "uncertain and unauthorised origins" – gained salience.[113] A history of government disinformation and propaganda, and an almost complete absence of reliable and trustworthy information, had laid the foundation. In May 1992, a Sebokeng resident called Peace Action – a violence monitoring organisation – about "a car that was seen driving around" and surmised that it might belong to Kheswa's gang.[114] A few days later, youth noticed "three suspicious cars" parked outside a house and threatened to burn them. They emphasised that "our enemy, the Vaal Monster (Khetisi) and his friends usually drive in cars, in their missions of terrorising residents."[115] Cars driving about at unusual times of the night therefore came to be viewed with suspicion.

Many households did not have a telephone, and residents had to go to a neighbour's house to make telephone calls. Consequently, community warning systems relied on networks of communal care and solidarity among neighbours. Moreover, information transmitted via telephone was often overheard and witnessed by several people; individual observations could rapidly translate into a rumour that spread through informal communication networks. Many people caught up in the violence expressed a sense of confusion and bewilderment re-

---

112 ZA HPRA AG2515E1, Peace Action, Report for June 1993, 2.

113 Gary A. Fine, "Rumour Matters. An Introductory Essay," in *Rumor Mills: The Social Impact of Rumor and Legends*, ed. Gary Fine, Véronique Campion-Vincent, and Chip Heath (New Brunswick: Aldine Transaction, 2005), 1.

114 ZA HPRA AG2515 L2.8.3, telephone monitoring form, Sebokeng, May 12, 1992.

115 ZA HPRA AG2515 L2.8.3, telephone monitoring form, Sebokeng, May 17, 1992.

garding violence; rumours produced "new truths" that aimed to interpret the world and to warn about impending attacks.[116] They constituted a coping mechanism to "mediate the existential uncertainty" of everyday life in a context of threat and violence.[117] In other instances, particular forms of dressing came to be associated with danger. In Thokoza, one man, alleged to be wearing a long overcoat, was seen wandering the streets, presumably hiding a rifle under his coat.[118] Rumoured to be invincible and immune against bullets, the man in the overcoat became symbolic of a deep distrust against anyone who looked or acted differently. Similarly, an IPF man allegedly wearing a red woman's dress was seen identifying targets for attack in Soweto.[119] Rumours of men dressing up as women signified the perceived inversion of norms and symbolised a deep-seated sense of vulnerability and suspicion that appearances could not be trusted. In Soweto, rumours began to circulate that ambulances were used as cover to shoot at residents. These rumours signified the erosion of the social fabric of society and reflected the pervasive sense of vulnerability; even the most trusted spaces, meant to protect and heal, came to be viewed as potentially dangerous. What was common to these rumours – the dress, the ambulance, the coat – was that mundane aspects of everyday life were evacuated of their meaning and ascribed new symbolic significance.

In numerous instances, police were accused of aiding the attackers. By then, allegations abounded of a third force fueling and participating in the violence. Ample evidence confirms the nefarious role that different outfits of the security forces played in arming and training the IFP, their bias against township communities, and their active participation in violence.[120] Furthermore, police rarely arrested perpetrators of mass violence in the Vaal Triangle. Consequently, many people refrained from calling the police in case of an attack, believing that the police were biased. Some people stated with suspicion that during attacks, the telephone lines of nearby police stations frequently appeared to be out of order, indicating a sinister collusion between attackers and police. Rumours abounded that whenever road barricades set up by SDUs were removed and their members

---

116 Ivana Maček, *Sarajevo under Siege: Anthropology in Wartime* (Philadelphia: University of Pennsylvania Press, 2009), 6, 35.

117 Sverker Finnström, *Living with Bad Surroundings. War, History, and Everyday Moments in Northern Uganda* (Durham: Duke University Press, 2008), 168.

118 ZA HPRA AG2515 L2.1.

119 Ibid.

120 Amnesty International, "South Africa: State of Fear: Security Force Complicity in Torture and Political Killings, 1990–1992," June 9, 1992, AFR 53/009/1992, https://www.amnesty.org/en/documents/afr53/009/1992/en/, accessed August 15, 2022.

arrested, an IFP attack was imminent.[121] Electricity cuts were interpreted as another sign that authorities were colluding with the IFP; in several instances, electricity cuts had preceded attacks.[122] This high level of distrust in the police further eroded their legitimacy and undermined the rule of law.

10.6 Conclusion

In May 1994, shortly after the first non-racial democratic elections took place in South Africa, Thabani Dhlamini called Peace Action to raise his concerns regarding ongoing violence in Thokoza.[123] Dhlamini had played a leading role in the IFP's paramilitary Self Protection Units and had therefore been centrally involved in the conflict. In May 1994, after elections had successfully taken place, violence in the Kathorus region and elsewhere remained out of control. Dhlamini's initiative was one among others of people across the divide in the Kathorus region to call for a halt to the violence. In late June 1994, local SPU and SDU members met in the presence of church leaders and political office holders to negotiate a ceasefire. Eventually, several programmes were implemented to demobilise the SDUs and SPUs and to develop the region. But despite these initiatives, violence continued beyond 1994 and peace remained fragile: in 1996, violence flared again as IFP supporters had to vacate houses they had occupied prior to the elections.[124] The ongoing violence in the Kathorus region after April 1994 brought into sharp relief the extent to which political contestations continued after the elections, and the diverse agendas of perpetrators of violence at the grassroots level: many of the SDUs and SPUs, by then, were largely beyond the control of political parties. Violence remained particularly acute in KwaZulu-Natal, where the conflict continued to ravage the region for years and threatened political stability.

The transition to formal democracy in South Africa has largely been written about as a "transition from above", emphasising state formation, critical turning points, and influential elites. Therefore, it predominantly appears as a linear success story that moves from the evils of apartheid to the first democratic elections in 1994. But patterns of violence at the grassroots call into question the periodisation of the transition era, and they highlight the significance of localised dynamics in shaping violent conflict. Shifting the focus to the perceptions, experiences

---

121 ZA HPRA AG2515 L2.8.3, telephone monitoring reports from Sebokeng.
122 ZA HPRA AG2515 L2.8.3, telephone monitoring report from Sebokeng, June 24, 1992.
123 Kathorus Simunye News, date unknown. Courtesy of Thabani Dhlamini.
124 "Political Conflict flares at Thokoza," *Mail & Guardian* (December 13, 1996).

and strategies of individuals and communities who lived through this period reveals that viewed from below, the transition was fractured, non-linear, and shot through with uncertainty. For many people in Thokoza, Katlehong, or Sebokeng, the transition era was an era of liminality: apartheid rule was being dismantled, but what would come in its place was uncertain. As the chapter has shown, violence was integral to the complex ways in which the transition was contested and experienced.

Understanding the significance of transition violence requires both an analysis of its roots and causes, as well as its consequences. For individuals and communities that lived in the war-torn townships of the PWV, violence shaped everyday life dramatically. It seeped into the social fabric of communities and manifested itself in forms of communication, the production of space, and the organisation of daily routines. Both the lived experiences of violence but also its pervasive potential structured people's strategies, coping mechanisms, and perceptions of their world.

Almost thirty years after the first democratic elections, political tensions have abated but the legacy of violence remains palpable. Hopes that the living conditions of both township residents and hostel residents would improve have been frustrated to a large extent. Today, Thokoka – like many other townships in South Africa – is scarred by desperate poverty, unemployment, and a lack of infrastructure and services. The three hostels along Khumalo street lack the most basic services and they remain volatile and unsafe. Trust in the police's ability to protect people from crime remains low. Many people are traumatised by what they experienced and witnessed during *udlame*.[125] As Jonny Steinberg recently noted, "I'm not sure that South Africa has yet reckoned with how horrible the violence of the 1980s and early 1990s was, before democracy in 1994. It's too ghastly to look in the eye."[126] At the local level, initiatives to commemorate the dead and to remember this violent past have been launched. Among them is a recent photographic project titled *Inganekwane* (story telling), which brings together sixteen photographers to engage with the history of violence that took place around Khumalo street. The photographs are a reminder that South Africa's transition to democracy, praised as a 'miracle', was far from peaceful.

---

125 These observations are based on my interactions and my time spent in Katlehong, Thokoza, Sebokeng and other townships ravaged by the violence. There is a significant scholarship on the legacy of violence in South Africa. See, for example, Barolsky, "Transitioning out of Violence".

126 Johnny Steinberg, "Winnie and Nelson. New book paints a deeply human portrait of the Mandela marriage and South Africa's struggle," *The Conversation* (May 17, 2023), https://theconver sation.com/winnie-and-nelson-new-book-paints-a-deeply-human-portrait-of-the-mandela-mar riage-and-south-africas-struggle-205505, accessed May 19, 2023.

References

Barolsky, Vanessa. *Transitioning out of Violence: Snapshots from Kathorus*. Johannesburg: Centre for the Study of Violence and Reconciliation, 2005.

Barolsky, Vanessa. "Childhood in the Shadow of Violence." In *Violence and Non-Violence in Africa*, edited by Pahl Ahluwahlia, Louise Bethlehem, and Ruth Ginio, 175–189. London and New York: Routledge, 2007.

Beinart, William. "Introduction: Political and Collective Violence in Southern African Historiography." *Journal of Southern African Studies*, 18/3 (Special Issue: Political Violence in Southern Africa, 1992), 455–486. https://doi.org/10.1080/03057079208708324.

Bond, Patrick. *Elite Transition – Revised and Expanded Edition: From Apartheid to Neoliberalism in South Africa*. London: Pluto Press, 2014.

Bonner, Philip, and Noor Nieftagodien. "The Truth and Reconciliation Commission and the Pursuit of 'Social Truth': The Case of Kathorus." In *Commissioning the Past. Understanding South Africa's Truth and Reconciliation Commission*, edited by Deborah Posel, and Graeme Simpson, 173–203. Johannesburg: Wits University Press, 2002.

Bonner, Philip, and Vusi Ndima. "The Roots of Violence and Martial Zuluness on the East Rand." In *Zulu Identities. Being Zulu, Past and Present*, edited by Benedict Carton, John Laband, and Jabulani Sithole, 363–382. Scottsville: UKZN Press, 2008.

Bonner, Philip. "Keynote Address to the 'Life after Thirty' Colloquium." *African Studies* 69/1 (2010): 13–27. https://doi.org/10.1080/00020181003647157.

Bonnin, Deborah. "Space, Place and Identity: Political Violence in Mpumalanga Township, KwaZulu-Natal, 1987–1993." PhD diss., University of the Witwatersrand, 2008.

Bordia, Prashant, and Nicholas DiFonzo. "Psychological Motivations in Rumor Spread." In *Rumor Mills: The Social Impact of Rumor and Legends*, edited by Gary Fine, Véronique Campion-Vincent, and Chip Heath, 87–102. New Brunswick: Aldine Transaction, 2005.

Bridger, Emily. *Young Women against Apartheid: Gender, Youth and South Africa's Liberation Struggle*. Woodbridge: James Currey, 2021.

Chipkin, Ivor. "Nationalism as Such: Violence during South Africa's Political Transition." *Public Culture* 16/2 (2004): 315–335. https://doi.org/10.1215/08992363-16-2-315.

Elder, Glen S. "Malevolent Traditions: Hostel Violence and the Procreational Geography of Apartheid." *Journal of Southern African Studies* 29/4 (2003): 921–35. https://doi.org/10.1080/0305707032000135897.

Ellis, Stephen. "The Historical Significance of South Africa's Third Force." *Journal of Southern African Studies* 24/2 (1998), 261–299. https://doi.org/10.1080/03057079808708577.

Everatt, David. "Analysing Political Violence on the Reef, 1990–1994." In *The Role of Political Violence in South Africa's Democratisation*, edited by Ran Greestein, 95–142. Johannesburg: Community Agency for Social Enquiry, 2003.

Fine, Gary A. "Rumour Matters. An Introductory Essay." In *Rumor Mills: The Social Impact of Rumor and Legends*, edited by Gary Fine, Véronique Campion-Vincent, and Chip Heath, 1–14. New Brunswick: Aldine Transaction, 2005.

Finnström, Sverker. *Living with Bad Surroundings. War, History, and Everyday Moments in Northern Uganda*. Durham: Duke University Press, 2008.

Gibbs, Timothy. "Inkatha's Young Militants: Reconsidering Political Violence in South Africa." *Africa* 87/2 (2017): 362–386. https://doi.org/10.1017/S0001972016001005.

Guelke, Adrian. "Political Violence and the South African Transition." *Irish Studies in International Affairs* 4 (1993): 59–68.

Hickel, Jason. *Democracy as Death: The Moral Order of Anti-Liberal Politics in South Africa*. Oakland: University of California Press, 2015.

Kelly, Jill. *To Swim with Crocodiles: Land, Violence and Belonging in South Africa, 1880–1996*. East Lansing: Michigan State University Press, 2018.

Khulumani Support Group, *Katorus Stories*. Johannesburg: Khulumani, 2007.

Kynoch, Gary. *Township Violence and the End of Apartheid: War on the Reef*. Woodbridge: James Currey, 2018.

Lissoni, Arianna, Noor Nieftagodien and Shireen Ally. "'Life after Thirty' – A Critical Celebration." *African Studies* 69/1 (2010): 1–12. https://doi.org/10.1080/00020181003647082.

Maček, Ivana. *Sarajevo under Siege: Anthropology in Wartime*. Philadelphia: University of Pennsylvania Press, 2009.

Manganyi, Chabani, and Andre du Toit, eds. *Political Violence and the Struggle in South Africa*. New York: Palgrave Macmillan, 1990.

Marks, Monique. *Young Warriors. Youth Politics, Identity and Violence in South Africa*. Johannesburg, Wits University Press, 2001.

Mchunu, Mxolisi. *Violence and Solace: The Natal Civil War in Late-Apartheid South Africa*. Charlottesville and London: University of Virginia Press, 2020.

Minnaar, Anthony. "East Rand Townships under Siege." *Indicator SA* 10/4 (1993): 67–70. https://hdl. handle.net/10520/AJA0259188X_187, accessed August 20, 2022.

Naidoo, Sasha. "Exploring the Challenges Facing Former Combatants in Post-Apartheid South Africa." MA thesis, University of the Witwatersrand, 2007.

Nieftagodien, Noor. "Life in South Africa's Hostels: Carceral Spaces and Places of Refuge." *Comparatives Studies of South Asia, Africa and the Middle East* 37/3 (2017): 427–436. doi:10.1215/ 1089201x-4279128.

Nieftagodien, Noor. "The Place of 'The Local' in History Workshop's Local History." *African Studies* 69/ 1 (2010): 41–61. https://doi.org/10.1215/1089201x-4279128.

Nuttall, Tim, and John Wright, "Exploring beyond History with a Capital' H'." *Current Writing: Text and Reception in Southern Africa* 10/2 (1998): 38–61. https://doi.org/10.1080/1013929X.1998.9678042.

Pigou, Piers. "The Apartheid State and Violence: What has the Truth and Reconciliation Commission Found?" *Politikon* 28/2 (2001): 207–233. https://doi.org/10.1080/02589340120091664.

Posel, Deborah. "Social History and the Wits History Workshop." *African Studies* 69/1 (2010): 29–40. https://doi.org/10.1080/00020181003647165.

Robinson, Jason. "Fragments of the Past: Homeland Politics and the South African Transition." *Journal of Southern African Studies* 41/5 (2015): 953–967. https://doi.org/10.1080/03057070.2015.1064297.

Rueedi, Franziska. "The Hostel Wars in Apartheid South Africa: Rumour, Violence and the Politics of Belonging." *Social Identities* 26/6 (2020): 756–773. https://doi.org/10.1080/13504630.2020. 1814235.

Rueedi, Franziska. "'Our Bushes are the Houses': People's War and the Underground during the Insurrectionary Period in the Vaal Triangle, South Africa." *Journal of Southern African Studies* 46/6 (2020): 615–633. https://doi.org/10.1080/03057070.2020.1771072.

Rueedi, Franziska. *The Vaal Uprising of 1984 & the Struggle for Freedom in South Africa*. Woodbridge: James Currey, 2021.

Seekings, Jeremy. *The UDF: A History of the United Democratic Front in South Africa, 1983–1991*. Cape Town: David Philip, 2000.

Segal, Lauren. "The Human Face of Violence: Hostel Dwellers Speak." *Journal of Southern African Studies* 18/1 (1992): 190–231. https://doi.org/10.1080/03057079208708311.

Sitas, Ari. "The New Tribalism: Hostels and Violence." *Journal of Southern African Studies* 22/2 (1996): 235–248. https://doi.org/10.1080/03057079608708489.

Skosana, Dineo. "Grave Matters: Dispossession and the Desecration of Ancestral Graves by Mining Corporations in South Africa." *Journal of Contemporary African Studies* 40/1 (2022): 47–62. https://doi.org/10.1080/02589001.2021.1926937.

Sparks, Allister. *Tomorrow Is Another Country: The Inside Story of South Africa's Road to Change.* New York: Hill and Wang, 1995.

Steinberg, Johnny. "Winnie and Nelson. New book paints a deeply human portrait of the Mandela marriage and South Africa's struggle." *The Conversation* (May 17, 2023).

Biographical Notes

Brigitta Bernet is a senior lecturer in modern history at Zurich University. After receiving her PhD (2013), she was a Research Fellow at the Science Studies Unit at the University of Edinburgh, at re: work at Humboldt University in Berlin and at Science Po's Centre d'Histoire in Paris. From 2017 to 2022 she was a Senior Researcher at the DFG Leibniz Research Group "The Contemporary History of Historiography" (Trier University). In addition to her academic work, Brigitta is responsible for science policy at a Swiss trade union. Her research interests include the political history of knowledge (especially of the human sciences and historiography), the history of work, and the history of political movements. She is co-editor of *What's Left of Marxism. Historiography and the Possibilities of Thinking with Marxian Themes and Concepts* (Berlin: De Gruyter 2020).

Etta Grotrian works at the intersection of data, emotion and storytelling. Currently at the Übersee-Museum in Bremen, she oversees several multidisciplinary collection-management projects. She has also set up partnerships with cultural and academic organisations in Northern Europe and Asia-Pacific. This includes NEO Collections and Oceania Digital/The Blue Continent. As a historian, Etta has researched museum history and theory, digital museum practice, and participatory approaches to historical research. She has worked as a curator of multimedia and online content at the Jewish Museum Berlin, and lectures on Public History at the Freie Universität Berlin and Universität Bremen. Etta is committed to the development of new museum practices on topics such as fair pay, diversity and inclusion, and decolonisation of museum institutions.

Menachem Klein is Professor Emeritus in the Department of Political Science at Bar-Ilan University, Israel. He studied Middle East and Islamic Studies at the Hebrew University of Jerusalem and was a fellow at Oxford University, a visiting professor in MIT, Fernand Braudel Senior Fellow at the European University Institute, Florence, a visiting scholar in Leiden University, Holland, and a Visiting Research Fellow in King's College London. His research focuses on the history of Palestine and Jerusalem since the late 19th century. His book *Lives in Common – Arabs and Jews in Jerusalem, Jaffa and Hebron* (2014) was recognised by the *New Republic* as one of best non-fiction books of 2014. *Lives in Common* has had German and Hebrew editions.

Yannick Lengkeek is a historian of everyday life under dictatorial rule, with a particular focus on the Portuguese Estado Novo regime. His published and forthcoming works cover histories of play and leisure, lived experiences of itinerant (ethnic and social) groups in Southern Europe, as well as comparative and global perspectives on dictatorships and far-right movements. He completed his PhD in Modern History in 2023 at the University of St Andrews, where he worked as a member of the ERC-funded project "Dictatorship as experience: A comparative history of everyday life and the 'lived experience' of dictatorship in Mediterranean Europe (1922–1975)". He previously studied at Leiden University and the University of Tübingen. He has worked with archives and collections in Portugal, Indonesia, the Netherlands, and Germany, and taught at the University of St Andrews and, more recently, the University of Birmingham.

Irit Carmon Popper is an art curator and scholar in the history and theory of visual culture. She earned her BA and MFA in Philosophy and Art History at The Hebrew University in Jerusalem, her Curatorial and Museum Studies at the Faculty of the Arts at Tel Aviv University, and her PhD at the Faculty of Architecture and Town Planning at the Technion IIT in Haifa. She holds a post-doctorate fellowship from

https://doi.org/10.1515/9783111522180-011

the Frankel Institute for Advanced Judaic Studies (LSA), University of Michigan, Ann Arbor, USA. Her interdisciplinary research explores the interchange between contemporary art and architectural preservation to safeguard cultural heritage in historical and contested sites, such as the Israeli-Palestinian conflict. This work has been recognised with an Honorable Mention for the Ben Halpern Award for Best Dissertation (AIS) and the Bruno Zevi Foundation Award in the Study of Architectural Culture (2020). Her most recent publication is included in the book "Dada and Its Later Manifestations in the Geographic Margins" (2024). She is an Associate Teaching Fellow at Haifa University; Technion IIT, Haifa; and Musrara School for Art and Society, Jerusalem. Her academic courses cover the history and theory of art, curation, design, and architecture. Her curatorial experience includes exhibitions in The Israel Museum, Jerusalem, Petach Tikva Museum of Art, Umm El-Fahem Art Gallery, Beit Ha'Gefen Arab-Jewish Culture Center in Haifa, and IKONA Gallery of Photography in Venice, Italy.

Olaf Kaltmeier is Professor of Iberoamerican History at Bielefeld University. He is director of CALAS, the Maria Sibylla Merian Center for Advanced Latin American Studies in the Humanities and Social Sciences and founding director of the Center for InterAmerican Studies (CIAS) at Bielefeld University. He has done research and teaching in Mexico, Ecuador, Chile, Bolivia, Peru, Argentina, and the USA.

Lutz Raphael is Professor emeritus of Contemporary History at the University of Trier. In 2013, he received the Wilhelm-Gottfried-Leibniz-Prize of the DFG. His research focuses on the contemporary history of historiography in time of globalisations and the social history of de-industrialisation in Western Europe since the 1970s. His recent publications include *Beyond Coal and Steel. A Social History of Western Europe after the Boom* (2023; original German version 2019); *Ordnungsmuster und Deutungskämpfe. Wissenspraktiken im Europa des 20. Jahrhunderts* (2018); *Professional Historians in Public. Old and New Roles Revisited* (2023, co-edited with Berber Bevernage); and *Vorgeschichte der Gegenwart.* (2016, co-edited with Anselm Doering-Manteuffel and Thomas Schlemmer).

Dario Di Rosa studied Anthropology in Italy (BA, MA) before leading on to a PhD in Pacific History at the Australian National University. For his PhD, he conducted extensive archival research in several countries and spent 15 months in Papua New Guinea conducting ethnographic fieldwork, working on contemporary Kerewo-speakers' narratives of their colonial past. The focus of his doctoral work was on the uses Kerewo people made of that past in order to make sense of their perceived "frustrated modernity". Given the interdisciplinary nature of his project, Dario has developed ever since a keen interest in exploring the epistemological strengths and limits of several historiographical strands, including their methodological implications. Dario is currently lecturing in History at the University of the South Pacific.

Franziska Rueedi is Senior Lecturer at the University of Zurich and a research associate at the History Workshop, University of the Witwatersrand. She holds a DPhil in Modern History from the University of Oxford and an MA in African Studies from the University of Basel. After completing her doctorate, she was a postdoctoral researcher at the University of the Witwatersrand and later, Deputy Professor of African History at the University of Bayreuth. Rueedi's research focuses on political violence and peacebuilding, protest movements, transnational activism, and the politics of truth commissions, transitional justice and historical knowledge production in South Africa. She has a special interest in the global connections between Africa and other regions. Her first monograph, *The Vaal Uprising of 1984 and the Struggle for Freedom in South Africa,* was published by Boydell & Brewer in 2021. The research for this project was funded by SNSF grant no. 186639 and no. 174427. She is currently working on her second monograph, *Between Violence and Peace: South Africa's Global Transition.*

Benjamin Zachariah is a member of the research staff at the Einstein Forum in Potsdam. He completed his undergraduate degree in history, philosophy and literature at Presidency College, Calcutta, and his PhD in history from Trinity College, Cambridge. His research interests include the politics of historical knowledge, historical theory and historiography, global fascism, transnational revolutionary networks, nationalisms, and memory. His publications include *Nehru* (2004), *Developing India: An Intellectual and Social History, c. 1930–1950* (2005), *Nation Games* (2020), and *After the Last Post: The Lives of Indian Historiography in India* (2019). He is co-editor of *The Internationalist Moment: South Asia, Worlds, and World Views 1917–1939* (2015), and of *What's Left of Marxism: Historiography and the Possibility of Thinking with Marxian Themes and Concepts* (2020).

Selected Bibliography

1 Classics

Dunbar-Ortiz, Roxanne. *An Indigenous Peoples' History of the United States*, Boston: Beacon Press, 2015.

Federici, Silvia. *Caliban and the Witch: Women, the Body and Primitive Accumulation*, USA: Autonomedia, 2004.

Fuentes, Marisa. *Dispossessed Lives: Enslaved Women, Violence, and the Archive*, Philadelphia: University of Pennsylvania Press, 2018.

Galeano, Eduardo. *Genesis: Memory of Fire*, Volume I–V, New York: W.W. Norton, 1998ff.

Genovese, Eugene. *Roll, Jordan, Roll! The World the Slaves Made*. New York: Pantheon, 1974.

Ginzburg, Carlo. *The Cheese and the Worms: The Cosmos of a Sixteenth-Century Miller*. London: Routledge & Kegan Paul, 1980 [1976].

Hill, Christopher. *The World Turned Upside Down: Radical Ideas in the English Revolution*, London: Penguin, 1972.

Hill, Christopher. *Revolution, 1640: An Essay*. London: Lawrence & Wishart, 1940.

James, C.L.R. *Black Jacobins: Toussaint L'Ouverture and the San Domingo Revolution*. London: Penguin, 2001 [1938].

Lefebvre, Georges. *The Coming of the French Revolution*. Princeton: Princeton University Press, 2015 [1939].

Levi, Giovanni. *Inheriting Power: The Story of an Exorcist*. Chicago: University of Chicago Press, 1988.

Linebaugh, Peter. *The London Hanged: Crime and Civil Society in the Eighteenth Century*. London: Verso Books, 1991.

Rediker, Marcus. *The Amistad Rebellion: An Atlantic Odyssey of Slavery and Freedom*, Penguin, 2012.

Rediker, Marcus and Peter Linebaugh, *The Many-Headed Hydra: Sailors, Laves, Commoners, and the Hidden History for the Revolutionary Atlantic*. Boston: Beacon Press, 2000.

Rowbotham, Sheila. *Hidden from History, 300 Years of Women's Oppression and the Fight Against it*, London: Pluto Press 1977.

Thompson, E.P. *The Making of the English Working Class*. London: Penguin, 1963.

van Onselen, Charles. *The Seed is Mine. The Life of Kas Maine, A South African Sharecropper 1894–1985*. New York: Hill and Wang, 1996.

Zemon Davis, Natalie. *The Return of Martin Guerre*. Cambridge, MA: Harvard University Press, 1982.

2 Critical Theory and Historiography

Aguirre Rojas, Carlos Antonio. *Microhistoria italiana: Modo de empleo*. Rosario: Prohistoria Ediciones, 2017.

Appadurai, Arjun. "The Past as a Scarce Resource." *Man* 16, no. 2 (1981): 201–19.

Barrett James R. *History from the Bottom Up and the Inside Out: Ethnicity, Race, and Identity in Working-Class History*, Durham and London: Duke University Press, 2017.

Benjamin, Walter. "Theses on the Philosophy of History (On the Concept of History)." In *Illuminations*, edited by Hannah Arendt, translated by Harry Zohn (Schocken Books: New York 2007), 253–264.

https://doi.org/10.1515/9783111522180-012

290 —— Selected Bibliography

Berg, Eberhard, and Martin Fuchs, eds. *Kultur, soziale Praxis, Text. Die Krise der ethnographischen Repräsentation*. Frankfurt am Main: Suhrkamp Verlag, 1995.

Bernet, Brigitta. "The Postwar Marxist Milieu of Microhistory: Heterodoxy, Activism and the Formation of a Critical Historiographical Perspective." In *What's Left of Marxism: Historiography and the Possibilities of Thinking with Marxian Themes and Concepts*, edited by Benjamin Zachariah, Lutz Raphael, and Brigitta Bernet, 37–64. Berlin: De Gruyter Oldenbourg, 2020.

Biersack, Aletta. "Local Knowledge, Local History: Geertz and Beyond." In *The New Cultural History*, edited by Lynn Hunt, 72–96. Berkeley – Los Angeles – London: University of California Press, 1989.

Bishop, Claire, ed. *Participation: Documents on Participatory Art*, London and Cambridge, Massachusetts: Whitechapel, The MIT Press, 2004.

Blackbourn, David. "Mikrogeschichte." In *Landschaften der deutschen Geschichte: Aufsätze zum 19. und 20. Jahrhundert*, edited by David Blackbourn, 353–367. Göttingen: Vandenhoeck & Ruprecht, 2016.

Burke, Peter. "Popular Culture Reconsidered." *Storia della Storiografia* 17 (1990): 40–49.

Burke, Peter. "The Cultural History of Intellectual Practices: An Overview." In *Political Concepts and Time: New Approaches to Conceptual History*, edited by Javier Fernándes Sebastián, 103–130. Santander: Cantabria University Press, 2011.

Carey, David. *Oral History in Latin America. Unlocking the Spoken Archive*. New York: Routledge, 2017.

Certeau, Michel de. *The Practice of Everyday Life*. Translated by Steven Rendall. Berkeley: University of California Press, 1984.

Cerutti, Simona. "Who is below? E.P. Thompson, historien des sociétés modernes: une relecture." *Annales. Histoire, Sciences Sociales* 70, no. 4 (2015): 931–956.

Charle, Christophe. "Micro-histoire sociale et macro-histoire sociale: Quelques réflexions sur les effets des changements de méthode depuis quinze ans en histoire sociale." *Histoire sociale – histoire globale? Actes du colloque de l'IHMC*, edited by Christophe Charle, 45–57. Paris: Editions de la MSH, 1993.

Corona Berkin, Sarah, and Olaf Kaltmeier, eds. *En diálogo. Metodologías horizontales en Ciencias Sociales y Culturales*. Barcelona: Gedisa, 2012.

Di Rosa, Dario. "Microstoria, Pacific History, and the Question of Scale: Two or Three Things That We Should Know About Them." *The Journal of Pacific History* 53, no. 1 (2018): 25–43.

Dirks, Nicholas B. "Is Vice Versa? Historical Anthropologies and Anthropological Histories' Terence." In *The Historic Turn in the Human Sciences*, edited by J. McDonald, 17–51. Ann Arbor: The University of Michigan Press, 1996.

Eley, Geoff. *History Made Conscious: Politics of Knowledge, Politics of the Past*. New York: Verso Books, 2023.

Felski, Rita. "The Invention of Everyday Life." *New Formations* 39 (2000): 15–31.

Ginzburg, Carlo, and Carlo Poni. "Was ist Mikrogeschichte?" *Geschichtswerkstatt* 6 (1985): 48–52.

Ginzburg, Carlo. "Clues: Roots of a Scientific Paradigm." *Theory and Society* 7/3 (May, 1979): 273–288.

Ginzburg, Carlo. "Microhistory: Two or Three Things I Know about it." *Critical Inquiry* 20 (Autumn, 1993): 10–35.

Gramsci, Antonio. *Selections from the Prison Notebooks*, ed. and trans. Quintin Hoare and Geoffrey Nowell Smith. New York: International Publishers, 1971.

Gribaudi, Maurizio. "La lunga marcia della microstoria." In *Microstoria: A venticinque anni da 'L'eredità immateriale'*, edited by Paola Lanaro, 9–23. Milano: Franco Angeli, 2011.

Hartman, Saidiya. "Venus in Two Acts." *small axe* 26 (2008), 1–14, https://warwick.ac.uk/fac/arts/history/research/centres/blackstudies/venus_in_two_acts.pdf, accessed November 09, 2024.

Heer, Hannes, and Volker Ulrich, eds. *Geschichte entdecken. Erfahrungen und Projekte der neuen Geschichtsbewegung*. Reinbek: Rowohlt, 1985.

Hobsbawm, Eric. "History from Below – Some Reflections." In *History from Below. Studies in Popular Protest and Popular Ideology* by Eric Hobsbwam, 12–28. Oxford: Basil Blackwell, 1988.

Kaltmeier, Olaf, and Sarah Corona Berkin, eds. *Methoden dekolonialisieren. Eine Werkzeugkiste zur Demokratisierung der Sozial- und Kulturwissenschaften*. Münster: Westfälisches Dampfboot, 2012.

Kroll, Thomas. "Die Anfänge der microstoria: Methodenwechsel, Erfahrungswandel und transnationale Rezeption in der europäischen Historiographie der 1970er und 1980er Jahre." In *Perspektiven durch Retrospektiven: Wirtschaftsgeschichtliche Beiträge*, edited by Jeanette Granda, and Jürgen Schreiber, 267–287. Köln: Böhlau, 2013.

Langhamer, Claire. "Who the Hell are Ordinary People? Ordinariness as a Category of Historical Analysis." *Transactions of the Royal Historical Society* 28 (2018): 175–95.

Levi, Giovanni. "On Microhistory." In *New Perspectives on Historical Writing*, edited by Peter Burke, 97–119. Cambridge: Polity Press, 2001.

Lindenberger, Thomas, and Michael Wildt. "Radikale Pluralität. Geschichtswerkstätten als praktische Wissenschaftskritik." *Archiv für Sozialgeschichte* 29 (1989): 393–411.

Lindqvist, Sven. *Dig Where You Stand. How to Research a Job*. New York: Watkins Media, 2023 [1978].

Lüdtke, Alf. *Eigen-Sinn. Fabrikalltag, Arbeitererfahrungen und Politik vom Kaiserreich bis in den Faschismus*. Hamburg: Ergebnisse Verlag, 1993.

Magnússon, Sigurdur Gylfi, and István M. Szijártó, eds. *What is Microhistory? Theory and Practice*. London, New York: Routledge, 2013.

Marin, C.G., and M. Roy. "Narrative Resistance: A Conversation with Historian Marcus Rediker." *Workplace* 30 (2018), 54–69.

Mignolo, Walter D. *Local Histories/Global Designs. Coloniality, Subaltern Knowledges, and Border Thinking*. Princeton: Princenton University Press, 2000.

Munro, Doug. *The Ivory Tower and Beyond: Participant Historians of the Pacific*. New Castle upon Tyne: Cambridge Scholars Publishing, 2009.

Nieftagodien, Noor. "The Place of 'The Local' in History Workshop's Local History." *African Studies* 69/1 (2010), 41–61, https://doi.org/10.1080/00020181003647181.

Peltonen, Matti. "How Marginal are the Margins Today? On the Historiographical Place of Microhistory." In *Microhistory and the Picaresque Novel: A First Exploration into Commensurable Practices*, edited by Binne de Haan, and Konstantin Mierau, 29–46. Newcastle upon Tyne: Cambridge Scholar Publishing, 2014.

Perks, Robert, und Alistair Thomson, eds. *The Oral History Reader*. London: Routledge, 2006.

Philipp, June. "Traditional Historical Narrative and Action-Oriented (or Ethnographic) History." *Historical Studies* 20, no. 80 (1 April 1983): 339–52. https://doi.org/10.1080/10314618308682932.

Pihlainen, Kalle. "The End of Oppositional History?" *Rethinking History: The Journal of Theory and Practice* 15/4 (2011), 463–488.

Posel, Deborah. "Social History and the Wits History Workshop." *African Studies* 69/1 (2010), 29–40. https://doi.org/10.1080/00020181003647165.

Rediker, Marcus. "The Poetics of History from Below." American Historical Association *Perspectives*, September 2010. https://www.historians.org/perspectives-article/the-poetics-of-history-from-below-september-2010/, accessed November 09, 2024.

Rosental, Paul-André. "Microstoria." In *Notionnaires*, Vol. II, 530–532. Paris: Encyclopaedia Universalis, 2005.

Samuel, Raphael. "People's History." In *People's History and Socialist Theory*, edited by Raphael Samuel, xv–xxxix. London: Routledge, 2016.

Sarkar, Sumit. "The Decline of the Subaltern in Subaltern Studies." In *Writing Social History*, edited by Sumit Sarkar, 92–108. Delhi: Oxford University Press, 1997.

Schnickmann, Alexander. "Unter einem anderen Mond: Carlo Ginzburg und die Hermeneutik der Risse." *Weimarer Beiträge: Zeitschrift für Literaturwissenschaft, Ästhetik und Kulturwissenschaften* 1 (2020), 17–35.

Schlumbohm, Jürgen, ed. *Mikrogeschichte – Makrogeschichte: Komplementär oder inkommensurabel?* Göttingen: Wallstein, 1998.

Schulze, Winfried, ed. *Sozialgeschichte, Alltagsgeschichte, Mikro-Historie: Eine Diskussion*. Göttingen: Vandenhoeck & Ruprecht, 1994.

Sharpe, Jim. "History from Below." In *New Perspectives on Historical Writing*, edited by Peter Burke, 24–41. Cambridge: Polity Press, 1991.

Sharpless, Rebecca. "The History of Oral History." In *Thinking about Oral History. Theories and Applications*, edited by Thomas Lee Charlton, Lois E. Myers, and Rebecca Sharpless, 7–32. Lanham: AltaMira Press, 2008.

Spivak, Gayatri Chakravorty. *A Critique of Postcolonial Reason. Toward a History of the Vanishing Present*. Cambridge: Harvard University Press, 1999.

Stoler, Ann Laura. *Along the Archival Grain. Epistemic Anxieties and Colonial Common Sense*. Princeton: Princeton University Press, 2008.

Thompson, E. P. "History from Below." *Times Literary Supplement*. 7 April 1966.

Trivellato, Francesca. "Microstoria/ Microhistoire/ Microhistory." *French Politics, Culture & Society* 33 (2015): 122–134.

Wood, Andy. "History from Below and Early Modern Social History." In: *The Many-Headed Monster: The History of 'The Unruly Sort of Clowns' and other Early Modern Peculiarities*. https://manyheadedmonster.com/2013/08/21/andy-wood-history-from-below-and-early-modern-social-history/, accessed November 20, 2023.

Index

academia, academic networks, academic field 5, 18–20, 29, 76, 80, 114, 117, 143, 156–158, 162, 164, 166–167

African National Congress (ANC) 24, 259

Afro-American Movements, African American 141, 153, 236, 242

agency, active agent paradigm 17, 19, 24, 46–47, 68, 115–116, 119, 124, 190, 227–253, 260

Agrarian society 16, 67, 70

Aguirre Rojas, Carlos Antonio 78–79

Al-alami, Musa 188–189

Alexander, Sally 6

Alfaro Reyes, Eloy 146

Alltagsgeschichte 5, 64, 77, 98–102, 107, 228

Alvarado Lincopi, Claudio 154–155

Amin, Idi 35

Amin, Shahid 40–41

Anderson, Peter 238

Andes, Andean Region 144–145, 148, 159

Annales School 64, 77

anthropology 6, 17, 22, 63, 65, 69, 113–114, 122–126, 128, 144–145, 150, 153, 155, 158–159, 162, 227, 278

anthropology, social 149–150, 153, 158–159

Anti-colonialism 22

Antileo Baeza, Enrique 154–155

Apartheid era 261, 264

Appadurai, Arjun 127

Arab jews 180–181, 183–185

Arab-Israeli conflict 184, 200

Arad, Arad Contemporary Art Center 217

Arbeitskreis Regionalgeschichte Konstanz (Working Group for the Regional History of Konstanz) 94–97

archaeology 216

archive 10–12, 37, 40, 42, 49, 66, 89, 94, 103, 106–107, 116, 142–143, 148–149, 151, 177, 184, 186–190, 192–193, 211, 227, 238, 270

Archive, Israeli State 187–188

Archive, Jerusalem Municipality Historical Archive 189

Argentina 78, 151, 165

Aristotle 50

art, artist 6, 12, 18, 23, 118, 153, 160, 197–198, 200, 211–212, 223

Australian National University (ANU) Canberra, Canberra School 114–115, 117–120, 122–123

Australian National University Canberra 31, 130, 132, 135

authenticity 16, 21, 29–53, 127, 158

authority 12, 31, 38, 42, 60, 131, 149, 152, 162–166, 168, 182, 186, 188, 215, 237, 247, 265, 273

Avci, Yasemin 186

Avissar, David 183

Azores 237

Azzali, Gianfranco 71

Bakhtin, Mikhail 70

Balfour Declaration 1917 181, 183

Bali 227

Barfußhistoriker (barefoot historians) 22, 47, 85–89, 98–102

Barolsky, Vanessa 260, 271

Bedouins 23, 198, 200–205, 212–213, 220, 224

Behar-Perahia, David 197, 213–214

Bellocchio, Piergiorgio 71

Ben Kiki, Haim 183

Bengal 37, 39, 43, 45

Benjamin, Walter 9–10, 21, 37

Berlin 6, 9, 12, 14–15, 35–36, 61, 69, 87–88, 98–100, 102, 104, 144

Berliner Volksuni 88, 105

Bermani, Cesare 71–72

Biersack, Aletta 124, 126

Billiards 229, 237, 243–253

BIMKOM–Planners for Plannings rights 205, 208

Bishop, Claire 198, 209–210

Black Lives Matter 36

Blackbourn, David 77–78

Boal, Augusto 5

Bolivia 141, 145–146, 150, 165–166, 286

Bologna, Sergio 72

Bosio, Gianni 71–72

Bourdieu, Pierre 19, 157, 248

Bourriaud, Nicolas 210

https://doi.org/10.1515/9783111522180-013

294 — Index

Brass, Tom 120–121
Brazil 5, 79, 161
Brecht, Bertolt 12–13
British Mass Observation Archive 227
Bruno Kreisky Forum Wien 179–180
Budeiri, Musa 188
Burgos, Claudio Hernández 238
Burgos-Debray, Elizabeth 154, 164
Buthelezi, Mangosuthu 259

Caillois, Roger 233–234
Calcutta 39, 78
Cambridge University 5, 34, 36, 114, 127, 130–131, 206, 233, 236
Camp David summit 2000 179
Canada 239, 244
capitalism 16, 34, 46, 48, 120, 134–135, 164, 228
Carey, David 145, 164, 167
Casas do Povo (People's Houses) 243
Castel, Yosef Haim 183
Catholic Church, Catholicism 70, 252
Centro de Estudios y Documentación Mapuche Liwen, temuco 146
Cerutti, Simona 76
Cham, Gerardo 153
Chappell, David 119
Chatterjee, Partha 40–41, 44
Checola, Giusy 209
Chicago 9, 32, 122, 125, 184, 216, 233, 235–236
Chinese Cultural Revolution 39
Chinese Revolution 6
Christian Democratic Party (DC) 65
Circoli di cultura 71
Circolo Gianni Bosio 72
Cirese, Alberto 71
class struggle, class, languages of 17, 22, 60, 65, 70, 253
Cold War 22, 35, 45–48, 235
Colombian Truth commission 147, 152
Colonial power 14, 113
colonialism, anti- 22
coloniality 141, 143, 152, 160, 168
Columbia University New York 7, 159, 181–182, 200, 206, 237, 248

Comisión de Verdad Histótrica y Nuevo Trato 147–148, 152
common people 4, 13–14, 19, 22, 24–25, 51, 133
Common view art collective 23, 197, 211–212, 223
Communist Party 13, 22, 34
Communist Party of Great Britain (CPGB) Historians' Group 4–5, 21, 33, 35
communitarian 14
Comunidad de Historia Mapuche 146, 155, 166
Condori Mamani, Gregorio 153
conservative 14, 51, 75, 77, 96, 129, 177, 180–181, 192, 221, 247
Cook, James 124
Cornejo Polar, Antonio 163
Corner, Paul 238
Corona, Sarah 144, 151–152, 156–157, 160–161, 163–164
Corris, Peter 119–121
counter-history 10, 23–24
Crapanzano, Vincent 162
Crespo, Carolina 165
Croce, Benedetto 65
Crocombe, Ron 127
cultural turn 18–19, 61–64, 69
culturalism 44–45, 134

Dann, Otto 95
Dar es Salaam, University of 73
Davidson, James W. 114–115, 117
Davin, Anna 6
Davis, Natalie Zemon 7, 11, 41, 78
De Certeau, Michel 192, 231, 235
De Cieza de Léon, Pedro 143
De la Vega, Garcilaso 144
De Martino, Ernesto 69–71, 75
De Sahagún, Bernardino 143
De Sousa Santos, Boaventura 141
decolonisation 15, 22–23, 126, 129–131, 141–169, 253
democracy 9, 15, 24, 38, 134, 146, 279–280
democratisation, democratising history 3–4, 29, 32, 146
Dening, Greg 122, 124
Deutscher Gewerkschaftsbund (DGB) 91

Index — **295**

dictatorship 15, 145–146, 229, 236, 238
Dolci, Danilo 74
dominant culture 6, 51, 222
Dostoevsky, Fjodor 227
Durutalo, Simione 116–117, 134

East India company 43
Eastern bloc 6, 31
Eastern Europe 5, 15
Ecuador 141, 161, 167
Egypt 35, 179, 185
EHESS, Paris 77
Eley, Geoff 8, 63, 95
Elias, Norbert 232
elitism 36, 45, 248
empiricism 121, 123
England 6, 33, 48, 85, 200
English Civil War 118
enlightenment 13, 47, 187, 232
Environmental Reconciliation 198, 213
equality 197, 205
Escalante Cutierrez, Carmen 154
escapism 229, 234, 236
Estado novo Portugal 24, 227–253
Ethnohistory 145
Eurocentrism 47, 141
events 16, 21, 65, 78, 93, 104, 106, 132, 147,
    149–150, 178, 185, 231, 234, 244
everyday culture, everyday life 16, 22, 51, 63–64,
    73–75, 85, 99, 104, 144–145, 161, 183–187, 190,
    193, 198, 229–239, 262, 264, 273, 278, 280
Èvora 240–241, 243–244
experience 4, 13, 17, 77, 93, 97, 178, 191, 205–206,
    209–210, 229–230, 235, 237, 239–240,
    259–260, 262, 266, 270–271, 275, 279–280
extractivism, colonial 155

Fabian, Johannes 159
facts 10, 20, 147–148, 150, 191, 206
Falklands War 51
Farberoff, Dan 197, 199, 204, 213–214,
    216–217, 220
fascism, fascist 13, 19, 75, 236, 239
Federal Republic of Germany 5–6, 85, 97, 101–102
feminism 5
Ferris, Kate 232–233, 236, 238

Feste dell'unità 66
Fiji 116, 129
Filer, Colin 130–131
Firstenberg Riegelhaupt, Joyce 237–238
Foucault, Michel 47, 231
France 5, 9, 19, 69, 78
fraternity 15
freedom 15, 24, 183, 236, 252, 262–264
Friedrich Ebert Stiftung 92

Galeano, Eduardo 7, 154
gambling 24, 229–230, 234–244, 247, 251–253
gaming 24, 228, 234
Gandhi, Mohandas 41
Geertz, Clifford 122–123, 125, 227, 234, 251
Geertz, Hildred 125
Genovese, Eugene 9
German Peasants' War 105
Germany, German romantic 14, 47, 61, 92,
    99–100, 167, 228
Germany, West Germany 22, 77, 85–108
Geschichte des kleinen Mannes. see common
    people
Geschichtswerkstätten (German history
    workshops) 85–108
Giebeler, Cornelia 161
Gilly, Adolfo 59–61, 79–80
Gilroy, Paul 50
Ginzburg, Leone 68–69
Giustizia e Libertà 68
Glienke, Dieter 90, 107
Global South 6, 15, 19–20, 52, 142
Godfrey, Mark 211
Gramsci, Antonio 7, 13, 29–30, 43, 64–65, 69, 78
Grandin, Greg 154
grass-roots 31, 68, 71–73, 92, 229, 261, 271, 279
Gräv där du star (Dig where you stand) 88,
    91–92, 103
Great Britain 4, 9, 18, 21, 33, 113, 180
Grendi, Edoardo 63
Gribaudi, Maurizio 61, 75–76
Gribetz, Jonathan 180
Gruppo Gramsci 73
Guaman de Ayala, Felipe 152
Guatemala 167
Guha, Ranajit 31, 37–41, 46, 123

296 —— Index

Hall, Catherine 47
Hamburg 86, 90–94, 98, 102, 106–107, 230
Hannah-Arendt-Institut für
    Totalitarismusforschung Dresden 102
Hau'ofa, Epeli 131–132
Hawai'i 116, 129
Heimat 14, 95–96, 100, 104
Henricks, Thomas S. 248
Herder, Johann Gottfried 114
hierarchy 20, 24, 40, 184, 273
Hill, Christopher 4, 7, 48–49, 118, 145
Hirschberg, Abraham Shmuel 181
historian 3–4, 6, 8–10, 12–13, 18–19, 21–22, 30,
    33–34, 37, 39, 42–43, 47, 49, 51–52, 59–60,
    69, 76–77, 85–86, 91, 95, 98–102, 108, 115,
    117–119, 121, 123, 125, 129, 131, 143–146,
    148–154, 165, 167, 177, 181, 184–186, 192,
    199, 205–207, 212, 228, 234, 236, 250–252
historical culture 21, 61–62, 65, 69, 72
historicism 9, 65
Historische Sozialwissenschaft 98–99
history workshop 6, 47, 71–73, 85–87, 94, 97–98,
    100, 102, 106, 146, 154, 166, 260–261
history workshop movement 6
history, Imperial History 22, 114–115
history, popularisation of 32
Hobsbawm, Eric 4, 9, 33–35, 64, 122, 145
Howe, Kerry 115, 117, 121, 124
Huizinga, Johan 227, 231, 234, 251
Husseini, Faisal 179

Identity
– local 182, 184–186
– national 23, 49
– politics 15, 145
Ilaquiche Licta, Raúl 146
Imperialism, cultural 142, 156
Inca Empire 144
indentured labour 119, 129
India 35, 37, 39, 43, 45–46, 78
indigeneity 141, 143–155, 168, 207
indigenous activists 146
indigenous movements 143
indigenous peoples 125, 145–147, 208
indigenous rights 129
indigenous scholars 114, 131
Indochina 6

industrial society 16, 87
inequality 22–24, 124, 156, 168
inheritance 41
Inkatha Freedom Party 24, 263
Institut für Zeitgeschichte München (Institute
    for Contemporary History Munich) 94
intellectual 17, 19, 21–22, 24, 32, 34, 36, 44, 50,
    52–53, 60–62, 68, 73, 77, 79, 116, 126–127,
    130, 141–142, 146, 164, 179, 206
internationalist 52
Intifada 179
Israel 23, 177–180, 184–189, 197–206, 208, 211,
    215–216, 223
Israel/Palestine 23, 179–185, 191, 201
Israeli-Palestinian conflict 184, 197, 223, 286
Italian communist Party (PCI) 60, 65–70, 72
Italian socialist Party (PSI) 74
Italy 5, 21–22, 35, 60–61, 65–73, 76–77, 236,
    238–239

James, C.L.R. 7
Japan 113
Jerusalem 23, 177–193
Johannesburg 24, 259–260, 263–264, 272–273, 276

Kapoor, Ilan 160
Kathorus 260, 263–268, 276, 279
Kautsky, Karl 66
Keesing, Roger 128
Kerr, Aphra 227–228
Khrushchev 5, 33–34
knowledge, geopolitics of 162, 168–169
knowledge, hegemonic 142
Kocka, Jürgen 98
Konstanz 94–97, 106
Kowii, Ariruma 142
Krankenhagen, Gernot 90, 93–94
Kroll, Thomas 61, 76
KwaZulu 259–260, 263, 265, 267, 269, 270, 272,
    276, 279
Kwon, Miwon 209

La Trobe University, Melbourne, Melbourne
    Group 121–122
Lal, Brij 115, 129
Lamb, Charles 227
Latin America 18, 23, 60, 78, 141–169

Le Roy Ladurie, Emmanuel 228
Leckie, Jacqueline 119, 122
Leenen-Young, Marcia 132
Lefebvre, Georges 7, 9
Lefebvre, Henri 192, 231–232
left 15–16, 18, 21–24, 32–33, 35, 44, 46, 51, 60,
    62, 67, 72, 74–76, 114, 124, 126–133, 154,
    163, 178, 187, 199, 201, 207, 260–261, 267,
    272, 275
Left Book Club 33
leisure 24, 75, 228–229, 231–234, 236, 239–244,
    248, 250
Lemir, Vincent 184, 186
Lenin, Vladimir I. 66
Lepetit, Bernard 77
Levi, Carlo 68–69
Levi, Giovanni 9, 63, 68, 73–75, 77–78
liberalism, liberal 15–16, 19, 47, 67–71, 133–134,
    221, 239
Lindenberger, Thomas 102, 107
Lindqvist, Sven 88–89, 91
Linebaugh, Peter 8, 47, 213
linguistic turn. *see* cultural turn
Linz, Juan J. 237
Lisbon 233, 237, 244, 247–248
Litherland, Benjamin 227–228, 234
Loach, Ken 5
local history 87, 106, 205–208, 211
Lockman, Zachary 182
longue durée 23, 124, 141, 160, 253
Lotta continua 74
Lüdtke, Alf 99, 228–229, 250

Malinowski, Branislaw 114
Mallon, Florencia 150, 156
Mao, Maoist 35–36, 38–39
Marcos, Subcomandante 59–60, 79
Marquesas 123–124
Marx, Karl; Marxian 9, 14, 16–17, 30–36, 45, 52
Marxist 7, 9, 32–38, 52, 60, 63, 65, 71, 75–76,
    78–80, 113–114, 118, 120, 134, 145, 155,
    205, 231
Max Planck Institute for history Göttingen 99
McKibbin, Ross 252
media 79, 153, 192, 234
mediation 31, 97, 162, 164, 221
Medick, Hans 77, 99

Melanesia 119–121, 129–130
Meleisea, Malama 133–134
Memmi, Albert 181
memorial group 19
memory 7, 32, 34, 40, 42, 49–51, 73, 86, 127, 142,
    147–150, 183, 187, 211, 235, 261, 271
Menchú, Rigoberta 154, 164
Meneses, Marina 161
Mexico, Chiapas 59–62, 79, 161, 252
México, Universidad Nacional Autónoma de 79,
    161, 252
Micronesia 113
Microstoria 59, 61, 77–78, 126
Middle East 178, 180–181, 184–185, 201
Mignolo, Walter 15, 141, 149, 168–169
Migrants, European migrants, settlers 117–118
Milan 61, 65, 69, 70–71, 74
modernity 183, 209
Montaldi, Danilo 72
moral economy 17
Morandi, Giuseppe 71
Morton, A.L. 33
Moscow 67
Movimiento Indígena-Campesino de
    Cotopaxi 168
Munro, Doug 115, 120
museum 90–93, 104, 189
Museum für Hamburgische Geschichte 91
Museum, Arbetets Museum (Museum of
    Labour), Norrköping 92
Museum, German Historical Museum 104
Mussolini, Benito 66

Naili, Falestin 186
Nakba 187, 200, 206
Nandy, Ashis 48
Narodniki 14, 68
Narokobi, Bernard 130
narratives 50
Nasser, Gamal Abdel 35
Natal 259–260, 262–263, 265, 267, 270, 276, 279
nation 34–35, 41, 144
National Socialism 9, 230
nationalism 21, 29–53, 182, 216, 234, 263–264
nation-building 22, 185, 216
native knowledge 14
Nazi Germany 233, 239

Ndlozi, George 272–273
Negev 23, 197, 200–206, 208, 214–216
Nehru 35, 45
Netherlands, Holland 285
Neumann, Klaus 131–132
New Economic History 64
New Left 5–6, 33, 35, 60, 62, 69–74, 144–145
New York 236
New Zealand 117–118, 132, 134
Niethammer, Lutz 107
North America 76, 78
Nouvelle histoire 77

oral history (movement) 5, 72
orality 23, 148, 163
ordinary people 3, 10, 13, 17, 23–24, 66, 75–76, 208, 232, 253, 261
    see also common people
Orient House, Jerusalem 179, 188
orientalism, orientalist 178
Oslo Agreement 1993 179
otherness 14–15
Ottoman Empire 182, 184, 186, 189, 192, 201–202, 214

Pacific History Association 127
Pacific Studies 126–127
Palermo 74
Palestine 27, 179–183, 185, 207
Palestine, British Mandatory period 201
Palestinian Liberation Organisation (PLO) 179
Panzieri, Raniero 73
Papua New Guinea 122, 130–131
Partito d'Azione 68–69
Pasolini Pier Paolo 68
Passerini, Luisa 63, 72–73, 75
Patai, Daphne 161
patriotism 182–185
Paulès, Xavier 251
peasantry (farmer) 13, 131, 134
people's history 3, 14, 16, 33, 51, 113, 117, 133
plebeian (culture) 17, 25, 34, 44, 47, 49, 52
Polícia Internacional e de Defesa do Estado (PIDE) 237
Polynesia 113, 129

Poma de Ayala, Guaman 144, 152
Pomata, Gianna 63, 76
Popper, Irit Carmon 218–221
popular culture 4, 14, 17–18, 60, 63–67, 70–72, 75, 80, 232, 253
Popular Front 51
populism, populist 3, 12, 14–16, 21, 24, 29, 32, 36, 39–40, 68, 80, 114, 130, 158
Portelli, Alessandro 72
Porto 241, 244–249
Portugal 229–230, 233, 239–240, 242, 244–246, 251–253
positionality 16, 32, 43
power, power networks 8, 13, 15–17, 20, 22–24, 29, 65, 79, 114, 116, 126, 128–129, 142, 153, 157, 162, 166, 168, 183, 197, 203, 207, 209, 211, 223, 227, 230–232, 234–236, 239, 244, 261, 264–267
Prakash, Gyan 44
Pratt, Mary Louise 153
Pre-industrial society 16
public 10, 15, 23–24, 29, 31, 41, 63, 76, 80, 88, 93–94, 99, 101, 105, 117, 155, 157, 166–167, 179, 183, 186–187, 198, 208–209, 213, 218, 220, 222, 247–251, 253, 261, 271–272, 277
publisher 18, 32, 164, 166, 192
Puerto Rico 5

Quaderni Rossi 73–74
Queensland 119

radical history 3
radicalism 233
Ramos Pacho, Abelardo 157
Rappaport, Joanne 157
reciprocity 23, 156, 161, 169
Rediker, Marcus 7–8
regionalist 14
Reinhard, Wolfgang 64
resilience 22, 24, 117, 233, 260
resistance 17–19, 22, 24, 47, 59–60, 66, 68, 70, 72–73, 75, 77, 103, 105, 160, 187, 201, 207, 222, 224, 230–231, 233, 249
Resistenza 66, 68–69, 72
Revel, Jacques 77

Ria~no, Yvonne 160
right 15, 20, 21, 24, 32, 38, 40, 42, 67, 73, 80, 103,
    129, 130, 153, 155, 164–165, 183, 186, 189,
    201–202, 207, 223, 227, 230, 240, 243, 251,
    253, 266
Rivera Cusicanqui Rivera, Silvia 146
romanticism 13, 19
Rossi-Doria, Manlio 68
Rowbotham, Sheila 9
Rufer, Mario 151, 165
rumours 276–279
rural classes 6
Ruskin College Oxford 6, 85, 94

Sabean, David W. 78
Sahlins, Marshall 122
Said, Edward W. 31, 47
Salazar, António de Oliveira 24, 229, 237,
    239–244, 247, 249, 251–253
Samoa 114, 132–134
Samuel, Raphael 6, 14, 16, 49, 52, 113
Sarkar, Sumit 40, 45–46
Sasson, Eliyahu 183
Savile, John 33–34
Scaraffia, Lucetta 75
Scarr, Deryck 119
Schlumbohm, Jürgen 77
Schoeffel, Penelope 132–133
Scotellaro, Rocco 68
Scotland 6
Scott, James 230
Second World War 3, 240, 263
Self Defense Units 265, 268
Self Protection units 267, 279
Sharpe, Jim 228
Sicart, Miguel 236
Siegfried, Detlef 105
slave, slave trade 7, 11, 119
social history 16, 47–48, 64, 75, 77, 99–100, 122,
    144–145, 167, 182, 205, 207, 229, 233
social learning 18
social movements 6, 18, 22, 66, 79, 88, 103, 105,
    143, 205
Solomon Islands 129
sources 10–12, 15–16, 20, 22, 31, 37, 39–43,
    47–52, 64, 79–80, 87, 95, 99, 105, 143,

    148, 150, 152, 154–156, 177, 181, 184,
    186–193, 238
South Africa 6, 9, 24, 259–280
South Asia 18, 36–44, 48
Soviet Union 33
Sozialdemokratische Partei Deutschlands (SPD) 92
Spain 233, 238–239
Spivak, Gayatri Chakravarty 41
sports 24, 233–234, 245, 248–250, 252–253
Stalin 35, 67, 233
Stalinist 31, 39, 233
state 10, 14, 23–24, 35, 37, 41, 43–44, 59–60,
    105, 113, 126, 128, 147–148, 152, 162, 177,
    179, 187–190, 192–193, 200–204, 206–207,
    213, 217, 224, 229, 233, 238, 242–243,
    248–250, 259, 261, 272, 274, 279
state archives 190, 192
state interventionism 24
Stedman Jones, Gareth 6
Steege, Paul 238
Steinberg, Jonny 280
Stephenson, Marcia 166
Stoll, David 154
subaltern classes 6, 16, 60, 64
Subaltern Studies (group) 5, 19, 21, 31, 36–48,
    52, 78, 145
subalternist 30, 42–45
subjectivity 30, 42, 105, 260, 276
sustainability 213, 220, 222, 224
Sutton-Smith, Brian 234
Sweden 5–6, 91–92
Switzerland 5, 160, 245

Taller Cultural Causanacunchic, Otavalo 146
Taller de Historia Oral Andina (THOA), La
    Paz 145, 166
Taussig, Michael 151
Tawney, R.H. 48
Tedlock, Dennis 159
testimony, testimonial literature 41, 49, 121,
    154, 268
Tevis, Walter 227
Thiele, Dieter 107
Third World 6, 19, 35–36, 68, 160
Thomas, Keith 125
Thompson, Dorothy 33

Thompson, E.P. 4, 7, 9–10, 17, 33–35, 44–48, 125, 145, 200, 228, 232, 250
Thompson, Nato 210
Tibán Guala, Lourdes 146
Ticona, Esteban 150, 163, 165
Togliatti, Palmiro 65–67
Tolstoy, Lev 8
Trask, Haunani-Kay 128
Trivellato, Francesca 78
Túpac Katari 145
Turin 60, 69, 72–75, 78
turn 4, 10–11, 16–19, 36, 42, 46–47, 60, 63, 69, 130, 141, 152, 157–158, 177, 228, 274, 277
turn, anthropological 16, 62

Udlame. *see* violence
Uganda 35
UK United Kingdom= Great Britain 4, 9, 18, 21, 33, 113, 180, 242
Universidad Andina Simón Bolívar, Quito 167
universities 18, 89, 100, 178. *see also* academia
University of Bielefeld 158, 167
University of Chicago 31
University of the South Pacific 127
University, Hebrew of Jerusalem 178
Uruguay 78
USA, United States of America 6, 9, 14, 19, 78, 113, 134, 145, 235, 239, 242, 253

Vaal Triangle 264, 276, 278
Valderrama Fernández, Ricardo 154
Van Onselen, Charles 9
Victoria University College, Wellington 117
Vietnam War 6

Viezzer, Moema 154
violence 20, 24, 142, 145, 148, 156, 162, 184–185, 259–280
violence, sexual 270–271
völkisch 14, 21

Wales 6
Wallraff, Günter 154
Walters, Ronald 125
Ward, Alan 121
Warren, James Francis 229
Weber, Max 16, 48
Wehler, Hans-Ulrich 98, 100–101
Wesley-Smith, Terence 131
Western Europe 6, 22, 60–61, 156, 236
women's history 99
work 4–5, 7, 10, 16, 22, 34, 45, 47, 63, 72, 75, 77–79, 86, 89–91, 93–95, 97–98, 106–108, 115–118, 121–123, 126, 129, 131, 144, 146–147, 150, 159–160, 166–167, 184, 189, 221, 228, 231, 248, 252, 268–269, 271–272
working class 4, 7, 18, 34–35, 74–75, 134, 229, 232–233, 243, 252–253
World War I 182
World War II (Second World War) 178, 209

Yugoslavia 5

Zang, Gert 94–95
Zapata, Claudia 146, 163
Zapatista 59
Zimmermann, Michael 107
Zionism 180–181, 206